Ocampo

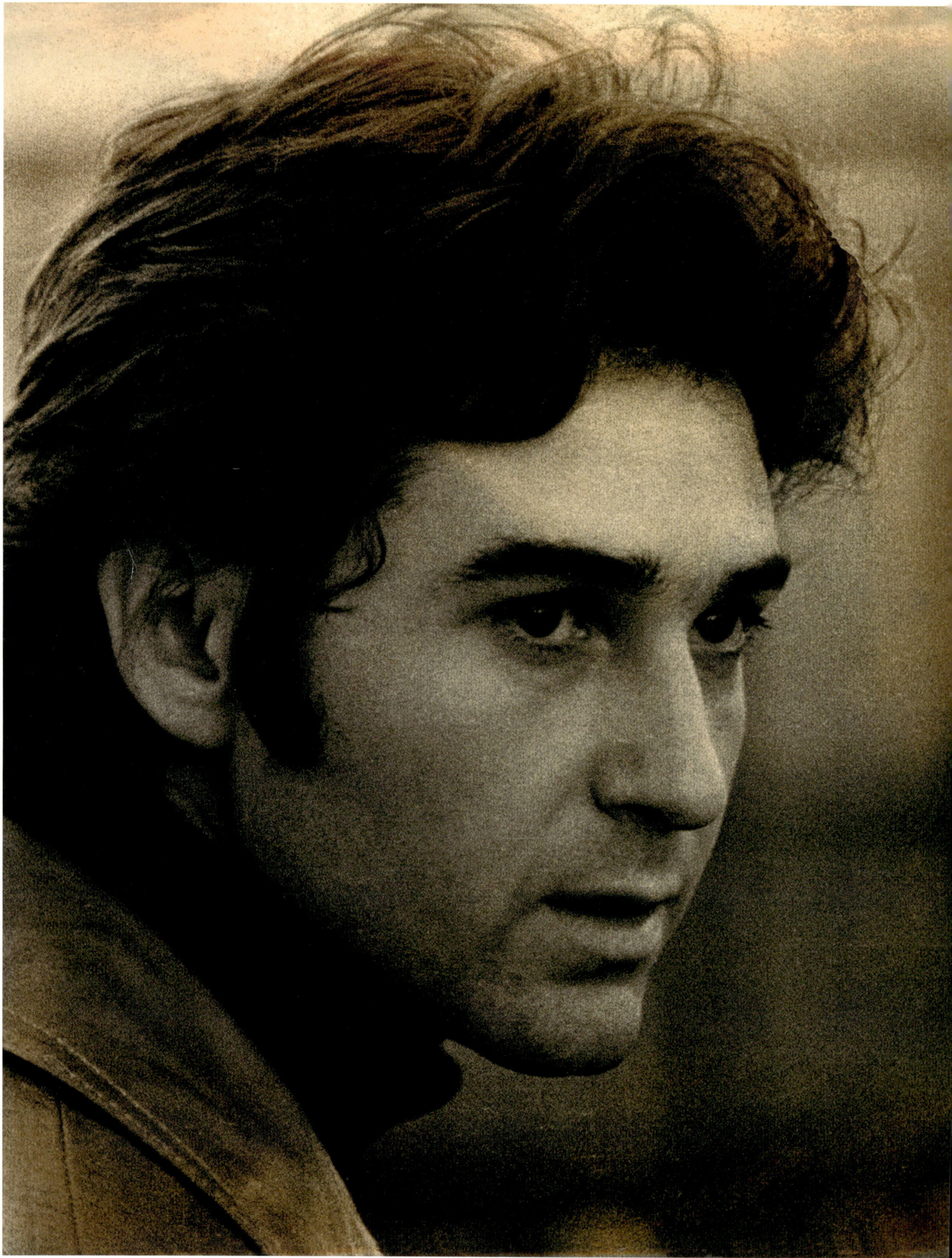

Octavio
Ocampo

Arte Metamórfico

EDITION OLMS ZÜRICH

EDITION OLMS AG
Willikonerstr. 10
CH-8618 Oetwil am See/Zürich
Switzerland

Mail: info@edition-olms.com
Web: www.edition-olms.com

ISBN 978-3-283-01212-0

International Edition
Translation: Eugene Edwards (GB),
Stefanie Kuballa-Cottone (D), Florence Bader (F), Lingo 24 (F)

Production, Design, Repro:
Weiß-Freiburg GmbH –
Graphik & Buchgestaltung

Bibliographische Information der Deutschen Bibliothek
Die Deutsche Bibliothek verzeichnet diese Publikation
in der Deutschen Nationalbibliografie; detaillierte bibliografische Daten
sind im Internet über http://dnb.ddb.de abrufbar

Acknowledgements:
Emmanuel Fouquet, Victoria Flores Verdad,
Iván Castellanos y Niklas Weiß.

Printed in Slovenia

OCTAVIO OCAMPO is represented in Europe/Suisse by
RANGEWOOD LTD., Emmanuel D. Fouquet,
rangewood@gmail.com, phone +33(0)6 08 94 22 63, +33(0)50 58 60 29

Octavio Ocampo

and the clouds | y las nubes | und Wolken | et les nuages

WHILE DRIVING the family car, mothers can have little inkling of the consequences when they ask their children to look out of the window to watch the clouds. "Look! That one looks like a tree, and that one over there looks like a dog chasing us!" At the time, Doña Octaviana, who used to create her own textile designs (also for the theatre in Celaya), was entirely unaware that she was planting the seeds of *metamorphic art* in her son Octavio.
Octavio continued to see women in flower vases or birds, pitchers made out of cows, flowers' mouths and houses that looked like apples, faces in the furrows of fields [...] Under the surface the boy created oceanic landscapes, covering an upper lip with a husk of wheat or wrapping a skull in fern fronds. And Iztaccihuatl, sharply outlined against the blue sky, is not actually a volcano, but the figure of a sleeping woman. Octavio could see sirens in bottles and guitars in furniture, discovered startling figures in the veins of marble, and transformed rock formations and the interwoven branches of trees into chairs.
Ocampo's whole family consisted [...] of artists; [...] they all drew and painted, and their talent was striking. From an early age, Don Ángel took his sons Ángel, Octavio, Eduardo and Gregorio to study at Salvador Zúñiga's Academy in Celaya. Zúñiga, sculptor and painter, created mojigangas, large, grotesque figures made of cardboard, with a person inside who danced to frighten the spectators or make them laugh. Sometimes two people got inside the mojigangas, and then they would grow and turn their heads round as if by magic. For children, these giant dolls on highly decorated floats opened up the door to a fantastic fairytale world, one that had little to do with everyday life.
Octavio in particular was beside himself with astonishment and fascination.

«One of my first drawings was a puppet kicking a ball, formed from my initials [Octavio Román Ocampo].»

He saw pictures in everything, just like with the cloud shapes of his childhood. He imagined the men and women cavorting in front of him were wearing bird's heads or lurch heads. Once, when one of his teachers [...] called him up to the blackboard to write the word vaca (cow), Octavio said: "the best thing is for me to paint one", and he painted a cow, but saw things in it others are not able to [...] At school, when not singing or dancing, he painted non-stop.
"Count me in, lady teacher," "I'll paint the decorations", "I'll manage it, but don't make me learn multiplication tables by heart, especially not the three times table, which is awful [...]".
At the Legionaries of Christ in *Tlalpan,* the young Octavio passionately wanted to be a saint, but the desire soon faded and he kept his distance. Even here, however, he caught people's attention by transforming the beautiful chapel into something heavenly. Here he would certainly have been baptized *Santo Niño Octavio de los Altar Barrocos* (Saint Octavio the Little of the Baroque Altar), but he found the earthly celebrations completely absorbing, and decorated the games room, transforming it into a beautiful, attractive but secular banqueting hall. The urge to embellish everything had nothing in common with the monastic frugality generally expected of saints and holy people.
From becoming the member of a seminary to a man of the theatre was a huge step, but Octavio took it in his stride. From the sensuality of church rituals, from altar and incense, pews and lily flowers, he took the theatrics and symbolic potency. After all, nothing evokes more intense emotions than a black confessional box. As an actor and set designer, with his mother Doña Octaviana at his side, he performed on stage, including a part in the play *Las salvajes criaturas* (Wild Creatures).

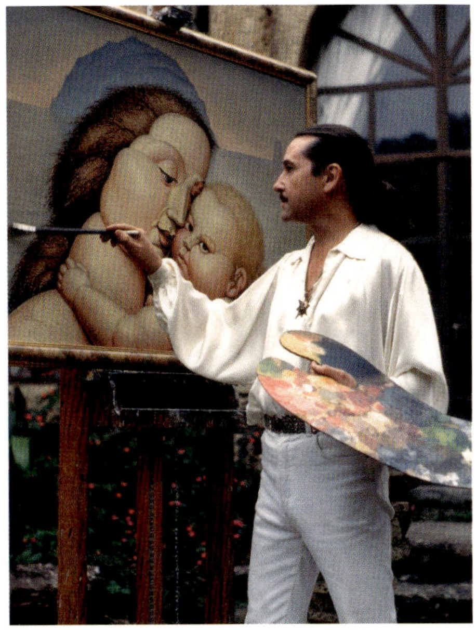

Ocampo painting – Ocampo pintando – Ocampo beim Malen – Ocampo peintre, 1989

Of paramount importance for Octavio was creating his first mural at school, which became the first step towards painting the staircase at Celaya's City Hall. Real recognition, however, was still slow to come, but he took a step in the right direction with the help of Ruth, Diego Rivera's favourite daughter. She managed to arrange a scholarship for him to study art in the capital. María Luisa *La China* Mendoza and Eduardo Deschamps admired his first murals, and *La China* vehemently begged Don Ángel [...]: „You have a responsibility to Mexico and to all humanity. Your son needs to go to Mexico City to study art!" No sooner said than done. *La China* made a lasting impression on the father, who not only sent Octavio to the *La Esmeralda* School of Art, but also Ángel, the eldest, to a course in craft and design at the *Escuela de la Ciudadela*. Octavio got top grades, and studied under the guidance of Feliciano Peña, Santos Balmori, Fernando Castro Pacheco, Jorge González Camarena and Antonio Rodríguez, graduating within five years.

Metamorphosis. | We are all diverse, but no man is an island. | We change overnight. We become older, we change, we transform ourselves. | Meanwhile, once peaceful lines are bringing the darker I to the surface. | Nothing is quite as it seems. A man and a woman who love one another are wearing a familiar face for their own sakes.

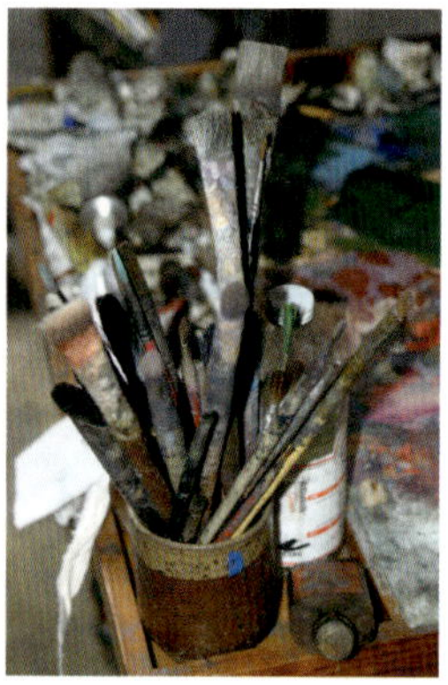
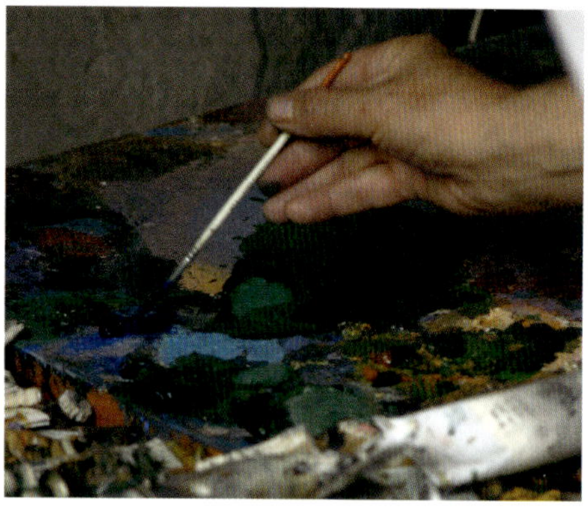
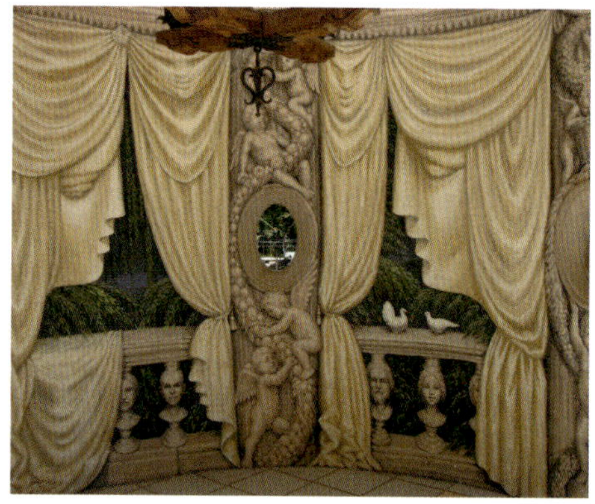

Casa de Tepoztlán (details) – Casa de Tepoztlán (detalles) – Casa de Tepoztlán (Details) – Casa de Tepoztlán (details), 1985

On the side, the two brothers found time to work together with Héctor Azar as draftsmen and designers, thereby enhancing the art of stage painting in Mexico by the power of two. Not only that, but the two brothers also became actors, under the direction of José Luis Ibáñez, Juan Jose Gurrola, Miguel Sabido, André Moreau and especially Julio Castillo. The brothers also felt attracted to the cinema, and Octavio was soon managing the props department of *Estudios América*. Using four stages and a small back lot, they produced 120 films. Between 1966 and 1969 together with Luis Alcoriza, Manuel Michel, Jorge Fons, Juan Ibañez and Archibaldo Burns they started making films like *Los Caifanes,* competing with Roberto Gavaldon, Emilio Gómez Muriel and Servando González. These were boom times for Mexican cinema! The Estudios América churned out films, sometimes four at a time! However, Octavio was soon tired of the chaos of filmmaking. Like Carlos Fuentes, he was on the verge of developing a stomach ulcer, and in order to avoid one, he escaped by travelling to Europe.

After his return, Octavio left the art of *metamorphosis* for a while, and instead took dance lessons with Guillermina Bravo, Ofelia Medina and Rosa Bracho. He sang under Mónica Miguel, put on plays with Julio Castillo and José Luis Ibáñez, and did a spell of acting both on stage and TV until deciding to visit his friend David Wiznievits in San Francisco.

He landed in the middle of the heated protests against nuclear weapons and the war in Vietnam, amid the hippies in Berkeley and the girls with long, golden legs, demonstrating for flower power and against bullets. He took classes at the San Francisco Art Institute, and teachers and students were amazed at the realism of his images. Hyperrealism was still largely unknown in the United States.

Childhood is our root, origin and provenance. In childhood we find everything we later become, when we have grown up. Childhood is also a catalyst, and so Octavio returned to what had inspired him so passionately in his early years. Along the way, he found unexpected shapes and forms, magic and miracles, as well as some new solutions.

Not that Ocampo despised reality; he merely wanted to transcend it. To prove it, he painted potentates like Carter, Alemán or De la Madrid (also López Portillo). He painted starlets like Dolores del Rio, Gloria Marín and María Douglas, and did a total of three portraits of Jane Fonda, who in turn recommended Cesar Chavez, the human rights activist. Posters were made from these paintings, and sold to raise money for the farm workers' movement and its followers. Octavio continued his optical experiments and noted that more and more elements were appearing to metamorphose his compositions.

What rider would not want to become the legs of his horse?
What woman would not be happy, if, instead of glaucoma, she had a horse rider in her right eye and a bullfighter in the left?
What monk would not like to illuminate his monastery, so as not to have to fumble about in the dark?
[...]
"I don't only paint figuratively, but multi-figuratively, polymorphically. I like to invite the observer to interact playfully with my paintings. First, I capture his attention, and try to communicate a sense of beauty or of something terrible. Then, on the second or third impression, the observer should be feeling something quite different.
In the tentative transition from one sensation to another, there is a magical moment in which I communicate on a different level, via the subconscious and the spirit."

Now a resident of Cuernavaca, today Octavio devotes all his time to creating the new realities of metamorphic art. How wonderful! I well

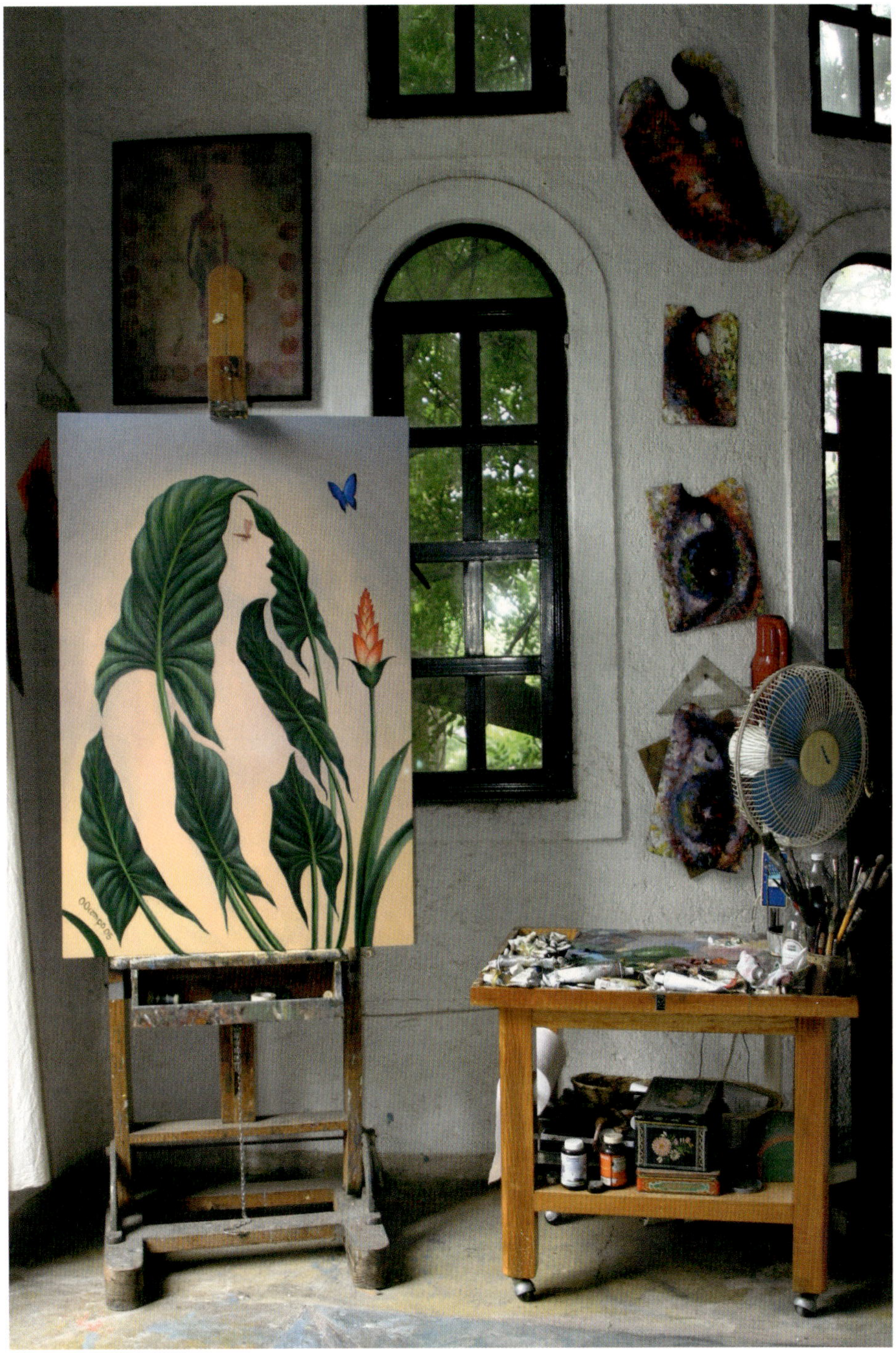

"Mariposa Azul" on the easel and eyes on palettes – «Mariposa Azul» en el caballete y ojos en paletas – „Mariposa Azul" auf der Staffelei und Augen auf Mischpaletten – «Mariposa Azul» sur le chevalet et des yeux sur palettes, 2005

remember sophisticated, elaborate paintings in which we (I was still a little girl then) had to search for the rabbit that was lost in the bushes, or find the girl with the angel face, or seek the dwarf hidden in the curtain, the guard dog, the evil witch, etc. It was a fascinating game, but it also made me scared. Had all that been hiding there all the time and we had not seen it? These images from children's books disturbed me so much that I could not sleep. Was it magic, witchcraft or the work of the devil to discover figures no one else could see, at least, not at first sight?

Suddenly nature took on a different, more threatening dimension: the tree was hostile, the house treacherous. Behind the door something was waiting for us, something challenging that we needed to face with resolve. Behind every human story lurked a trap door, an unknown level, uncontrollable emotions. Dorian Gray might suddenly appear round the next corner! With his metamorphic painting, what Octavio Ocampo teaches his audience, the curious, emotional and visually receptive individual, is how to liberate the unconscious, to trust our intuition, to follow the mystique and transformative power of metamorphic art to raise our sense of awareness. Only then can we be greater than ourselves.

Elena Poniatowska.

Metamorfosear. | Todos somos múltiples, nadie es uno solo.
Cambiamos de la noche a la mañana. | Envejecemos, nos alteramos, nos transmutamos.
Mientras líneas antes apacibles hacen surgir al otro yo. | Gatos por liebres.
Un hombre y una mujer que se aman tienen un rostro por ellos conocido

LAS MADRES nunca saben lo que pueden suscitar cuando les dicen a sus hijos que vean las nubes por la ventanilla del automóvil: «Mira, esta tiene forma de árbol, aquella nos sigue como perro».

Allá en Celaya doña Octaviana, artista por derecho propio (textiles y teatro), no imaginó que al señalarle las nubes a su hijo Octavio estaba sembrando en él la semilla del *arte metamórfico*.

El niño siguió viendo mujeres jarrón, mujeres ave, jarras vaca, bocas flor, casas como manzanas, rostros como surcos. [...] Dentro de la piel humana el niño dibujaba paisajes mentales, cubría un labio superior de trigo, un cráneo de helechos. En realidad el *Iztaccihuatl* que todavía podía verse sobre el cielo azul no era un volcán sino una mujer dormida. Octavio veía sirenas botella, muebles aguitarrados y encontraba figuras asombrosas en las manchas de los mármoles, en las formas de la piedra, en los cerros que se vuelven sillas y en los árboles que entretejen sus ramas.

La familia de Ocampo se compone de artistas [...], todos dibujan y salta a la vista su talento para las artes. Desde muy pequeños, don Ángel llevó a sus hijos Ángel, Octavio, Eduardo y Gregorio a la Escuela de Artes Plásticas del escultor y pintor Salvador Zúñiga, en Celaya. El maestro hacía grandes y grotescas figuras de cartón, en cuyo interior una persona bailaba haciendo reír o asustando un poco a los mirones. A veces cabían dos personas y entonces la *mojiganga* crecía mágicamente y volvía la cabeza para todos lados. Para los niños las *mojigangas* eran el acceso a un mundo fantástico, de carros alegóricos, decoraciones fabulosas que poco tenían que ver con la vida de todos los días, Octavio sobre todo, no cabía en sí del asombro y del deslumbramiento.

Como en las nubes, en todo seguía viendo otra imagen. A los hombres y a las mujeres que se movían frente a él, mentalmente les ponía cabezas de pájaros o de batracios .

Una vez cuando una de sus maestras [...] lo pasó al pizarrón para que escribiera la palabra *vaca* el niño solicitó «mejor la dibujo». El niño Octavio dibujó una vaca, pero en la vaca veía otras cosas que los demás no sabían ver. [...]

En la escuela se la pasaba dibujando y si no cantando y bailando. [...]

«Yo salgo maestra», «yo pinto el decorado», «maestra o yo barro, maestra, todo con tal de no memorizar las tablas de multiplicación, sobre todo la del 3 que es horrible [...].»

Internado con los Legionarios de Cristo en *Tlalpan*, el joven Octavio quiso ser santo, pero pronto desistió. También allí destacó en los celestiales trabajos de decoración de la capilla. Allí si lo hubieran beatificado *Santo Niño Octavio de los Altares Barrocos*, pero también le gustaban otras fiestas más terrenales como decorar el salón de juegos y convertirlo en un esplendoroso salón de fiestas, terrestre y apetitoso y este afán por embellecerlo todo, nada tenía que ver con la frugalidad monástica que se le exige a los santos.

De aspirante a seminarista a hombre de teatro hay más que un paso y Octavio lo dio con éxito. Del altar y del incienso, los reclinatorios y los ramos de azucenas, de la voluptuosidad contenida de los rituales conservó la teatralidad y el impacto. Nada más evocativo que un negro confesionario. Escenógrafo, actor junto a doña Octaviana, su madre, participó en la obra *Las salvajes criaturas*, entre otras.

Sin embargo, para Octavio lo más importante fue pintar en la escuela su primer mural. Este le permitió más tarde pintar en la escalera de acceso a la Presidencia Municipal de *Celaya*. De allí al reconocimiento dio otro paso con la ayuda de Ruth, la hija más querida de Diego Rivera, quien le consiguió una beca para estudiar en la capital. María Luisa *La China* Mendoza y Eduardo Deschamps admiraron esos primeros murales y *La China*, con vehemencia , conminó a don Ángel «Usted tiene una responsabilidad con México y con la humanidad entera. ¡Su hijo debe ir a México D.F. a estudiar arte!»

Dicho y hecho impresionado por *La China*, envío no solo a Octavio a *La Esmeralda* sino a Ángel, el mayor a aprender diseño y artesanías en la *Escuela de la Ciudadela*.

Allí si Octavio sacó las mejores calificaciones guiado por sus maestros Feliciano Peña, Santos Balmori, Fernando Castro Pacheco, Jorge González Camarena y Antonio Rodríguez. Terminó su carrera en cinco años.

A los dos hermanos Octavio y Ángel todavía les dio tiempo de trabajar con Héctor Azar y la escenografía mexicana ganó entonces a dos extraordinarios diseñadores. Y no solo eso, también a dos actores a las órdenes de José Luis Ibáñez, Juan José Gurrola, Miguel sabido, André Moreau y sobre todo Julio Castillo.

El cine también atrajo a los hermanos y Octavio dirigió el departamento de escenografía de los *Estudios América*. Ciento veinte películas se filmaron en cuatro foros y un pequeño *backlot*. Entre 1966 y 1969 junto con Luis Alcoriza. Manuel Michel, Jorge Fons, Juan Ibañez y Archibaldo Burns empezaron a hacer películas como *Los Caifanes* compitiendo con Roberto Gavaldón, Emilio Gómez Muriel y Servando González. ¡Ah qué tiempos esperanzados para el cine! Los *Estudios América* no paraban y se filmaban al mismo tiempo cuatro películas. Octavio se cansó de este *pandemónium*; como Carlos Fuentes, estuvo a punto de contraer ulcera y para que no le diera escogió zarpar hacia Europa.

Al regreso, Octavio adictó a la *metamorfosis*, tomó danza con Guillermina Bravo, Ofelia Medina y Rosa Bracho, cantó con Mónica Miguel, hizo

«Una de las primeras firmas fue un muñeco pateando una pelota formado con mis iniciale [Octavio Román Ocampo].»

"Amistad del Quijote" (sketch, boceto, Skizze, esquisse)
"Amistad del Quijote", Oil on canvas – Óleo sobre tela – Öl auf Leinwand – Huile sur toile, 1999

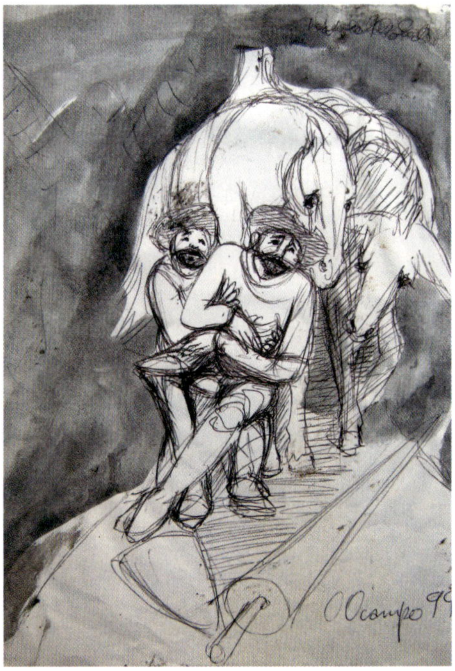

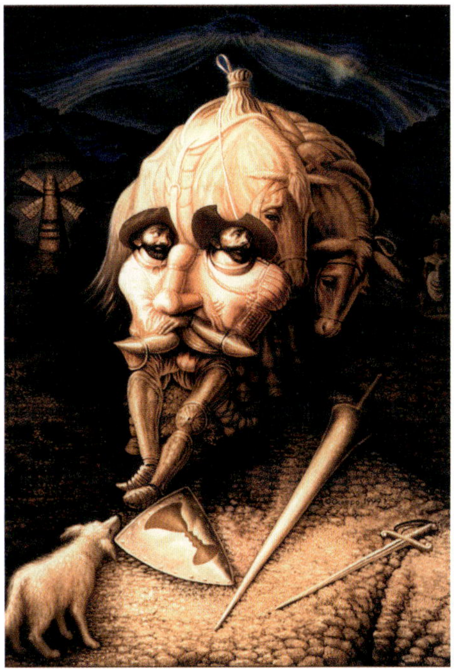

teatro con Julio Castillo y José Luis Ibáñez y actuó para teatro y televisión, hasta que decidió visitar a su amigo en San Francisco, David Wiznievits.

Cayó parado en medio de los días fervorosos de protesta contra la guerra de Vietnam y las bases nucleares, los hippies en Berkleley y las muchachas de piernas largas y doradas que ofrecían flores en vez de balas en las plazas públicas.
Tomó cursos en el Instituto de Arte de san Francisco y maestros y alumnos se sorprendieron del realismo de sus composiciones. Todavía no surgía el *hiperrealismo* en los Estados Unidos.

La infancia es raíz y origen. En la infancia se encuentra todo lo que seremos de grandes. La infancia es catalizadora. Octavio volvió a sus obsesiones de los primeros años, encontrando formas inesperadas, sortilegios y milagros en sus caminos, aportando nuevas soluciones.

No es que Ocampo despreciara la realidad, es que deseaba ir más allá. Para demostrar que no la despreciaba, pintó a potentados, Carter, Alemán, De la Madrid (a López Portillo tambiéné).
Captó a luminarias como Dolores del Río, Gloria Marín, María Douglas, e hizo tres retratos de una sola Jane Fonda, quien le encomendó al líder Cesar Chávez.
De esa pintura se hicieron carteles para recaudar fondos para la causa del guía campesino y sus seguidores. Octavio sigue haciendo experimentos ópticos y se dio cuenta que aparecían cada vez más elementos que *metamorfoseaban* sus composiciones.

¿A qué jinete no le gustaría ser la pata de su caballo?
¿A qué mujer no le llenaría de gozo tener un charro en el ojo derecho y un torero en el izquierdo, en vez de un glaucoma?
¿Qué monja no prefiere ser candil de su convento y no oscuridad de su convento?

í«No solo soy figurativo, sino multifigurativo, polimórfico. Me gusta invitar al espectador a jugar y con eso capto su atención al dar una impresión de belleza o de horror en la primer imagen; otra al descubrir que hay una segunda y hasta una tercera imagen.
Entre el frágil paso de una a otra existe un momento mágico en el cual me comunico con el espectador a otro nivel por medio del subconsciente y del espíritu.»

¡Qué bueno que Octavio, quien ahora vive en *Cuernavaca*, se dedique solo a inventar una nueva realidad, la de la metamorfosis!De niña, recuerdo unos dibujos alambicados, laboriosos, en los que teníamos que encontrar al conejo perdido en el matorral, a la niña con cara de ángel, al gnomo en la cortina, al perro guardián, a la bruja maldita. Era un juego fascinante que daba miedo.
¿Así es que todo esto estaba ahí escondido y no lo habíamos visto?
El dibujo en las planas del periódico infantil inquietaba tanto que producía insomnio.
¿Era cosa de magia o era cosa infernal encontrar figuras que nadie más podía hallar, al menos a primera vista?
De pronto la naturaleza adquiría otro sentido, el árbol ya no era inocente ni la casa confiable. Algo más nos esperaba atrás de la puerta, algo que nos retaba y teníamos que completar.

Tras de todo acontecimiento humano había una trampa, un nivel desconocido, un impulso incontrolable. A la vuelta de la esquina podíamos descubrir de golpe y porrazo a Dorian Gray.
Lo que enseña Octavio Ocampo en su pintura metamórfica es a liberar el inconsciente, a tenerle fe a los impulsos, al misticismo, a los poderes de la mutación y, sobre todo, a darnos cuenta — curiosos y emocionados espectadores visuales — que podemos ser más grandes que nosotros mismos.

Elena Poniatowska.

Metamorphosieren. | Wir alle sind vielgestaltig, niemand ist einer allein.
Wir verändern uns über Nacht. | Wir werden älter, wir ändern uns, verwandeln uns.
Unterdessen bringen einst friedfertige Zeilen das andere Ich an die Oberfläche.
Nichts ist so, wie es scheint [...].

MÜTTER HABEN JA keine Ahnung, was alles passieren kann, wenn sie ihren Kindern während der Fahrt vorschlagen, sie sollten durchs Fenster schauen und die Wolken betrachten: «Schau, die hier sieht aus wie ein Baum, und die da drüben rennt uns hinterher wie ein Hund.» — Damals in Celaya ahnt Doña Octaviana — die ihre eigene textile Kunst entwirft, auch am Theater — nicht, dass sie ihrem Sohn Octavio damit das Samenkorn der *metamorphischen Kunst* einpflanzt. Der Junge sieht auch weiterhin in Blumenvasen oder Vögeln Frauen, er sieht Krüge, die aus Kühen geformt sind, Blumenmünder, Häuser, die wie Äpfel aussehen, Gesichter in Ackerfurchen [...] Unter der Oberfläche lässt der Junge Seelenlandschaften entstehen, bedeckt eine Oberlippe mit Weizen oder hüllt einen Schädel in Farnwedel. Und der *Iztaccihuatl*, der vor dem blauen Himmel zu sehen ist, ist eigentlich gar kein Vulkan, sondern eine schlafende Frau. Octavio sieht Sirenen in Flaschen und gitarrenhafte Möbel, er entdeckt verblüffende Figuren in den Maserungen des Marmors, in den Formen der Felsbrocken, in Hügeln, die sich in Sessel verwandeln, und im verflochtenen Geäst der Bäume.

[...] Ocampos Familie besteht [...] aus Künstlern [...] alle malen und zeichnen, ihre künstlerische Begabung springt ins Auge. Von klein auf bringt Don Ángel seine Söhne Ángel, Octavio, Eduardo und Gregorio zur Kunstakademie des Bildhauers und Malers Salvador Zúñiga in Celaya. Dieser fertigt *mojigangas* — große, groteske Figuren aus Pappe, in deren Inneren sich eine Person verbirgt, die tanzt und die Schaulustigen zum Lachen bringt oder erschreckt. Manchmal stecken auch zwei Personen in den Figuren, dann wächst die *mojiganga* wie durch Zauberhand und dreht den Kopf nach allen Seiten. Für die Kinder öffnen diese Riesenpuppen das Tor zu einer phantastischen Welt aus märchenhaft geschmückten Festwagen, einer Welt, die wenig mit dem alltäglichen Leben zu tun hat. Vor allem Octavio ist außer sich vor Erstaunen und Faszination. In allem sieht er ein Bild, wie bei den Wolken. Den Männern und Frauen, die sich vor ihm tummeln, setzt er im Geiste anstelle der Gesichter Vögel- oder Lurchköpfe auf. Einmal, als eine seiner Lehrerinnen [...] ihn an die Tafel ruft, um das Wort *vaca* (Kuh) zu schreiben, sagt Octavio: «Am besten male ich eine»; und er malte eine Kuh, sah in ihr aber Dinge, die die anderen nicht sehen können [...] In der Schule malt er die ganze Zeit, wenn er nicht gerade singt oder tanzt [...].

«Ich mache mit, Frau Lehrerin», «Ich male die Deko», «Ich fege, alles, nur nicht die Multiplikationstabellen auswendig lernen, vor allem nicht die von der 3, die ist furchtbar [...]».

Bei den Legionären Christi in *Tlalpan* will der junge Octavio so gerne ein Heiliger werden, geht aber bald wieder auf Abstand. Doch auch dort macht er durch eine himmlisch schöne Umgestaltung der Kapelle auf sich aufmerksam. Man würde ihn dort sicherlich *Santo Niño Octavio de los Altares Barrocos* taufen (Heiliger kleiner Octavio der barocken Altäre), aber er findet an den irdischen Festen großen Gefallen; so dekoriert er beispielsweise das Spielzimmer und verwandelt es in einen prächtigen, einladend-weltlichen Festsaal. Dieser Drang, alles zu verschönern, hat nichts mit der mönchischen Genügsamkeit gemein, die man allgemein von Heiligen erwartet.

Vom Seminaristen, der er werden wollte, zum Theatermenschen, ist es mehr als nur ein Schritt, doch Octavio geht diesen Weg erfolgreich. Von Altar und Weihrauch, von Betstuhl und Lilienstrauß, von der *Sinnlichkeit* des kirchlichen Rituals bewahrt er sich seine Theatralik und die Zuneigung zu starker Wirkung. Nichts beschwört mehr Emotionen herauf als ein schwarzer Beichtstuhl. Als Bühnenbildner und Schauspieler wirkt er, an der Seite seiner Mutter, Doña Octaviana, unter anderem bei dem Stück *Las salvajes criaturas* (Wilde Kreaturen) mit. Von größter Bedeutung für Octavio war, in der Schule sein erstes Wandgemälde zu malen; ein erster Schritt zur späteren Bemalung des Treppenaufgangs im Rathaus von *Celaya*. Von dort zur tatsächlichen Anerkennung ist es ein weiterer Schritt, den er mit der Unterstützung von Ruth, der Lieblingstochter von Diego Rivera, geht. Sie besorgt ihm ein Stipendium für das Kunststudium in der Hauptstadt. María Luisa *La China* Mendoza und Eduardo Deschamps bewundern diese ersten Wandgemälde, und *La China* beschwört Don Ángel mit [...] Vehemenz: «Sie tragen eine Verantwortung gegenüber Mexiko und der ganzen Menschheit. Ihr Sohn muss nach Mexiko-Stadt und dort Kunst studieren!»

«Eine meiner ersten Zeichnungen war eine Puppe, die gegen einen Ball trat, geformt aus meinen Initialen [Octavio Román Ocampo].»

Gesagt, getan. Der von La China nachhaltig beeindruckte Vater schickt nicht nur Octavio an die Kunsthochschule *La Esmeralda*, sondern auch Ángel, den Ältesten, zum Design- und Kunsthandwerkstudium an die *Escuela de la Ciudadela.* Dort bekommt Octavio die besten Noten; er lernt bei Feliciano Peña, Santos Balmori, Fernando Castro Pacheco, Jorge González Camarena und Antonio Rodríguez und schließt das Studium innerhalb von fünf Jahren ab.

Nebenbei finden die beiden Brüder Zeit, um mit Héctor Azar zusammenzuarbeiten, wodurch die mexikanische Bühnenmalerei um zwei außergewöhnliche Zeichner und Gestalter reicher wird. Und nicht nur das, auch zwei neue Schauspieler werden geboren, unter der Regie von José Luis Ibáñez, Juan José Gurrola, Miguel Sabido, André Moreau und vor allem Julio Castillo. Auch vom Kino fühlen sich die Brüder angezogen, und Octavio leitet bald die Requisitenabteilung der *Estudios América.* Auf vier Bühnen und einem kleinen *Backlot* werden 120 Filme gedreht. Zwi-

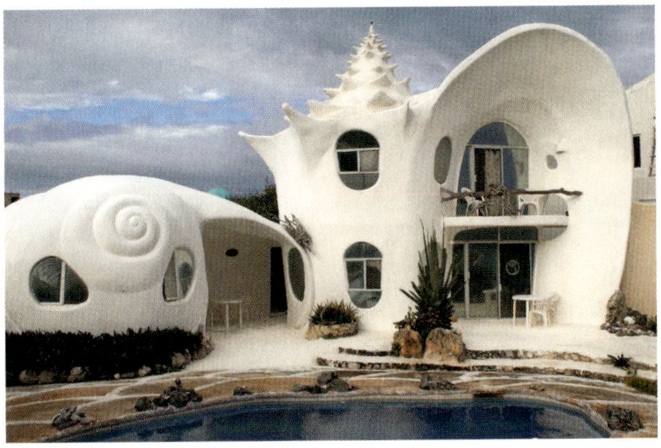

The Shell House, Casa Caracol, Das Schneckenhaus, La Maison Escargot, Mexico

Arte Metamórfico (Pancarta Exposición en Puerto Rico), Acrylic on canvas – Acrílico sobre tela – Acryl auf Leinwand – Acrylique sur toile, 1990

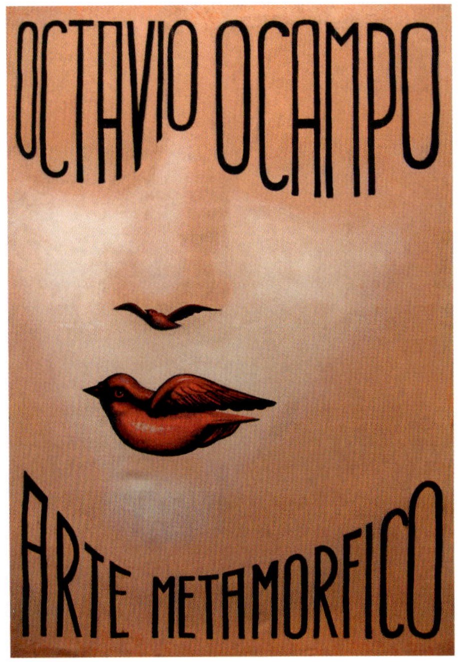

schen 1966 und 1969 mit Luis Alcoriza. Manuel Michel, Jorge Fons, Juan Ibañez und Archibaldo Burns fangen an, Filme wie *Los Caifanes* zu drehen und wetteifern mit Roberto Gavaldón, Emilio Gómez Muriel und Servando González. Ach, welch hoffnungsvolle Zeiten für das Kino! Die *Estudios América* filmen am laufenden Band, zum Teil vier Filme gleichzeitig. Octavio wird jedoch dieses *Pandämoniums* bald überdrüssig. Wie Carlos Fuentes, steht er auch irgendwann kurz vor einem Magengeschwür, und um dem zu entgehen, macht er sich aus dem Staub und schifft sich ein nach Europa.

Nach seiner Rückkehr verfällt Octavio der *Metamorphose,* nimmt Tanzunterricht bei Guillermina Bravo, Ofelia Medina und Rosa Bracho, singt bei Mónica Miguel, macht mit Julio Castillo und José Luis Ibáñez Theater und schauspielert für Theater und Fernsehen, bis er sich entscheidet, seinen Freund David Wiznievits in San Francisco zu besuchen.

Er landete inmitten der hitzigen Proteste gegen den Vietnamkrieg und die Stationierung von Atomwaffen, inmitten der Hippies in Berkeley und den Mädchen mit den langen, goldenen Beinen, die auf öffentlichen Plätzen für Blumen statt Gewehrkugeln werben. Er nimmt Unterricht am Kunstinstitut von San Francisco, und Lehrer wie Schüler staunen über den Realismus seiner Bilder. Der Hyperrealismus war in den USA noch nicht aufgekommen.

Die Kindheit ist die Wurzel, ist Ursprung und Herkunft. In der Kindheit findet sich alles, was wir sein werden, wenn wir groß sind. Die Kindheit ist ein Katalysator. Octavio kehrt zu dem zurück, was ihn in den ersten Jahren so leidenschaftlich begeistert hatte; er findet unerwartete Formen, Zauberei und Wunder auf seinem Weg — und neue Lösungen.

Nicht, dass Ocampo die Realität geringschätzt: Er will aber über sie hinaus. Um zu beweisen, dass er sie nicht geringschätzt, malt er Potentaten wie Carter, Alemán oder De la Madrid (auch López Portillo). Er malt Filmsternchen wie Dolores del Río, Gloria Marín, María Douglas, und malt allein drei Porträts von Jane Fonda, die ihn dem Menschenrechtsverfechter Cesar Chávez empfahl. Von diesem Gemälde werden Plakate gedruckt, um Geld für die Landarbeiterbewegung und ihre Gefolgsleute zu sammeln. Octavio fährt mit seinen optischen Experimenten fort und stellt fest, dass immer mehr Elemente auftauchen, die seine Bildkompositionen *metamorphisieren.*

Welcher Reiter wäre nicht gerne das Bein seines Pferdes? Welche Frau würde es nicht mit Freude erfüllen, einen Reiter im rechten und einen Torero im linken Auge zu haben, statt eines Glaukoms?

Welcher Mönch würde sein Kloster nicht gerne erleuchten, statt in demselben im Dunkeln zu tappen? [...] «Ich male nicht nur figürlich, sondern multifigürlich, polymorph. Ich mag es, den Betrachter zum Spielen einzuladen. Ich fessele seine Aufmerksamkeit, vermittele ihm in der ersten Bildebene ein Gefühl von Schönheit oder von etwas Schrecklichem, und in einer zweiten oder sogar dritten Ebene verspürt er dann etwas ganz Anderes.

In dem tastenden Übergang von dem einen Sinneseindruck zum anderen gibt es einen magischen Moment, in dem ich mit dem Betrachter auf einer anderen Ebene kommuniziere, über das Unterbewusstsein und über den Geist.»

Wie gut, dass Octavio, der heute in *Cuernavaca* lebt, seine ganze Zeit nur darauf verwendet, eine neue Realität zu erfinden: die der Metamorphose! Ich erinnere mich an ausgeklügelte, aufwendige Bilder, in denen wir, als ich noch ein kleines Mädchen war, das Kaninchen suchen sollten, das sich im Gebüsch verirrt hatte, oder das Mädchen mit dem Engelsgesicht, den Zwerg im Vorhang, den Wachhund, die böse Hexe. Es war ein faszinierendes Spiel, das mir aber auch Angst machte. All das war also die ganze Zeit dort versteckt und wir hatten es nicht gesehen? Diese Bilder aus der Kinderzeitung beunruhigten mich so sehr, dass ich nicht mehr schlafen konnte. War es Zauberei oder Teufelswerk, Figuren zu entdecken, die sonst niemand sehen konnte, zumindest nicht auf den ersten Blick? Plötzlich erhielt die Natur eine andere Dimension, der Baum war nicht mehr harmlos, das Haus nicht mehr vertrauenswürdig. Hinter der Tür wartete noch etwas Anderes auf uns, etwas, das uns herausforderte und das wir auflösen, vervollständigen mussten. Hinter jeder menschlichen Begebenheit lauerte eine Falltür, eine unbekannte Ebene, eine unbeherrschbare Regung. Es konnte passieren, dass hinter der nächsten Ecke urplötzlich Dorian Gray auftauchte.

Was Octavio Ocampo uns durch seine metamorphische Malerei lehrt, ist, das Unbewusste zu befreien, auf unsere Impulse, die Mystik und die Macht der Verwandlung zu vertrauen und, vor allem, uns — den neugierigen, emotionalen und visuell empfänglichen Bildbetrachtern — bewusst zu machen, dass wir größer sein können als wir selbst.

Elena Poniatowska

Métamorphoser. Nous sommes tous multiformes, personne n'est qu'un seul individu. Nous nous transformons durant la nuit. Nous devenons plus âgés, nous changeons, nous nous métamorphosons. Parallèlement, des lignes autrefois pacifiques conduisent l'autre Moi à la surface. Rien n'est ce qu'il semble [...].

LES MÈRES n'ont aucune idée de tout ce qui peut se produire lorsqu'elles proposent durant un voyage à leurs enfants de regarder par la fenêtre et de contempler les nuages : « Regarde, celui- ci ressemble à un arbre, et celui- là, de l'autre côté, nous poursuit comme un chien. » – À l'époque, à Celaya, Doña Octaviana – qui créait son propre art textile, également au théâtre – ne se doutait pas qu'elle venait ainsi de planter la graine de *l'art métamorphique* dans la tête de son fils, Octavio. Mais ensuite, le garçon voit aussi des femmes dans des vases ou dans des oiseaux, des carafes en forme de vaches, des fleurs en forme de bouches, des maisons qui ressemblent à des pommes, des visages dans les sillons des champs [...] Sous la surface, le jeune garçon fait naître des paysages animiques, il couvre une lèvre supérieure de blé ou enveloppe un crâne de branches de fougères. Quant à *l'Iztaccihuatl* qui se dresse dans le ciel bleu, ce n'est pas un volcan, mais une femme endormie. Octavio voit des sirènes dans des bouteilles et des meubles en forme de guitare, il découvre des silhouettes stupéfiantes dans les veines du marbre, dans les formes de morceaux de rocher, dans des collines qui se transforment en fauteuils et dans les branches entrelacées des arbres.

la magie et tourne la tête dans toutes les directions. Pour les enfants, ces poupées géantes ouvrent les portes d'un monde fantastique avec des charrettes de défilé fabuleusement décorées, un monde qui n'a quasiment rien à voir avec la vie quotidienne. Plus que les autres, Octavio est submergé de surprise et de fascination.

Il voit une forme en chaque chose, comme dans les nuages. Il remplace mentalement les visages des hommes et des femmes qui s'activent devant lui par des têtes d'oiseaux ou d'amphibiens. Un jour, alors que l'une de ses institutrices [...] l'appelle au tableau pour écrire le mot *vaca* (vache), Octavio déclare : « Il vaut mieux que j'en dessine une » ; et il dessine une vache, mais voit en elle des choses que les autres ne peuvent voir [...] A l'école, il peint tout le temps, s'il n'est pas en train de chanter ou de danser [...].

« Je participe, maîtresse », « Je peins la décoration », « Je balaierai, je ferai tout ce que vous voulez, mais je ne veux pas apprendre les tables de multiplication par cœur, surtout pas celle de 3, elle est terrible [...] ».

Chez les légionnaires du Christ à *Tlalpan*, le jeune Octavio aimerait tellement devenir un saint, mais il prendra cependant très vite de la distance par

« L'un de mes premiers dessins était une poupée qui tapait du pied dans un ballon formé à partir de mes initiales. [Octavio Román Ocampo].»

[...] La famille d'Ocampo est une famille [...] d'artistes [...] tous peignent et dessinent, leur talent artistique saute aux yeux. Dès leur enfance, Don Ángel emmène ses fils, Ángel, Octavio, Eduardo et Gregorio à l'école des beaux-arts du sculpteur et peintre Salvador Zúñiga à Celaya. Ce dernier fabrique des *mojigangas* – de grandes figures burlesques en carton à l'intérieur desquelles se cache une personne qui danse et qui fait rire ou effraie les curieux. Quelquefois, ce sont deux personnes qui se trouvent à l'intérieur des figures, alors le *mojiganga* grandit comme sous l'effet de

rapport à ce projet. Là aussi, il attire l'attention en transformant la chapelle, lui conférant une beauté céleste. On l'y baptiserait certainement *Santo Niño Octavio de los Altares Barrocos* (Saint Enfant Octavio des Autels Baroques), mais il prend un grand plaisir aux fêtes terrestres ; ainsi, il décore par exemple la salle de jeux et la transforme en une splendide salle des fêtes, très engageante et mondaine. Ce besoin de tout embellir n'a rien en commun avec la tempérance monastique que l'on attend généralement des saints. Du séminariste qu'il voulait devenir à l'homme de théâtre,

il y avait plus d'un pas à faire, mais Octavio emprunta ce chemin avec succès. De l'autel et de l'encens, du prie-Dieu et des bouquets de lys, *de la sensualité* du rituel religieux, il conservera la théâtralité et une inclination pour les effets puissants. Rien ne suscite plus d'émotions qu'un confessionnal noir. En tant que scénographe et acteur, il participera à des pièces aux côtés de sa mère, Doña Octaviana, entre autres à *Las salvajes criaturas* (Les créatures sauvages).

Pour Octavio, peindre son premier mural à l'école était de la plus haute importance ; un premier pas vers la décoration ultérieure de la montée des escaliers de l'Hôtel de ville de *Celaya*. À partir de là et jusqu'à la véritable reconnaissance, il lui restait un autre pas qu'il effectua avec le soutien de Ruth, la fille préférée de Diego Rivera. Elle lui procura une bourse pour des études d'art dans la capitale. María Luisa *La China* Mendoza et Eduardo Deschamps admiraient ces premières peintures murales, et *La China* conjura Don Ángel avec [...] véhémence : « Vous portez une responsabilité à l'égard du Mexique et de toute l'humanité. Votre fils doit se rendre à Mexico pour y étudier l'art ! » Aussitôt dit, aussitôt fait. Fortement impressionné par *La China,* le père envoie non seulement Octavio à *La Esmeralda,* l'école supérieure des arts, mais aussi Ángel, l'aîné, à la *Escuela de la Ciudadela* pour y suivre des études de design et des métiers de l'art. Octavio obtient les meilleures notes ; il apprend chez Feliciano Peña, Santos Balmori, Fernando Castro Pacheco, Jorge González Camarena et Antonio Rodríguez, et termine ses études en cinq ans.

Parallèlement, les deux frères trouvent du temps pour collaborer avec Héctor Azar, et grâce à cela, la scénographie mexicaine s'enrichit de deux dessinateurs et créateurs extraordinaires. Et ce n'est pas tout, car deux nouveaux acteurs sont également nés, sous la direction de José Luis Ibáñez, Juan José Gurrola, Miguel Sabido, André Moreau et surtout Julio Castillo. Les deux frères se sentent également attirés par le cinéma, et Octavio dirige bientôt le service des accessoires *d'Estudios*

Ocampo and "Maternidad" – Ocampo con "Maternidad" – Ocampo und "Maternidad" – Ocampo et "Maternidad", 1989

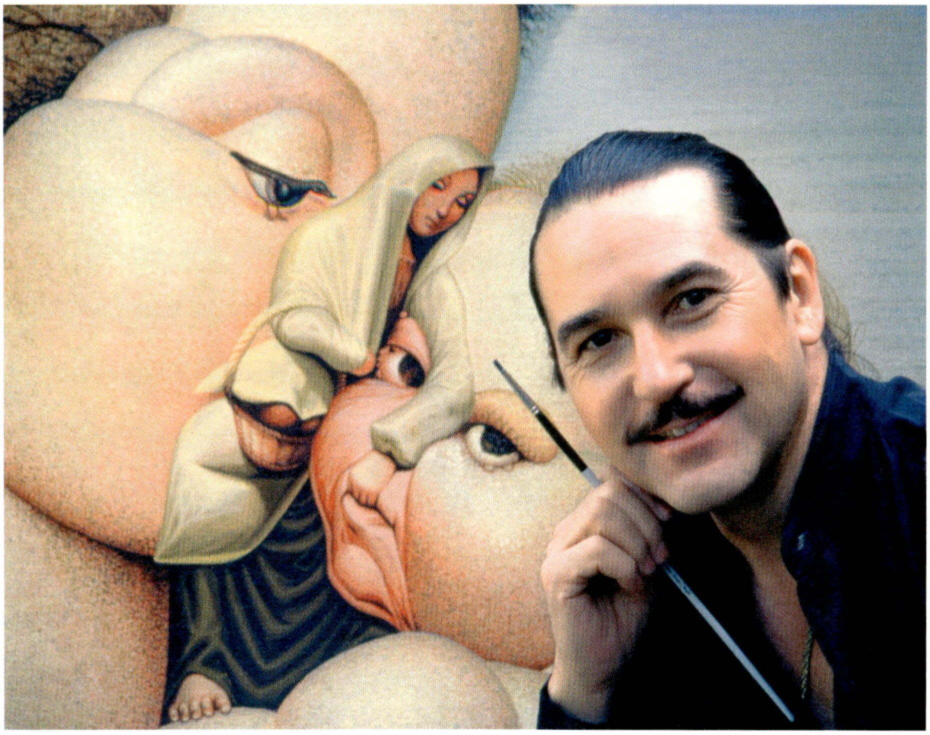

América. 120 films sont tournés sur quatre scènes et un petit *Backlot.* De 1966 à 1969 avec Luis Alcoriza. Manuel Michel, Jorge Fons, Juan Ibañez et Archibaldo Burns commencent à tourner des films tels que *Los Caifanes* et rivalisent avec Roberto Gavaldón, Emilio Gómez Muriel et Servando González. Ah, quels temps prometteurs pour le cinéma ! Les studios *Estudios América* filment continuellement, quelquefois quatre films en même temps. Toutefois, Octavio est bientôt lassé de ce *Pandémonium.* Tout comme Carlos Fuentes, il est un jour sur le point de souffrir d'un ulcère de l'estomac, et pour lui échapper, il tire sa révérence et prend un bateau pour l'Europe.

Après son retour, Octavio entre dans la *métamorphose,* prend des cours de danse chez Guillermina Bravo, Ofelia Medina et Rosa Bracho, chante chez Mónica Miguel, fait du théâtre avec Julio Castillo et José Luis Ibáñez et travaille comme acteur pour le théâtre et la télévision jusqu'à ce qu'il décide de rendre visite à son ami David Wiznievits à San Francisco.
Il atterrit au milieu des véhémentes protestations contre la guerre du Vietnam et le stationnement d'armes nucléaires, au milieu des hippies à Berkeley et des filles aux longues jambes dorées qui appellent sur les places publiques à remplacer les balles des fusils par des fleurs. Il prend des cours à l'institut des arts de San Francisco, et tant les professeurs que les élèves s'étonnent du réalisme de ses peintures. L'hyperréalisme n'avait pas encore fait son apparition aux États-Unis.
L'enfance est la racine, elle est l'origine et la source. C'est durant l'enfance que l'on trouve tout ce que nous serons lorsque nous serons grands. L'enfance est un catalyseur. Octavio revient à ce qui l'avait si passionnément enthousiasmé dans ses premières années ; il trouve des formes inattendues, de la magie et des miracles sur son chemin – et de nouvelles solutions.

Ce n'est pas qu'Ocampo méprise la réalité : mais il veut sortir d'elle. Pour prouver qu'il ne la méprise pas, il peint des puissants tels que Carter, Alemán ou De la Madrid (ainsi que López Portillo). Il peint des starlettes du cinéma comme Dolores del Río, Gloria Marín, María Douglas, et réalise trois portraits de Jane Fonda que Cesar Chávez, défenseur des droits de l'homme, lui a recommandée. Des affiches sont imprimées à partir de ce tableau afin de collecter de l'argent pour le mouvement des ouvriers agricoles et de leurs partisans. Octavio poursuit ses expériences d'optique et constate que de plus en plus d'éléments apparaissent, qui *métamorphosent* ses compositions visuelles.

Quel cavalier n'aimerait être la jambe de son cheval ? Quelle femme ne serait comblée de bonheur d'avoir un cavalier dans l'œil droit et un torero dans l'œil gauche plutôt qu'un glaucome ?
Quel moine ne préfèrerait illuminer son cloître plutôt que d'y avancer à tâtons dans l'obscurité ?
[...] « Je ne peins pas seulement de manière figurative, mais aussi multifigurative, polymorphe. J'aime inviter le spectateur à jouer. Je captive son attention, je lui procure au premier plan du tableau un sentiment de beauté ou de quelque chose de terrible, puis, au second ou même au troisième niveau, il éprouve quelque chose de tout à fait différent.
Dans le passage à tâtons d'une impression sensorielle à l'autre, il y a un moment magique pendant lequel je communique avec le spectateur à un autre niveau, par le subconscient et par l'esprit. »

Il est formidable qu'Octavio, qui vit aujourd'hui à *Cuernavaca,* consacre tout son temps à l'invention d'une nouvelle réalité : celle de la métamorphose ! Je me souviens des tableaux élaborés et complexes dans lesquels, lorsque j'étais encore une petite fille, nous devions chercher le lapin qui s'était égaré dans les broussailles, ou la fille avec un visage d'ange, le nain dans le rideau, le chien de garde, la vilaine sorcière. C'était un jeu fascinant, mais il m'effrayait aussi. Tout cela y était resté caché tout ce temps et nous ne l'avions pas vu ? Ces images du journal pour enfants m'inquiétaient tellement que je ne parvenais plus à dormir. Était-ce de la magie ou l'oeuvre du diable de découvrir des silhouettes que personne d'autre ne pouvait voir, tout au moins pas au premier regard ? Soudain, la nature prenait une autre dimension, l'arbre n'était plus inoffensif, la maison n'inspirait plus confiance. Derrière la porte, autre chose nous attendait encore, quelque chose qui nous défiait et que nous devions résoudre, compléter. Derrière chaque réalité humaine nous guettait une trappe, un niveau inconnu, un mouvement non maîtrisable. Peut-être même que Dorian Gray allait surgir du prochain recoin.
Ce qu'Octavio Ocampo nous enseigne à travers sa peinture métamorphique est de libérer l'inconscient, de faire confiance à nos impulsions, à la mystique et au pouvoir de la transformation, et surtout, il nous permet de prendre conscience – nous, les spectateurs curieux et réceptifs sur le plan émotionnel et visuel – du fait que nous pouvons être plus grands que nous-mêmes.

Elena Poniatowska

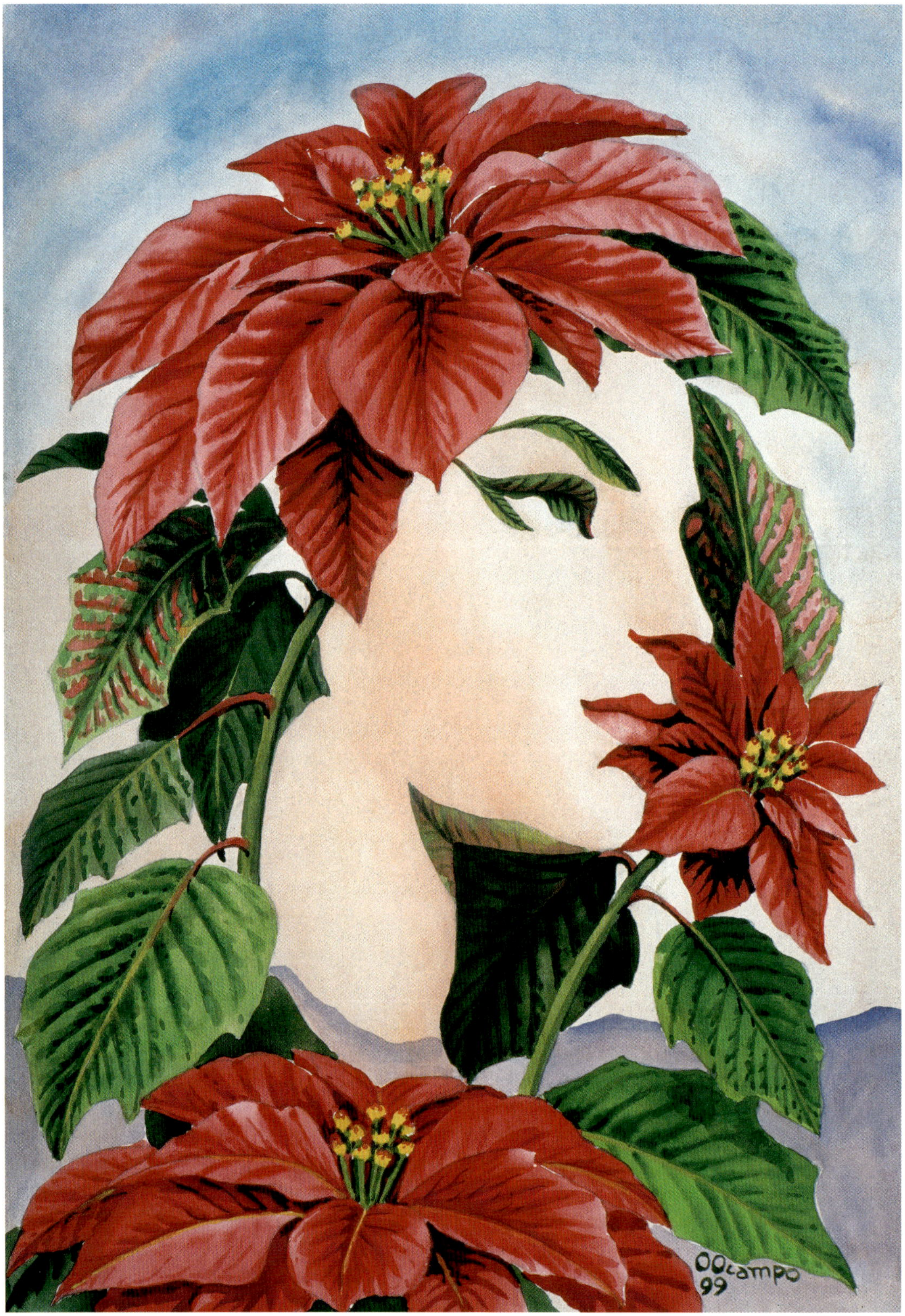

MUJER NOCHEBUENA II 1999 (36 × 52*)

Watercolor on paper – Acuarela sobre papel – Aquarell auf Papier – Aquarelle sur papier

** Dimensions in centimetres – Dimensiones en centimetros – Maße in Zentimeter – Dimensions en centimetres*

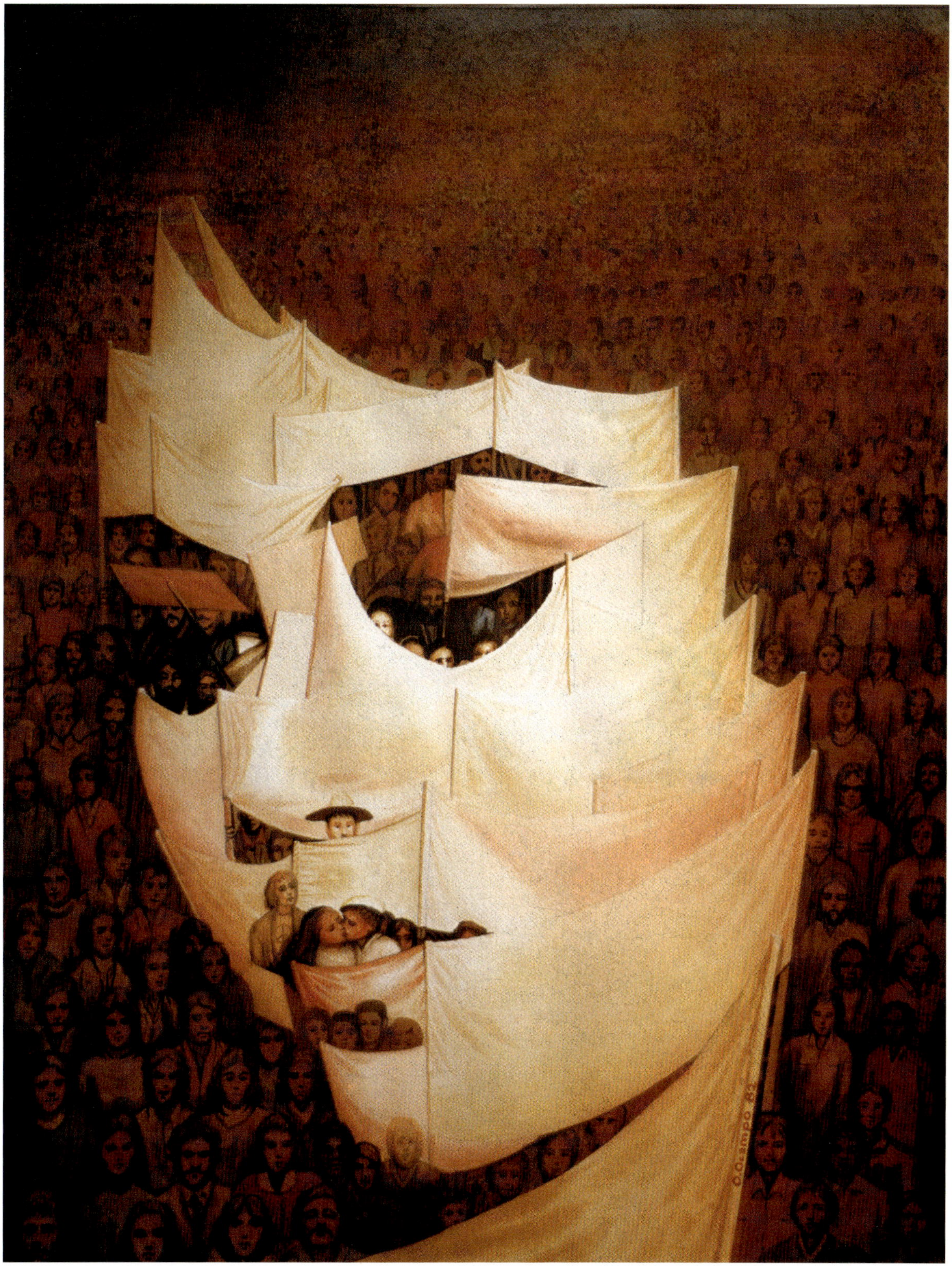

JANE FONDA 1982 (38 x 51)

Watercolor on cardboard – Acuarela sobre cartón – Aquarell auf Karton – Aquarelle sur carton

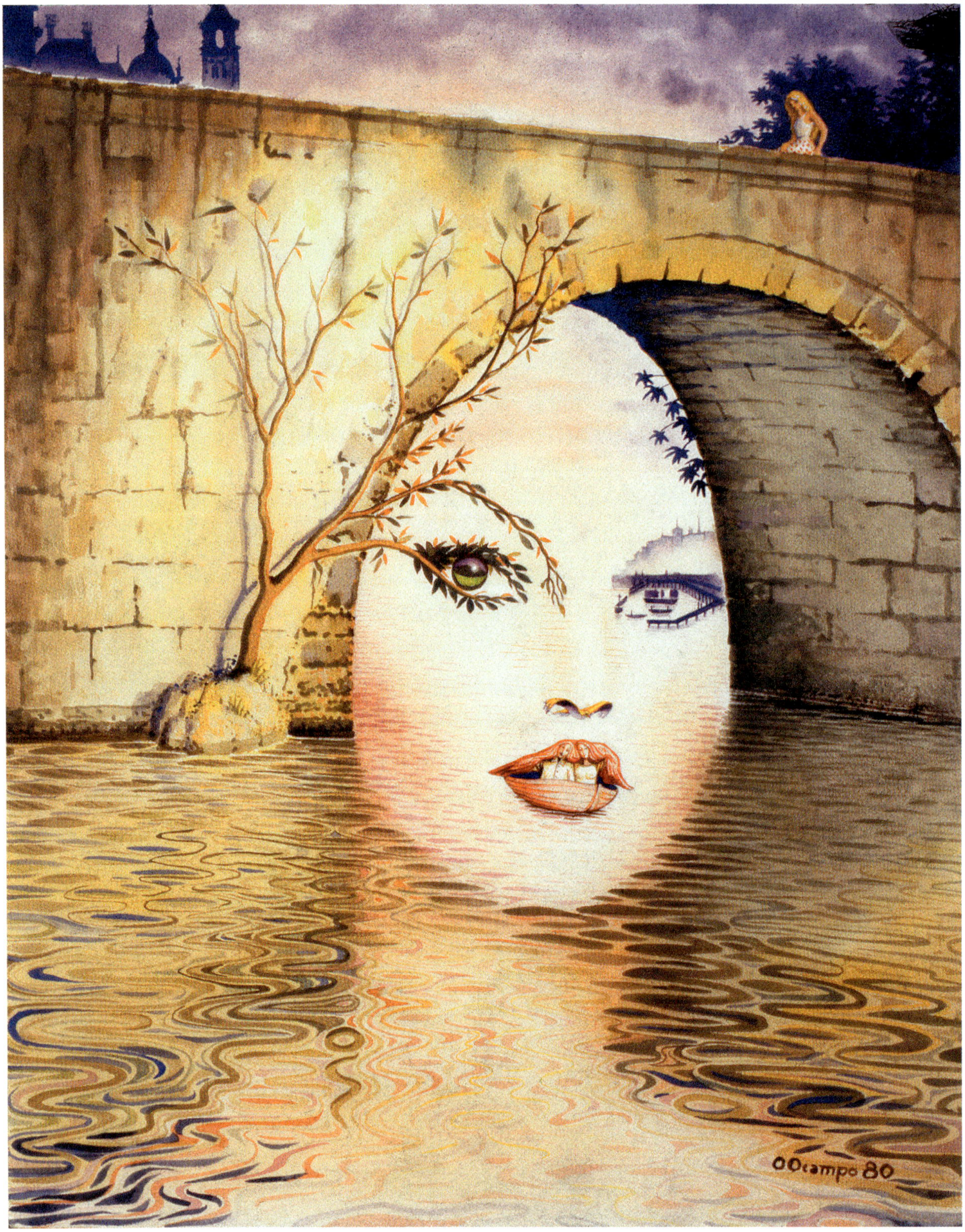

BRIGITTE ON THE BRIDGE 1980 (30 × 40)

Watercolor on paper – Acuarela sobre papel – Aquarell auf Papier – Aquarelle sur papier

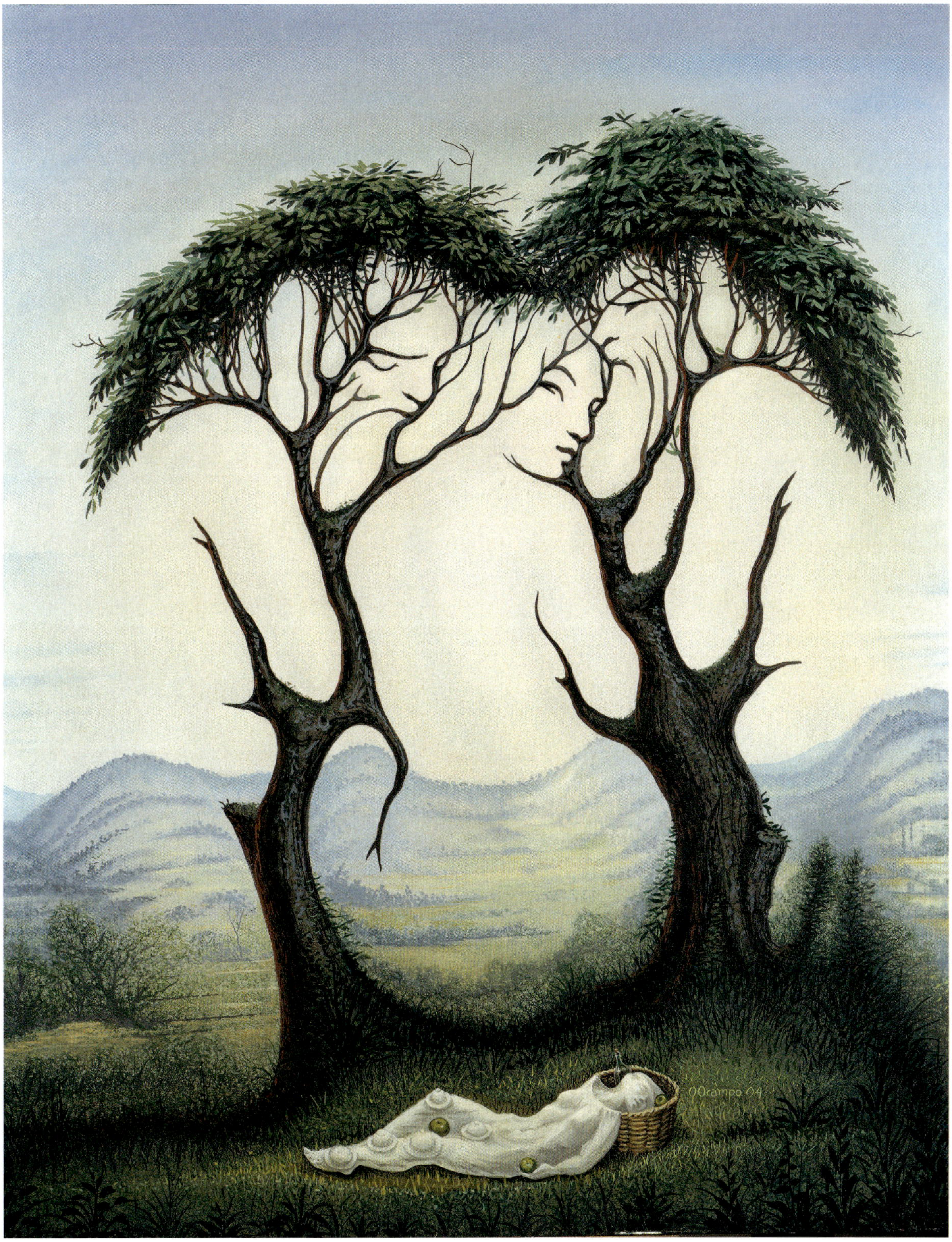

SUSANA Y LOS VIEJOS 2004 (80 × 110)

Oil on canvas – Óleo sobre tela – Öl auf Leinwand – Huile sur toile

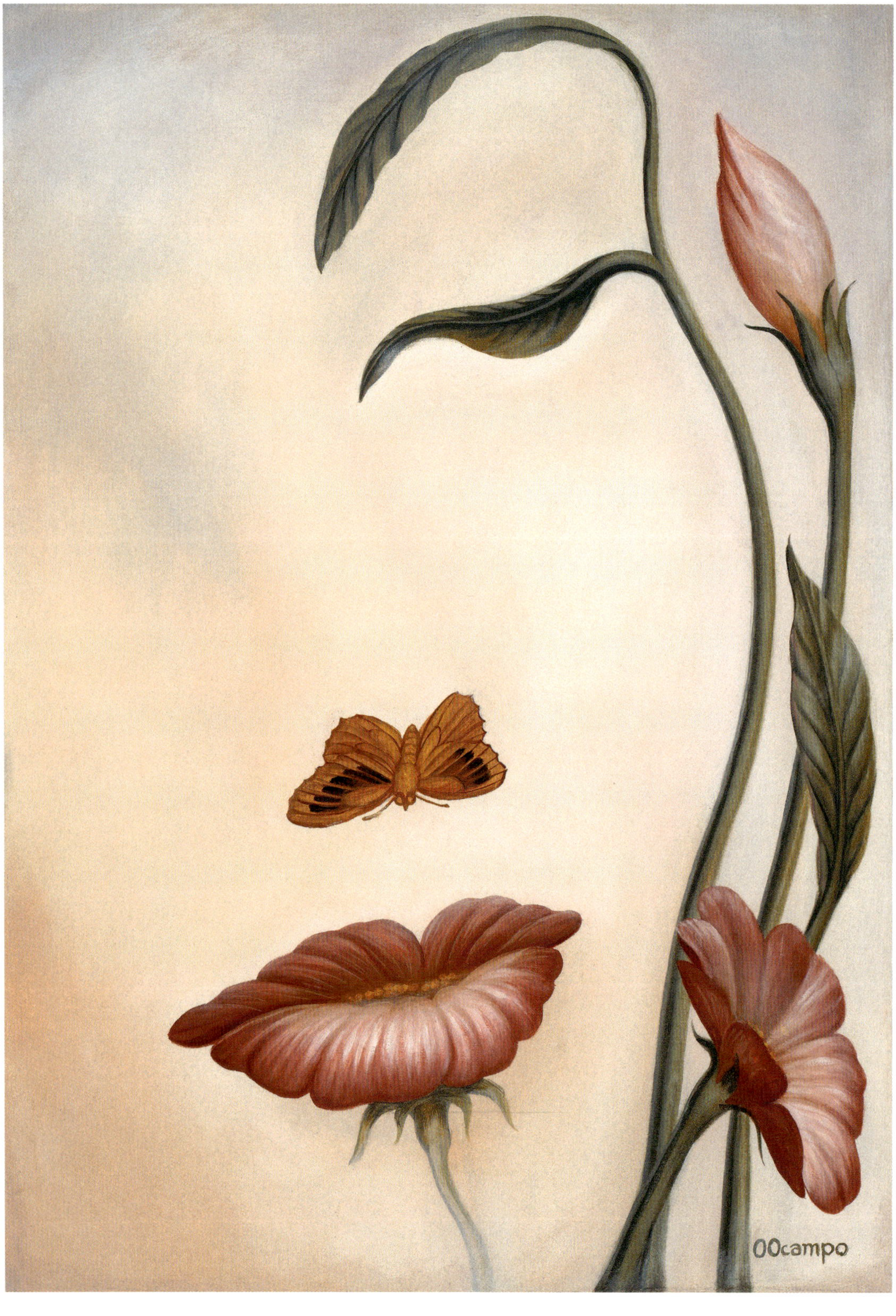

BOCA FLOR 1983 (40 × 60)

Oil on canvas – Óleo sobre tela – Öl auf Leinwand – Huile sur toile

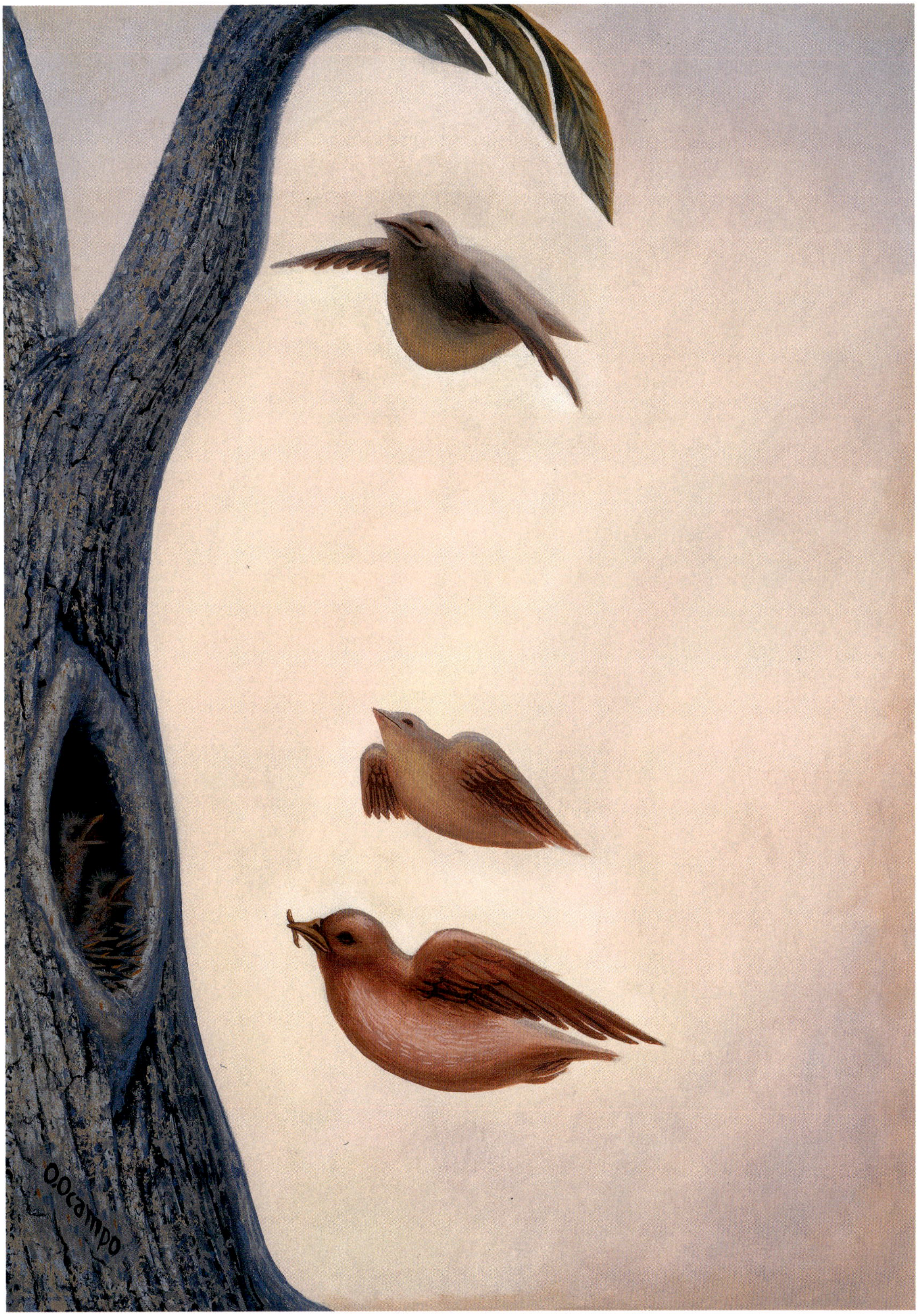

FAMILIA DE PÁJAROS 2000 (40 × 60)

Oil on canvas – Óleo sobre tela – Öl auf Leinwand – Huile sur toile

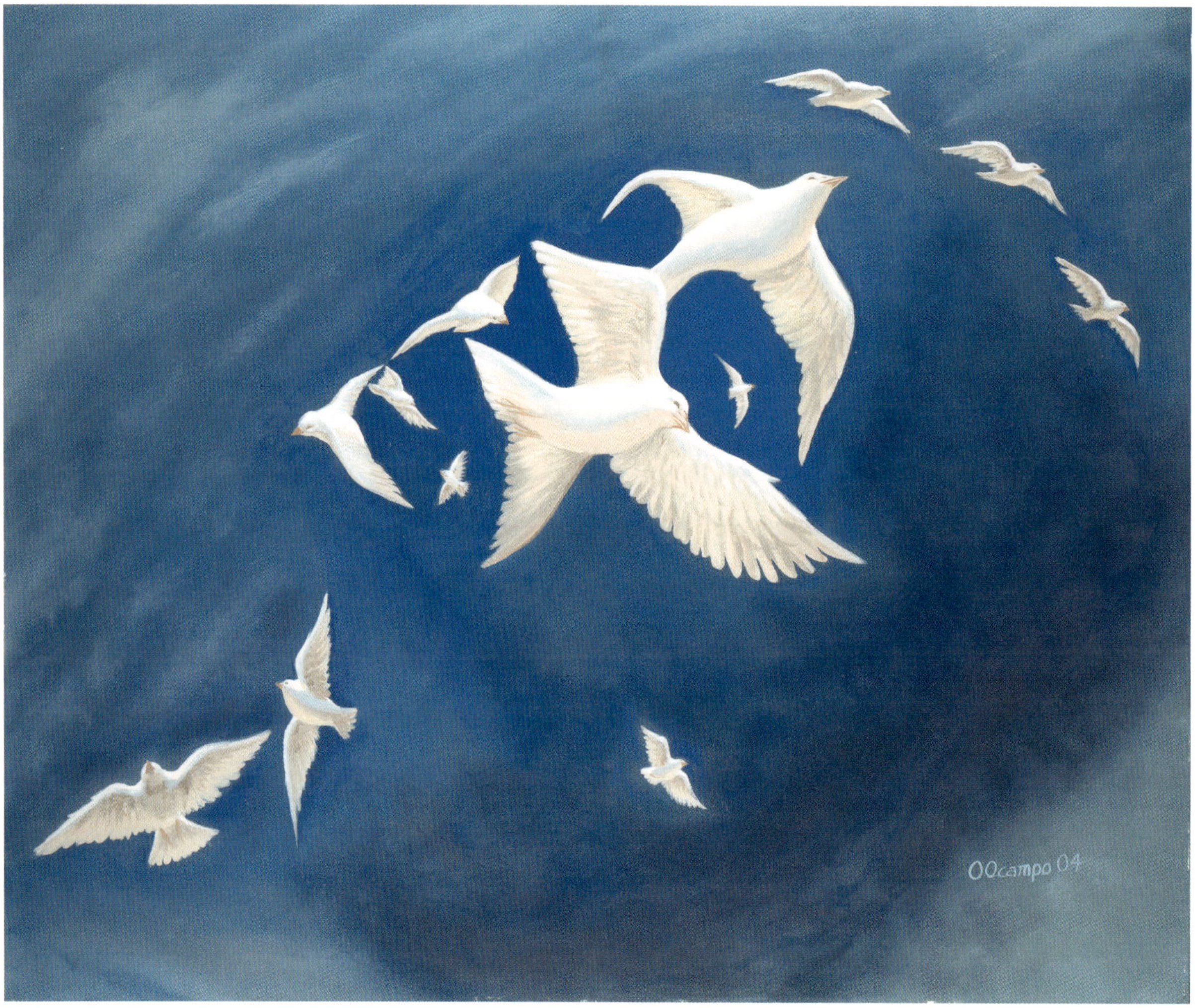

RUDY 2004 (120 × 90)
Oil on canvas – Óleo sobre tela – Öl auf Leinwand – Huile sur toile

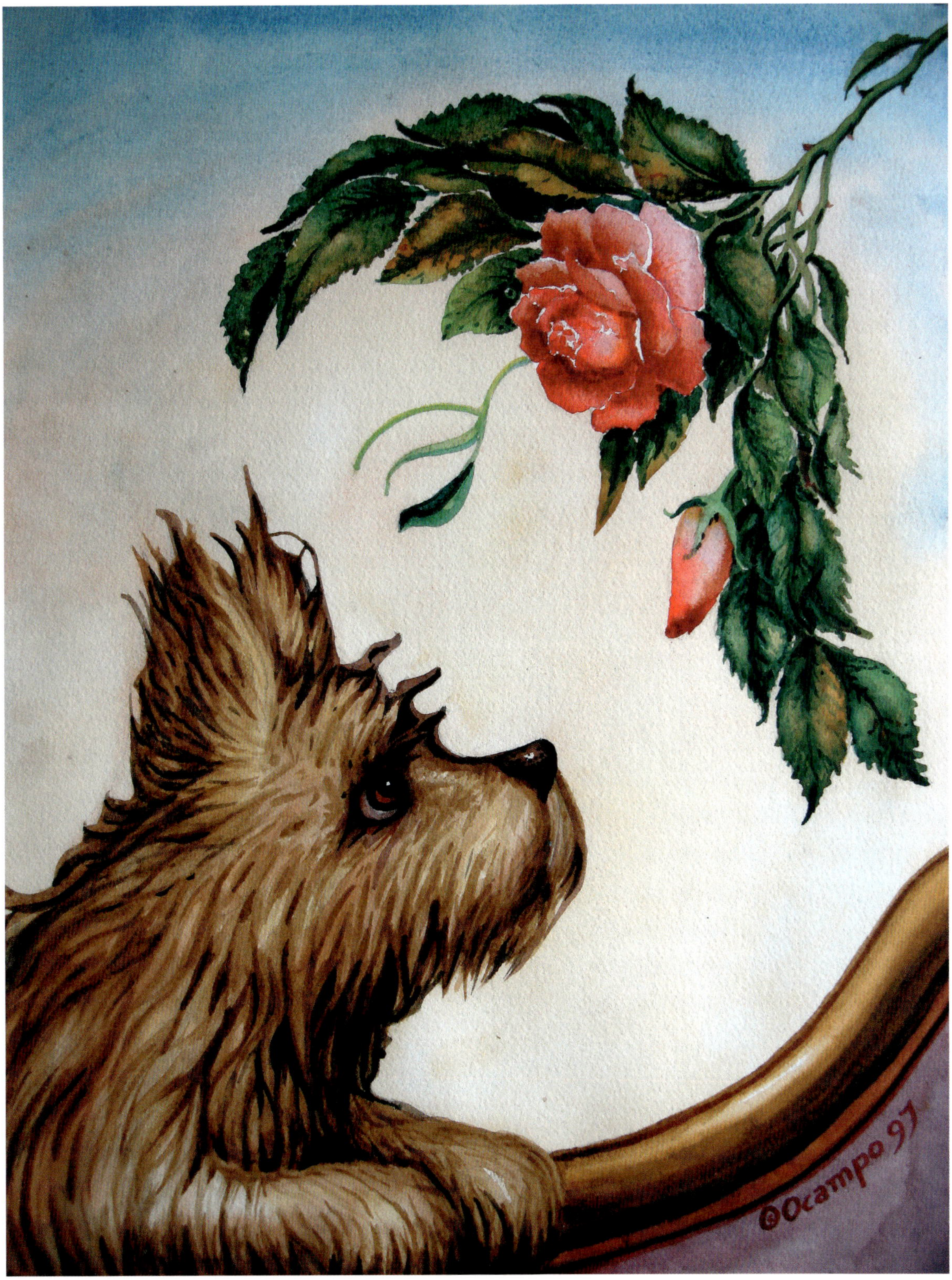

EL PERRO Y LA ROSA 1997 (31 × 41)

Watercolor on paper – Acuarela sobre papel – Aquarell auf Papier – Aquarelle sur papier

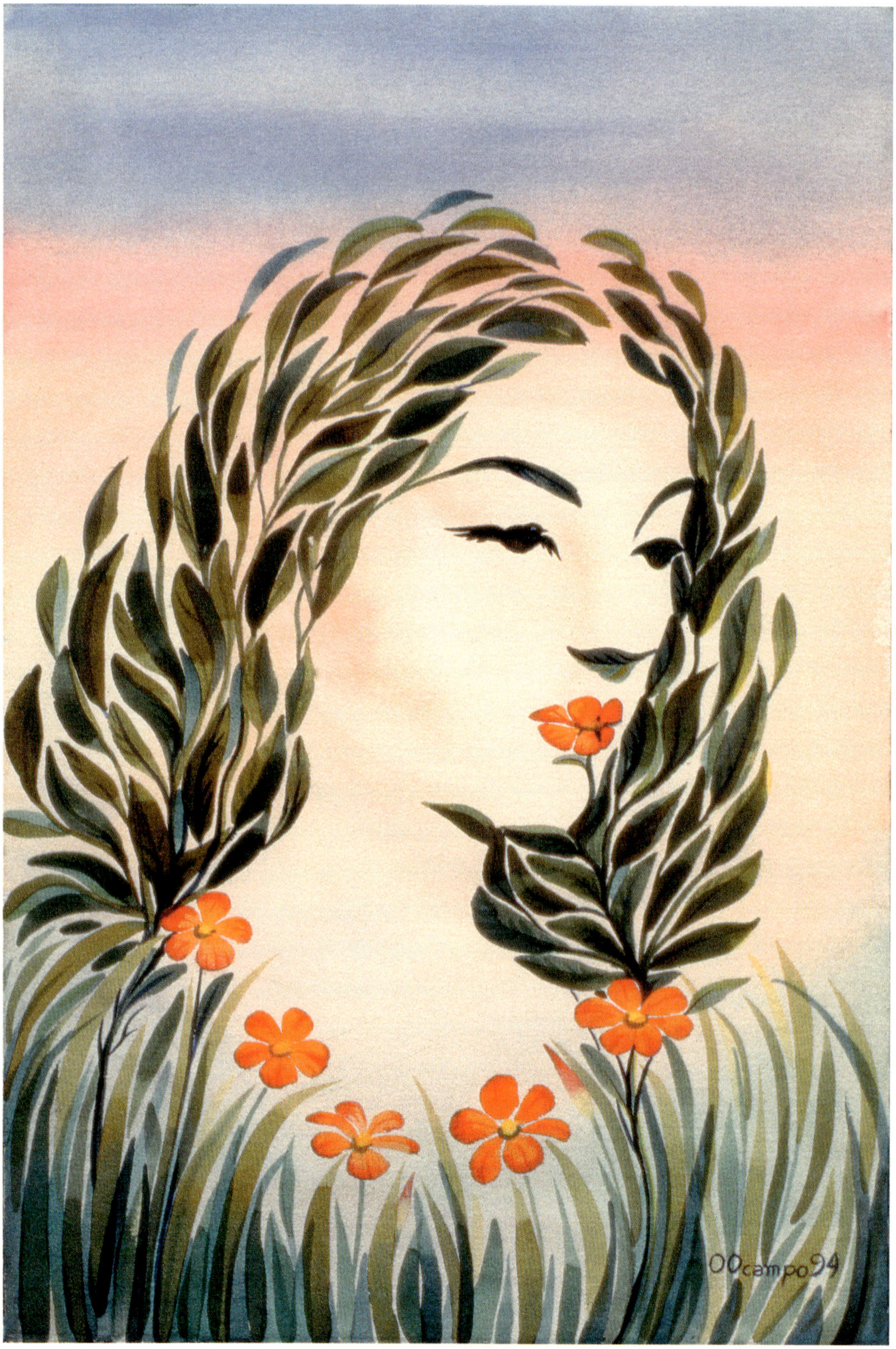

BELÉN 1994 (38 × 51)

Watercolor on paper – Acuarela sobre papel – Aquarell auf Papier – Aquarelle sur papier

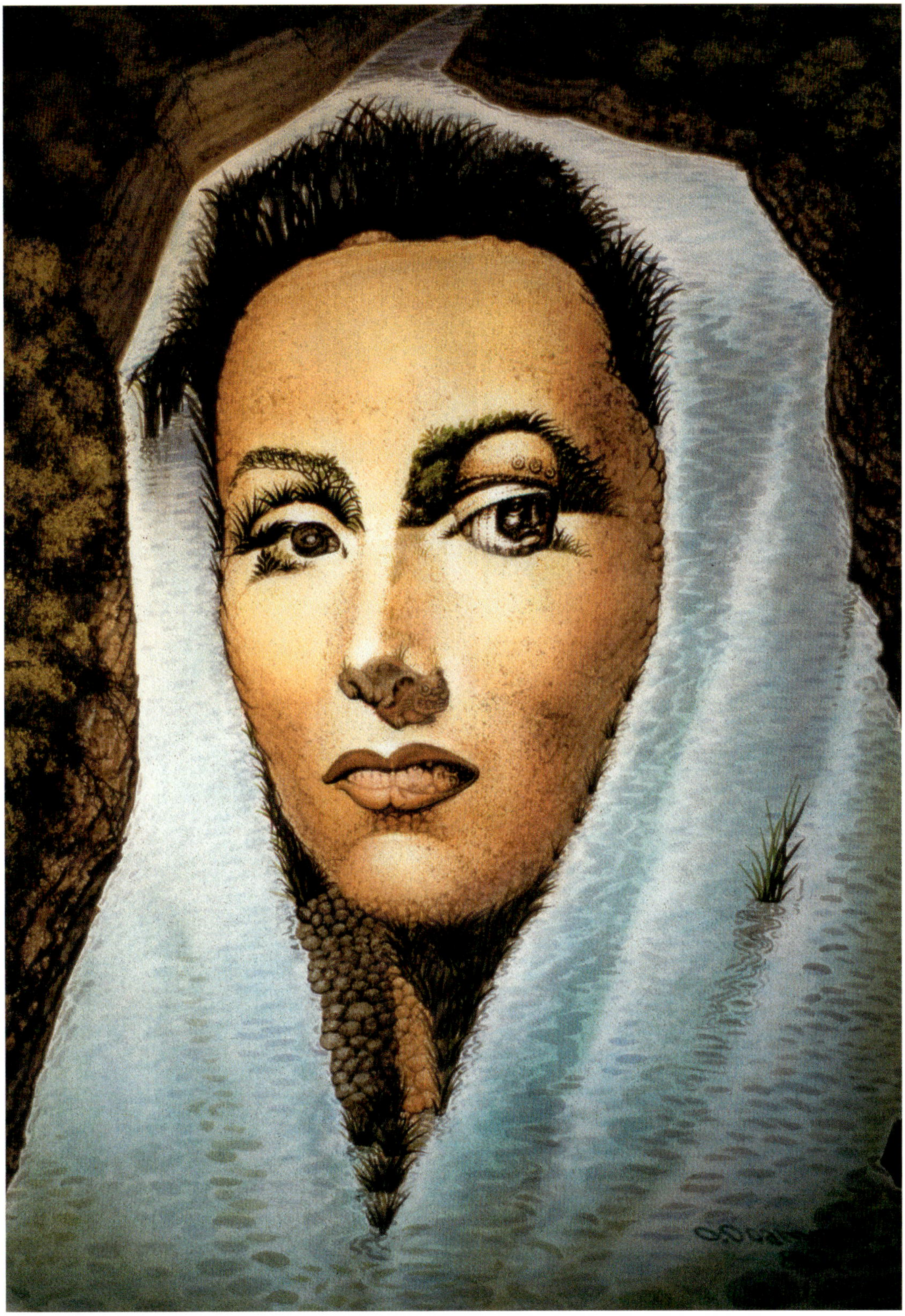

DOLORES DEL RÍO 1982 (38 × 51)

Watercolor on paper – Acuarela sobre papel – Aquarell auf Papier – Aquarelle sur papier

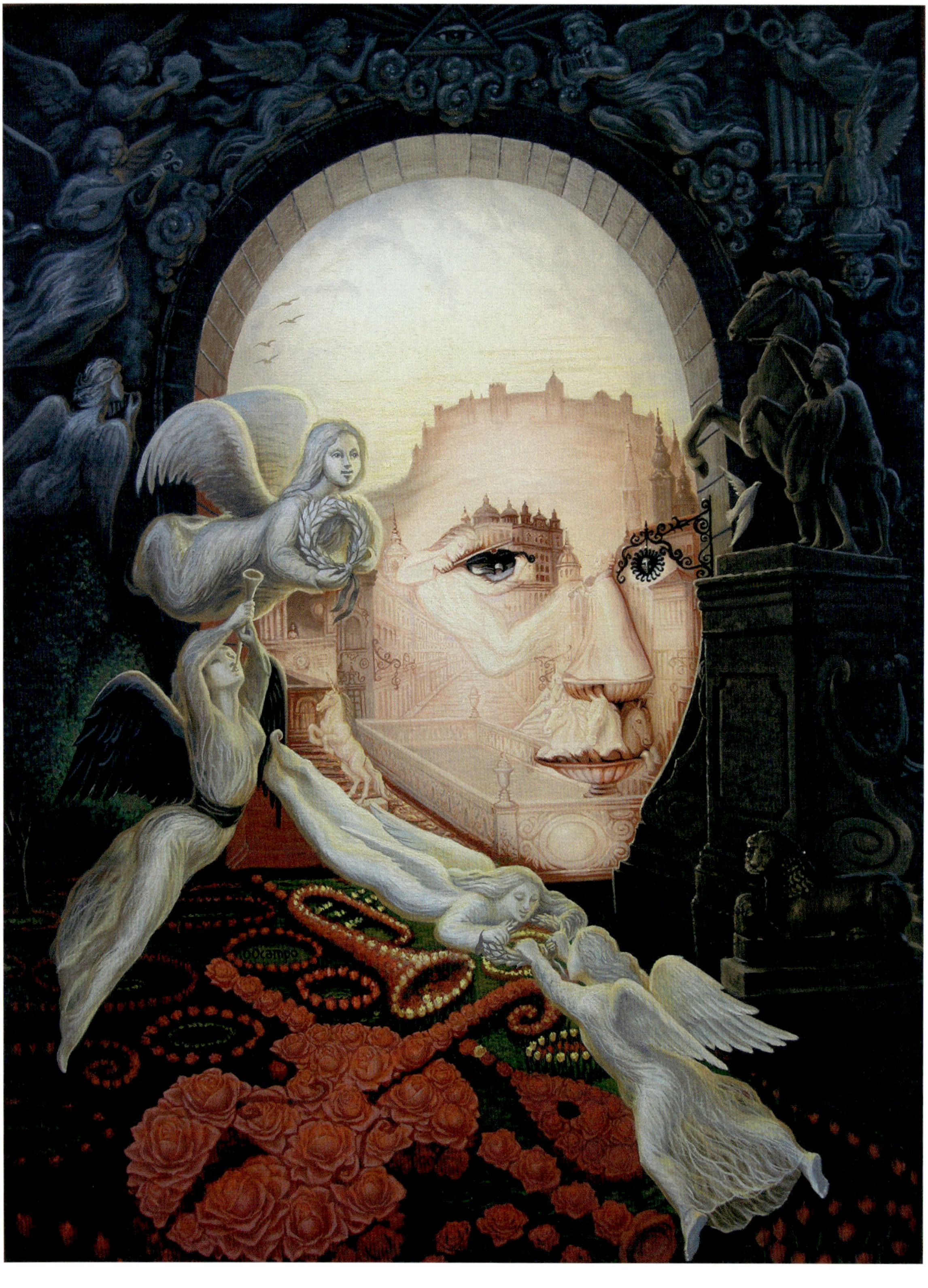

A. MOZART 2006 (90 × 120)

Oil on canvas – Óleo sobre tela – Öl auf Leinwand – Huile sur toile

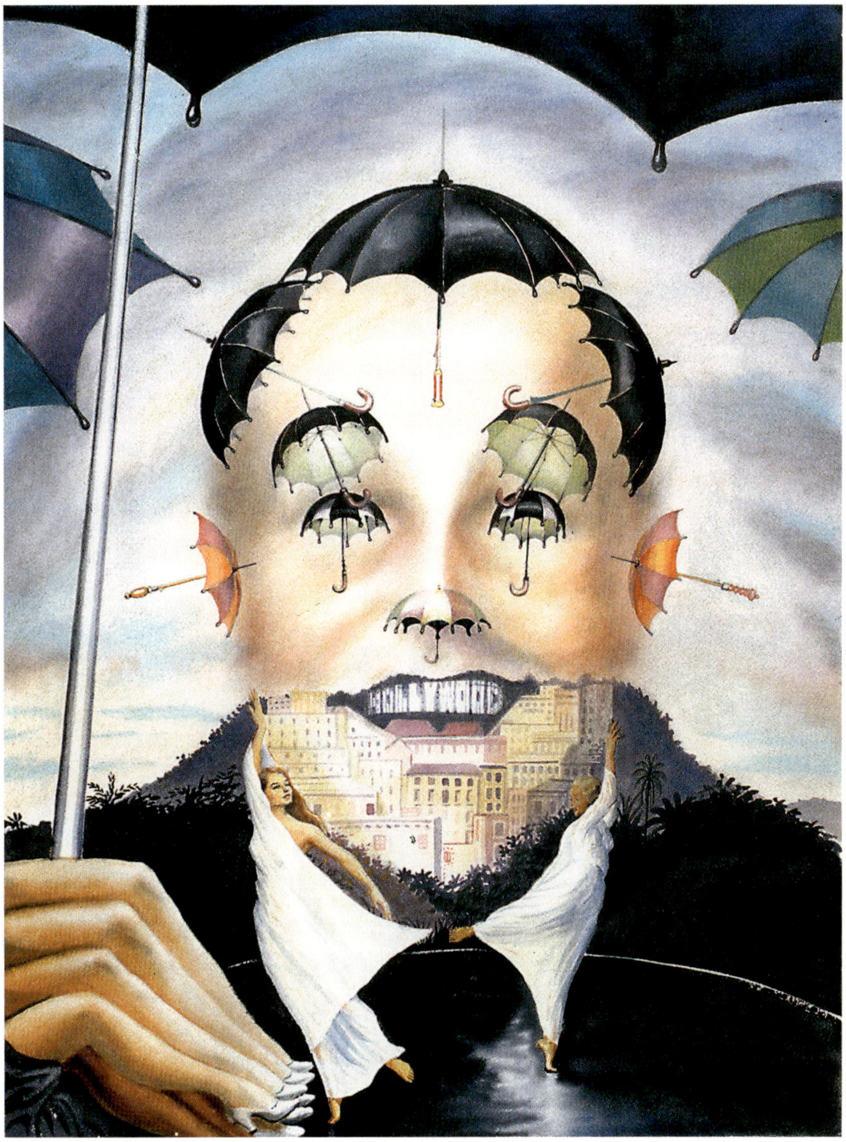

GENE KELLY 1981 (80 × 100)

Oil on canvas – Óleo sobre tela – Öl auf Leinwand – Huile sur toile

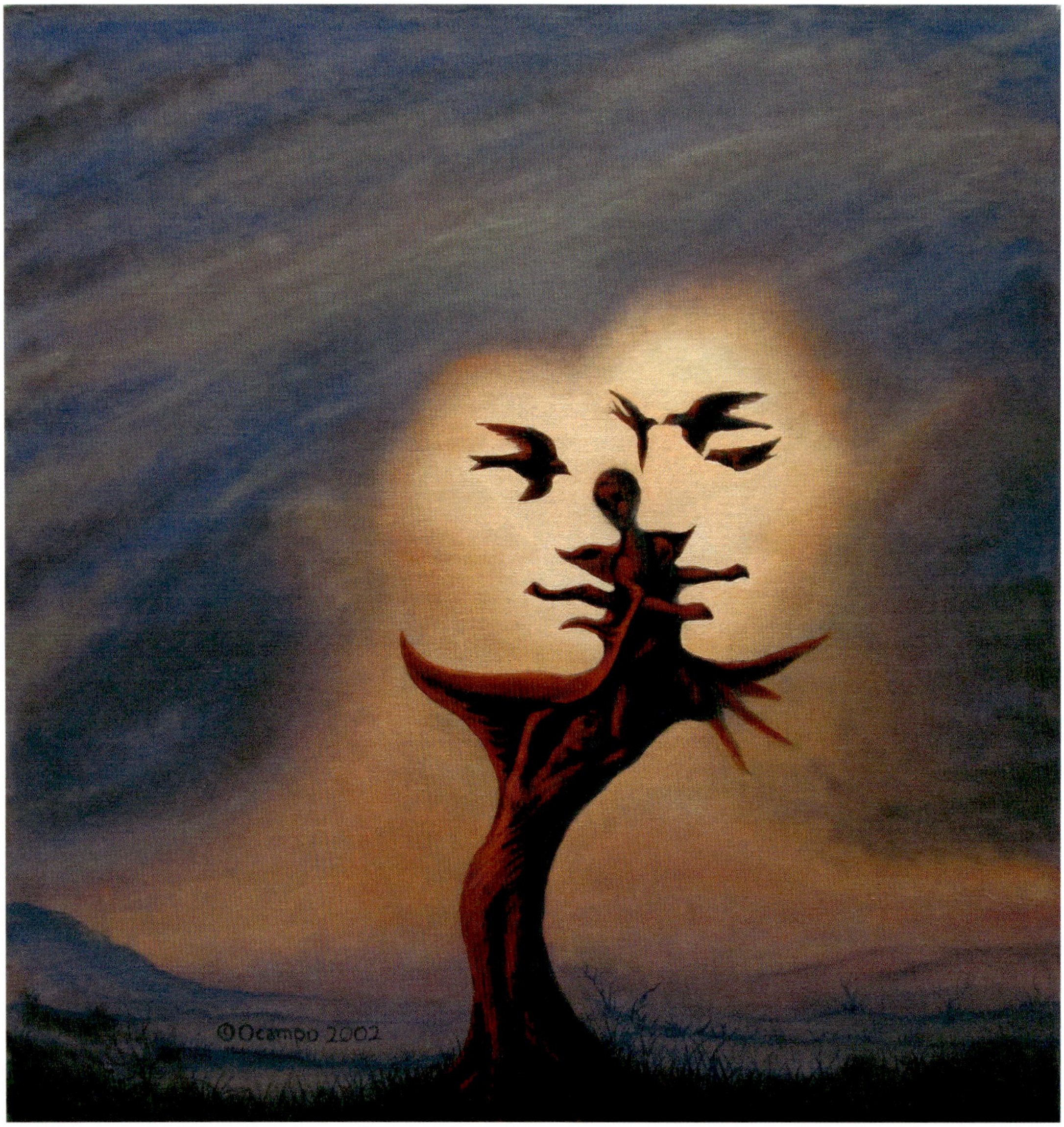

AMOR AL VUELO 2002 (61 × 58)

Oil on canvas – Óleo sobre tela – Öl auf Leinwand – Huile sur toile

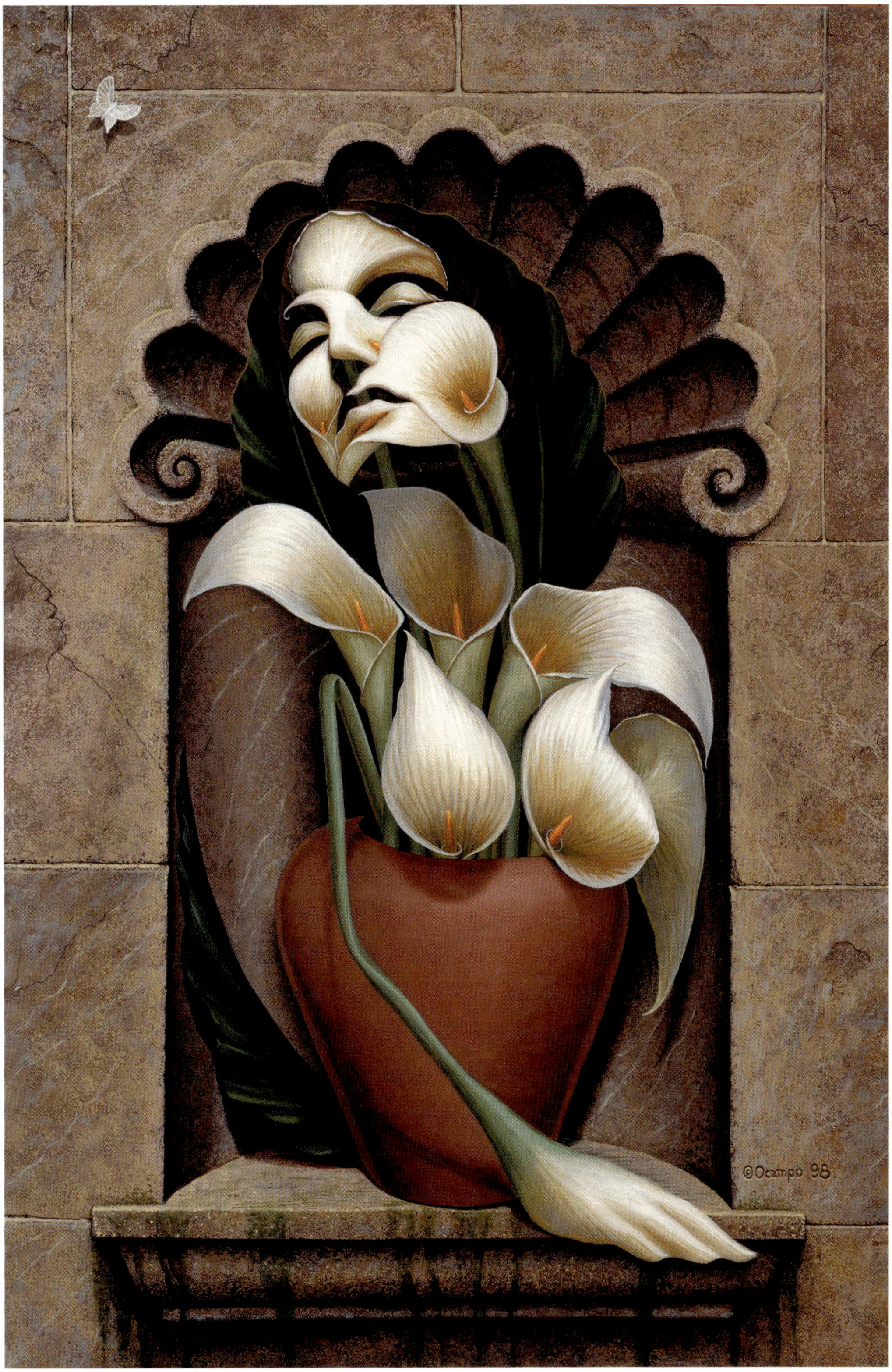

ÉXTASIS DEL ALCATRAZ 1998 (80 × 120)

Oil on canvas – Óleo sobre tela – Öl auf Leinwand – Huile sur toile

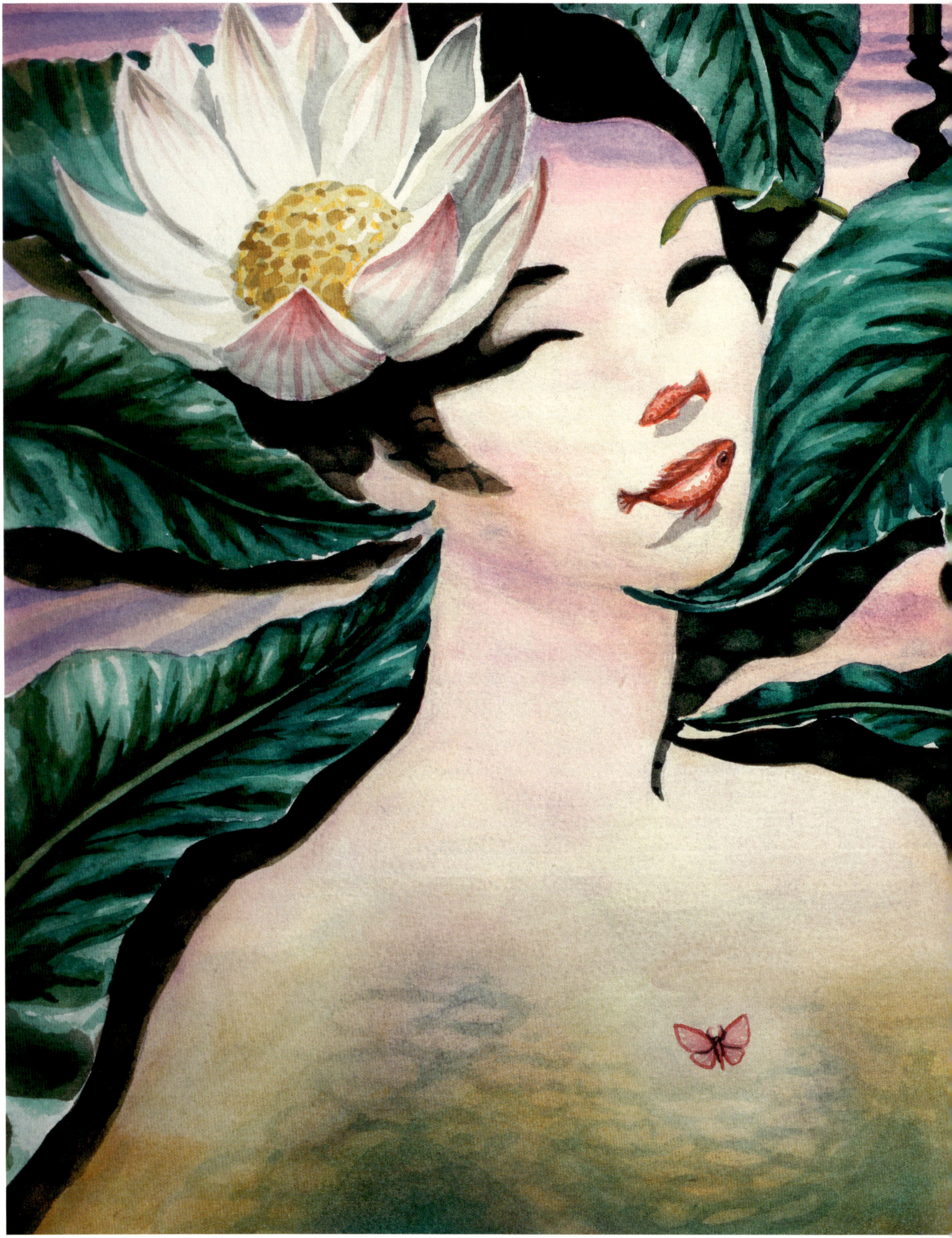

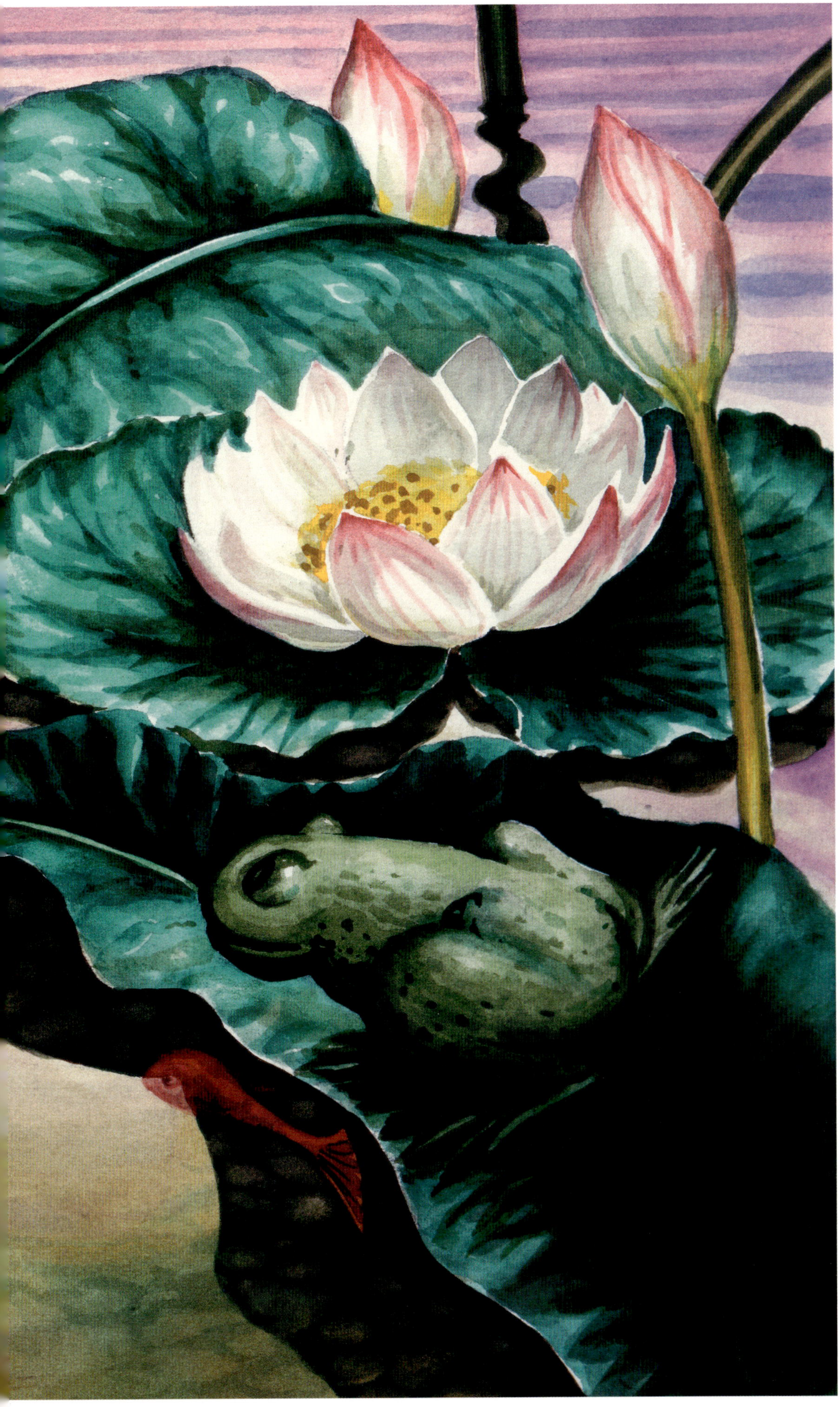

LOTOS, PECES, RANA Y ABALLOS 1998 (48 × 34)

Watercolor on paper – Acuarela sobre papel – Aquarell auf Papier – Aquarelle sur papier

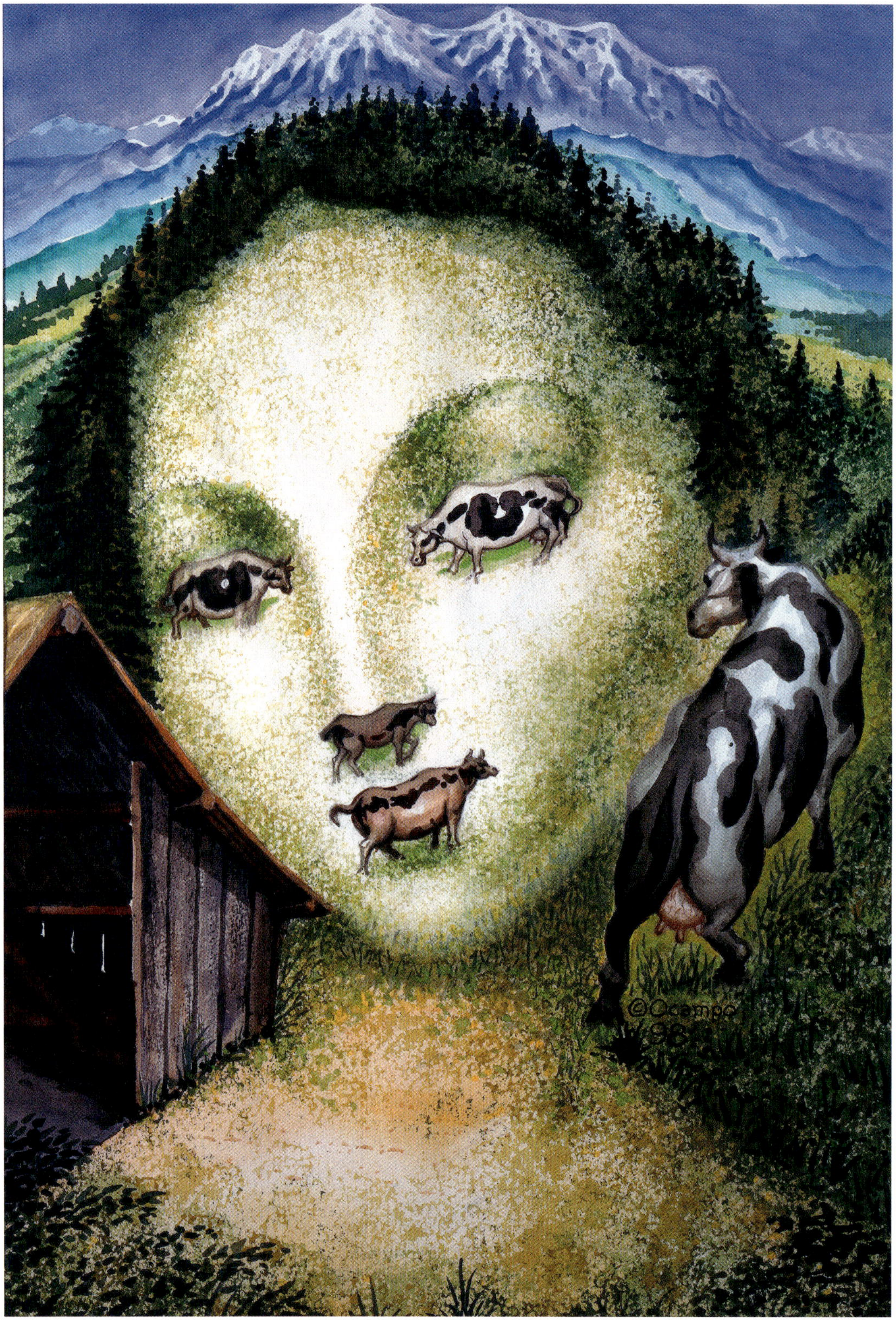

LA GRANJA 1998 (31 × 41)

Watercolor on paper – Acuarela sobre papel – Aquarell auf Papier – Aquarelle sur papier

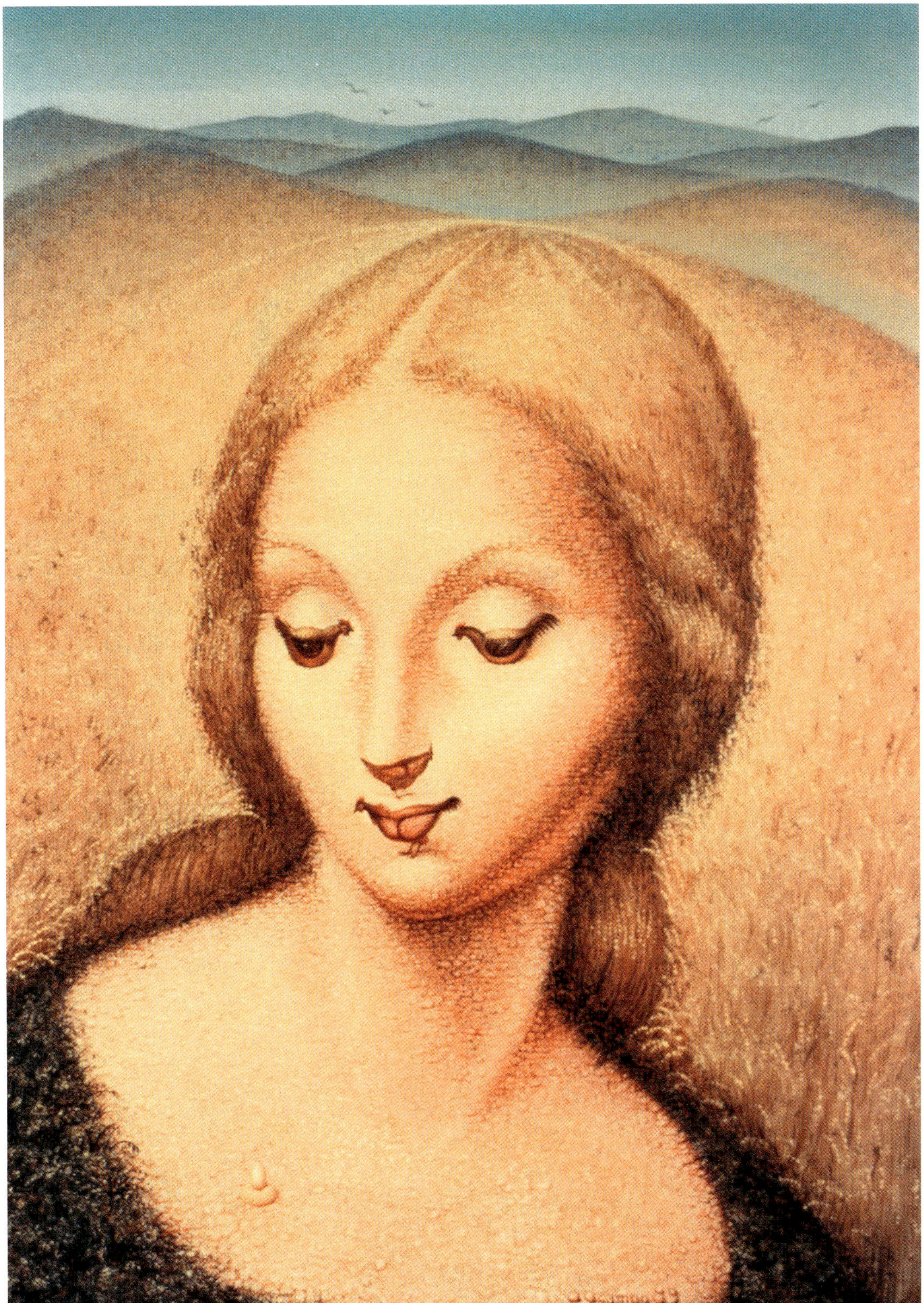

EL PRINCIPIO 1989 (70 × 100)

Oil on canvas – Óleo sobre tela – Öl auf Leinwand – Huile sur toile

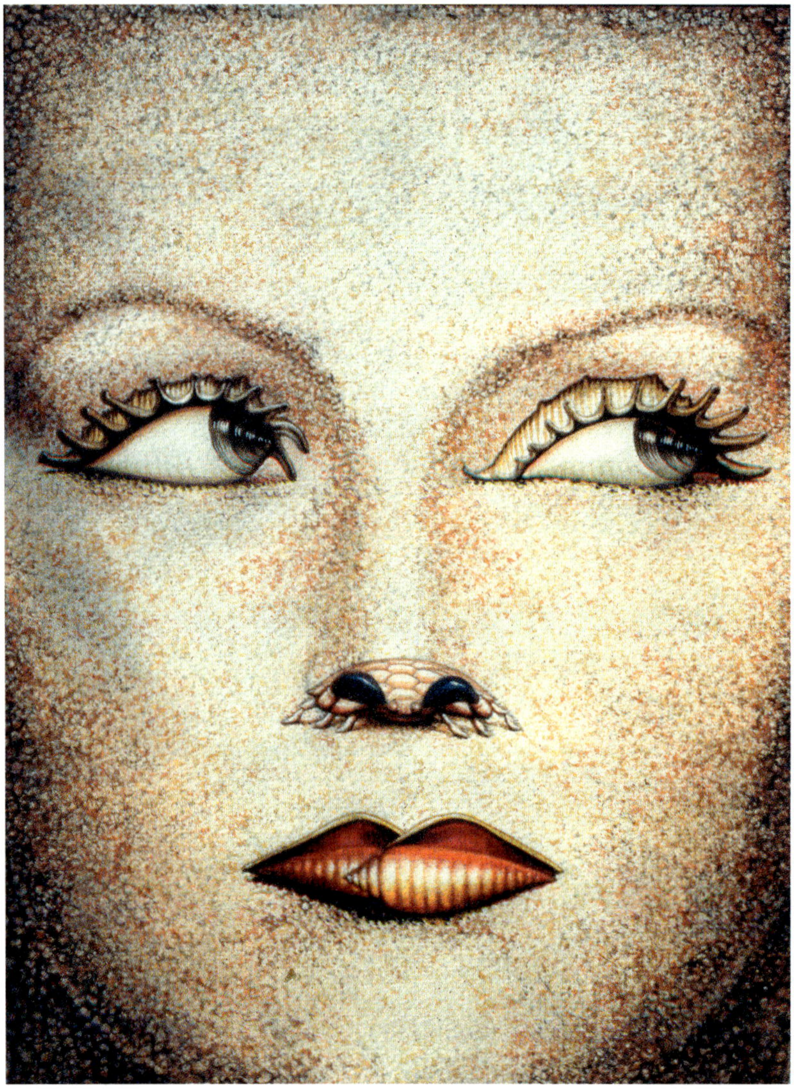

CARACOLES GRETA 1986 (38 × 51)

Watercolor on paper – Acuarela sobre papel – Aquarell auf Papier – Aquarelle sur papier

MARGARITA 1979 (80 × 100)

Oil on canvas – Óleo sobre tela – Öl auf Leinwand – Huile sur toile

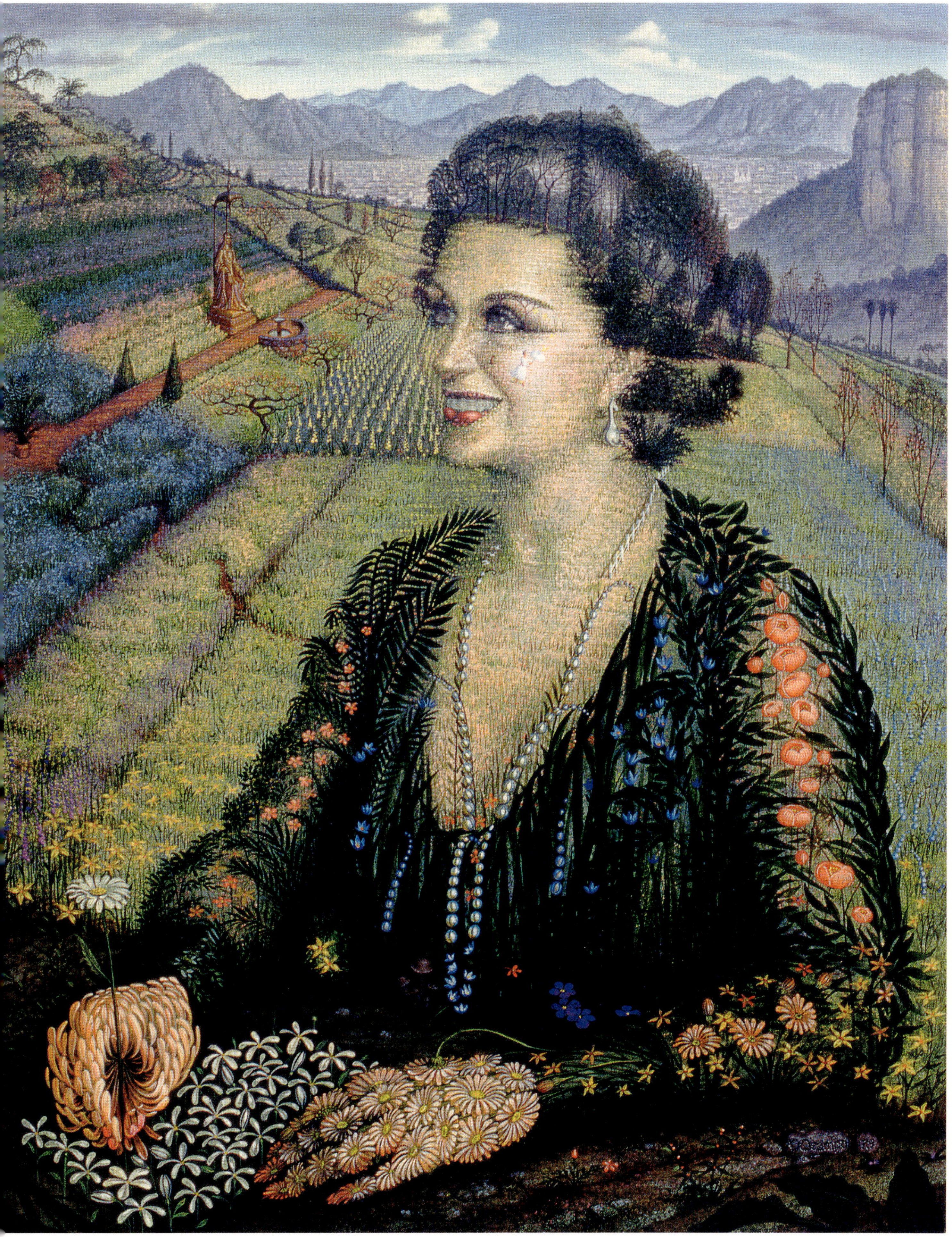

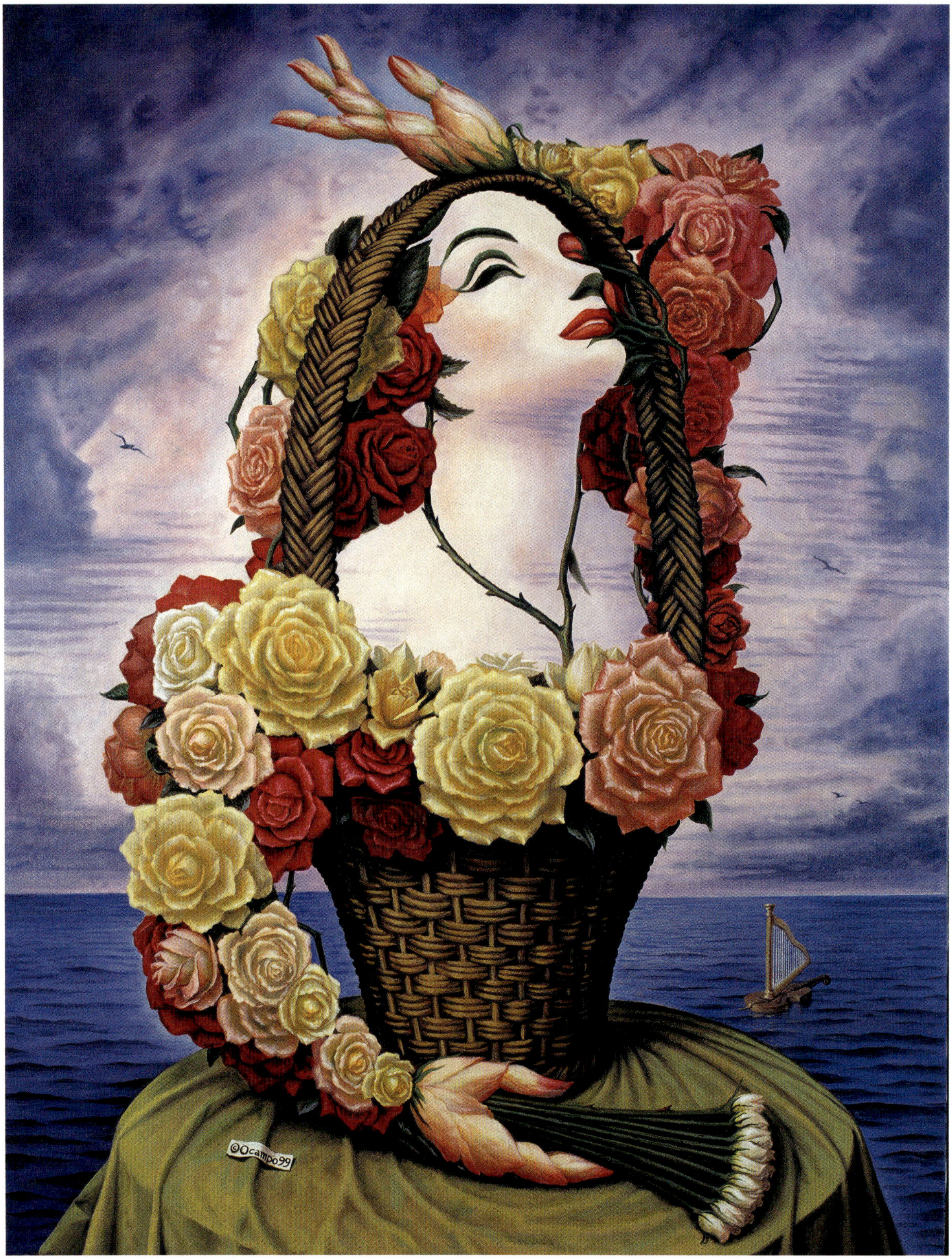

CANASTA DE ROSAS 1999 (90 × 120)

Oil on canvas – Óleo sobre tela – Öl auf Leinwand – Huile sur toile

JIMMY CARTER 1979 (80 × 100)

Oil on canvas – Óleo sobre tela – Öl auf Leinwand – Huile sur toile

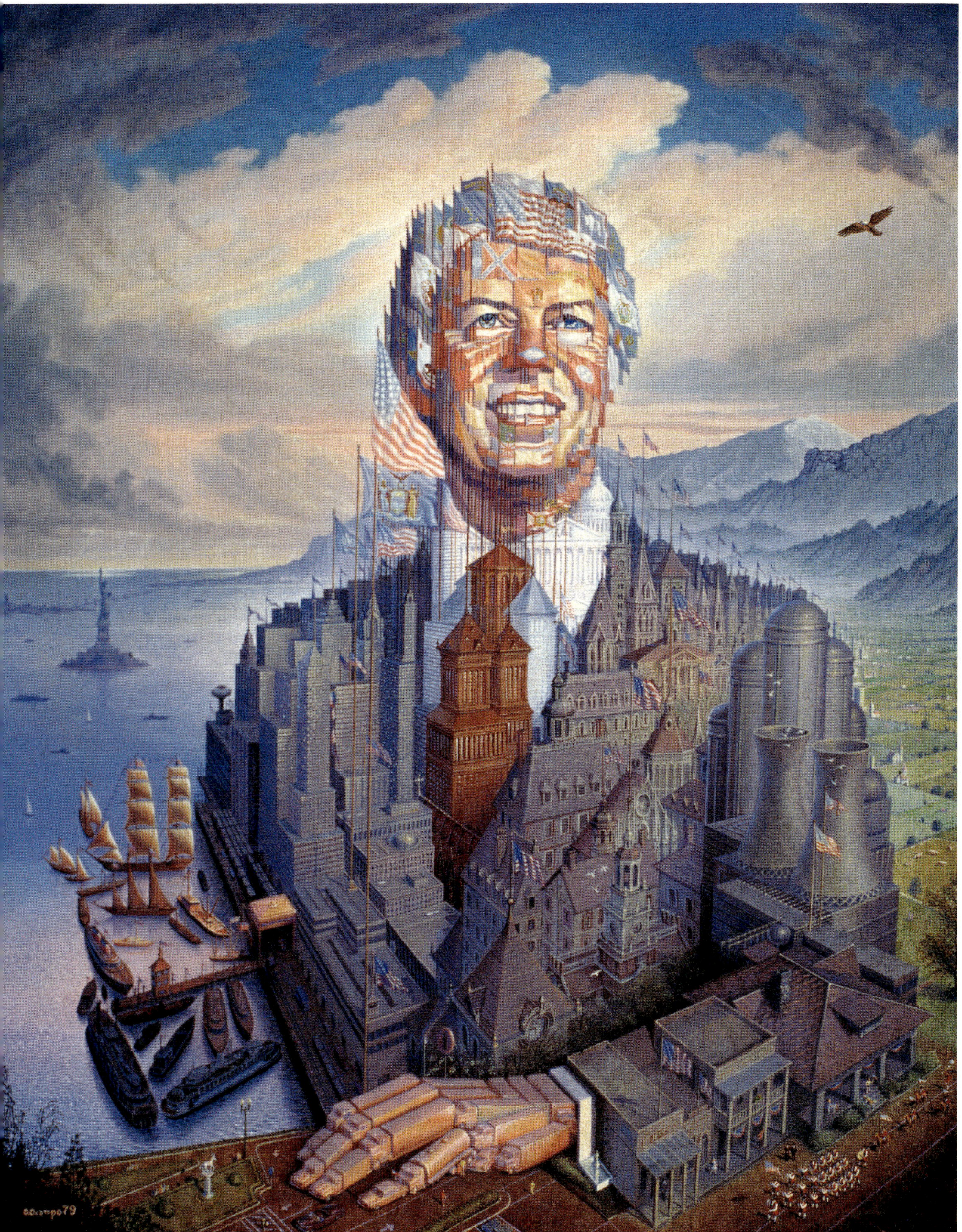
ocampo79

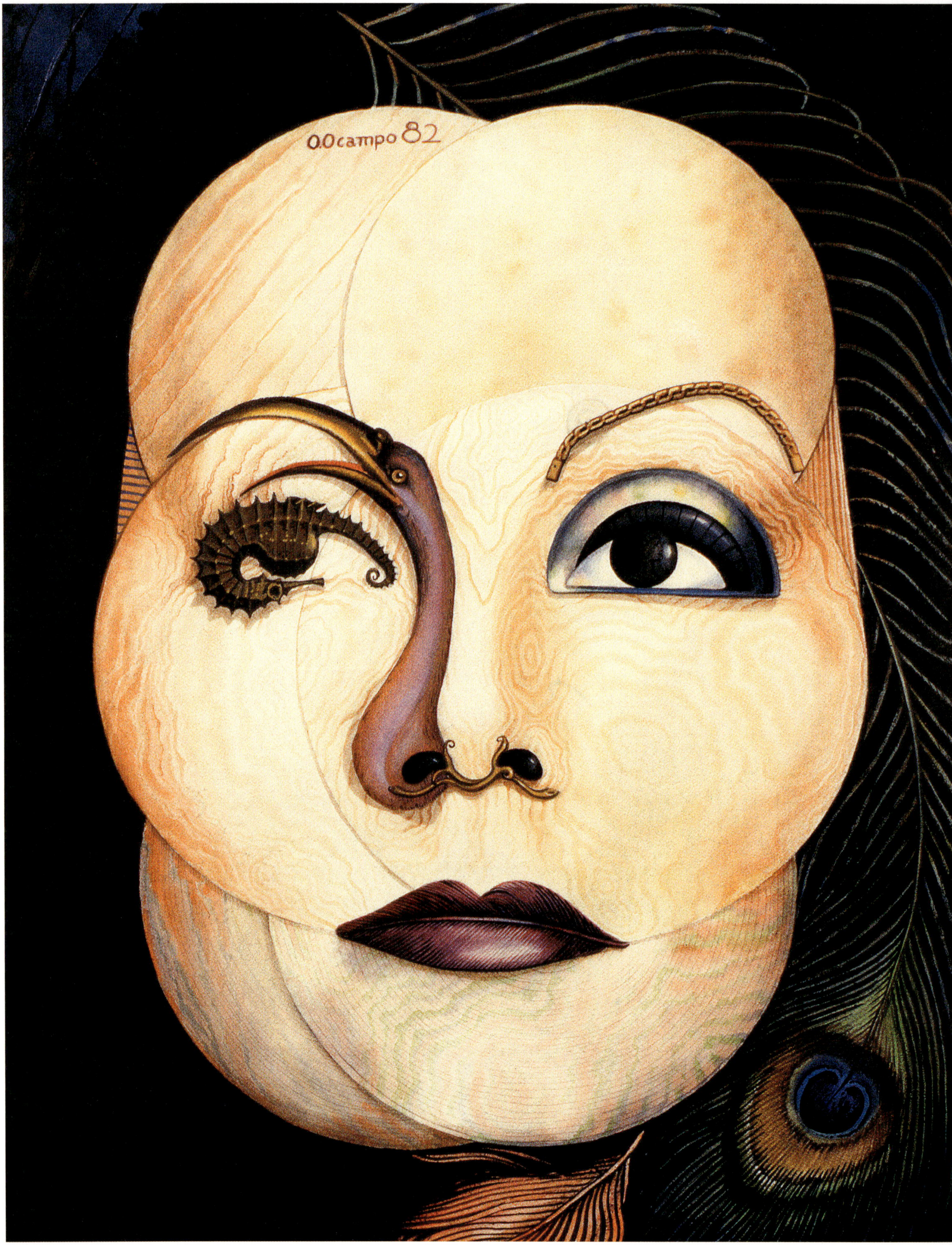
O.Ocampo 82

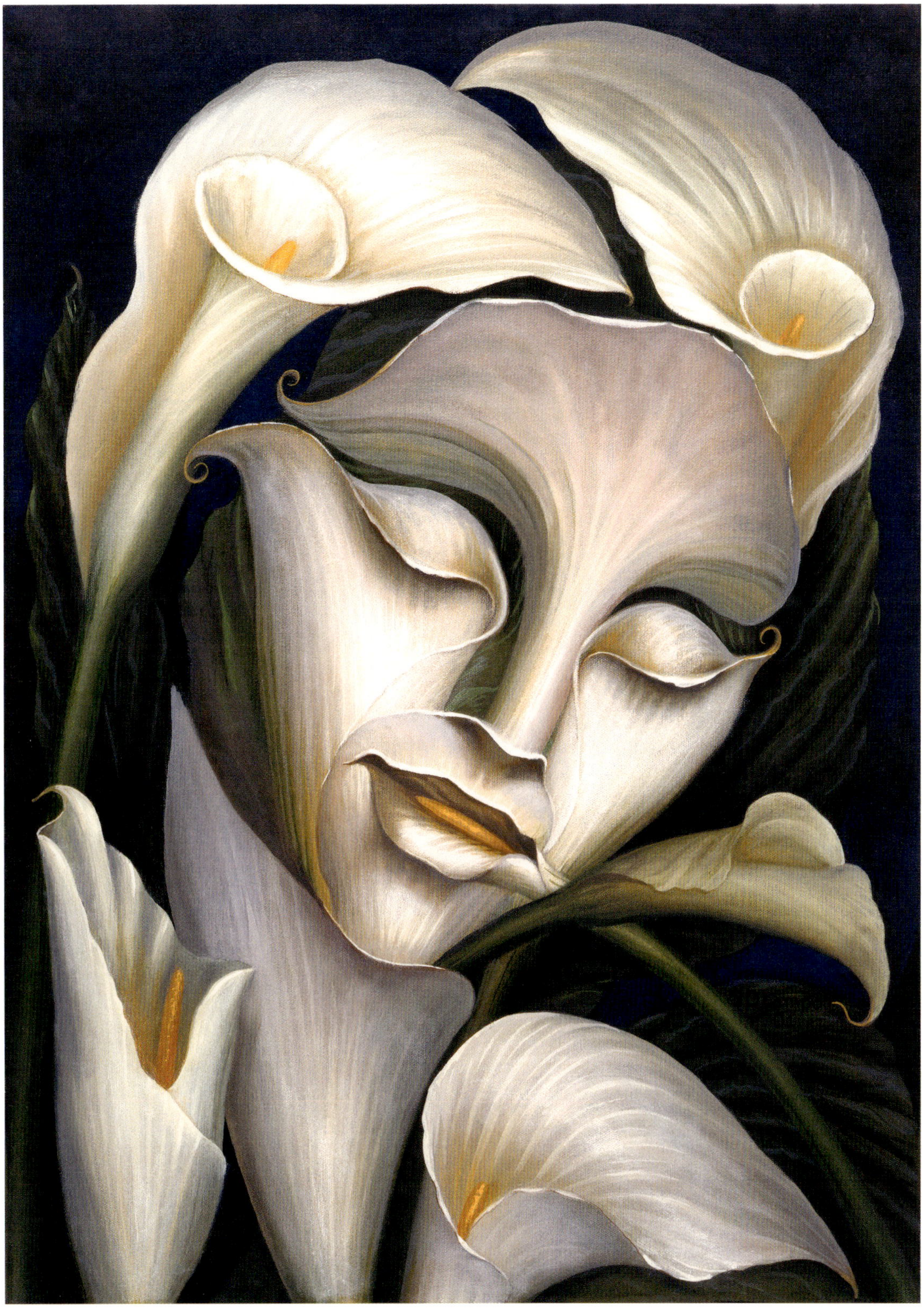

ALCATRAZ ENAMORADA 2001 (50 × 70)

Oil on canvas – Óleo sobre tela – Öl auf Leinwand – Huile sur toile

LOS FETICHES DE GRETA 1982 (57 × 76)

Watercolor on paper – Acuarela sobre papel – Aquarell auf Papier – Aquarelle sur papier

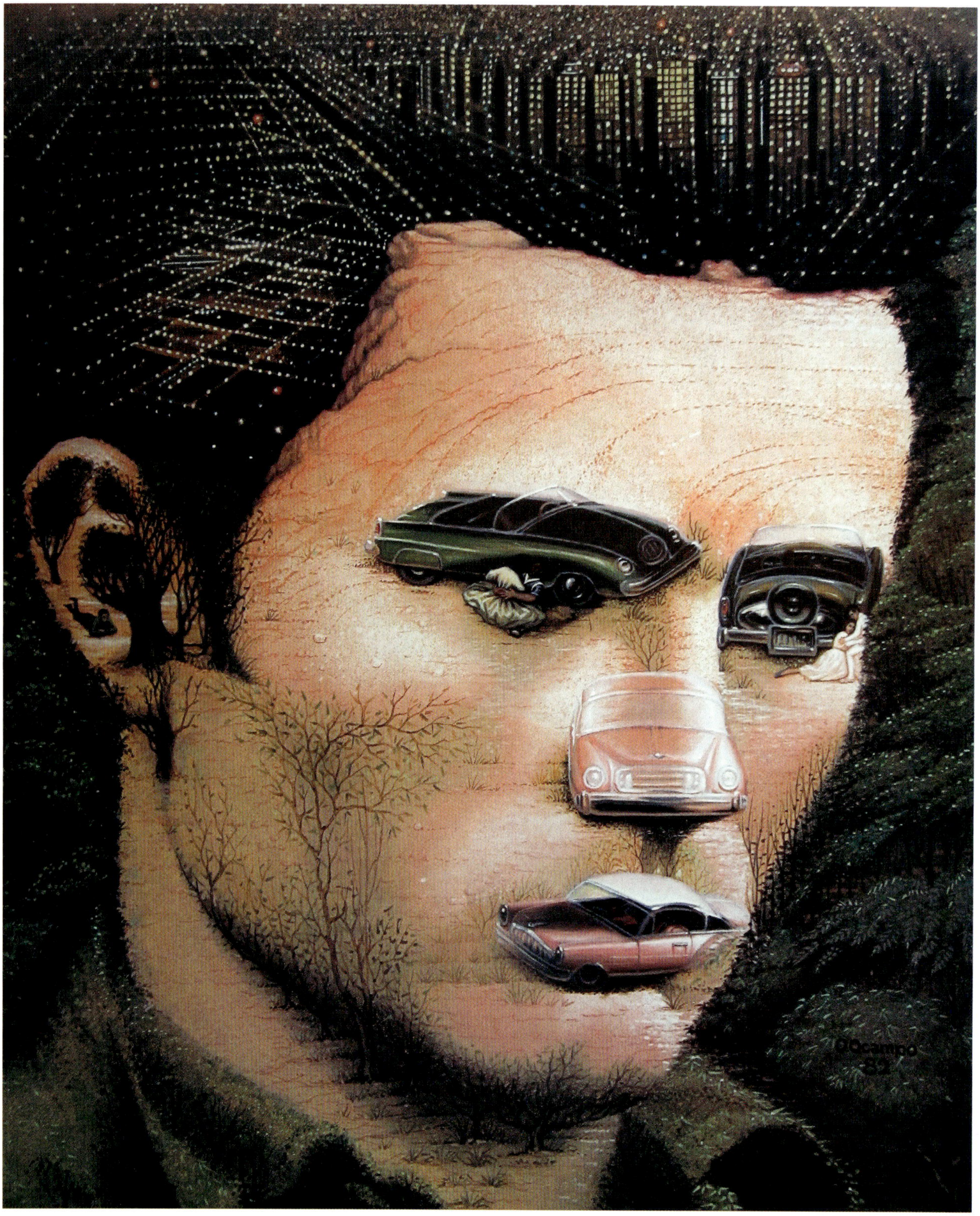

JAMES DEAN 1982 (80 × 100)

Oil on canvas – Óleo sobre tela – Öl auf Leinwand – Huile sur toile

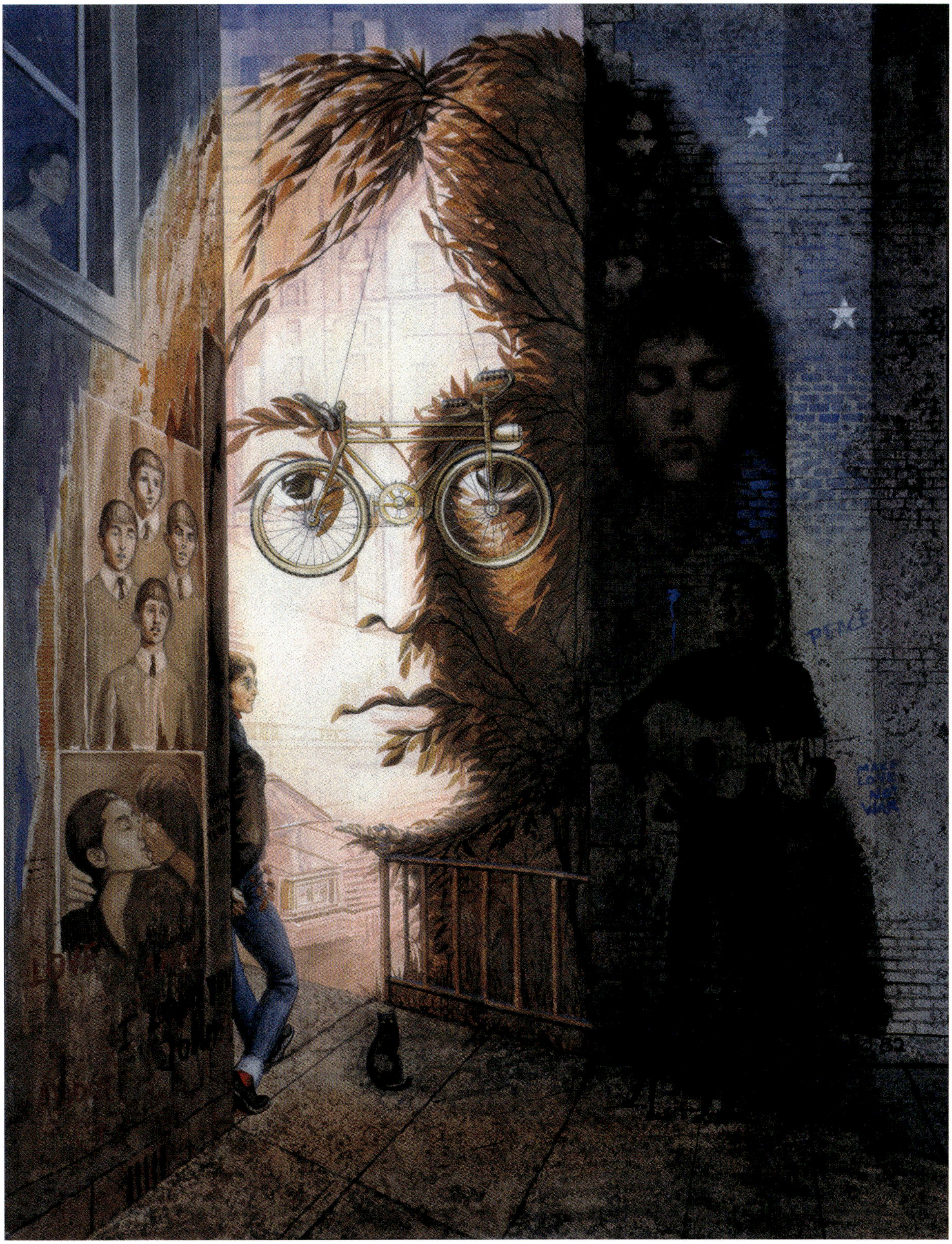

TE AMO JOHN 1982 (37 × 46)

Watercolor on paper – Acuarela sobre papel – Aquarell auf Papier – Aquarelle sur papier

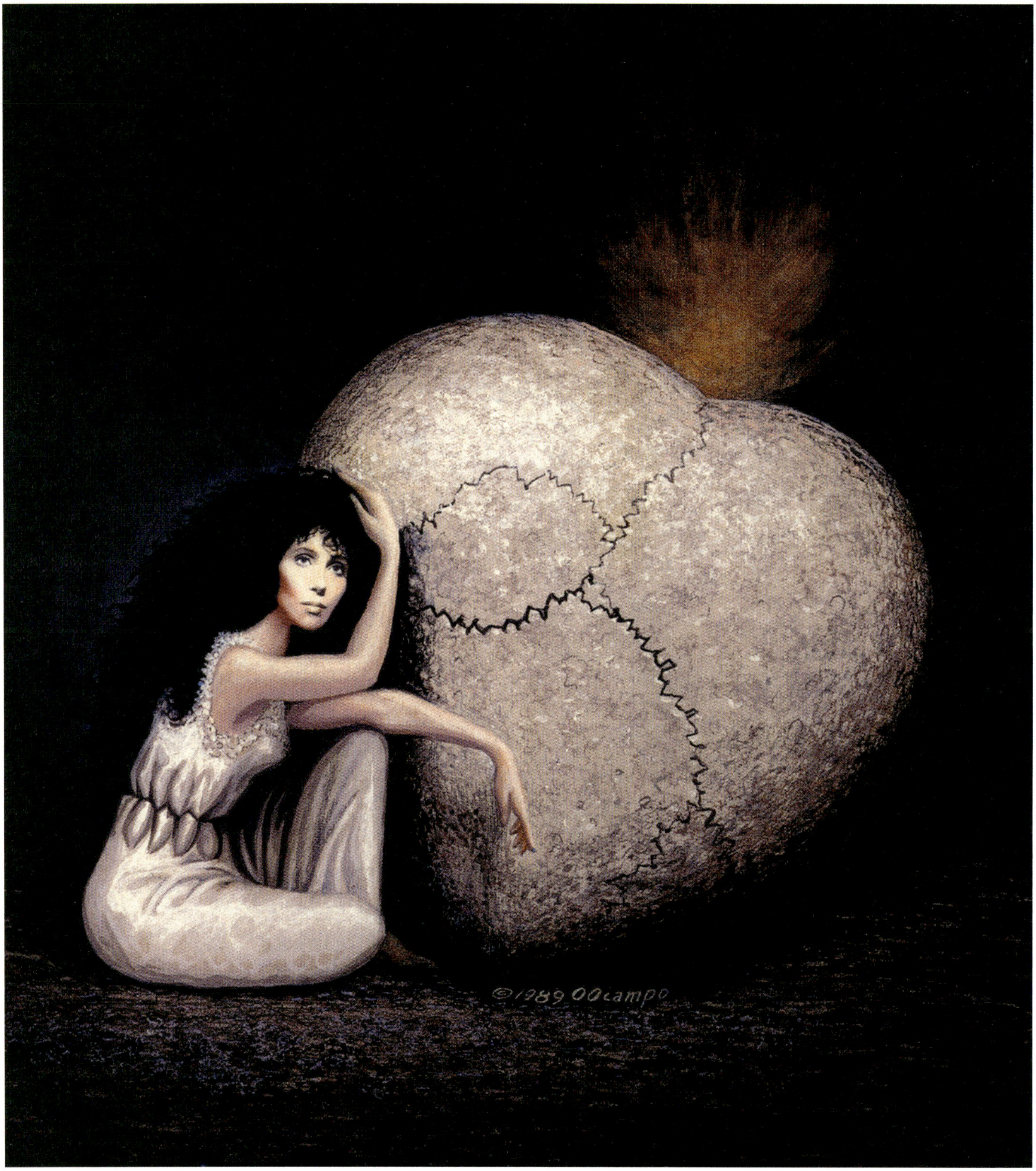

CORAZÓN DE PIEDRA 1989 (91 × 121)

Oil on canvas – Óleo sobre tela – Öl auf Leinwand – Huile sur toile

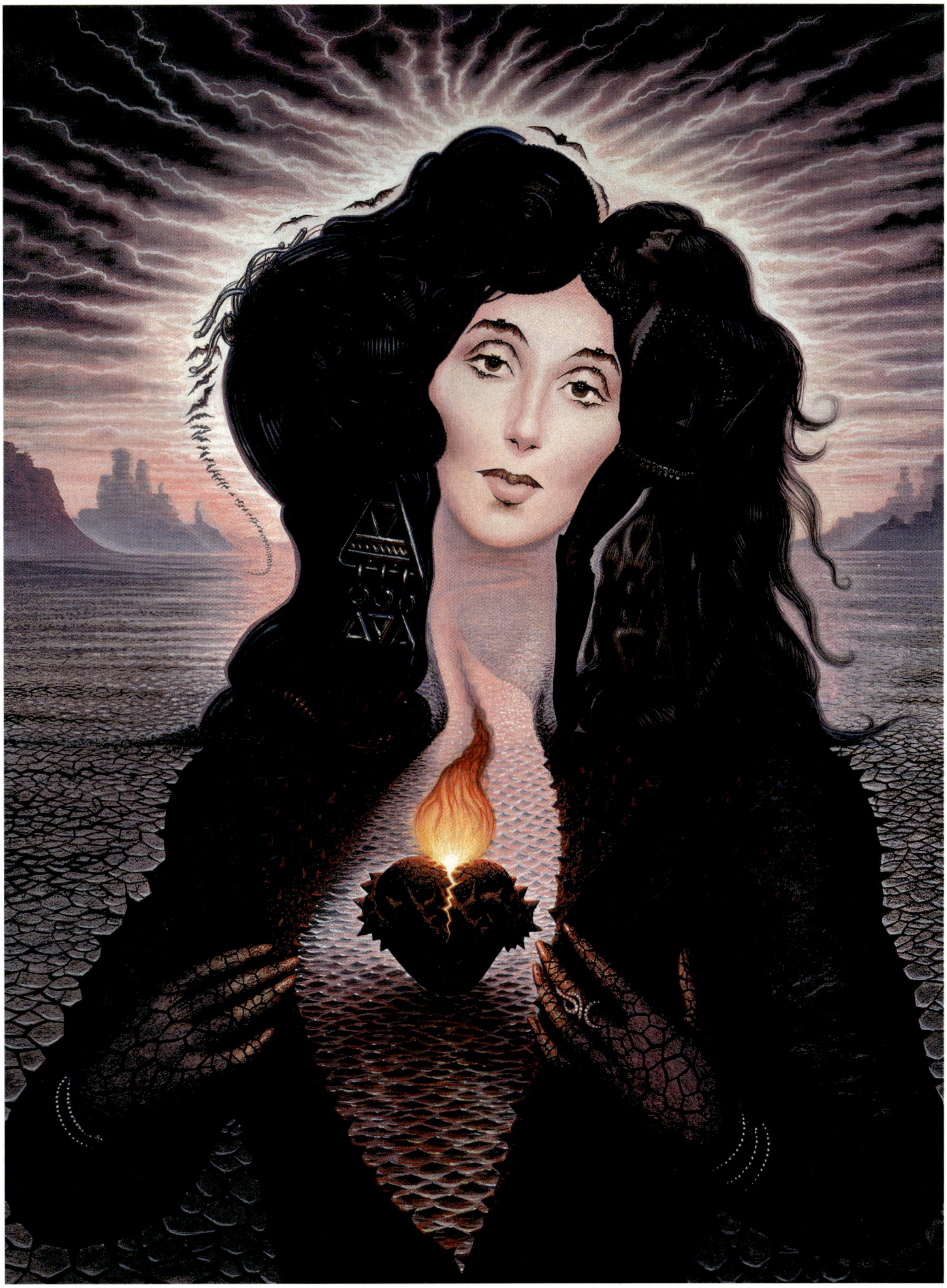

CHEROKEE 1989 (90 × 110)

Oil on canvas – Óleo sobre tela – Öl auf Leinwand – Huile sur toile

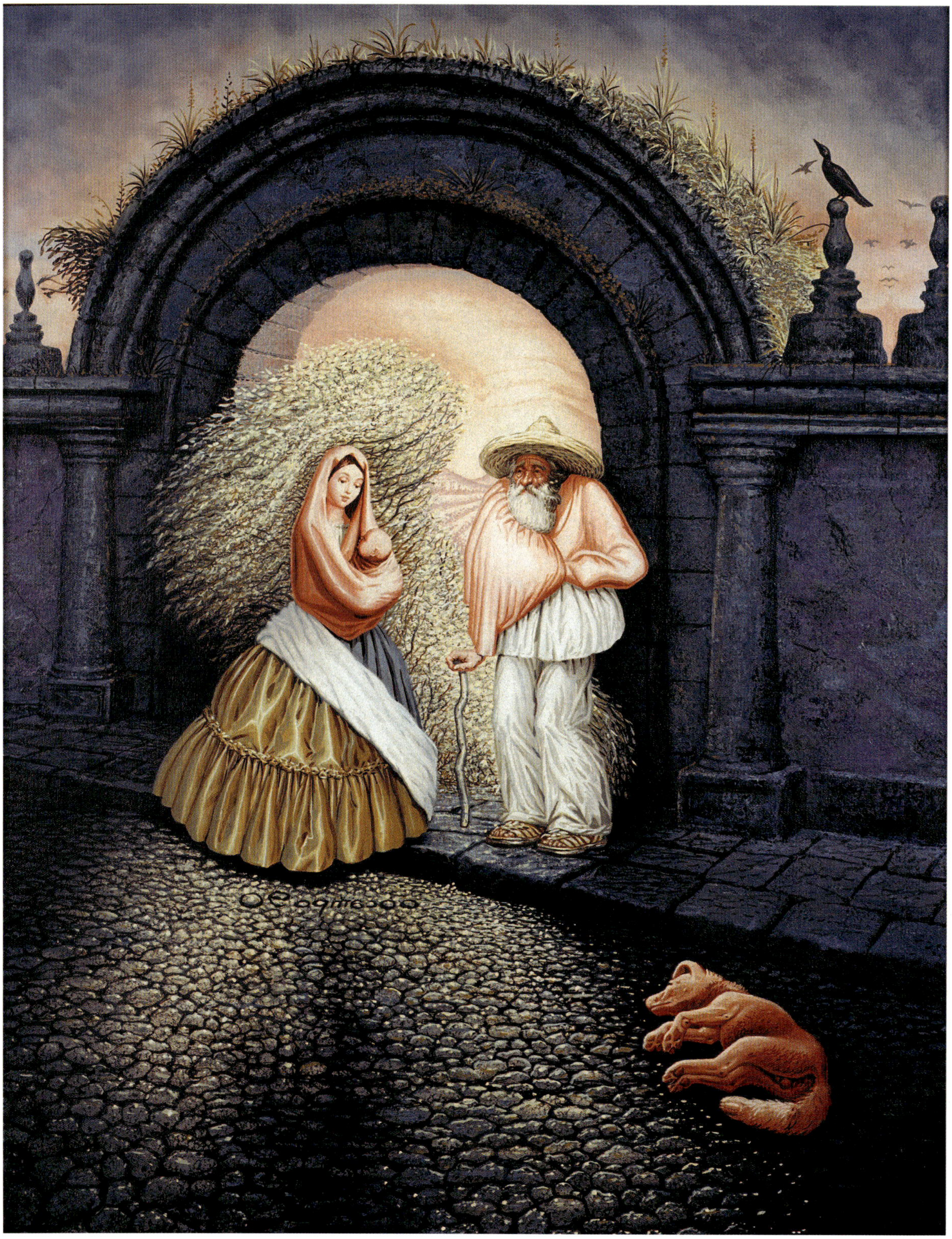

LA FAMILIA DEL GENERAL 1990 (51 × 65)

Oil on canvas – Óleo sobre tela – Öl auf Leinwand – Huile sur toile

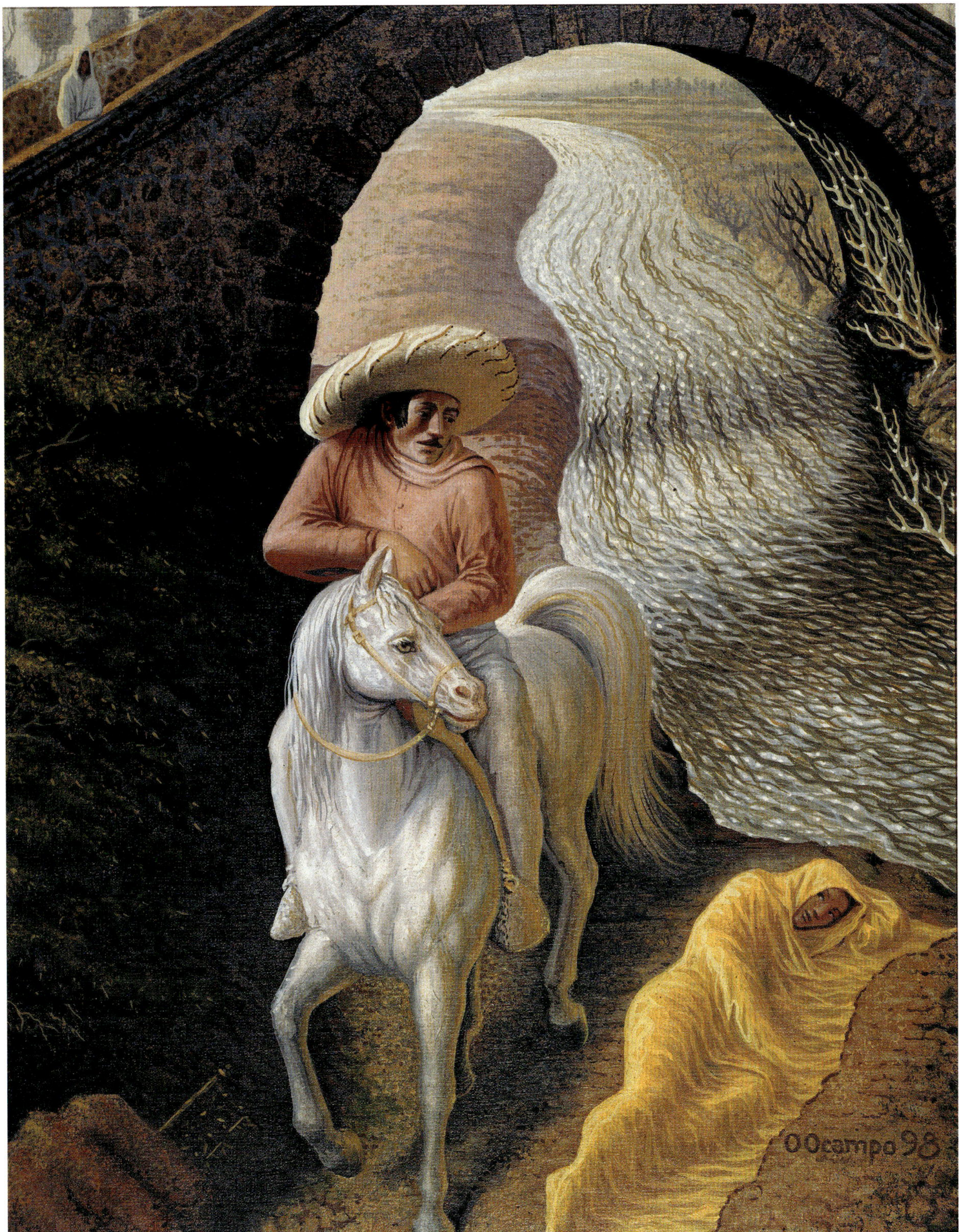

EL VIEJO Y EL RIO 1998 (51 × 65)

Oil on canvas – Óleo sobre tela – Öl auf Leinwand – Huile sur toile

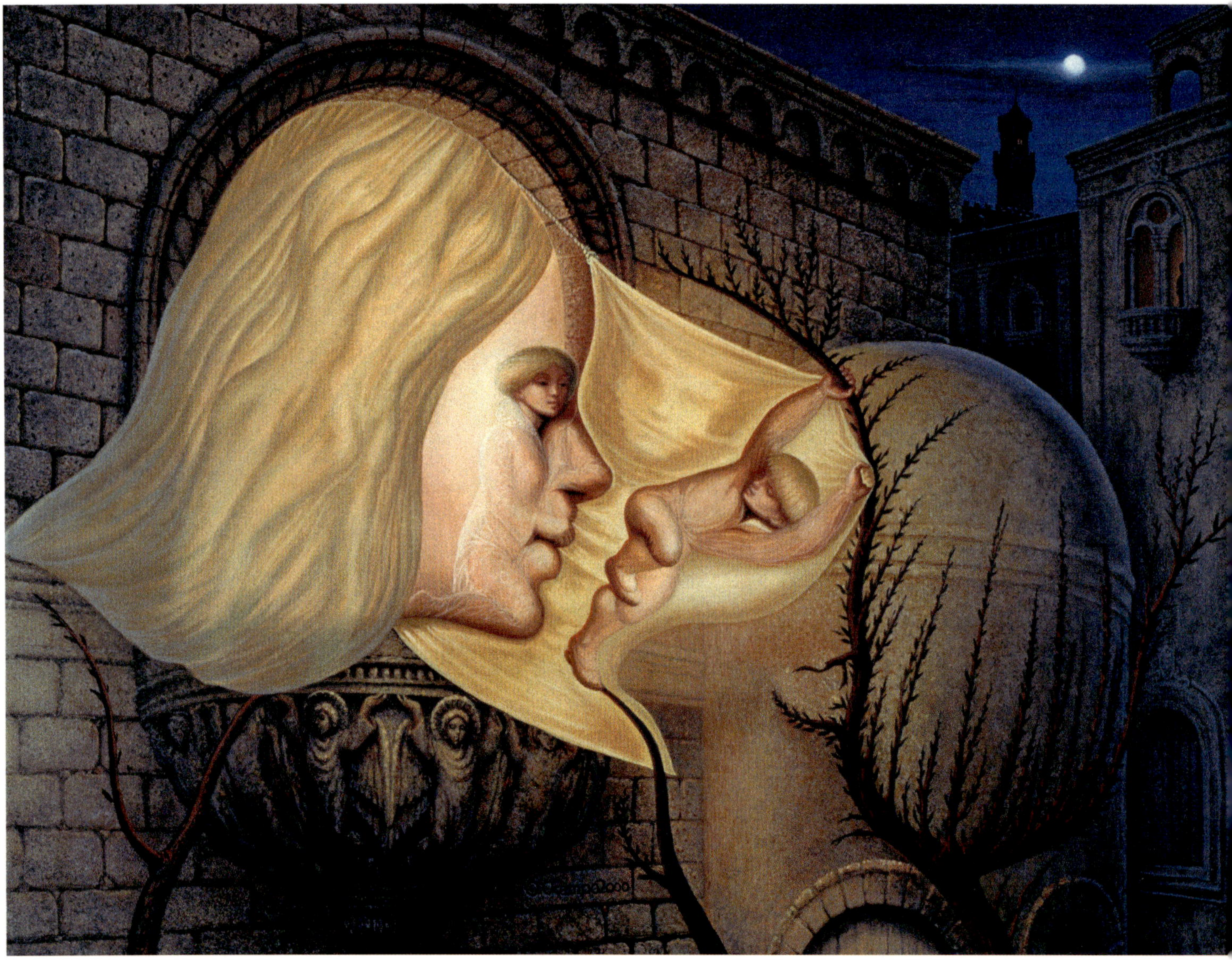

ROMEO Y JULIETA 2000 (90 × 120)

Oil on canvas – Óleo sobre tela – Öl auf Leinwand – Huile sur toile

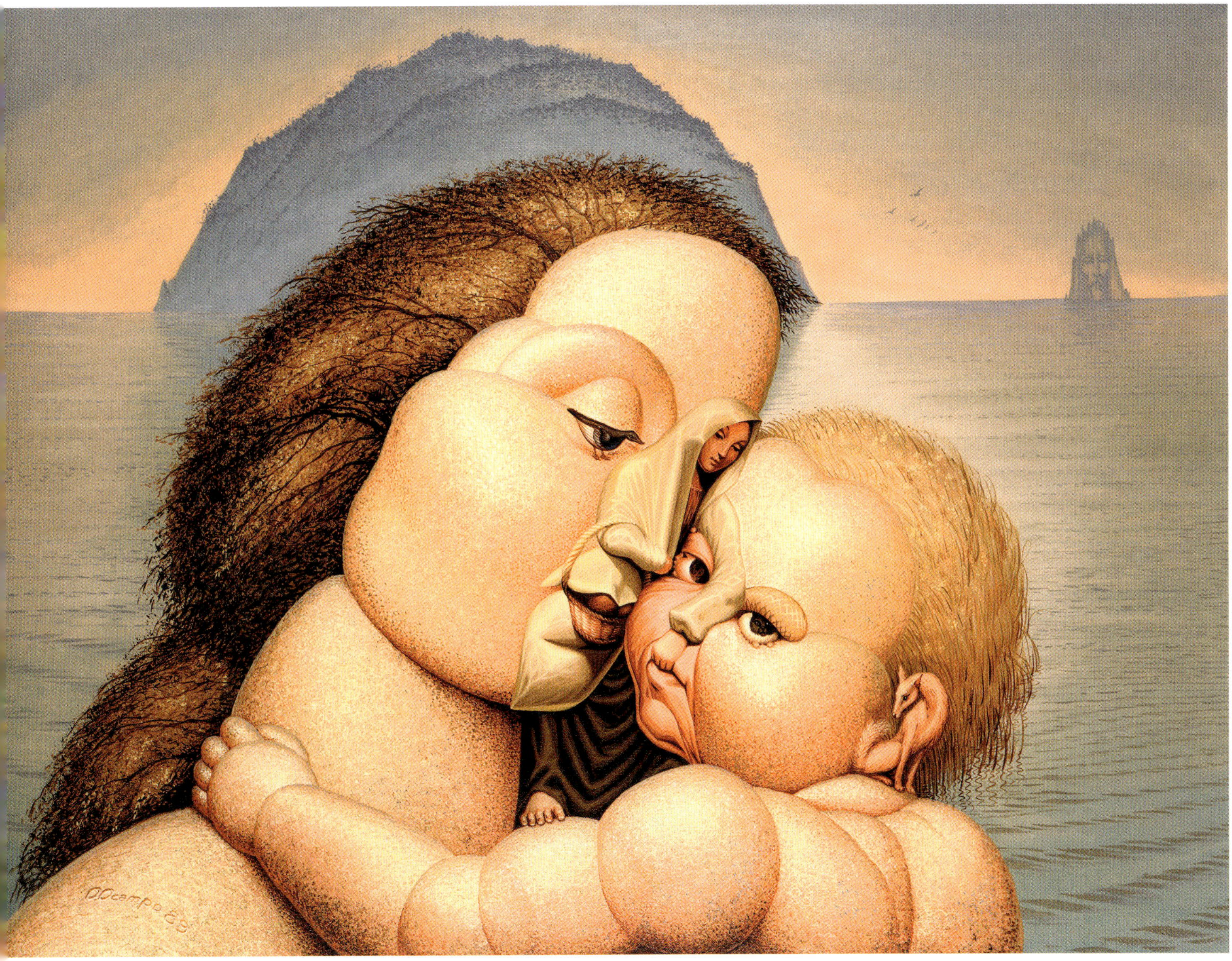

MATERNIDAD 1989 (90 × 120)

Oil on canvas – Óleo sobre tela – Öl auf Leinwand – Huile sur toile

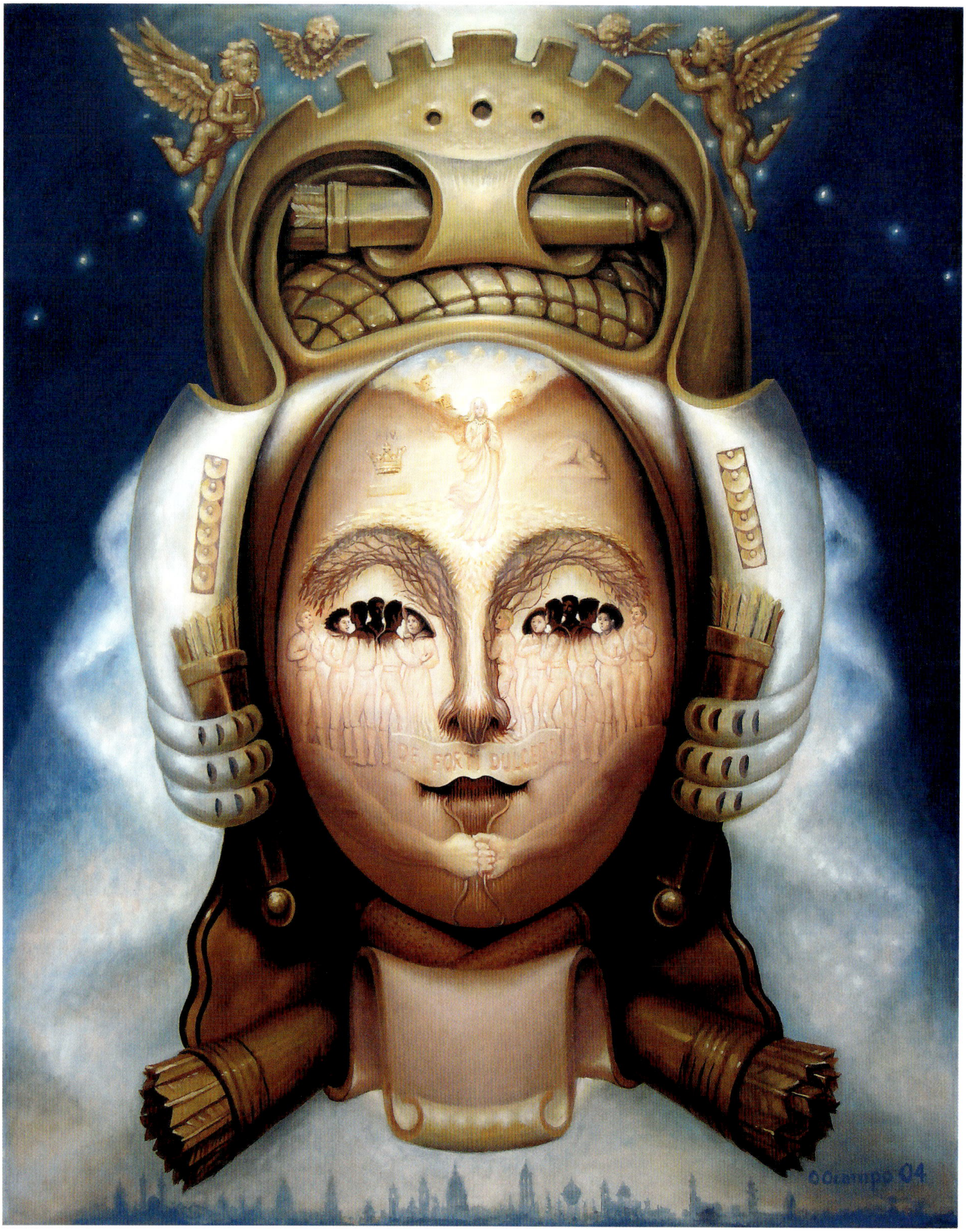

PURÍSIMA Y ESCUDO DE CELAYA 2004 (90 × 120)

Oil on canvas – Óleo sobre tela – Öl auf Leinwand – Huile sur toile

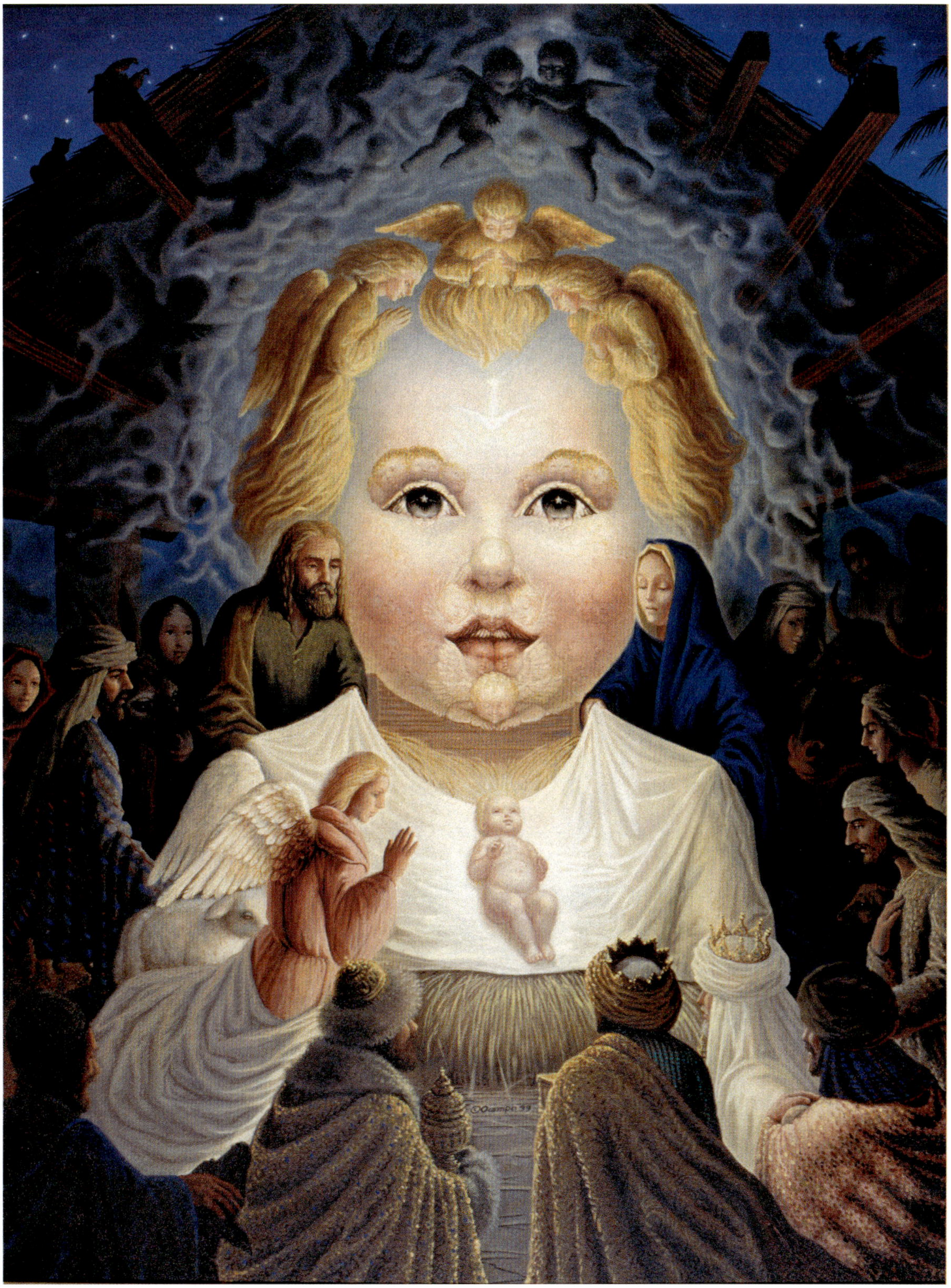

NATIVIDAD 1999 (90 × 120)

Oil on canvas – Óleo sobre tela – Öl auf Leinwand – Huile sur toile

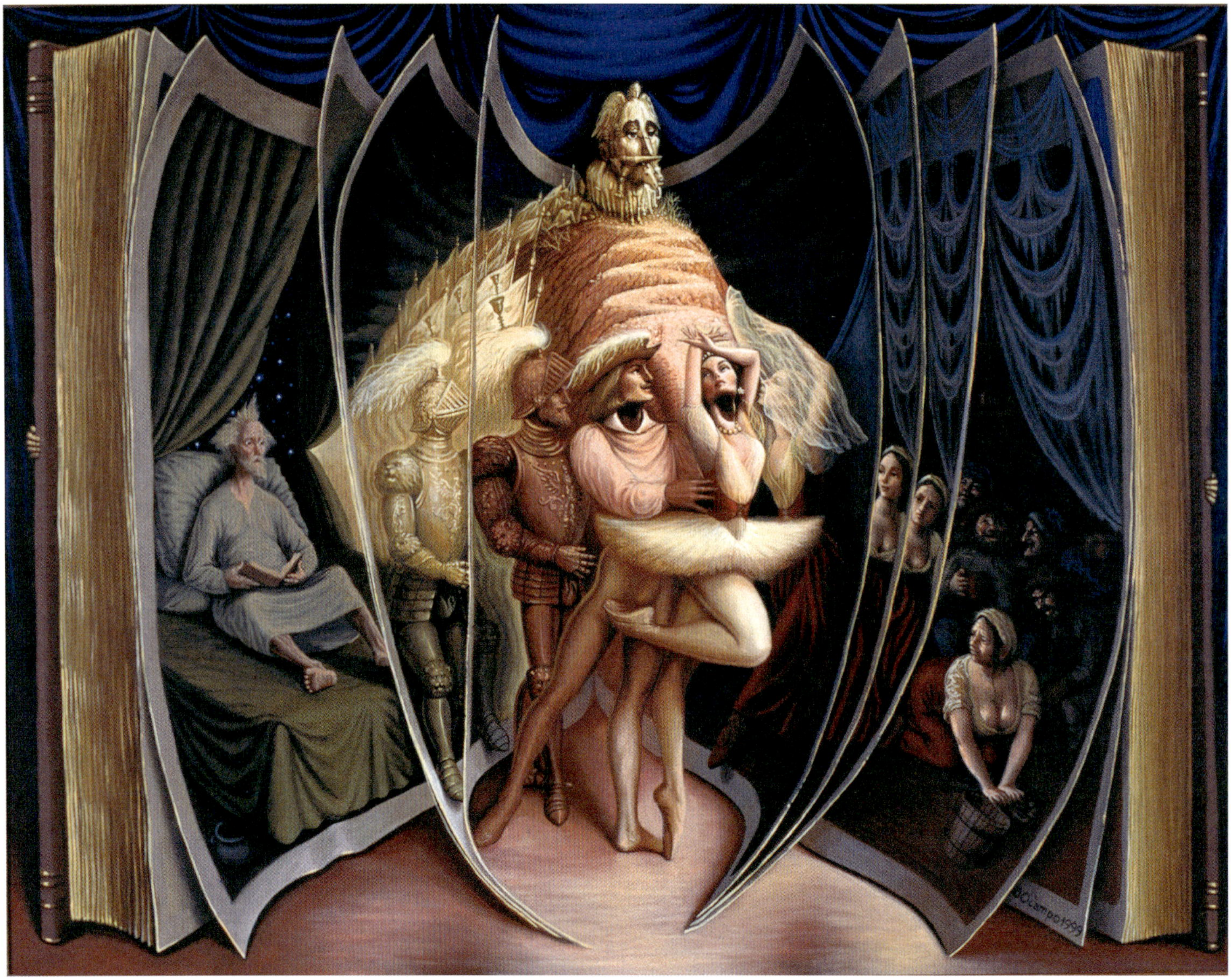

METAMORFOSIS POR AMOR 1999 (120 × 80)

Oil on canvas – Óleo sobre tela – Öl auf Leinwand – Huile sur toile

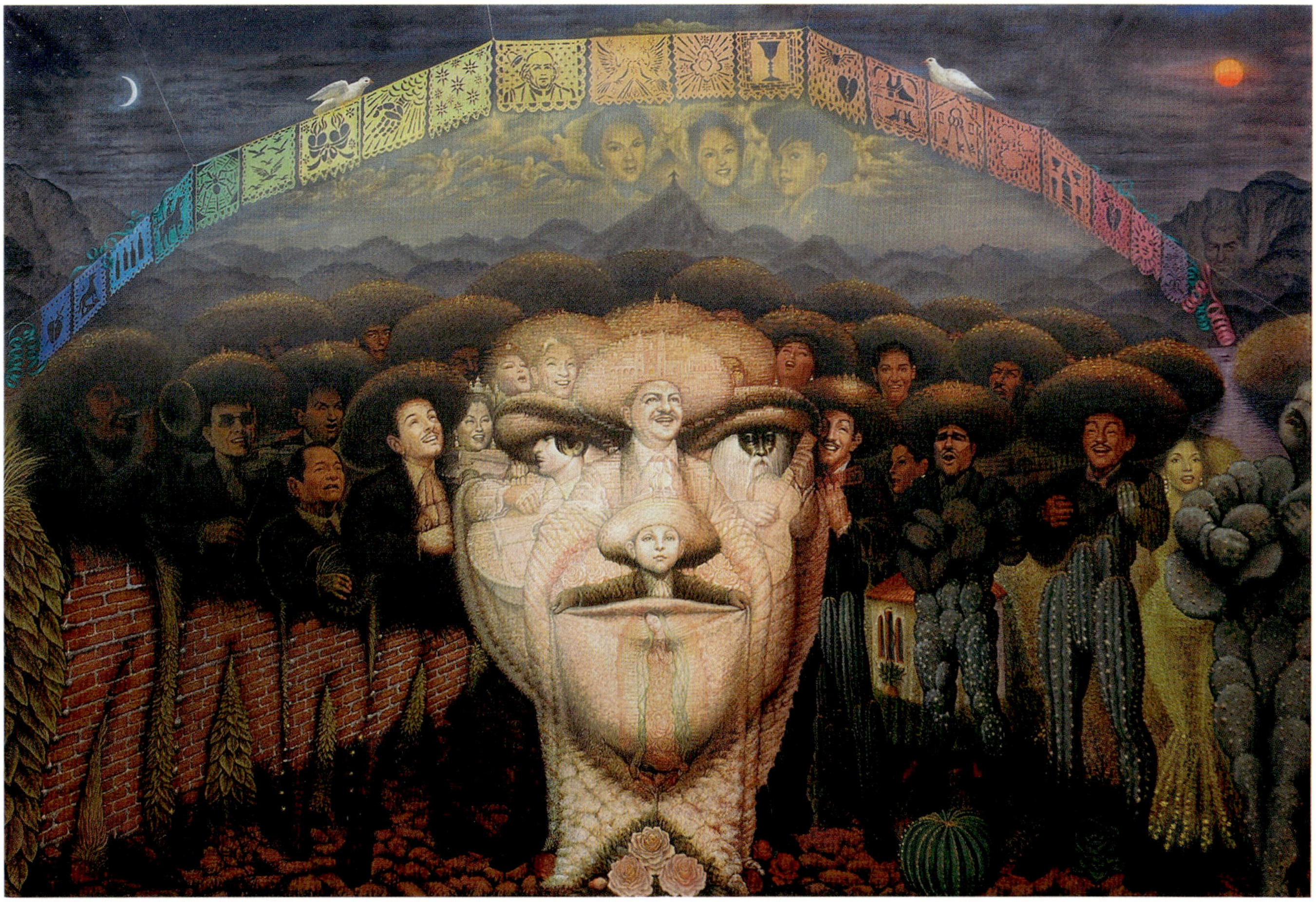

JOSÉ ALFREDO 2002 (300 × 200)

Oil on canvas – Óleo sobre lino – Öl auf Leinwand – Huile sur toile

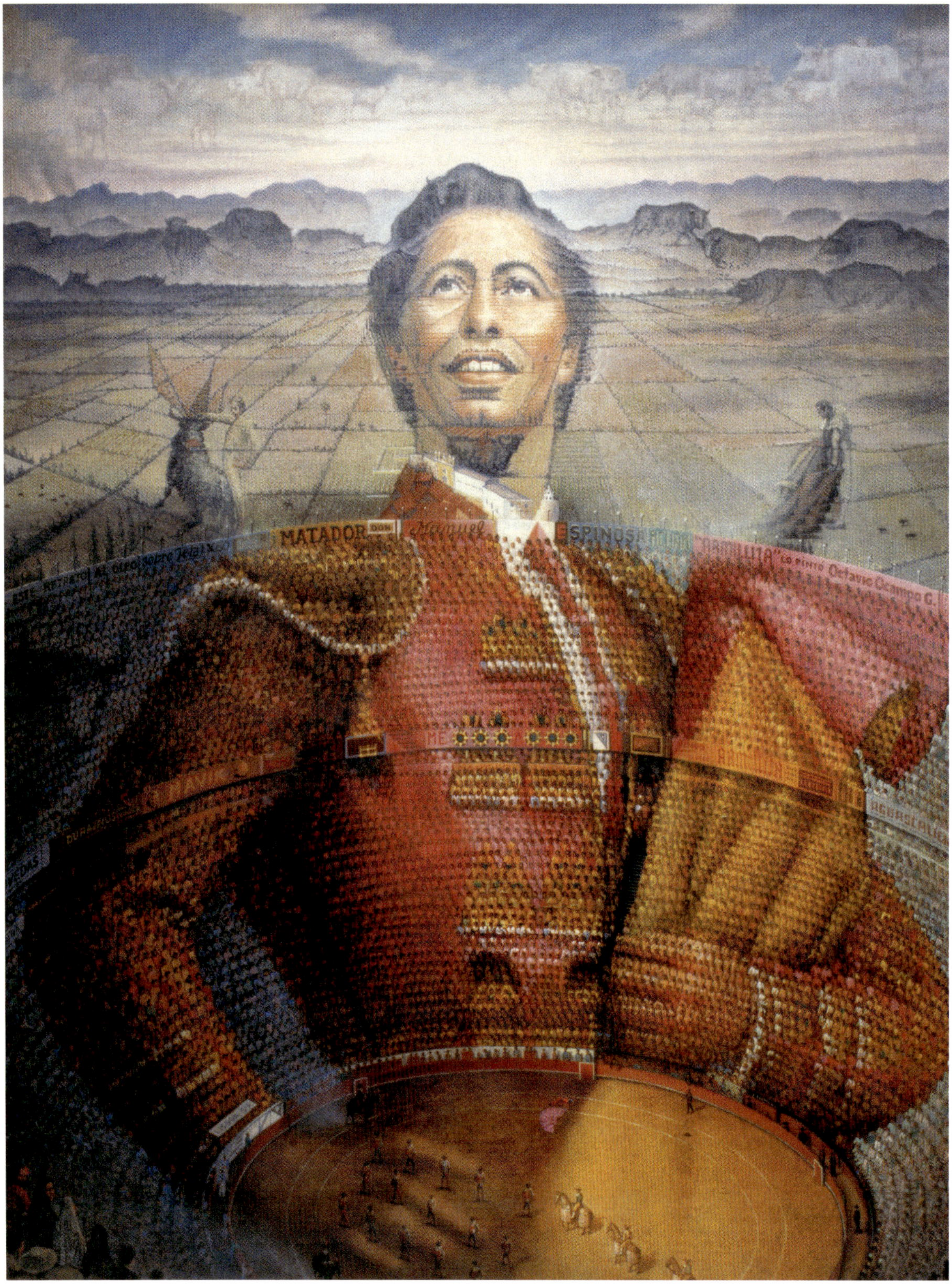

MANUEL ESPINOZA "ARMILLITA" 1979 (80 × 100)

Oil on canvas – Óleo sobre tela – Öl auf Leinwand – Huile sur toile

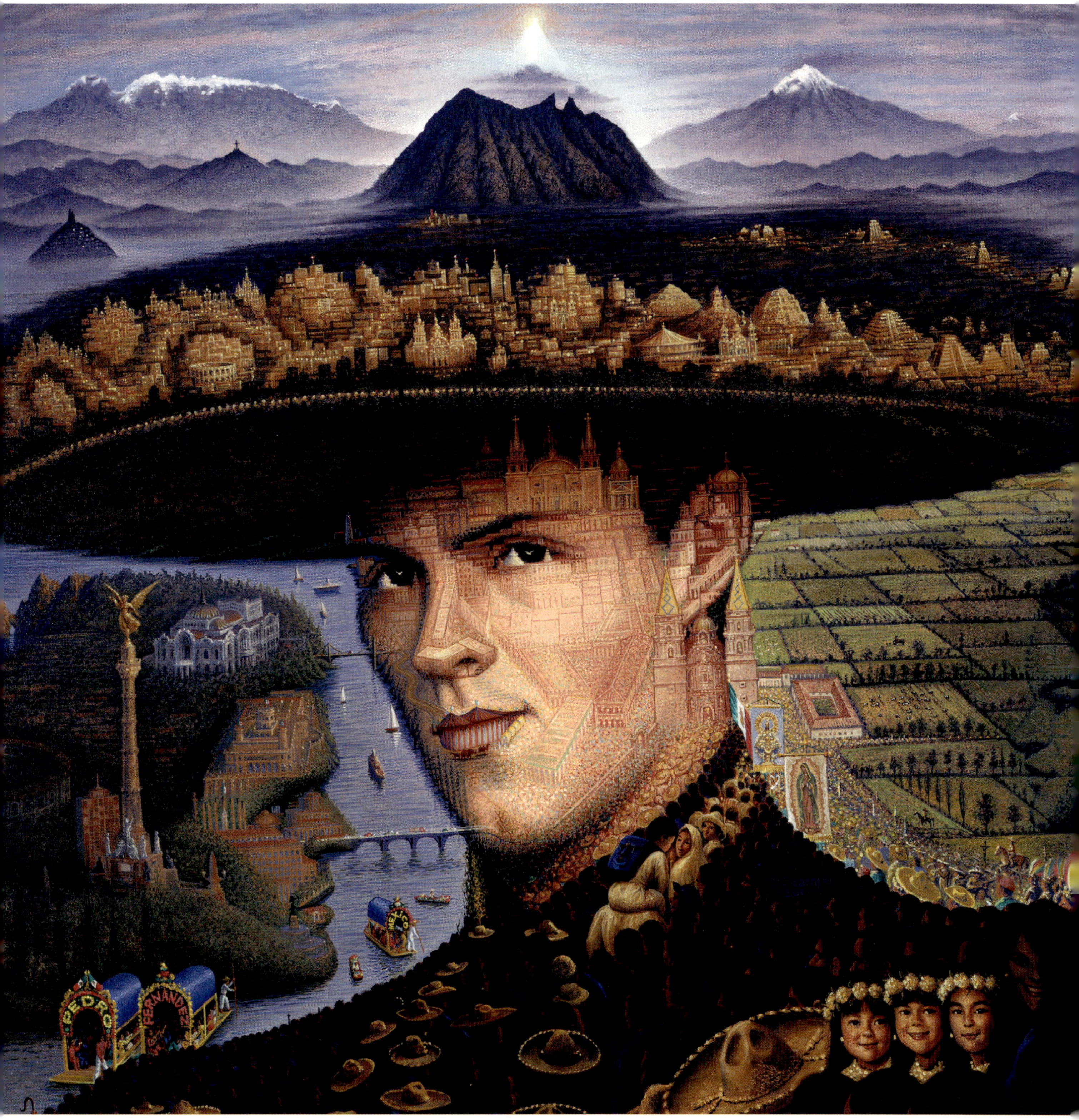

PEDRO FERNÁNDEZ 2002 (100 × 100)

Oil on canvas – Óleo sobre tela – Öl auf Leinwand – Huile sur toile

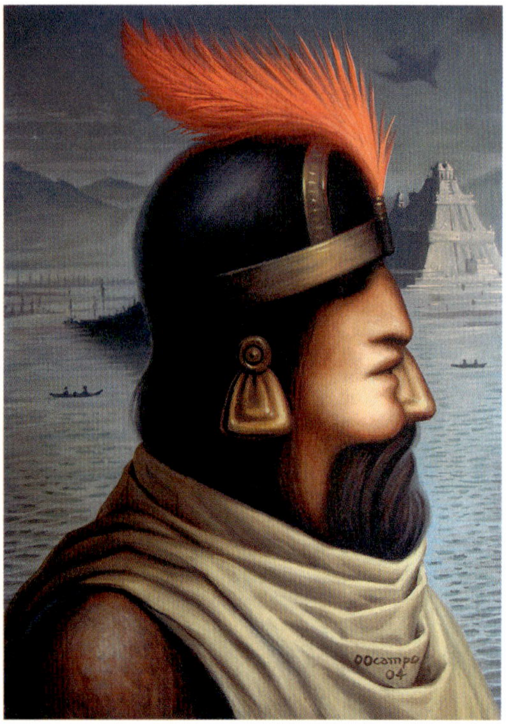

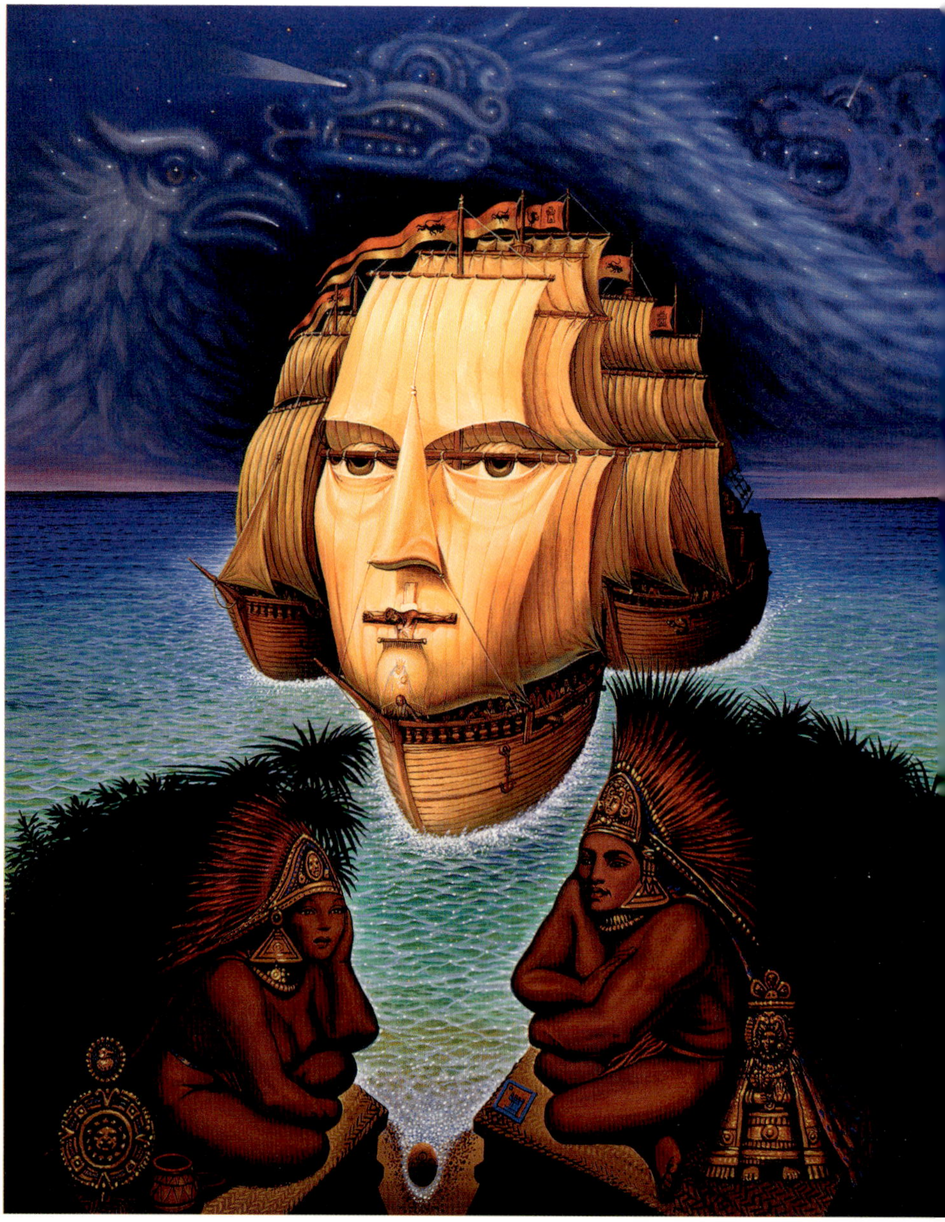

CUAUHTÉMOC Y CORTÉS 2004 (45 × 65)

Oil on canvas – Óleo sobre tela – Öl auf Leinwand – Huile sur toile

ENCUENTRO (CRISTÓBAL COLÓN) 1992 (100 × 120)

Oil on canvas – Óleo sobre tela – Öl auf Leinwand – Huile sur toile

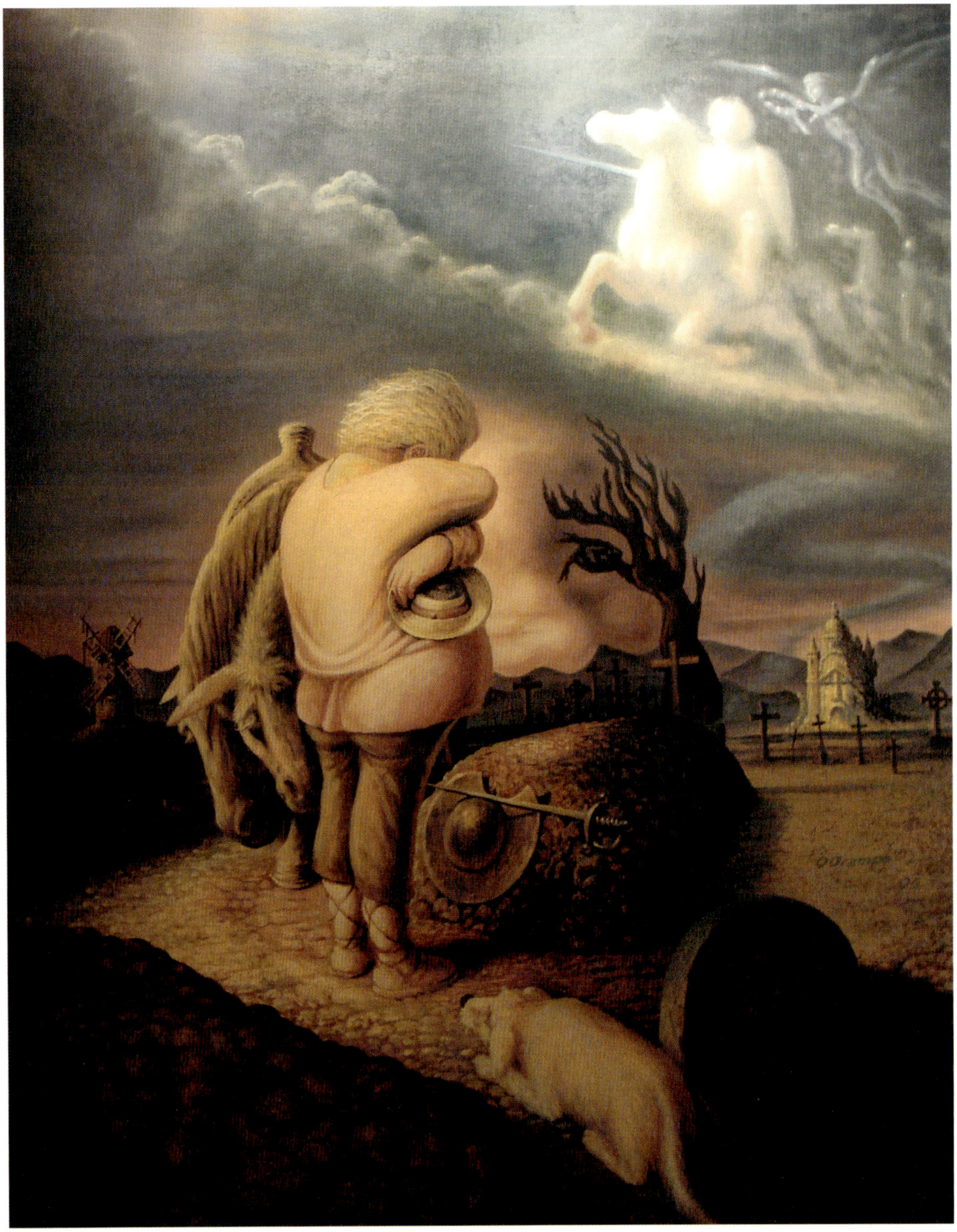

SANCHO EN DUELO 2005 (80 × 110)

Oil on canvas – Óleo sobre tela – Öl auf Leinwand – Huile sur toile

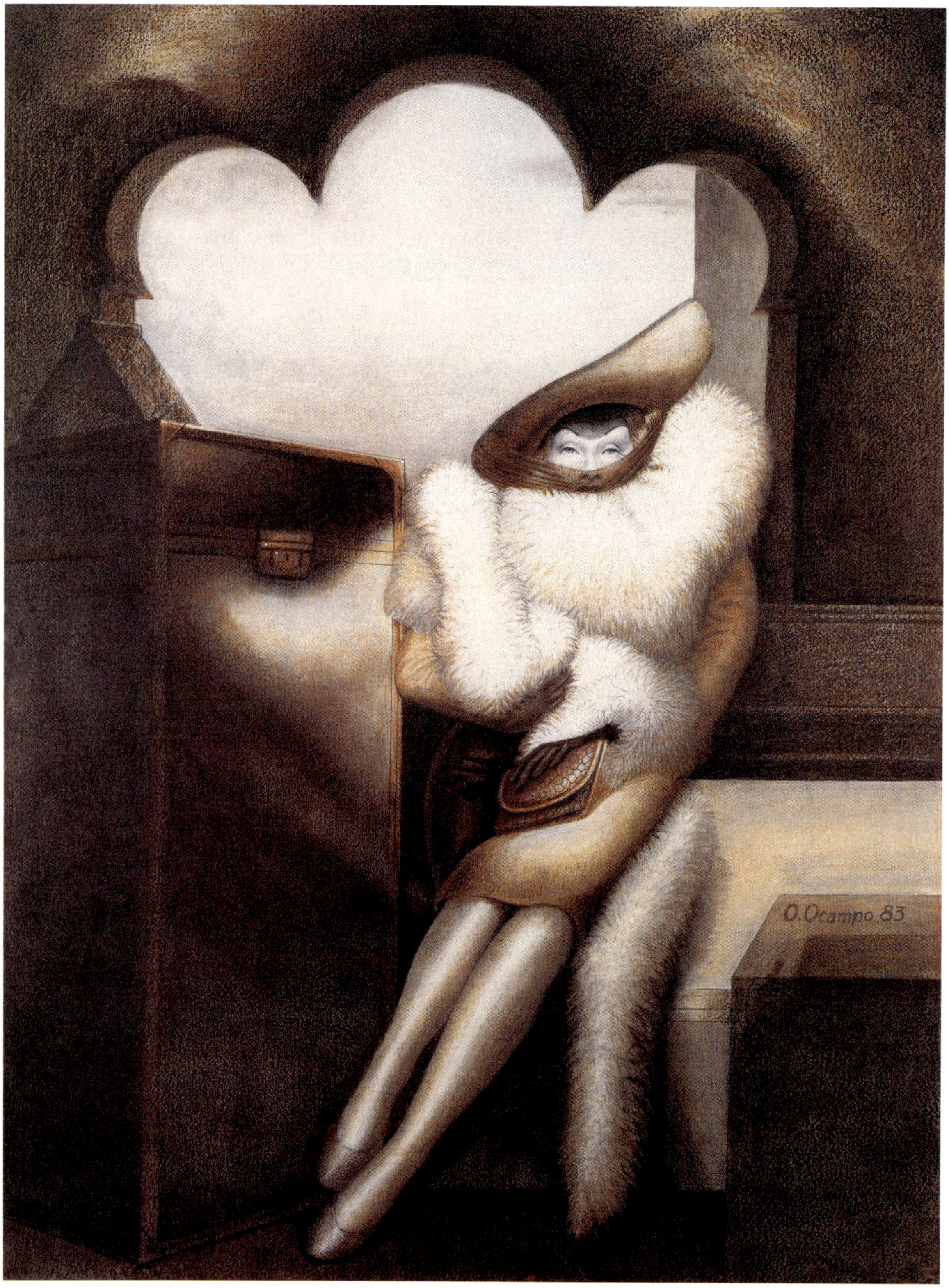

MARLENE 1983 (112 × 129)

Oil on canvas – Óleo sobre tela – Öl auf Leinwand – Huile sur toile

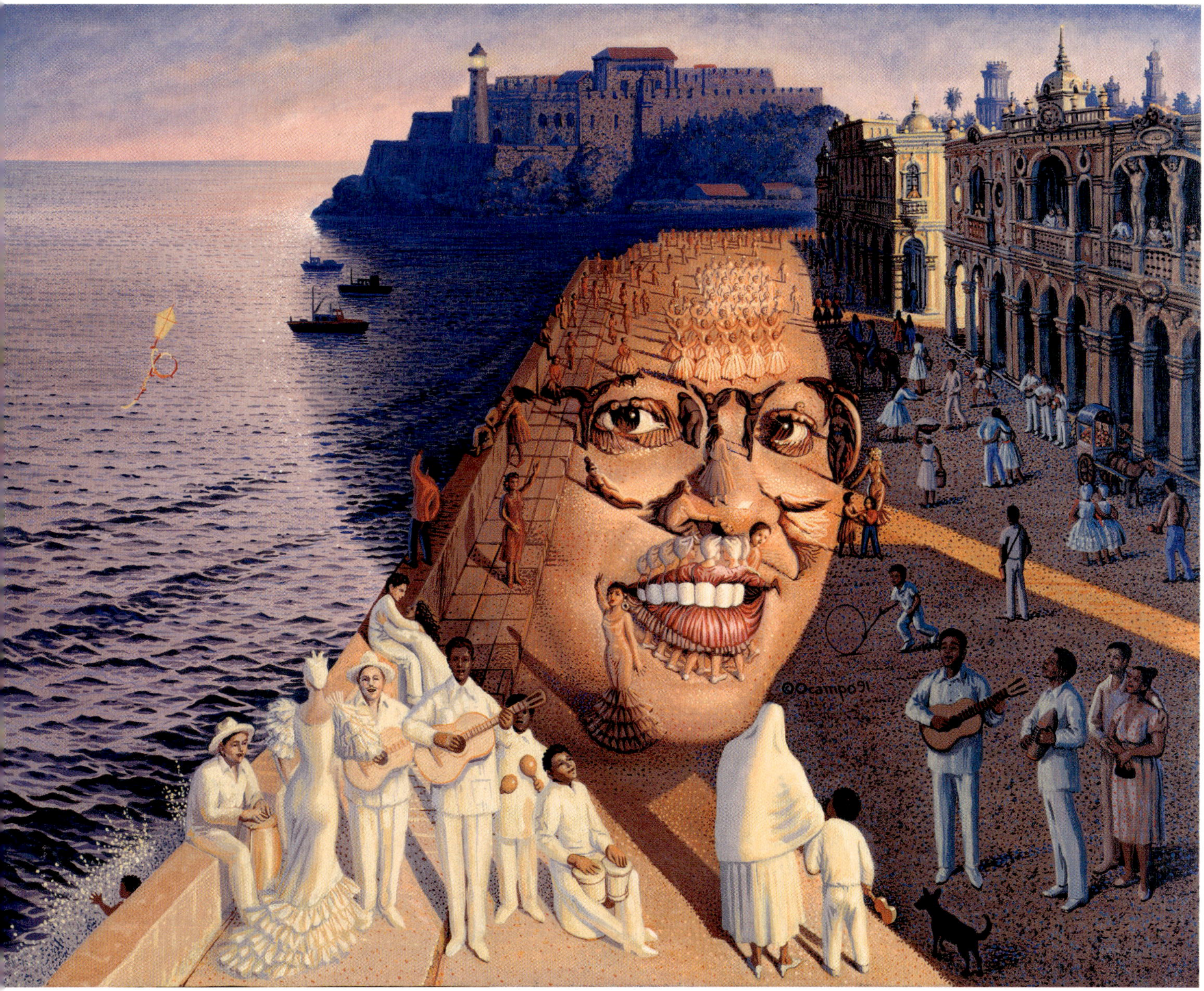

PABLO MILANÉS 1991 (110 × 90)

Oil on canvas – Óleo sobre tela – Öl auf Leinwand – Huile sur toile

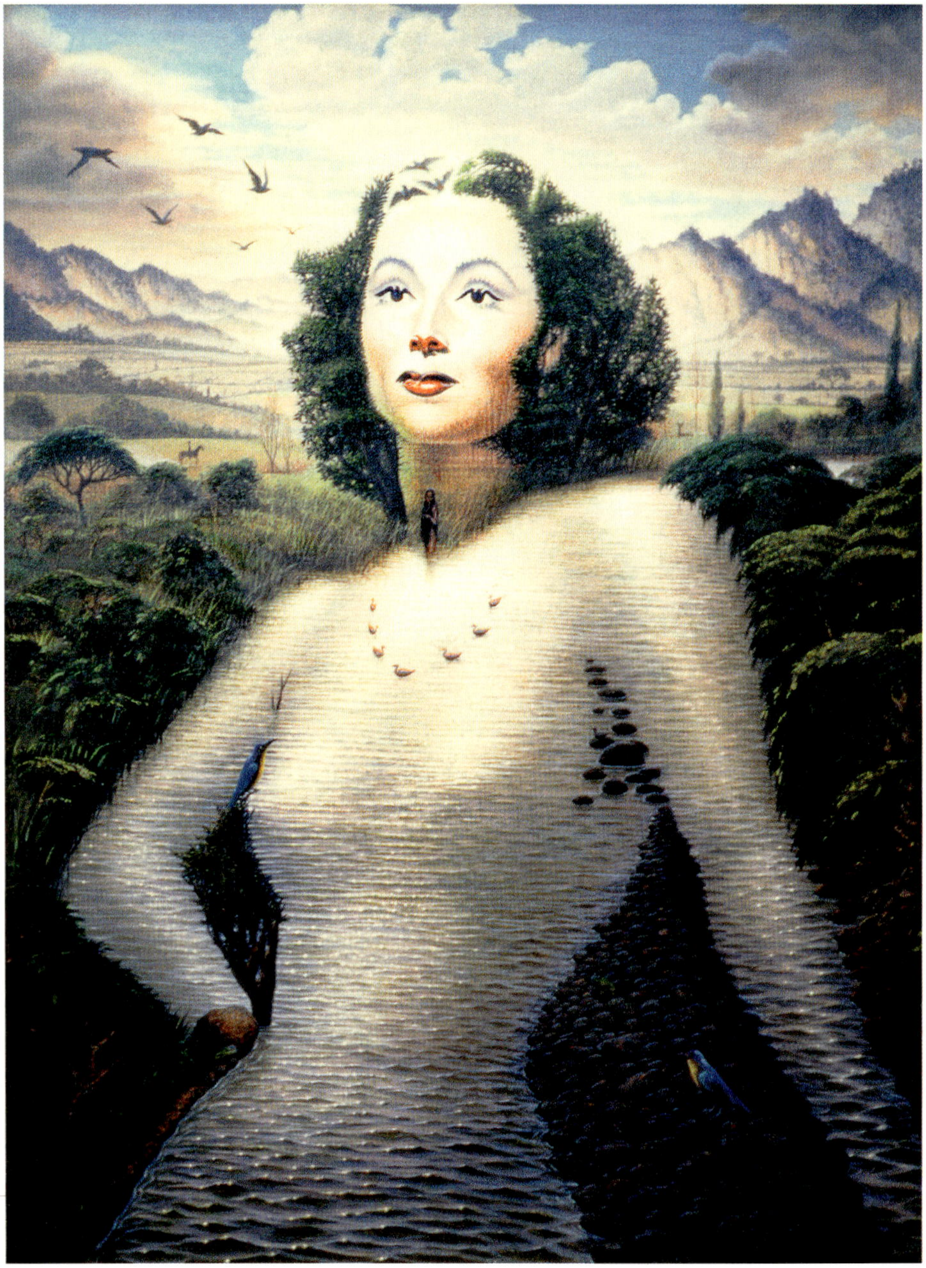

DOLORES DEL RÍO 1982 (90 × 120)

Acrylic on canvas – Acrílico sobre tela – Acryl auf Leinwand – Acrylique sur toile

SILENCIO 2004 (100 × 100

Oil on canvas – Óleo sobre tela – Öl auf Leinwand – Huile sur toil

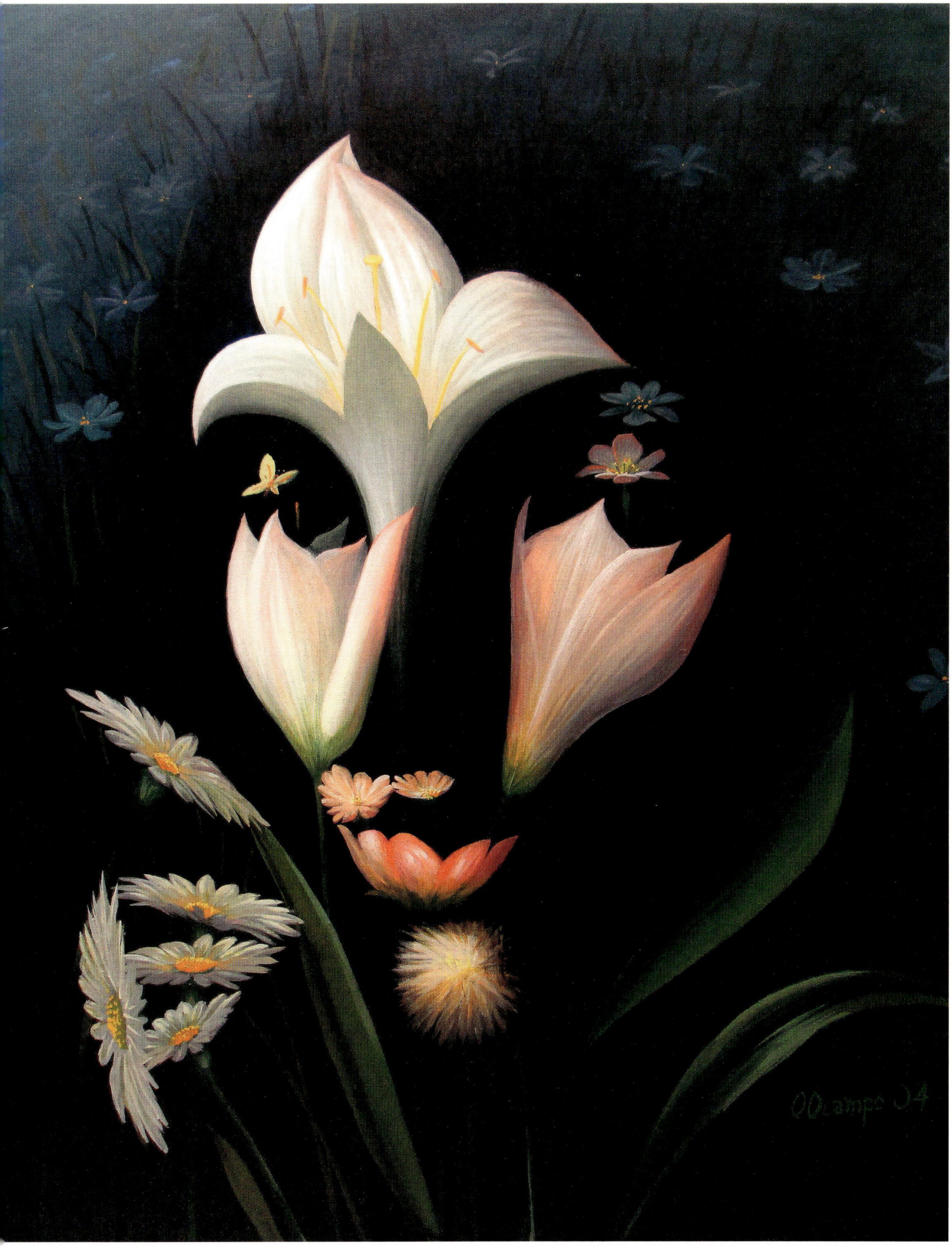
OOcampo 04

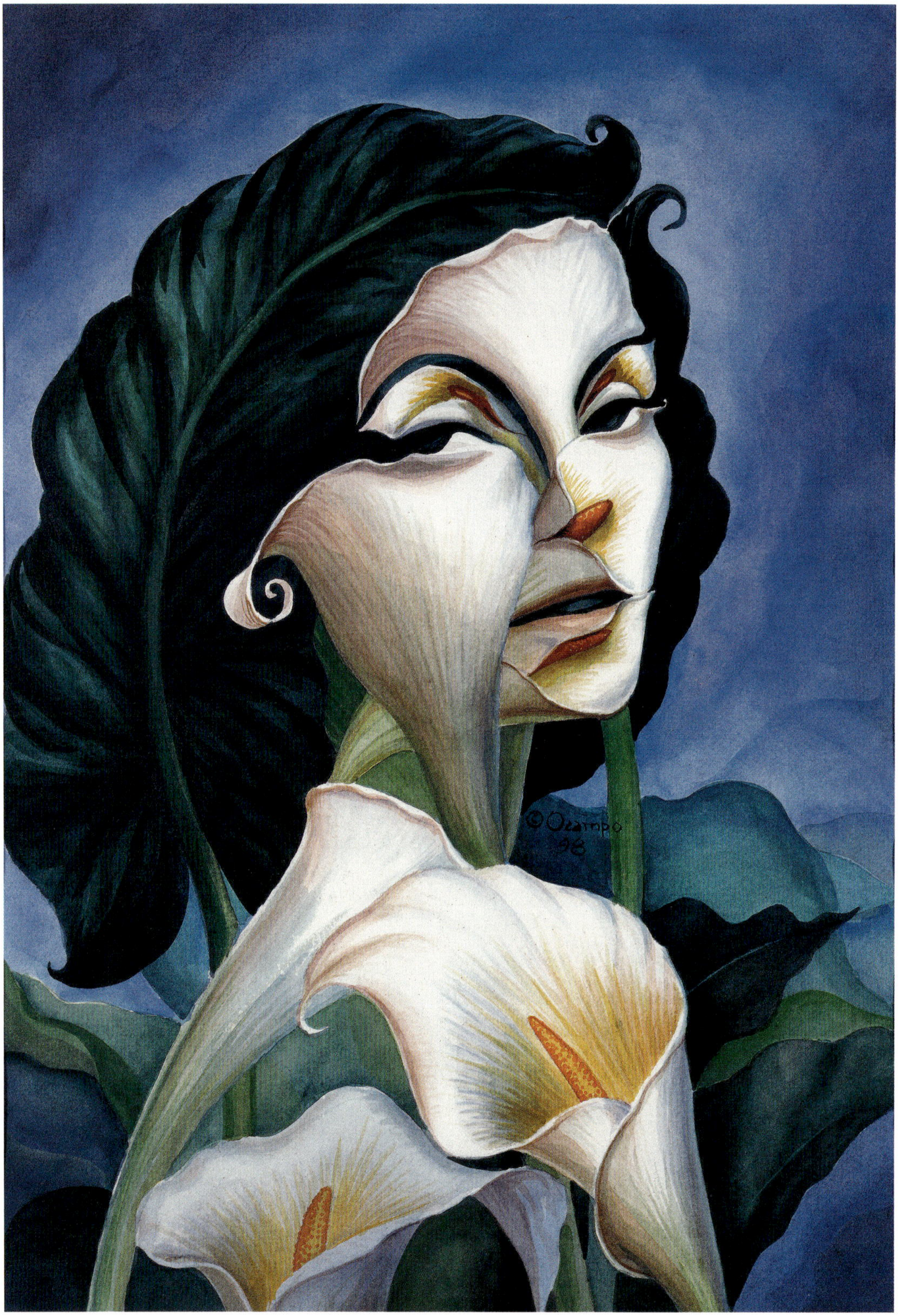

LA SOBERBIA DEL ALCATRAZ 1998 (38 × 51)

Watercolor on paper – Acuarela sobre papel – Aquarell auf Papier – Aquarelle sur papier

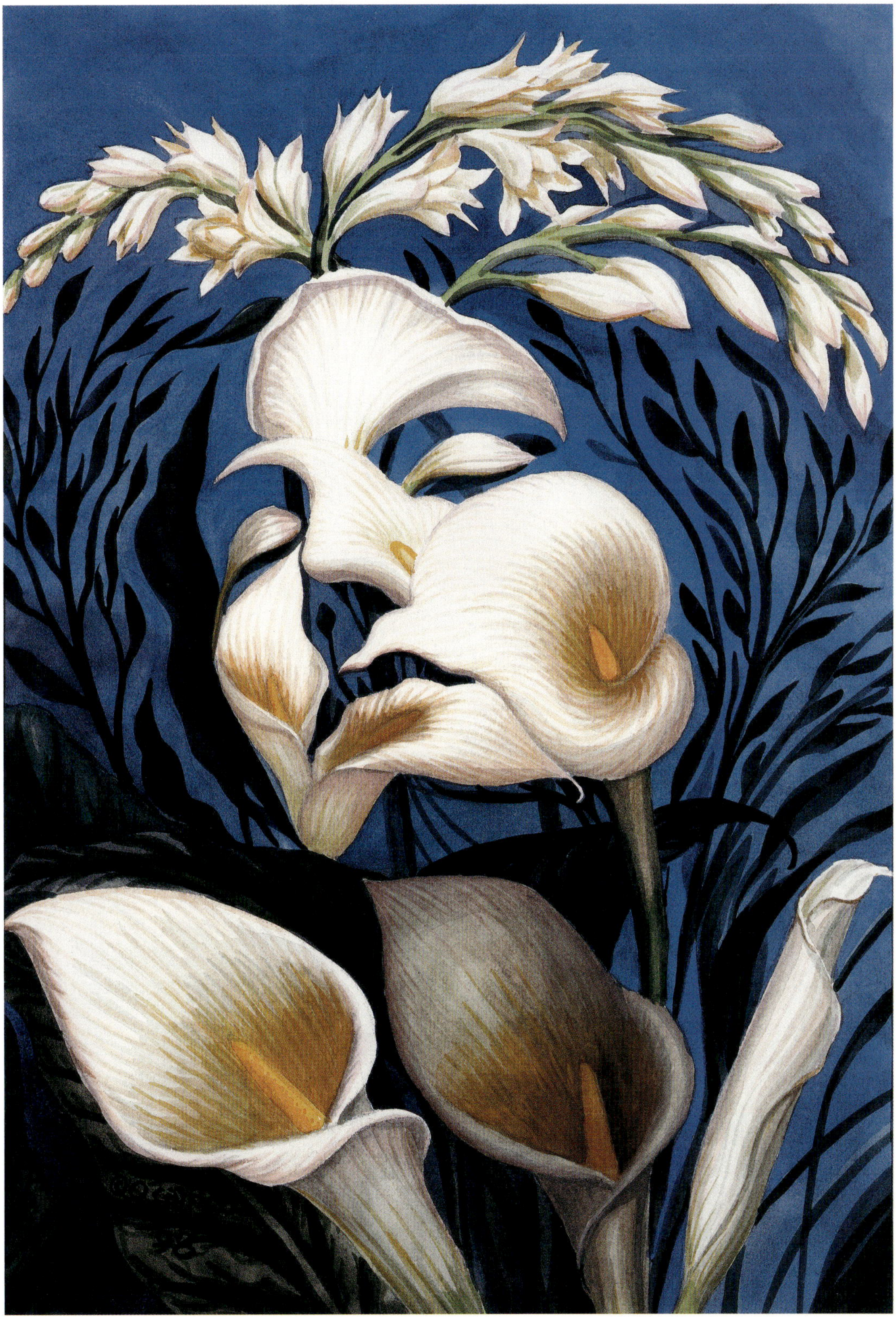

LA PASIÓN DEL ALCATRAZ 1998 (38 × 51)

Watercolor on paper – Acuarela sobre papel – Aquarell auf Papier – Aquarelle sur papier

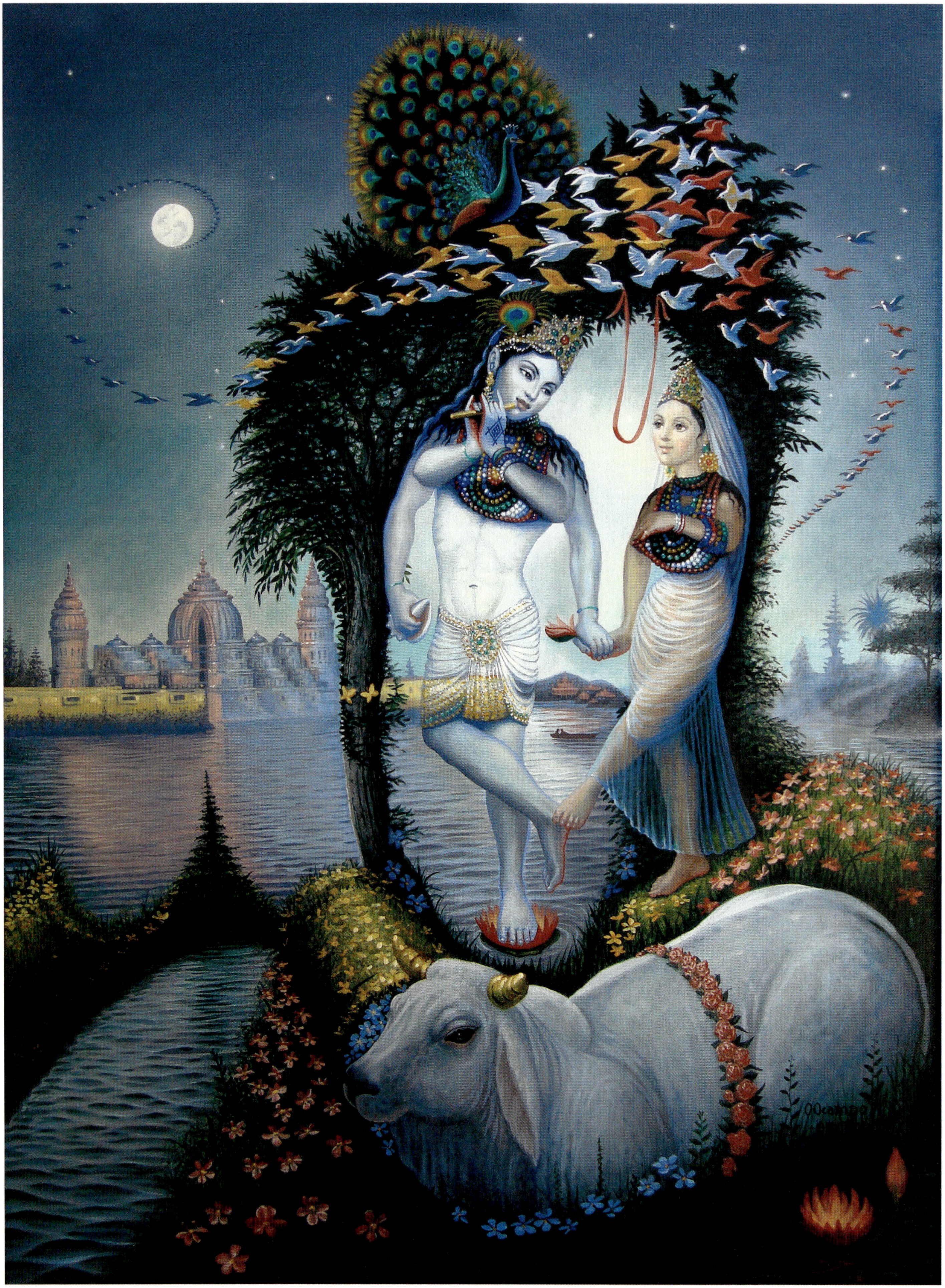

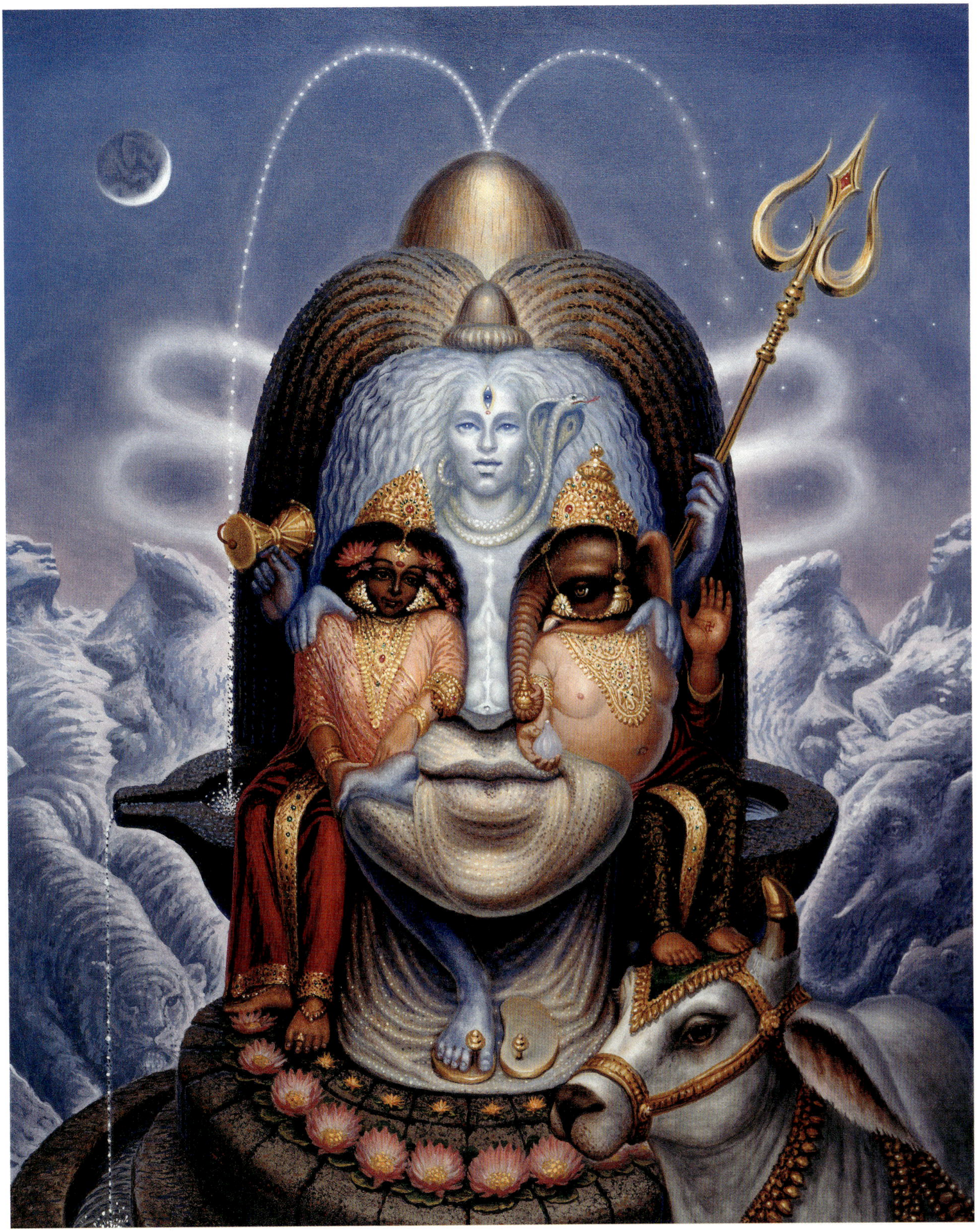

SHIVA 2002 (90 × 100)

Oil on canvas – Óleo sobre tela – Öl auf Leinwand – Huile sur toile

KRISHNA 2003 (90 × 120)

Oil on canvas – Óleo sobre tela – Öl auf Leinwand – Huile sur toile

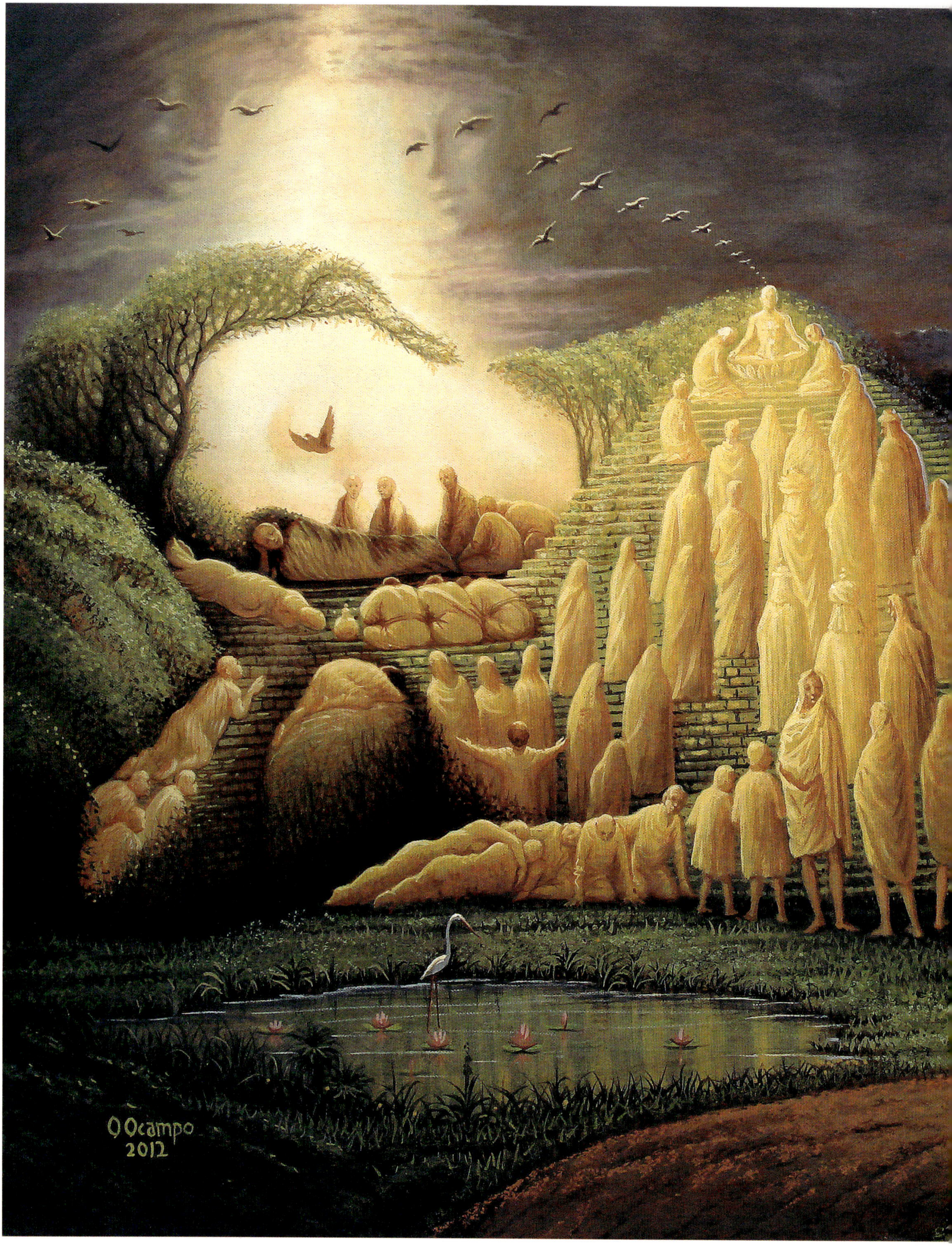
O Ocampo
2012

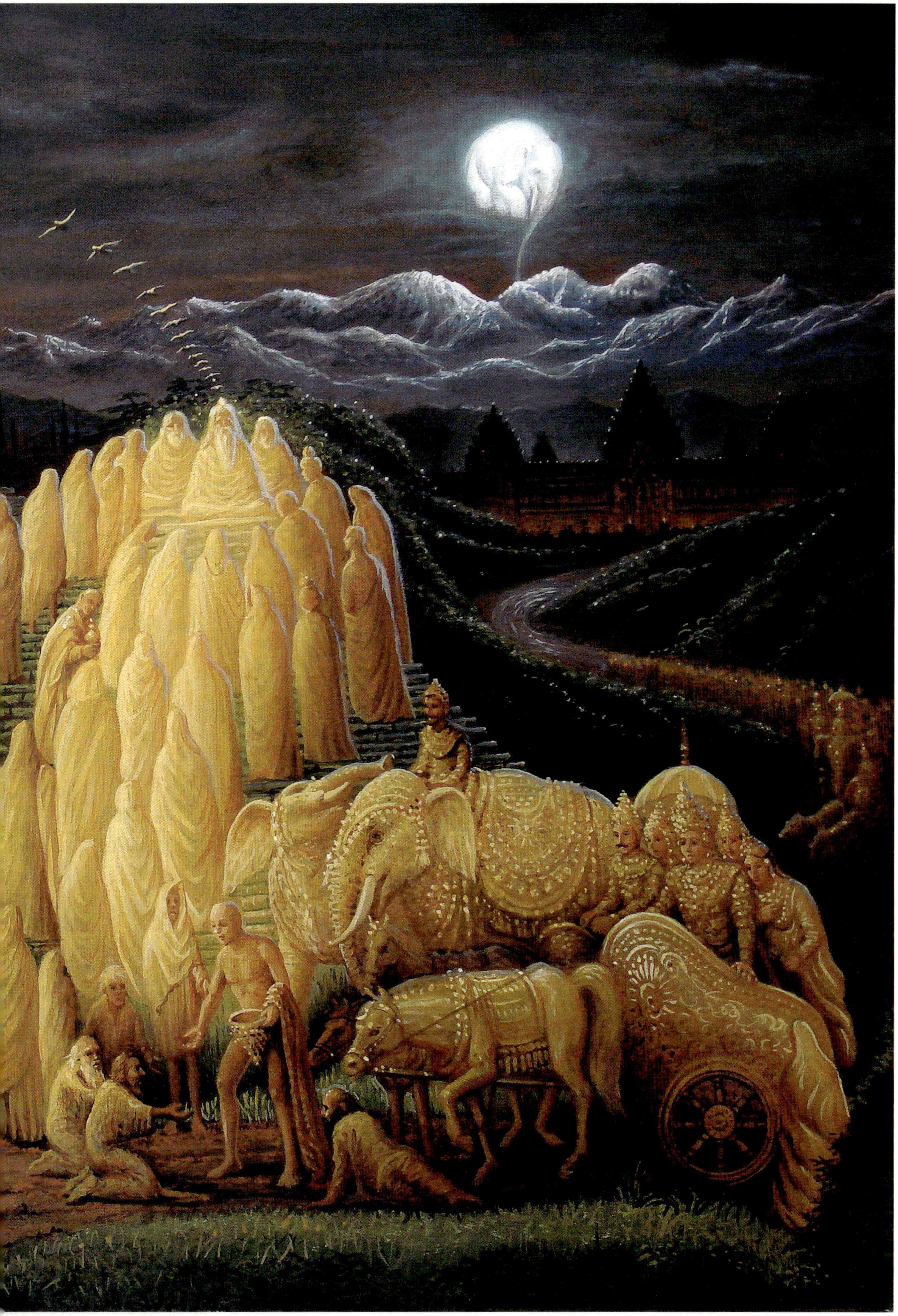

SIDDARTHA 2012 (120 × 80)
Oil on canvas – Óleo sobre tela – Öl auf Leinwand – Huile sur toile

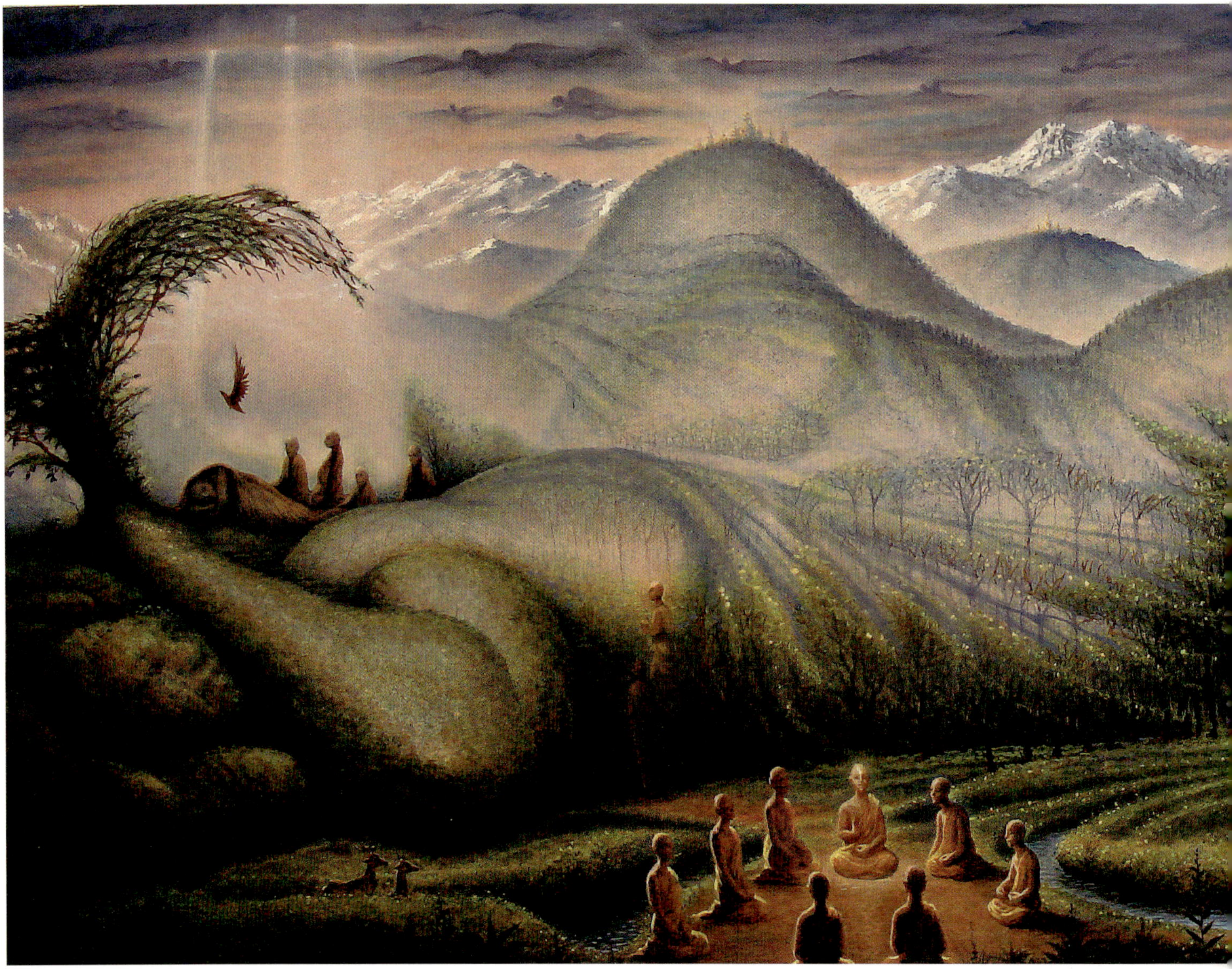

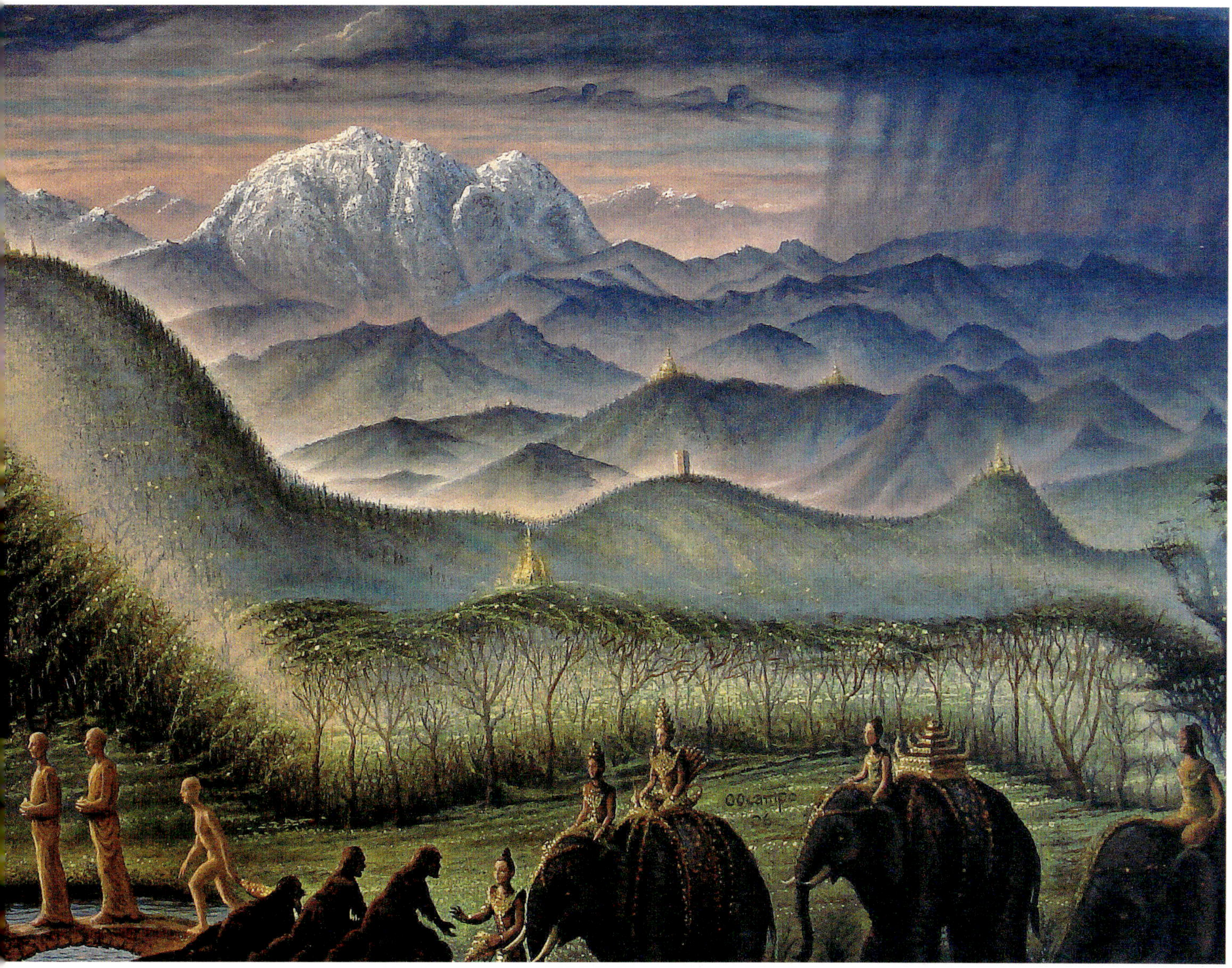

BUDA RECLINADO 2006 (183 × 68)

Oil on canvas – Óleo sobre tela – Öl auf Leinwand – Huile sur toile

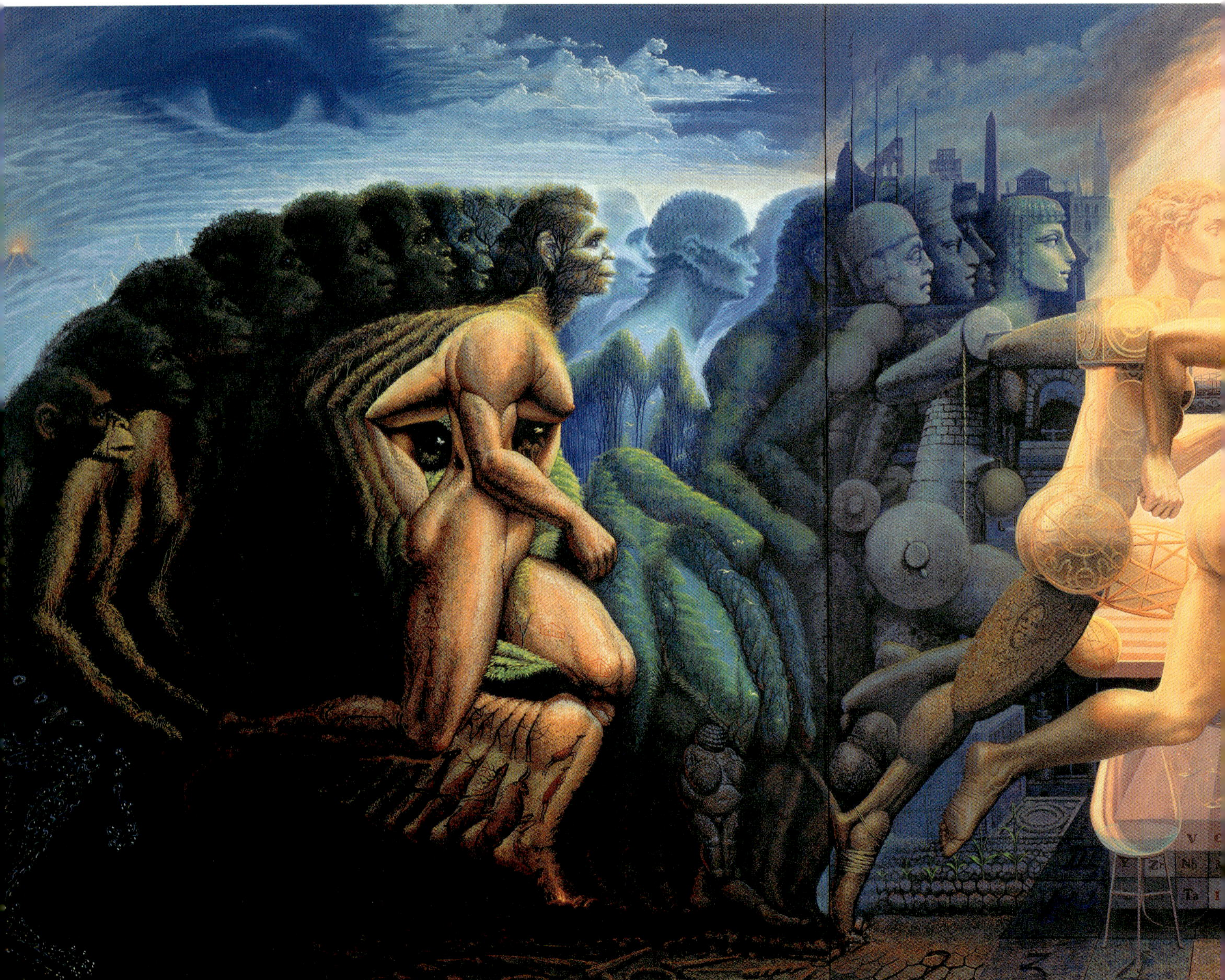

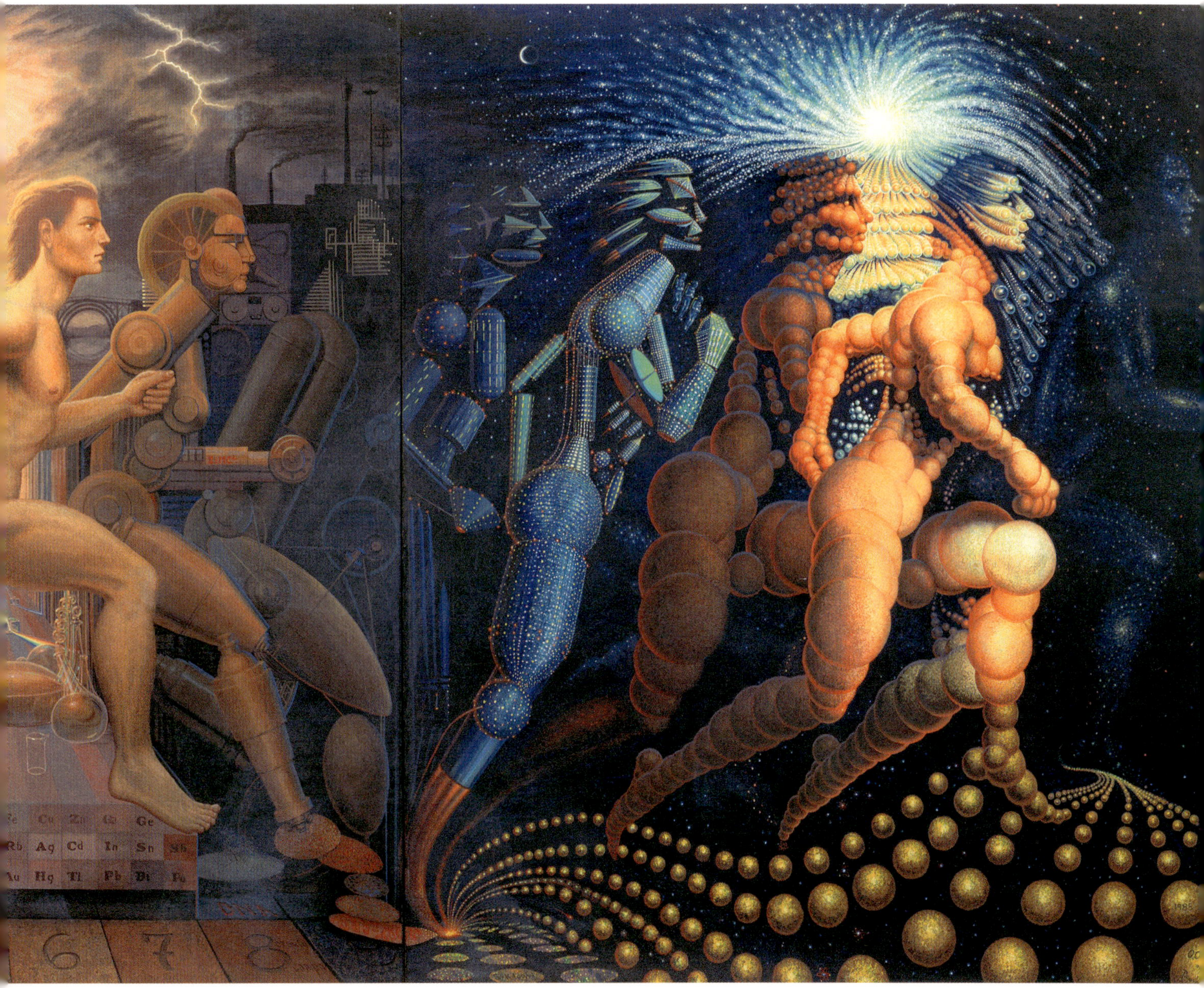

EVOLUCIÓN DEL HOMBRE 1996 (240 × 150)

Acrylic on canvas – Acrílico sobre tela – Acryl auf Leinwand – Acrylique sur toile

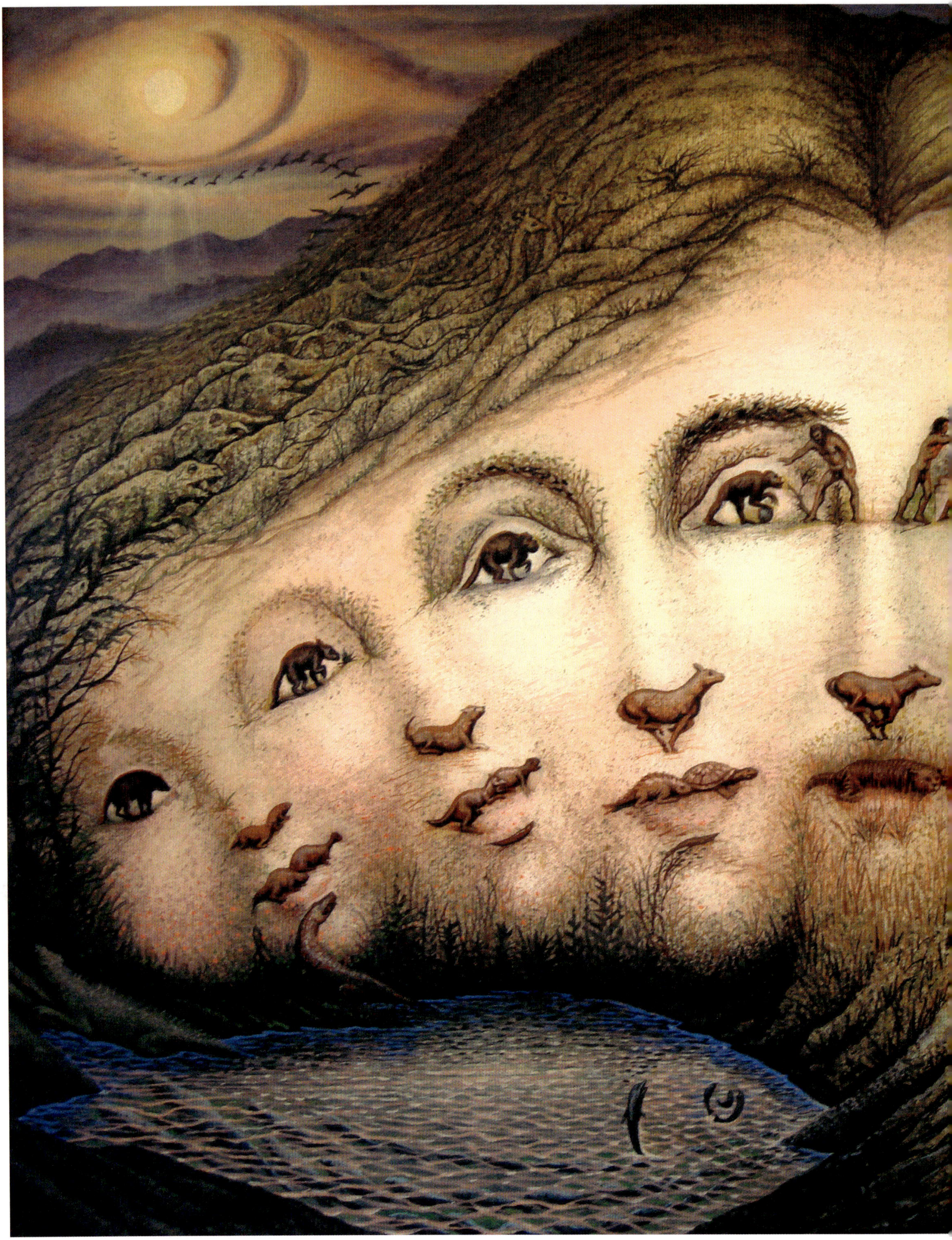

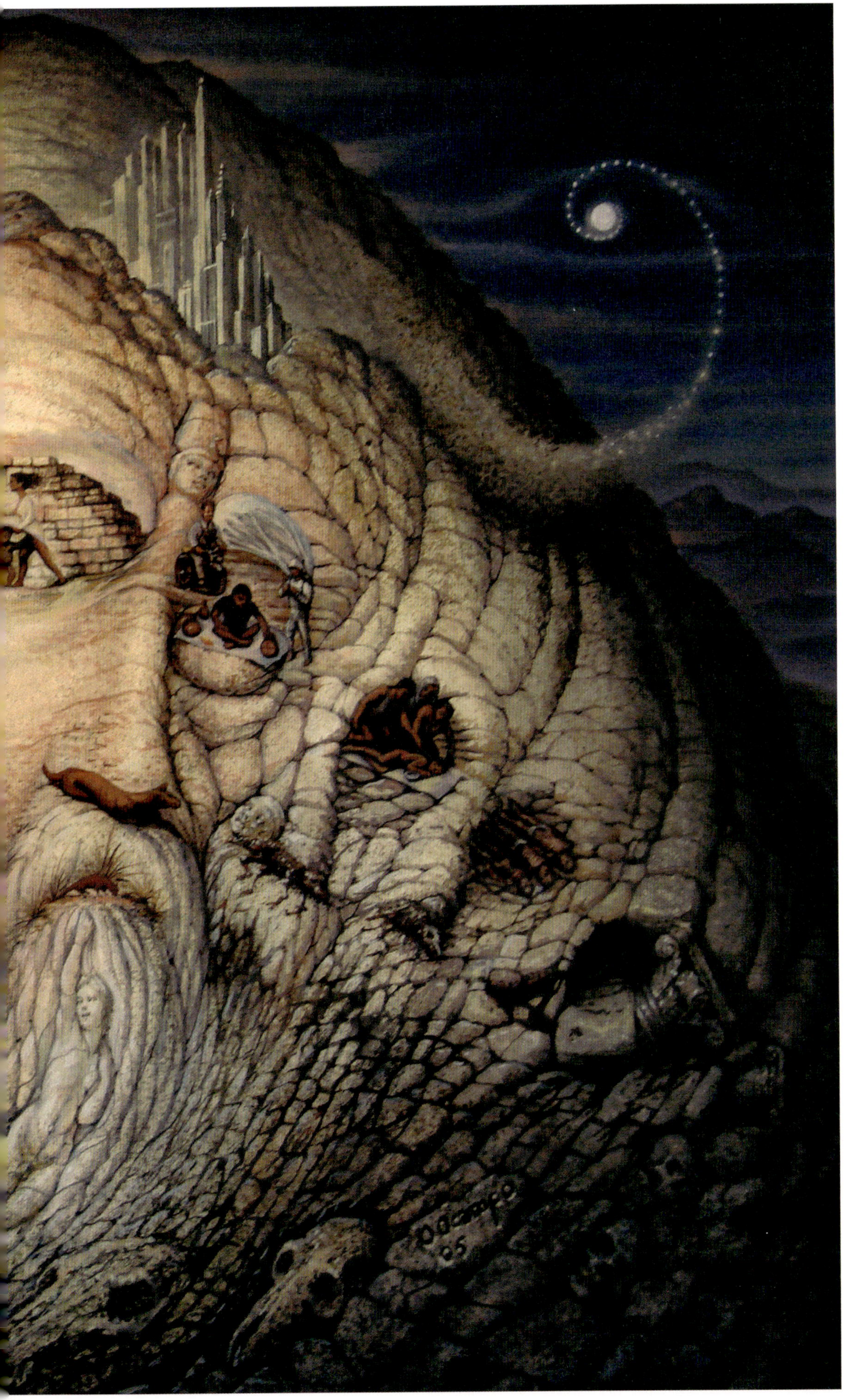

EVOLUCIÓN 2005 (120 × 80)
Oil on canvas – Óleo sobre tela – Öl auf Leinwand – Huile sur toile

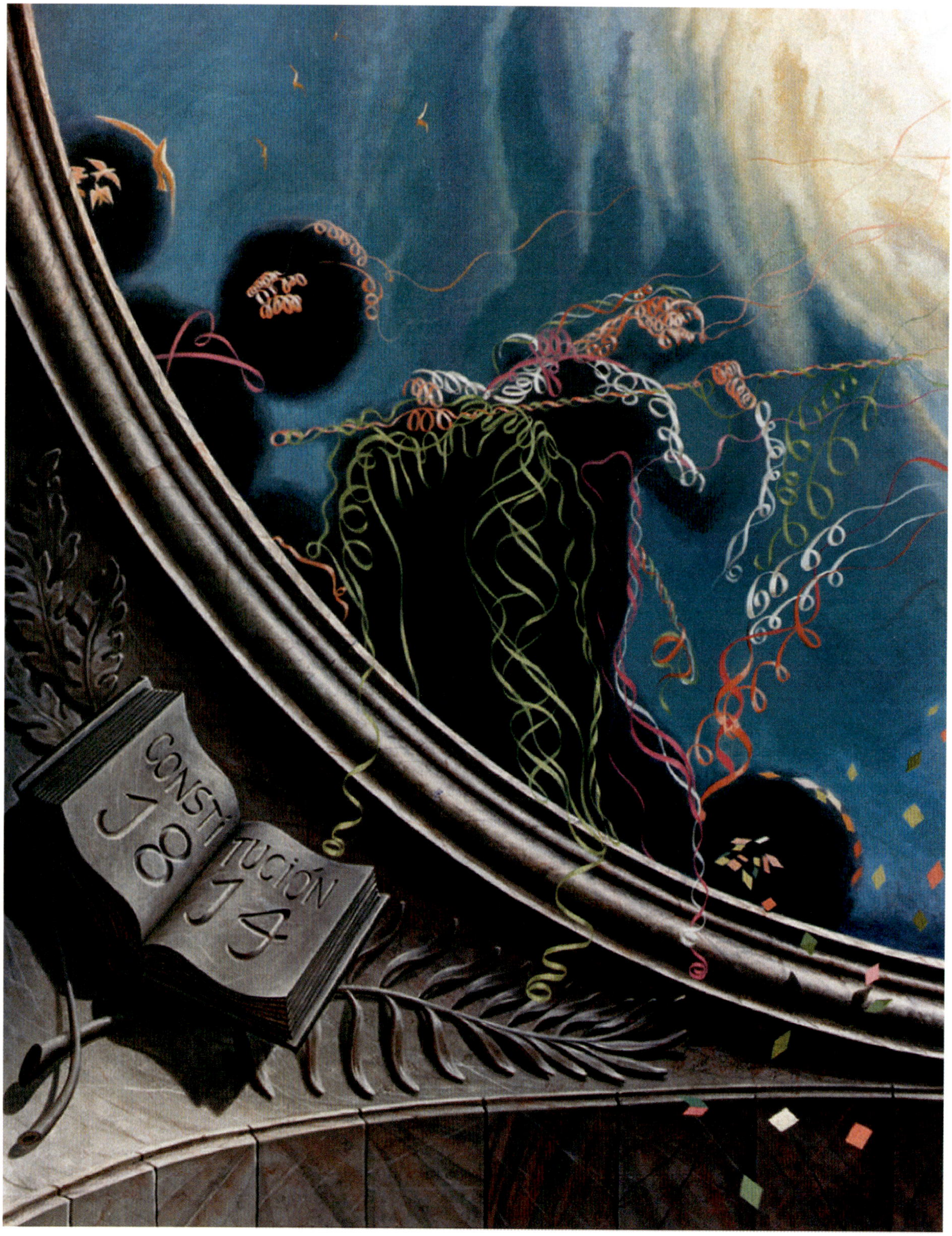

CONSTITUCION 1814 – PLAFON 2–4 1980 (200 × 180)

Acrylic on canvas – Acrílico sobre tela – Acryl auf Leinwand – Acrylique sur toile

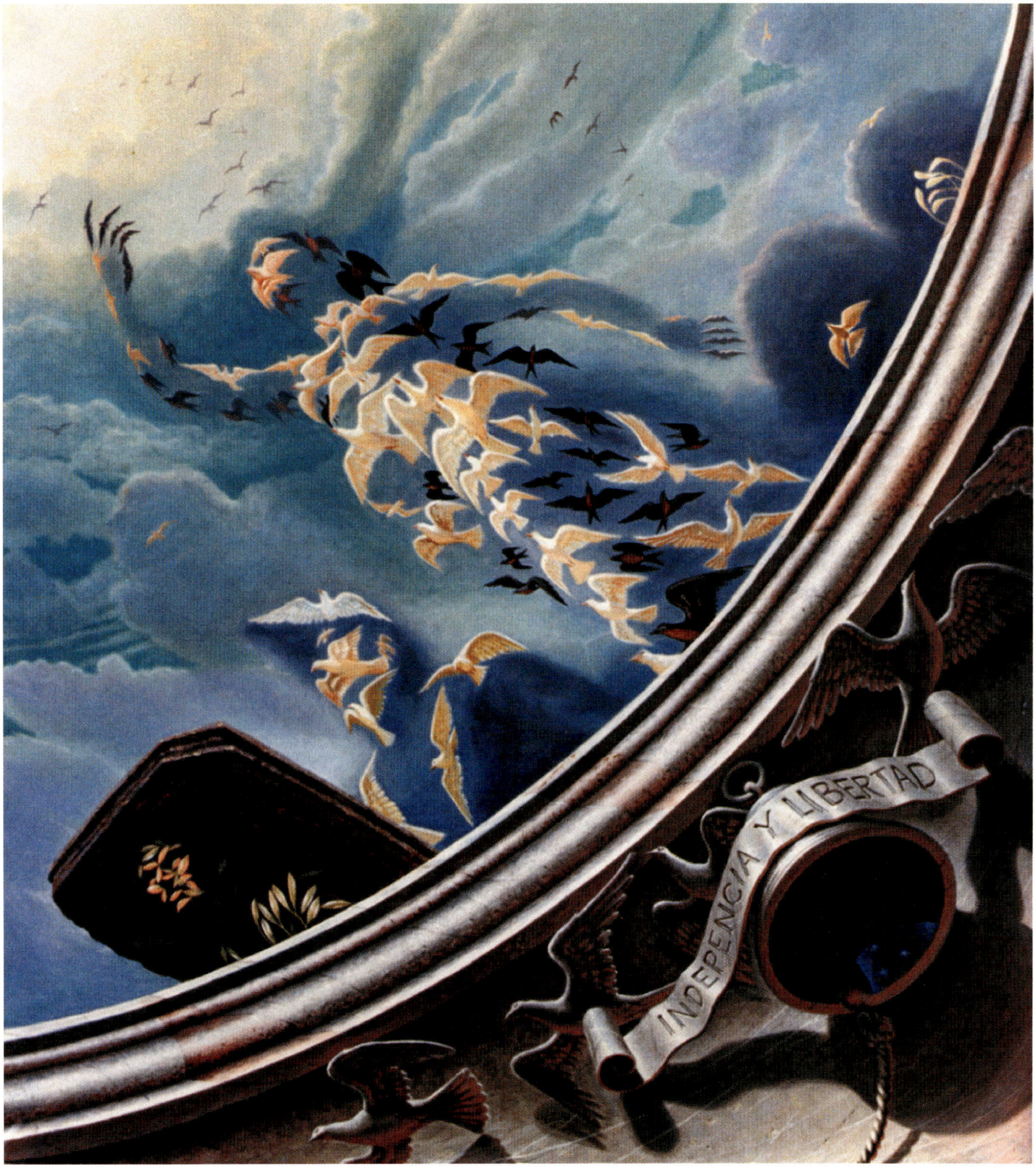

INDEPENDENCIA Y LIBERTAD – PLAFON 1–4 1980 (200 × 190)

Acrylic on canvas – Acrílico sobre tela – Acryl auf Leinwand – Acrylique sur toile

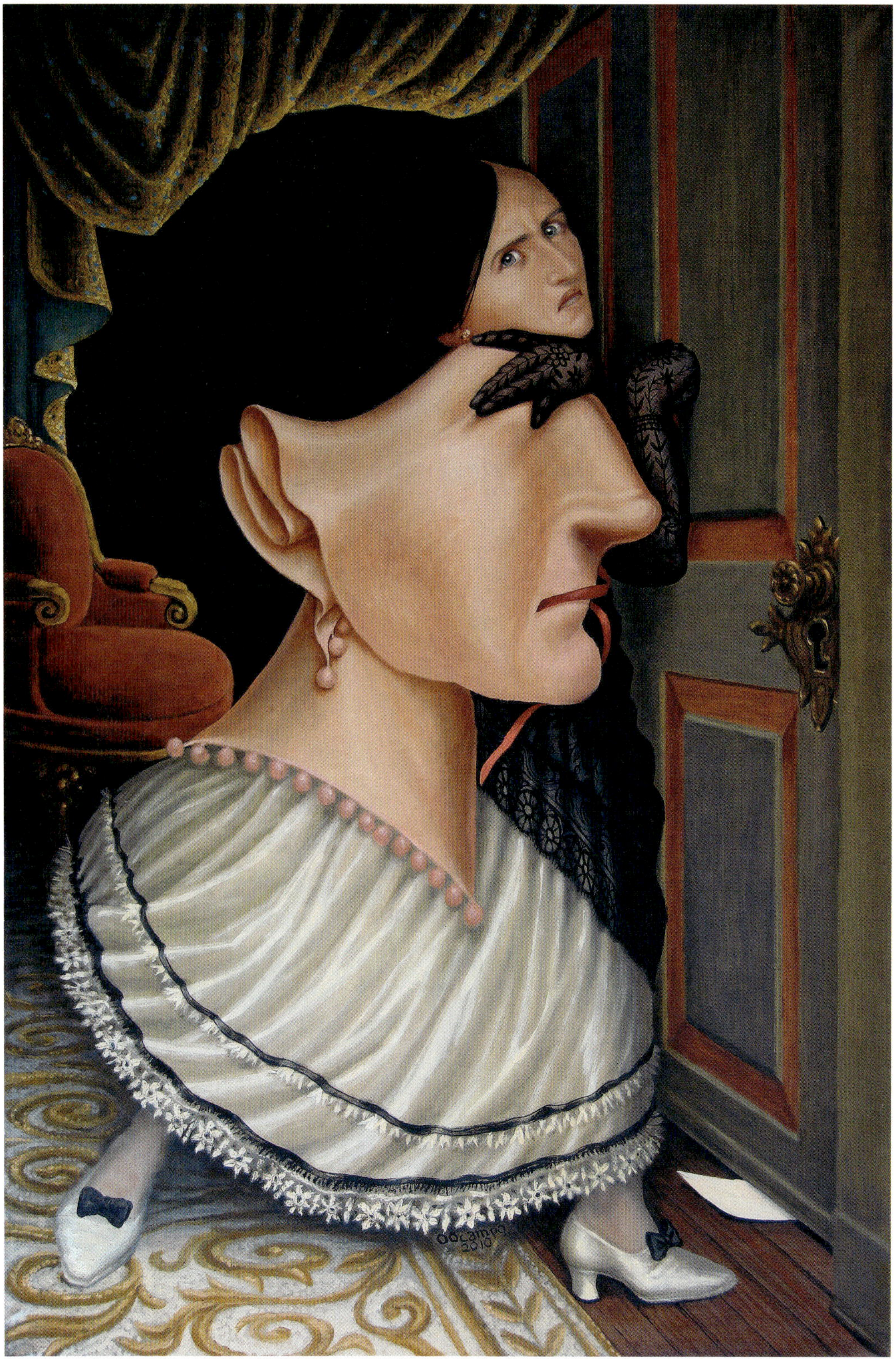

NOS DESCUBRIERON (CORREGIDORA) 2010 (80 × 120)

Oil on canvas – Óleo sobre tela – Öl auf Leinwand – Huile sur toile

ALLENDE 2010 (90 × 115

Oil on canvas – Óleo sobre tela – Öl auf Leinwand – Huile sur toi

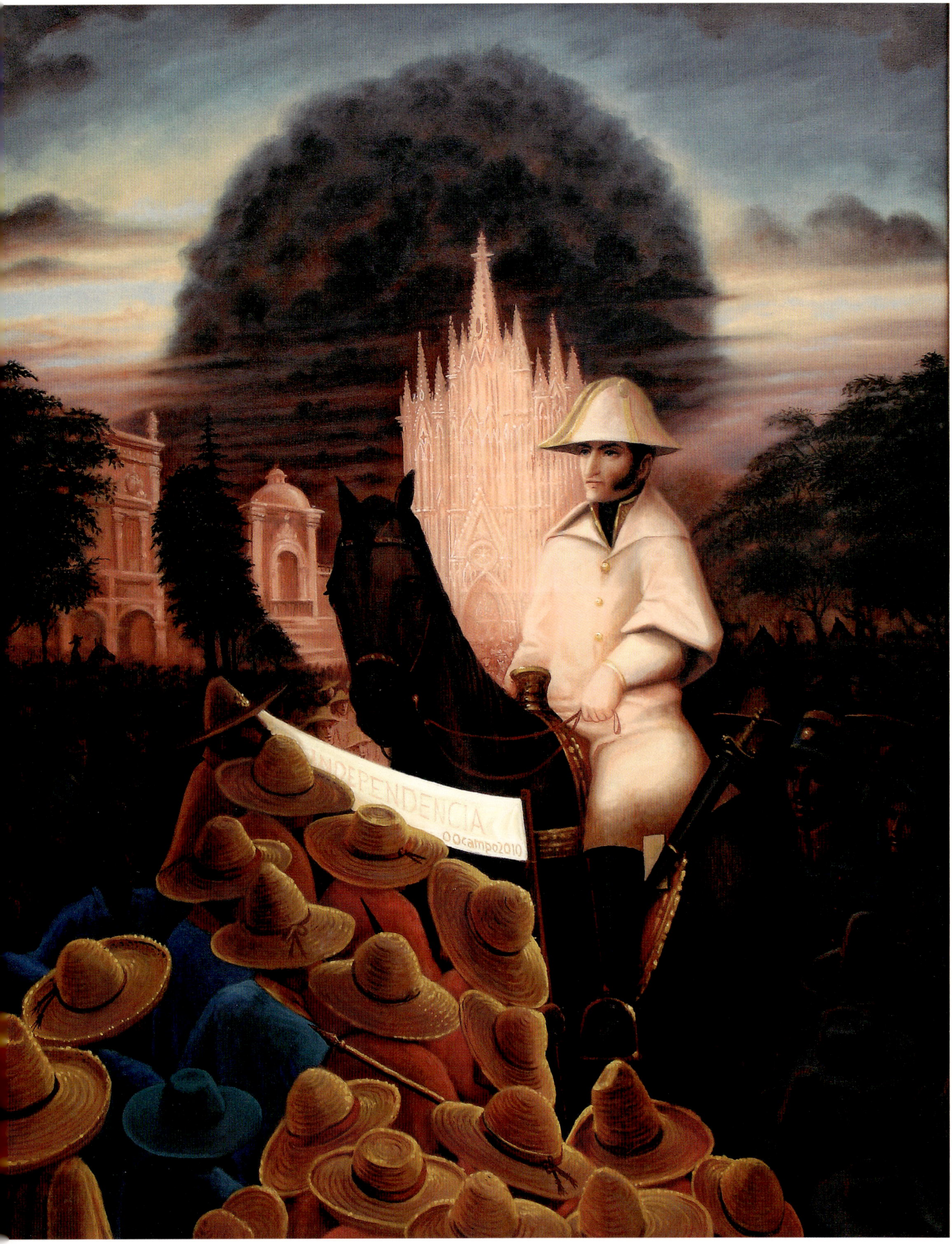
INDEPENDENCIA
O.Ocampo2010

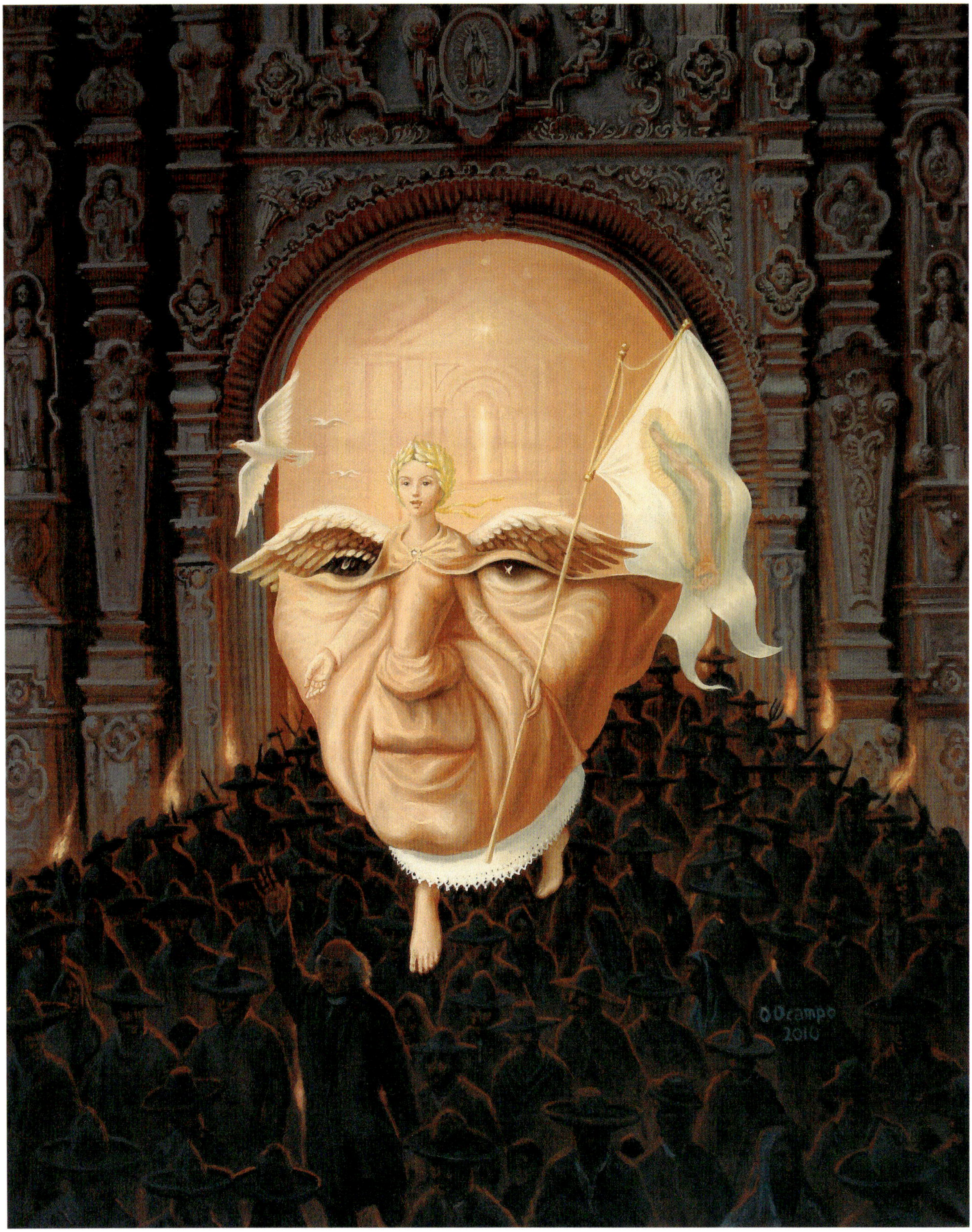

VIVA LA INDEPENDENCIA 2010 (80 × 100)

Oil on canvas – Óleo sobre tela – Öl auf Leinwand – Huile sur toile

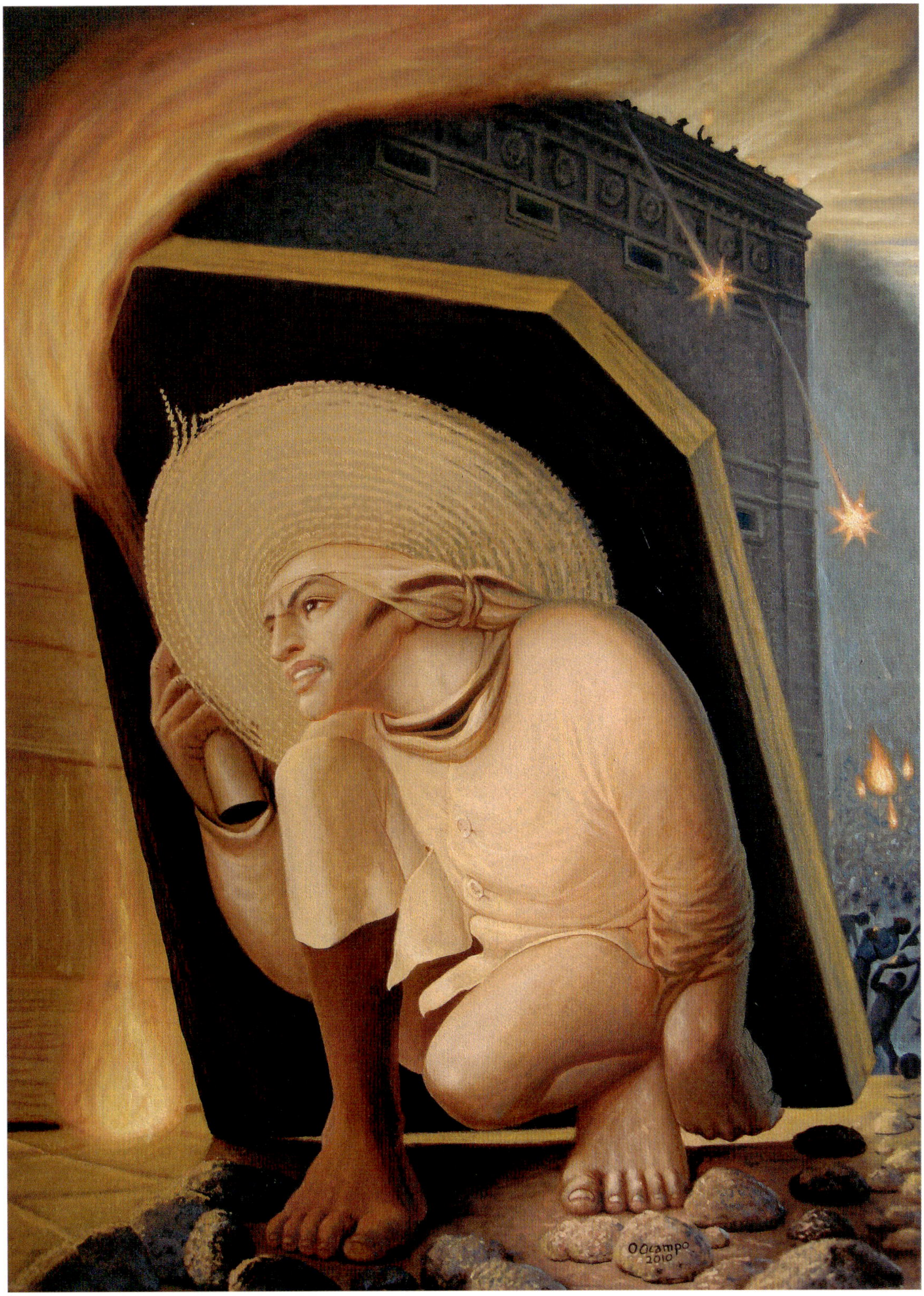

EL PÍPILA 2010 (80 × 110)

Oil on canvas – Óleo sobre tela – Öl auf Leinwand – Huile sur toile

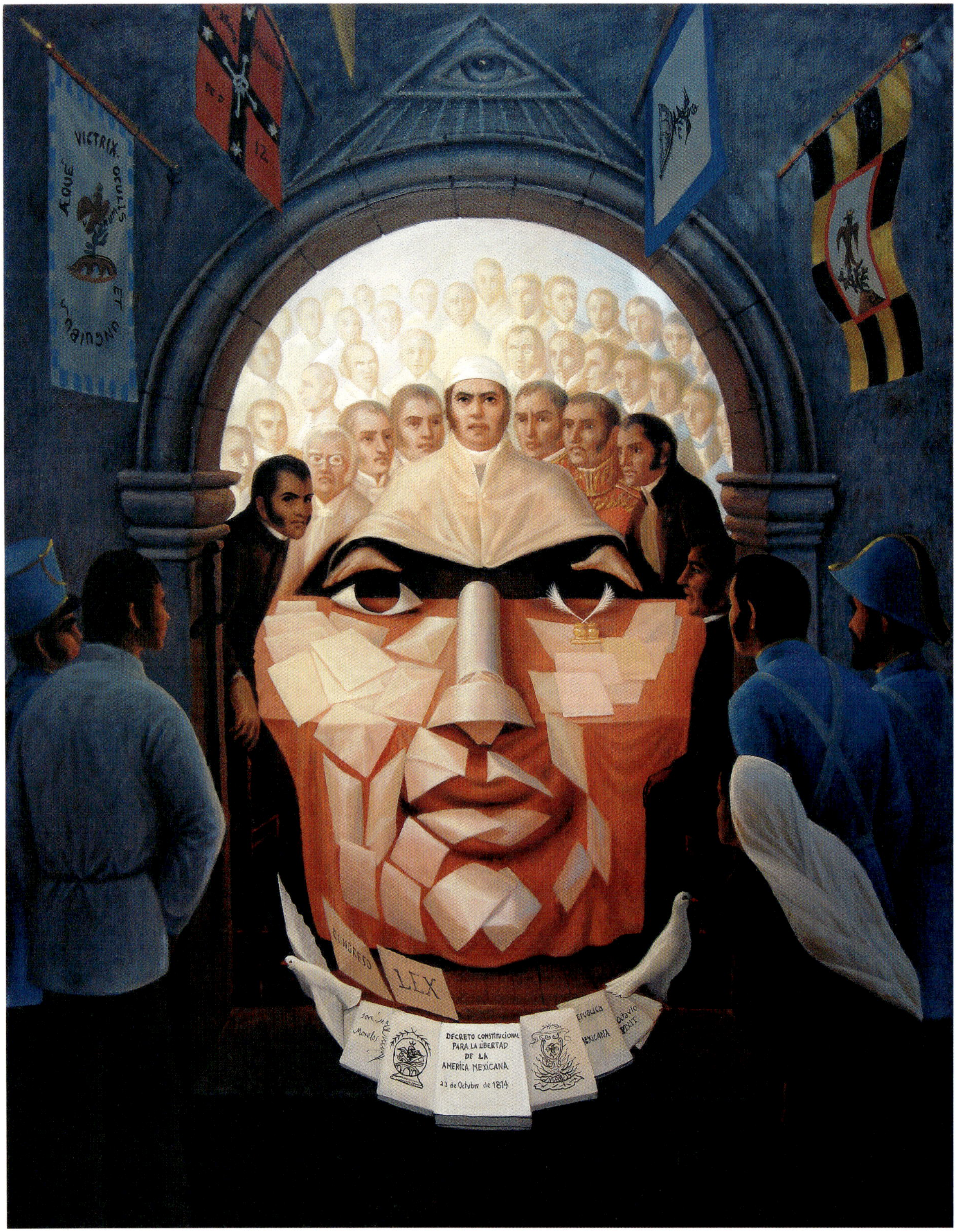

CONSTITUCIÓN DE MORELOS 2010 (90 × 115)

Oil on canvas – Óleo sobre tela – Öl auf Leinwand – Huile sur toile

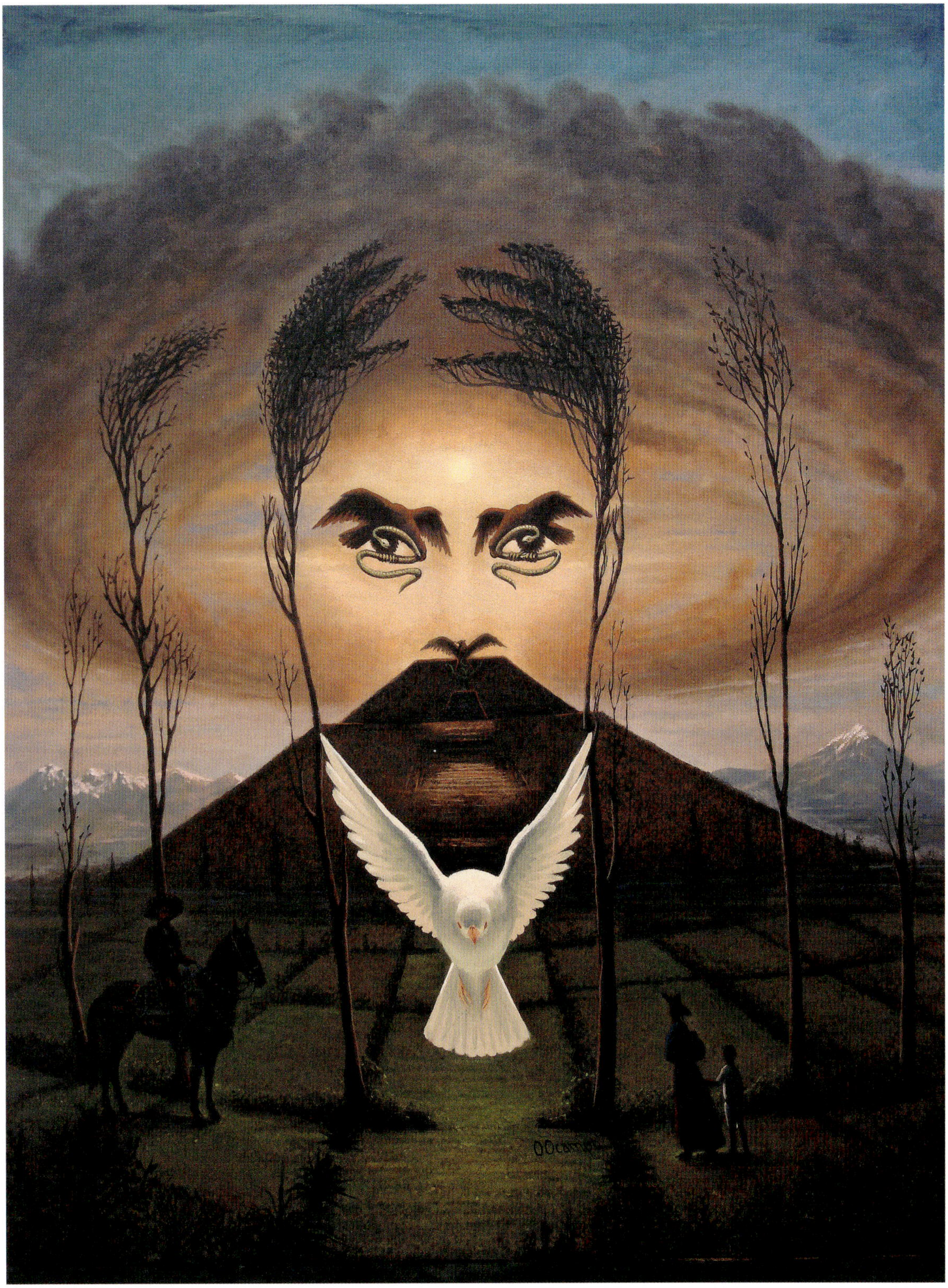

ZAPATA Y LIBERTAD 2010 (60 × 90)

Oil on canvas – Óleo sobre tela – Öl auf Leinwand – Huile sur toile

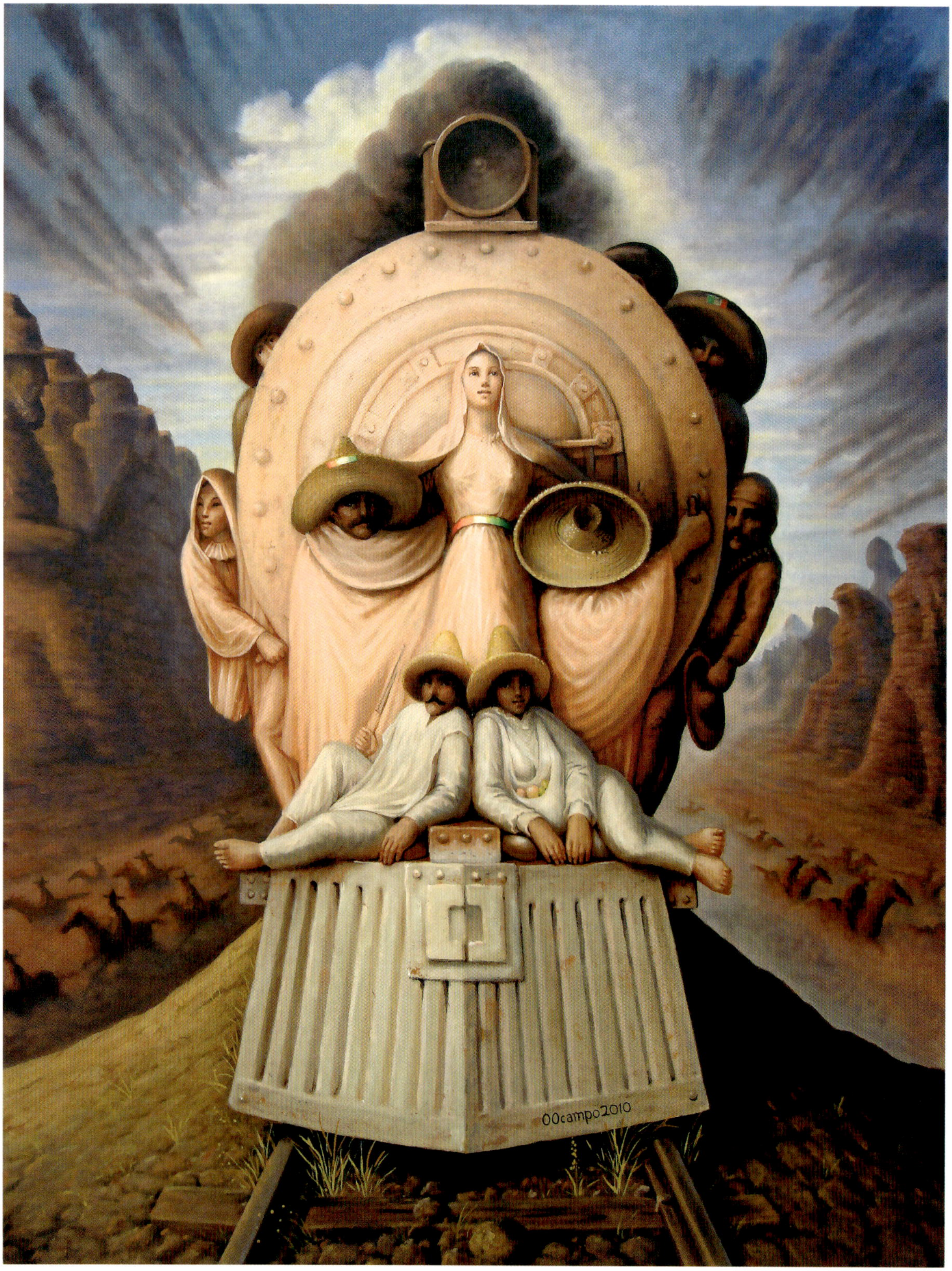

LOCOMOTORA DE CARRANZA 2010 (90 × 115)

Oil on canvas – Óleo sobre tela – Öl auf Leinwand – Huile sur toile

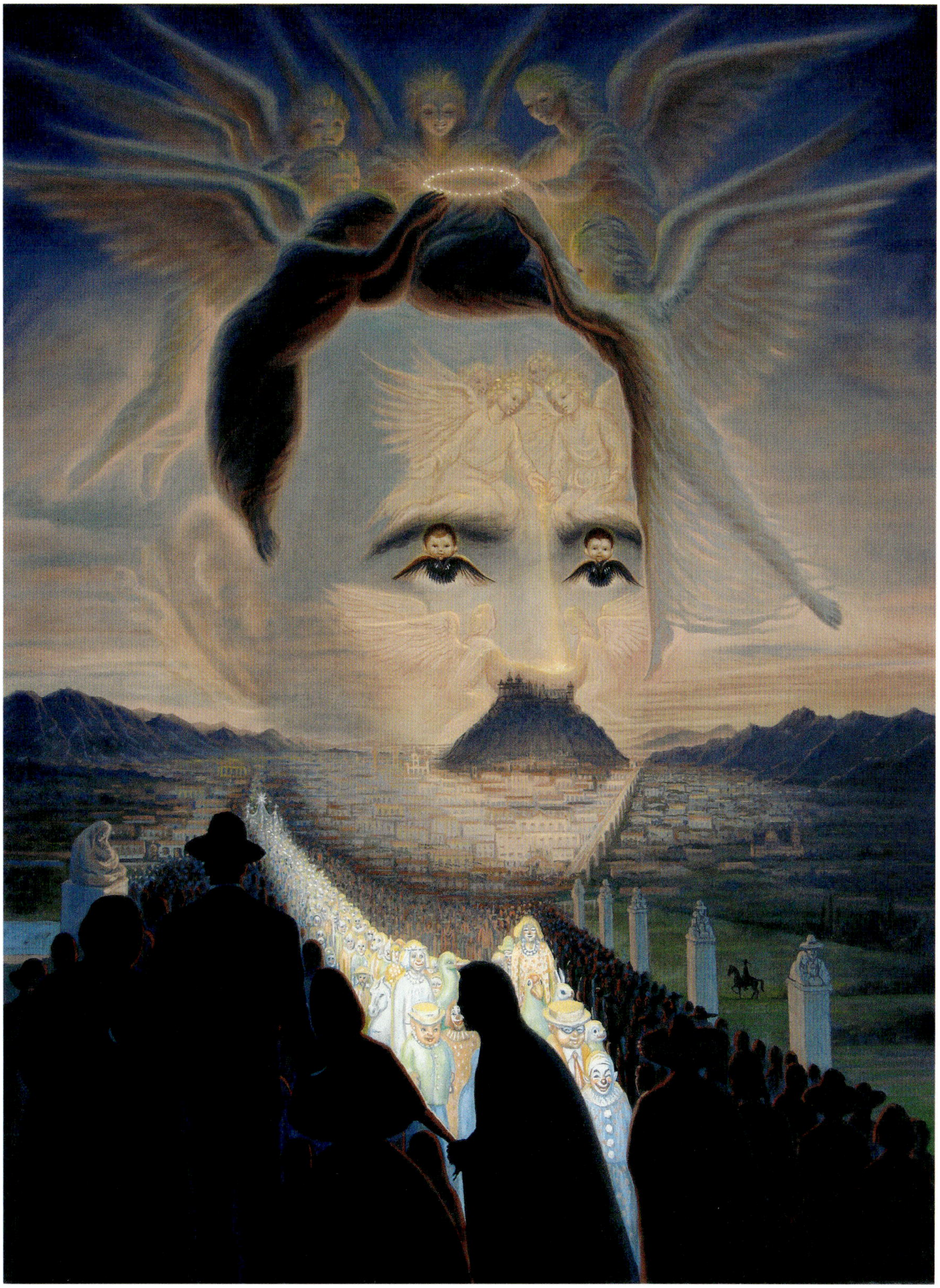

A MI MAESTRO SALVADOR ZÚÑIGA 2008 (90 × 120)

Oil on canvas – Óleo sobre tela – Öl auf Leinwand – Huile sur toile

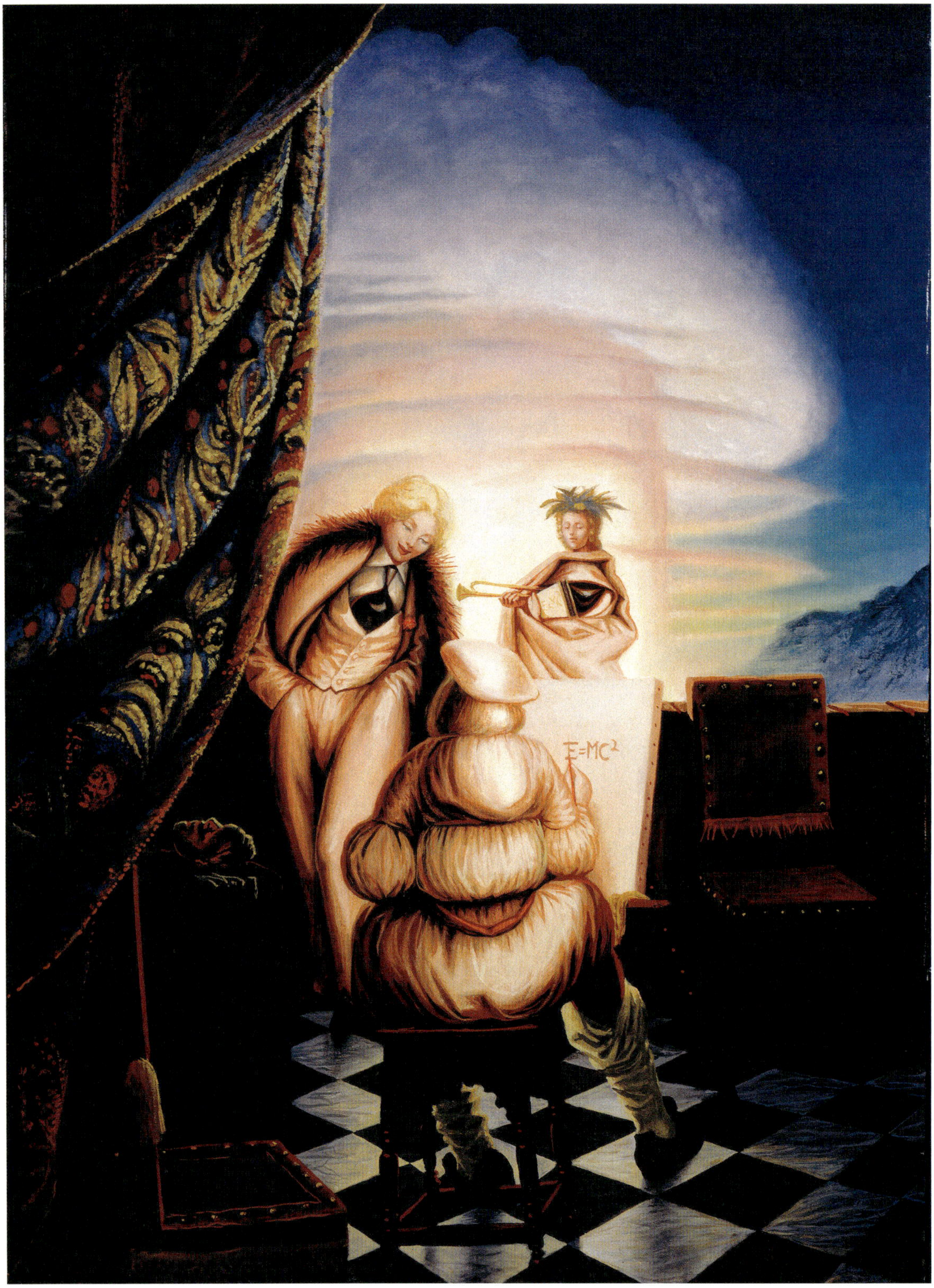

RELATIVIDAD DE EINSTAIN 2004 (90 × 120)

Oil on canvas – Óleo sobre tela – Öl auf Leinwand – Huile sur toile

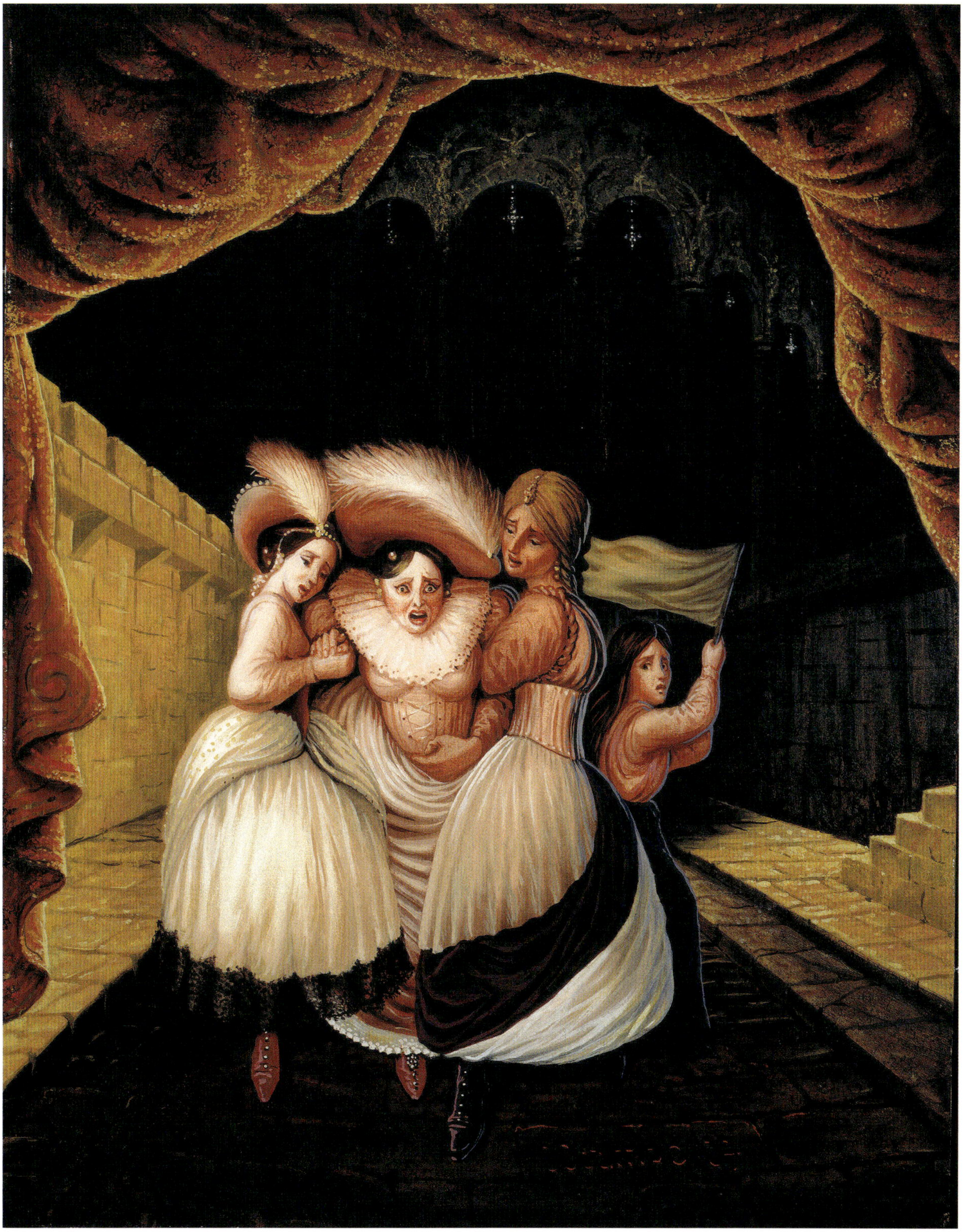

VERDI 2004 (90 × 100)

Oil on canvas – Óleo sobre tela – Öl auf Leinwand – Huile sur toile

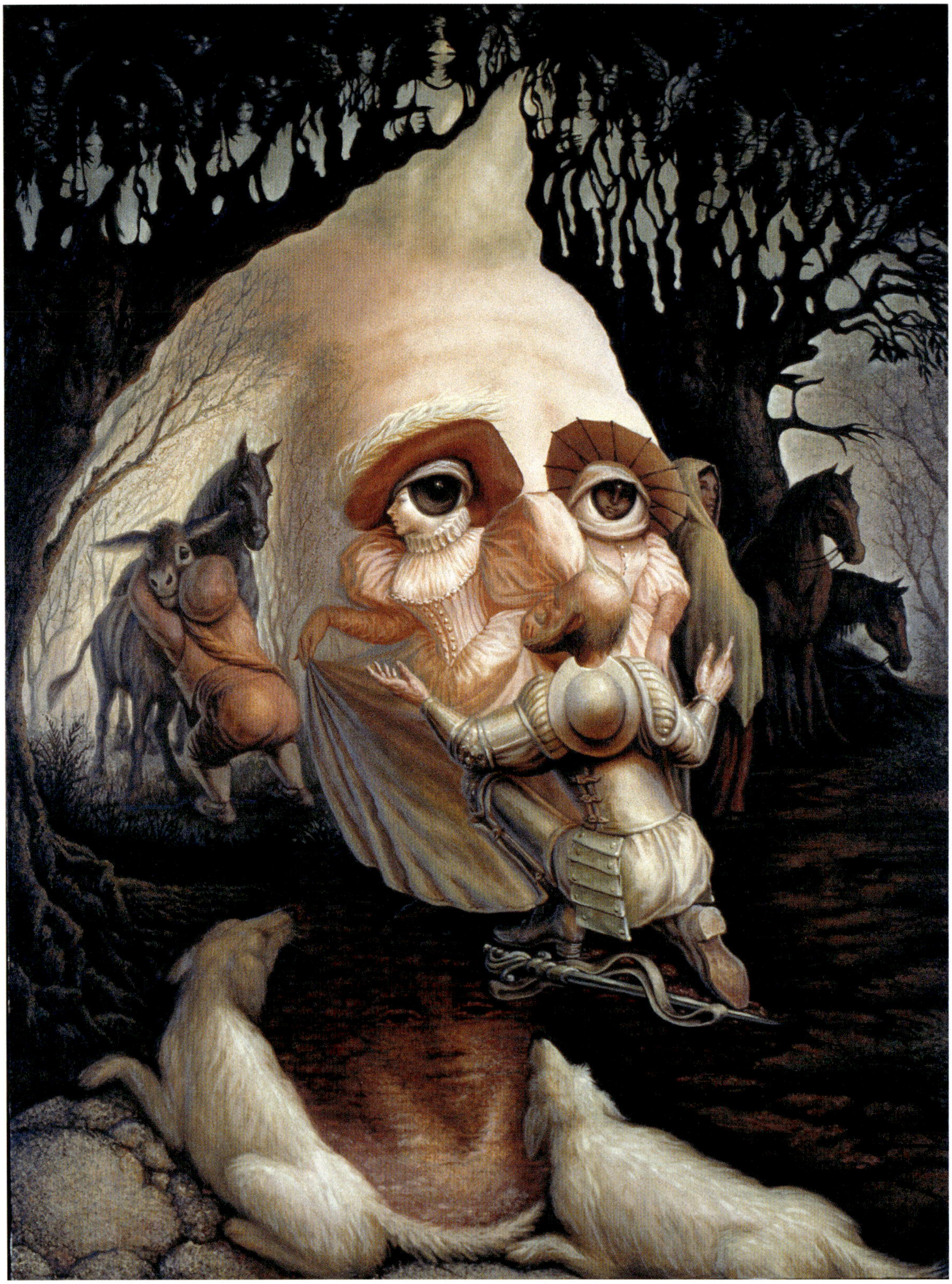

CORTEJO 2000 (80 × 100)

Oil on canvas – Óleo sobre tela – Öl auf Leinwand – Huile sur toile

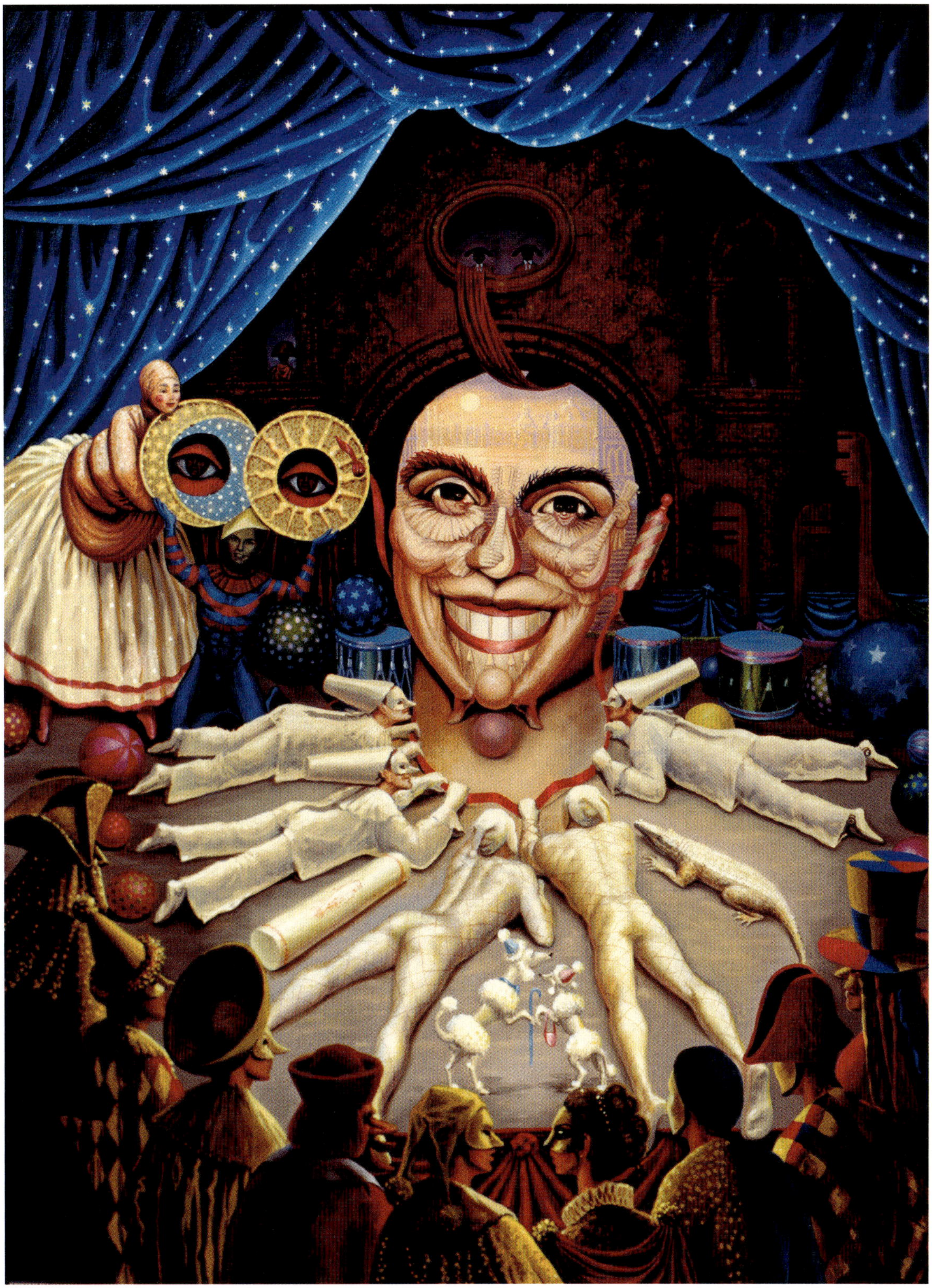

EL AMOR DEL ARLEQUÍN 1997 (80 × 120)

Oil on canvas – Óleo sobre tela – Öl auf Leinwand – Huile sur toile

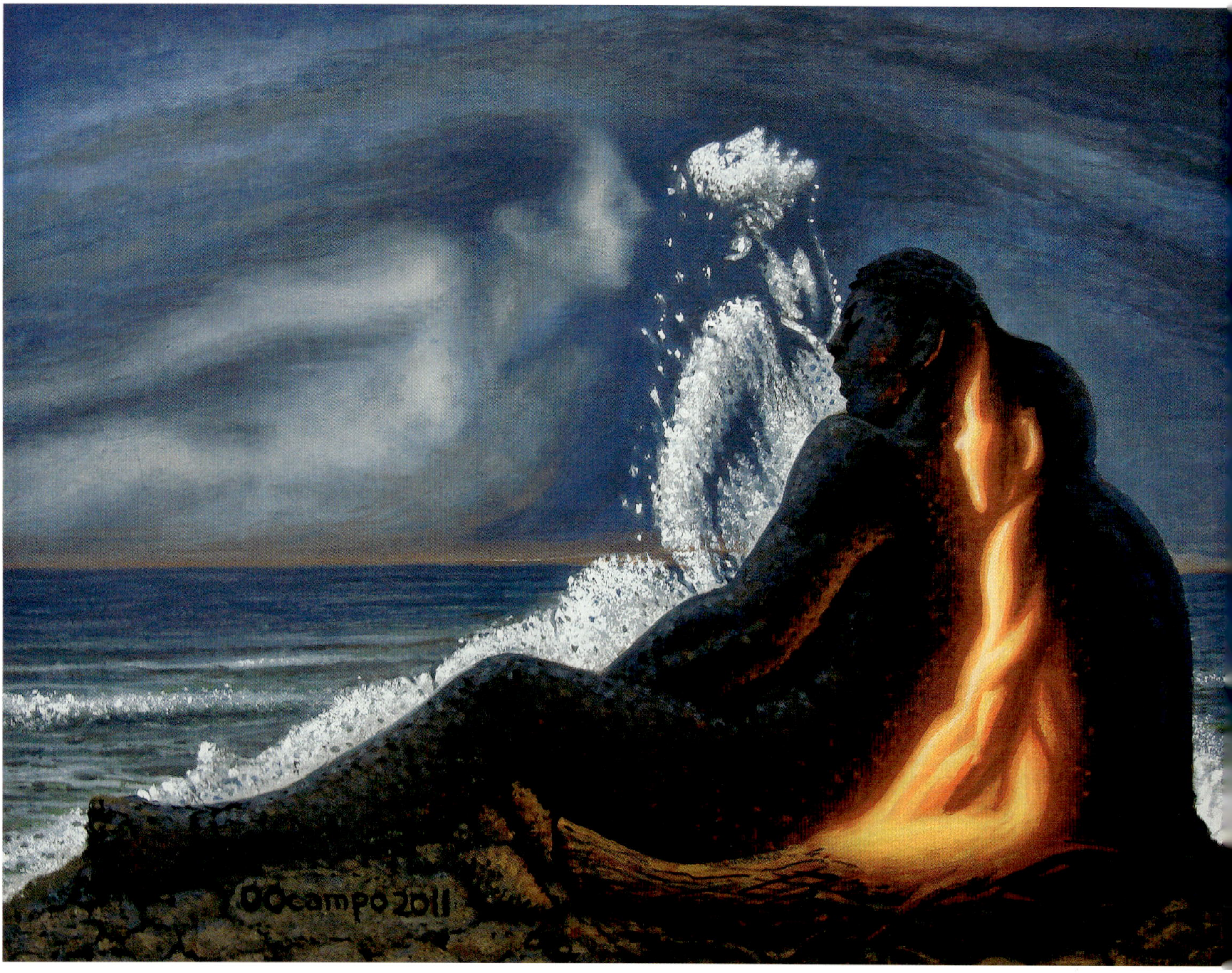

ELEMENTOS ENAMORADOS 2011 (60 × 40)

Oil on canvas – Óleo sobre tela – Öl auf Leinwand – Huile sur toile

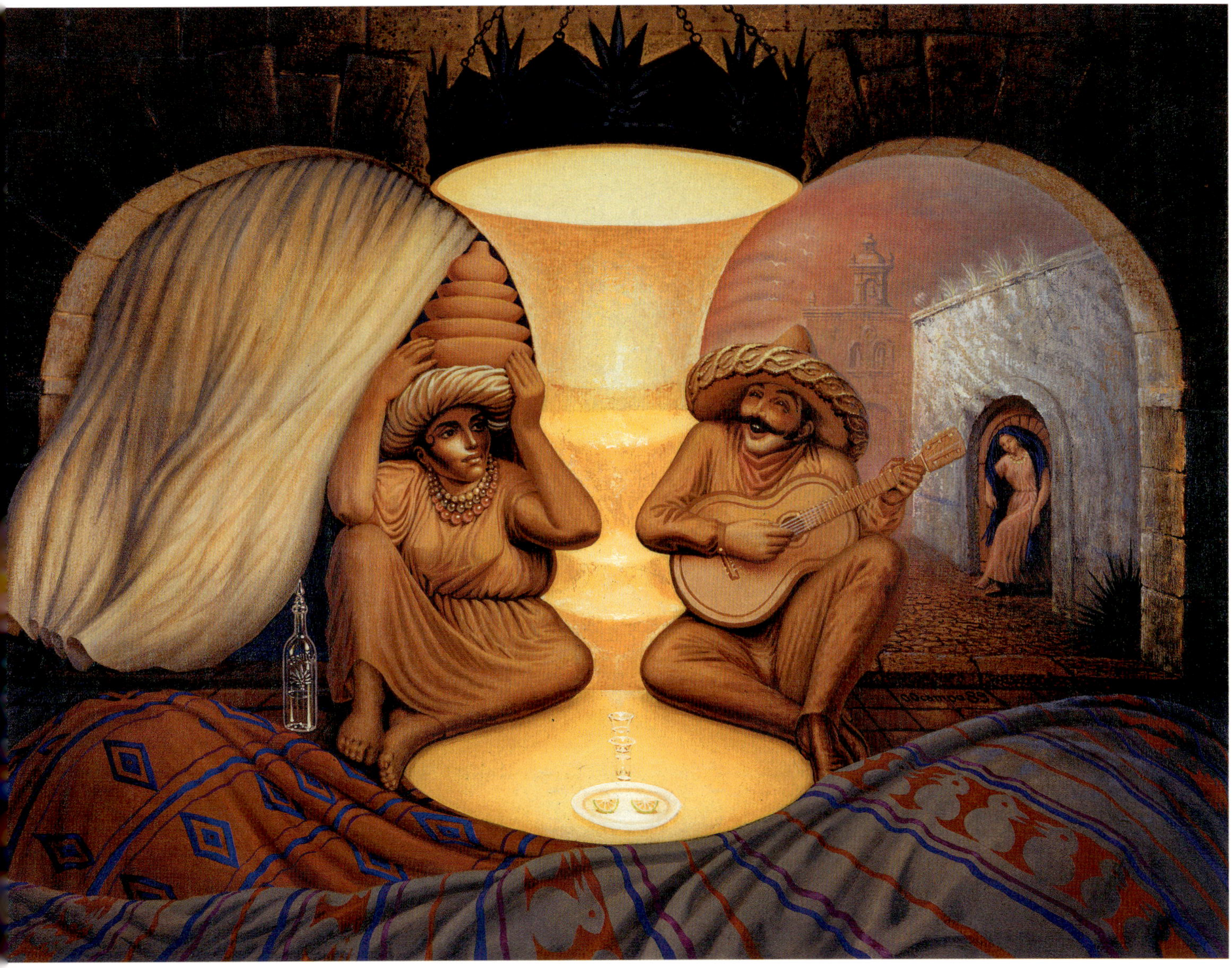

SOLOS PARA SIEMPRE 1985 (120 × 90)

Oil on canvas – Óleo sobre tela – Öl auf Leinwand – Huile sur toile

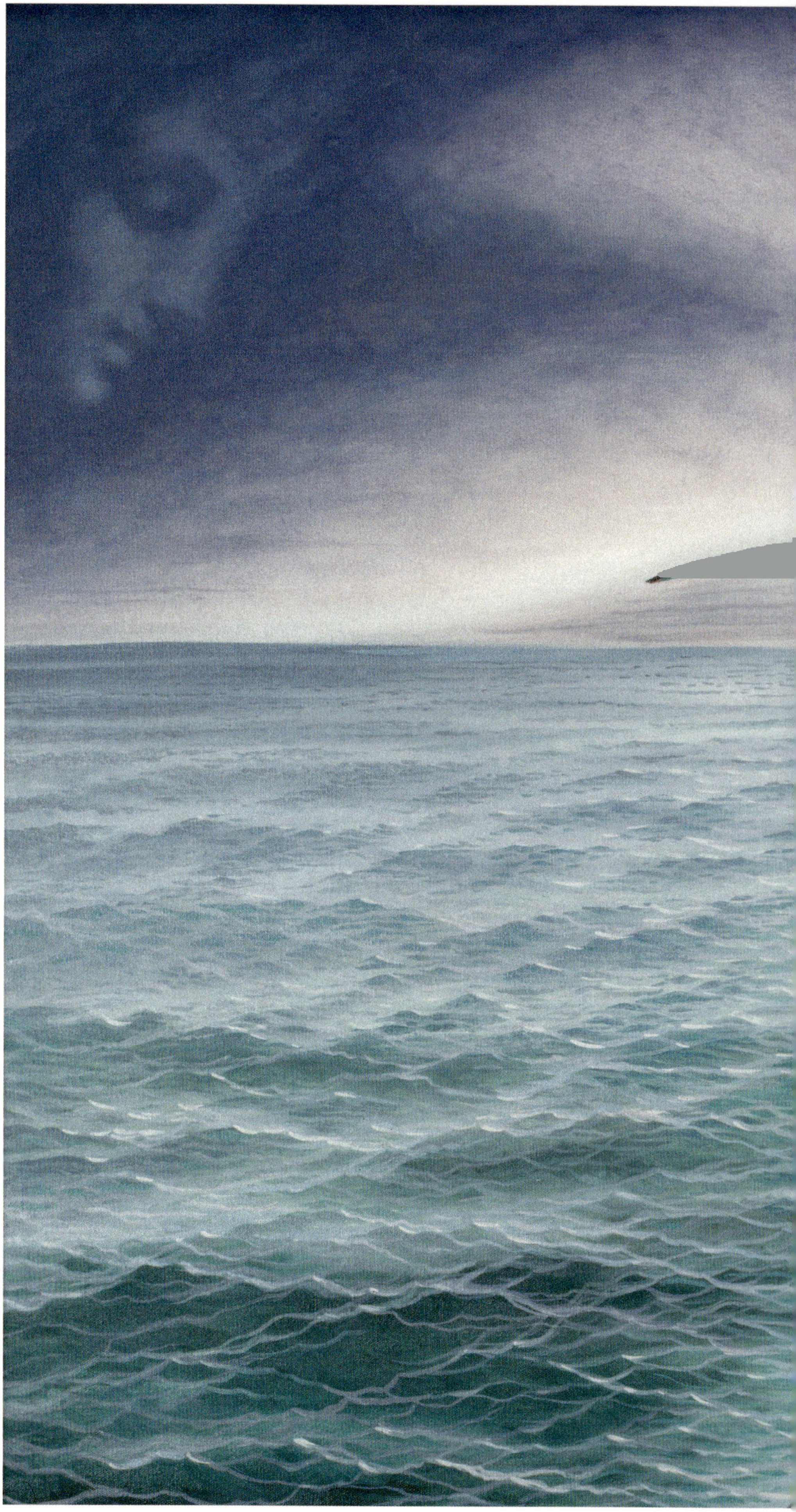

BESO DEL MAR 2001 (120 × 80)
Oil on canvas – Óleo sobre tela – Öl auf Leinwand – Huile sur toile

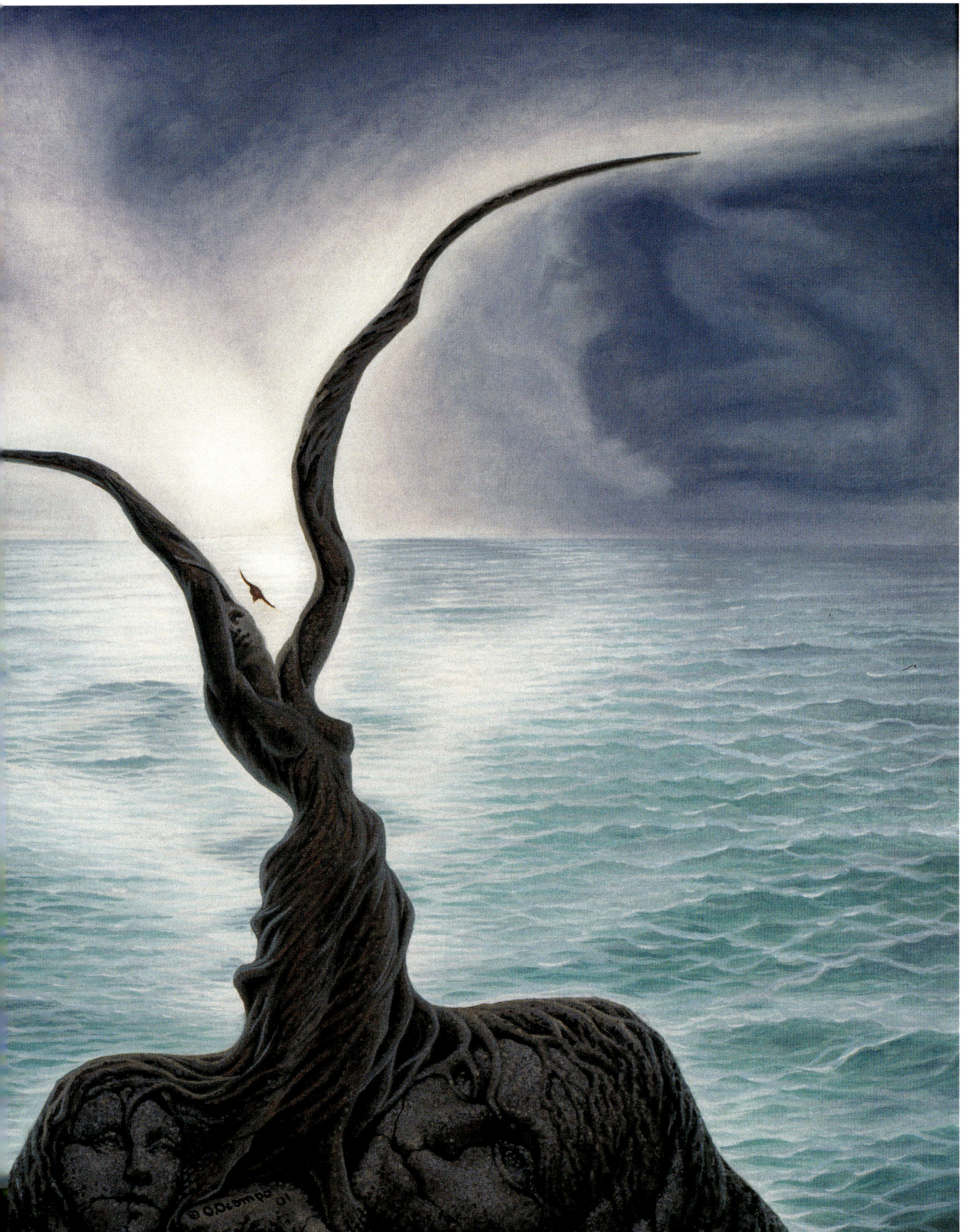

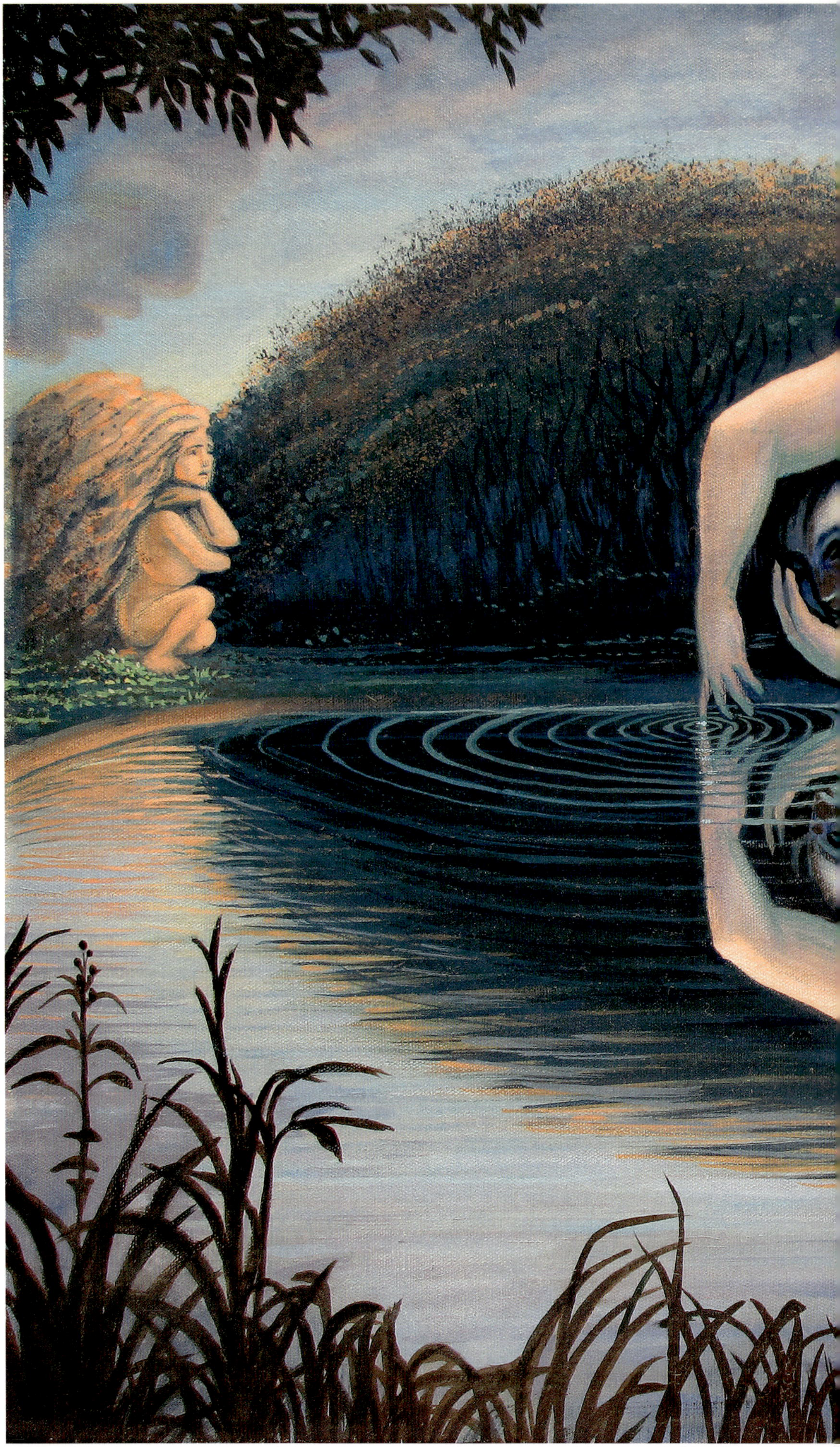

NARCISO 2007 (70 × 50)
Oil on canvas – Óleo sobre tela – Öl auf Leinwand – Huile sur toile

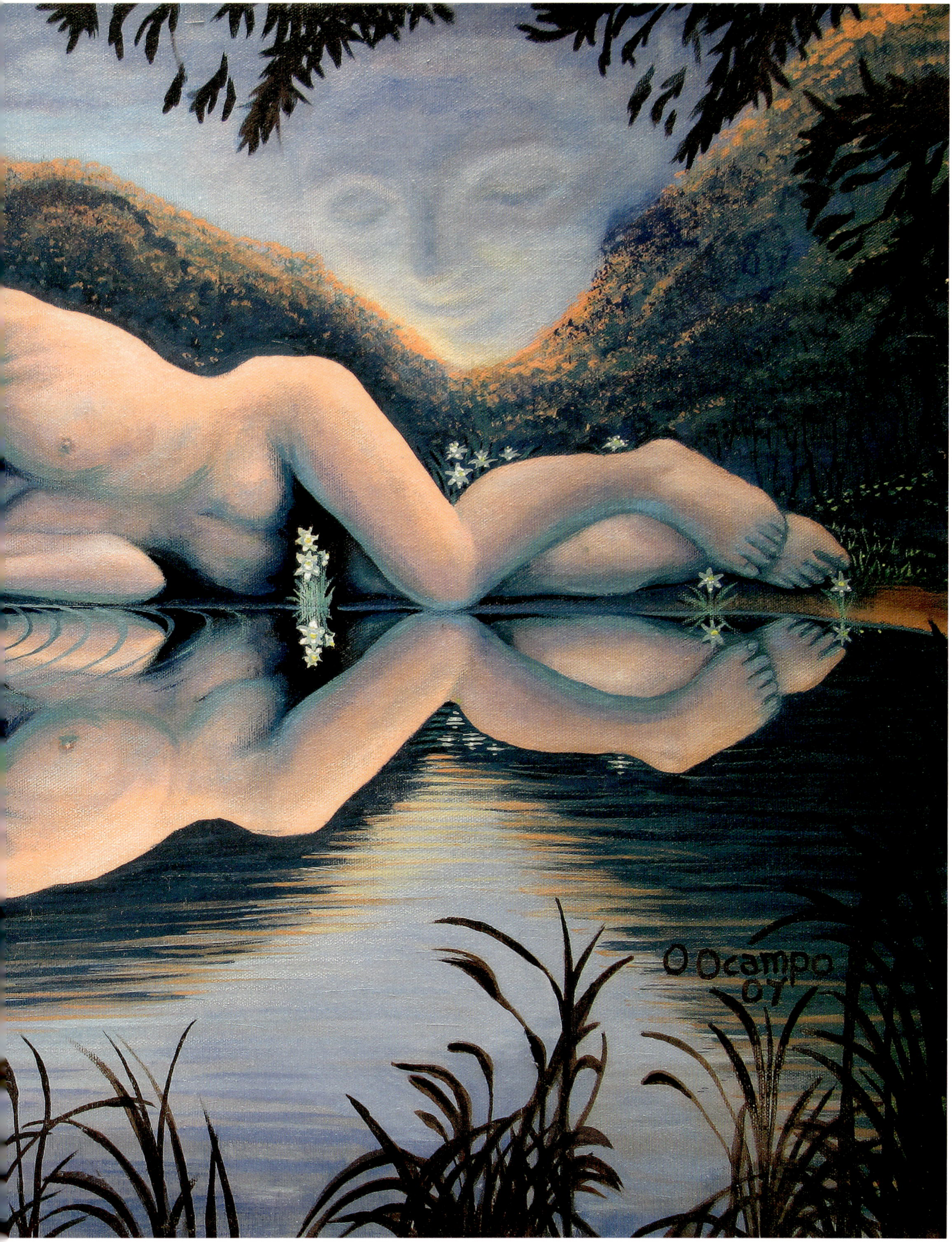
O Ocampo
07

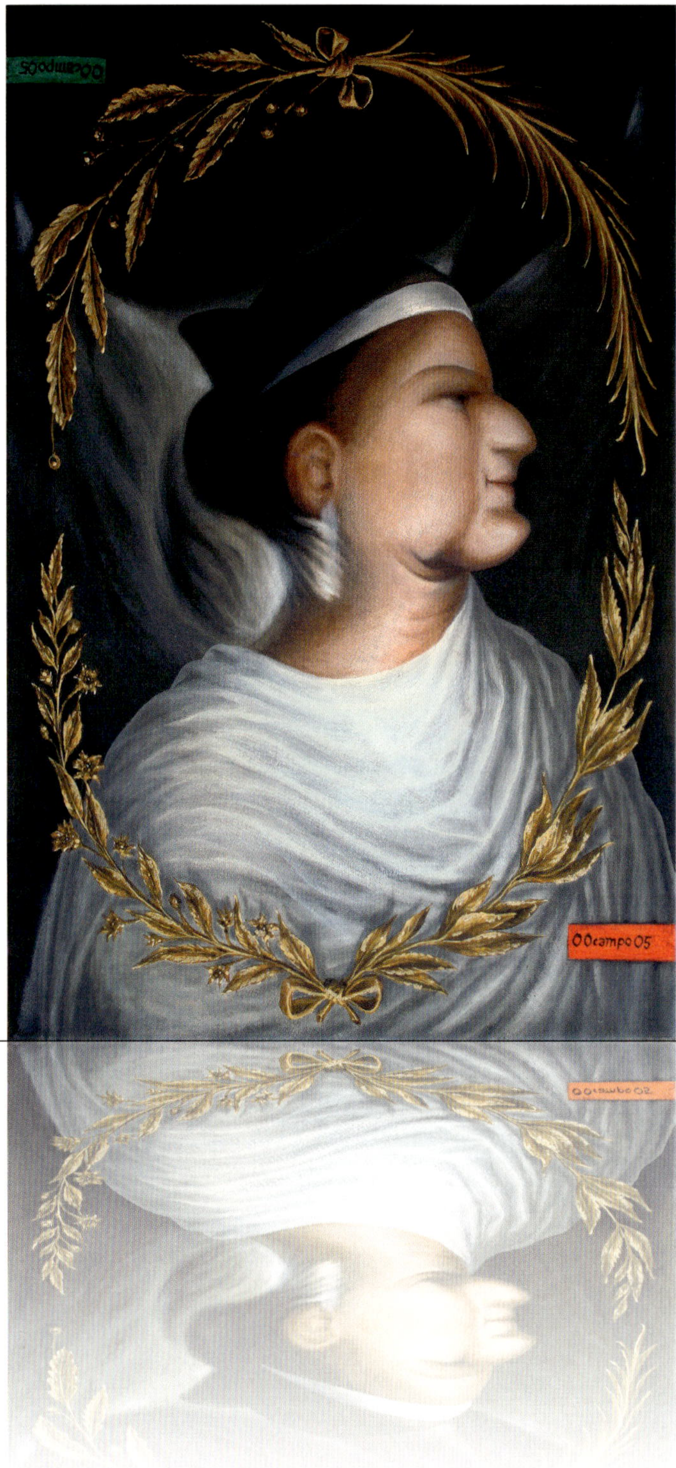

DOÑA JOSEFA Y DON MIGUEL 2005 (50 × 75)

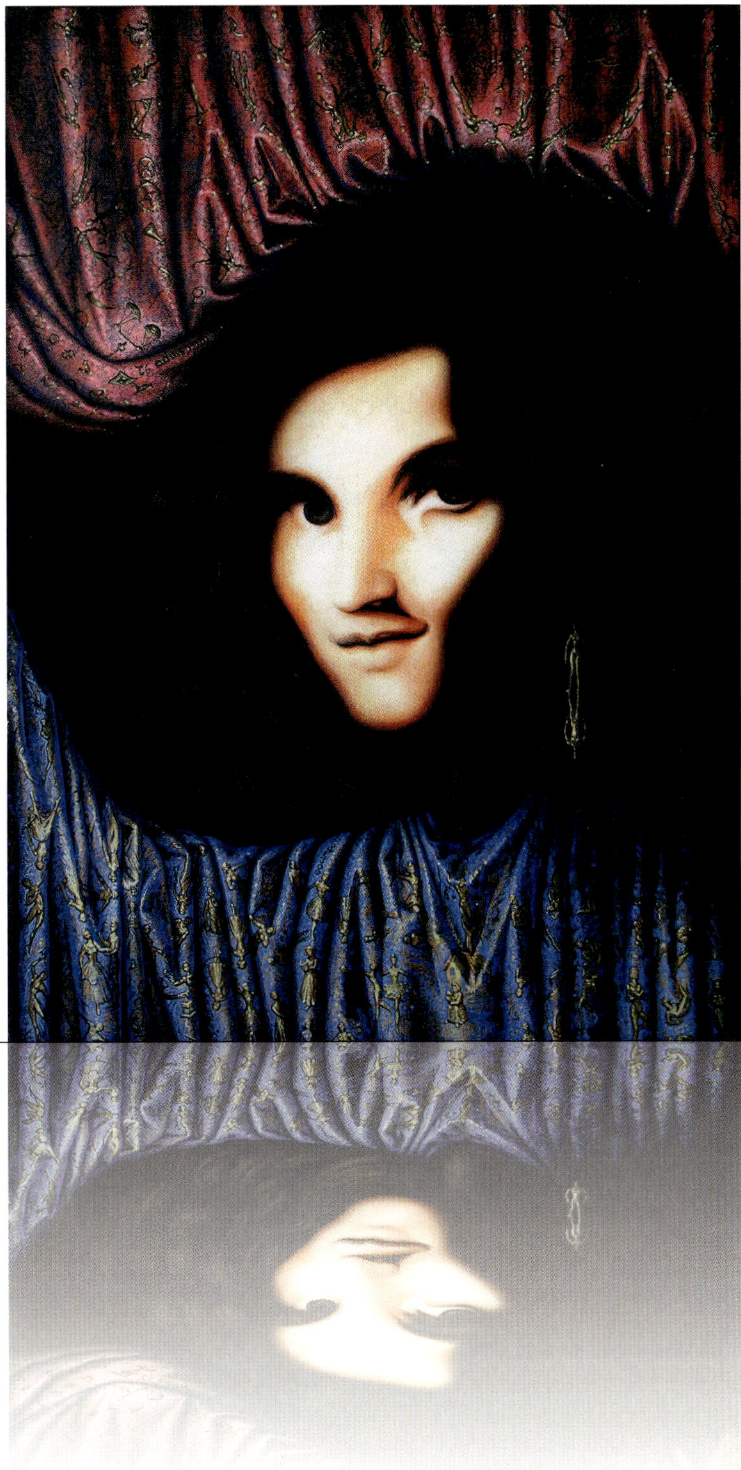

IGUALDAD 1992 (80 × 110) (TURNABLE)

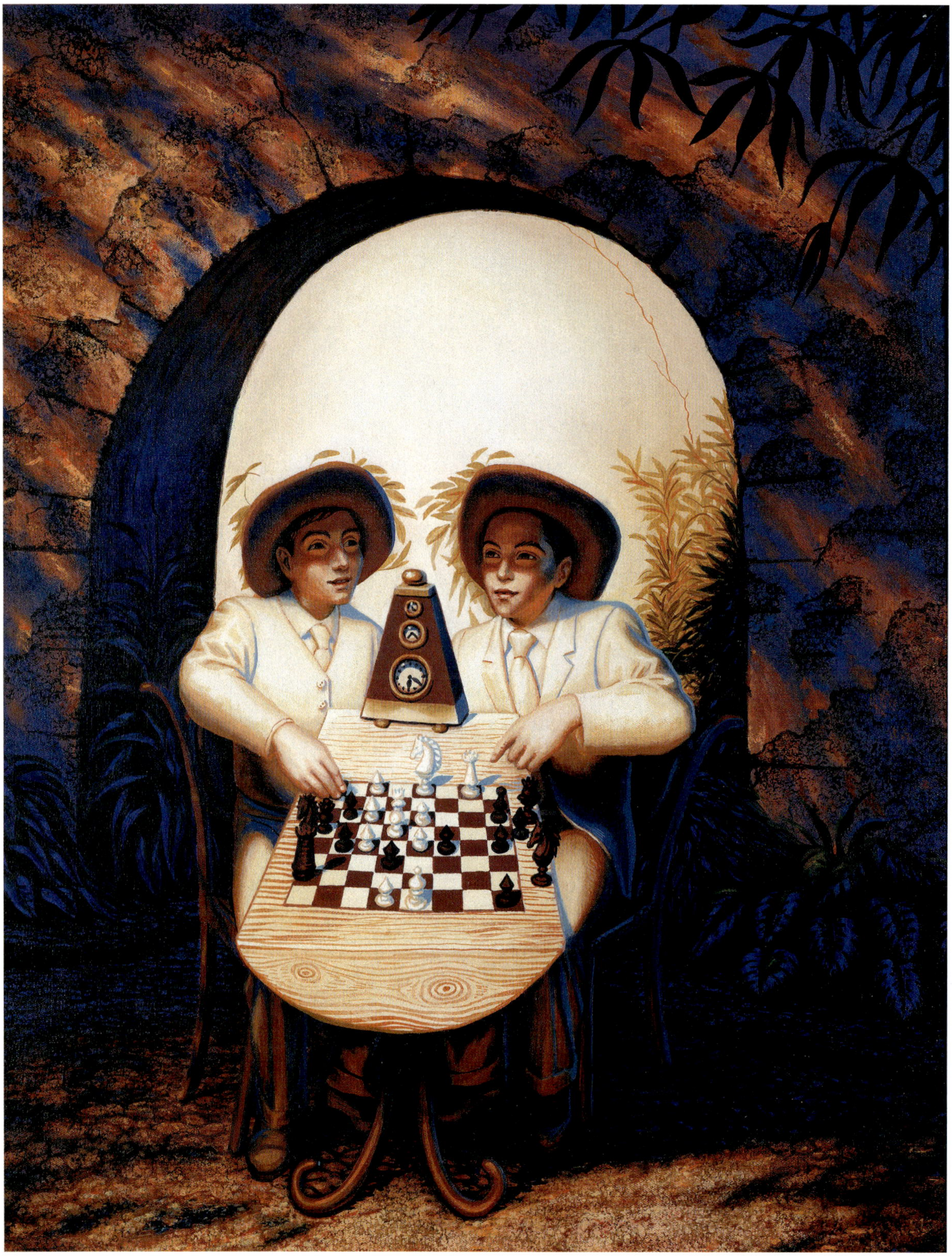

JAQUE MATE 1990 (80 × 100)

Oil on canvas – Óleo sobre tela – Öl auf Leinwand – Huile sur toile

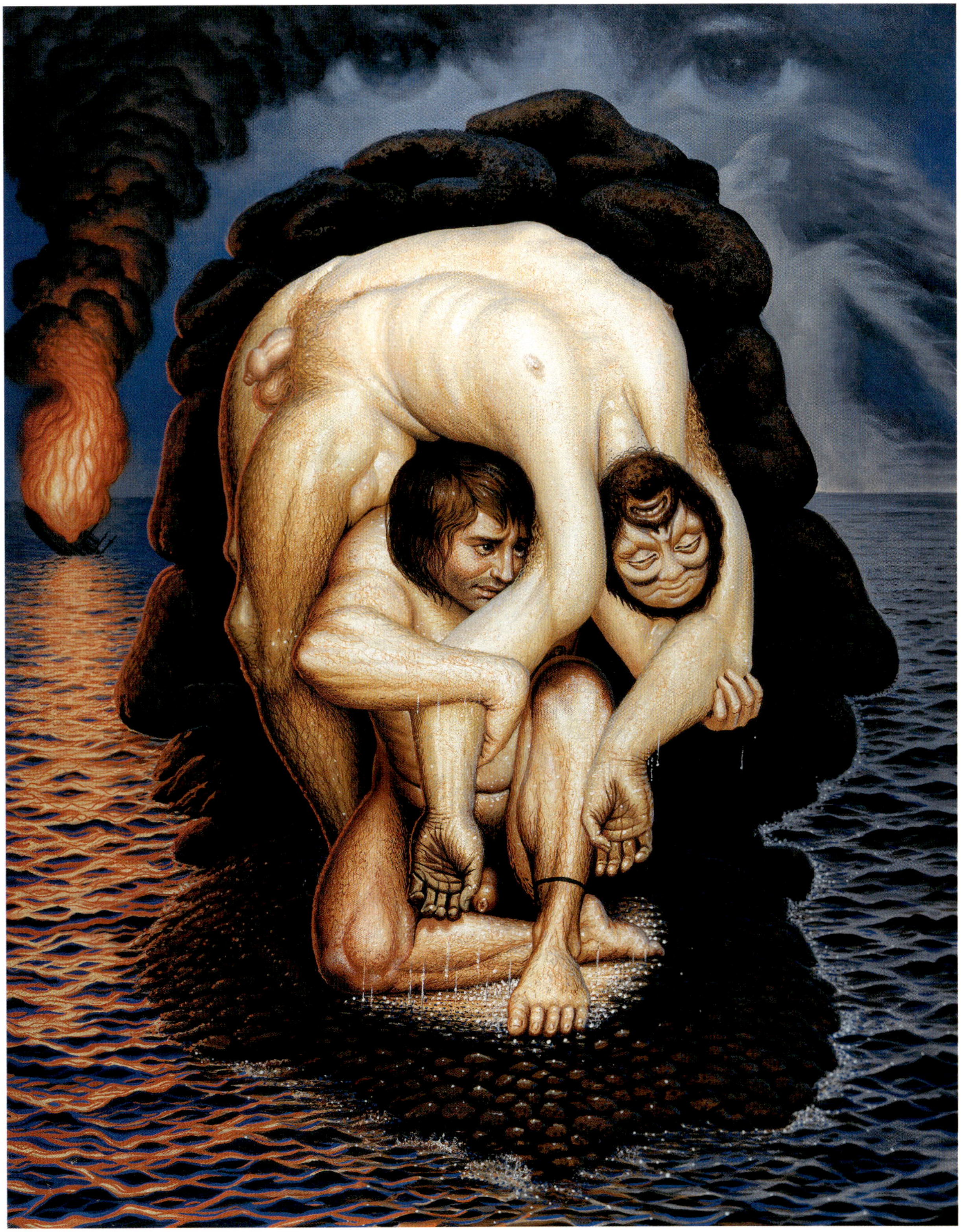

NAUFRAGIO 1990 (80 × 100)

Oil on canvas – Óleo sobre tela – Öl auf Leinwand – Huile sur toile

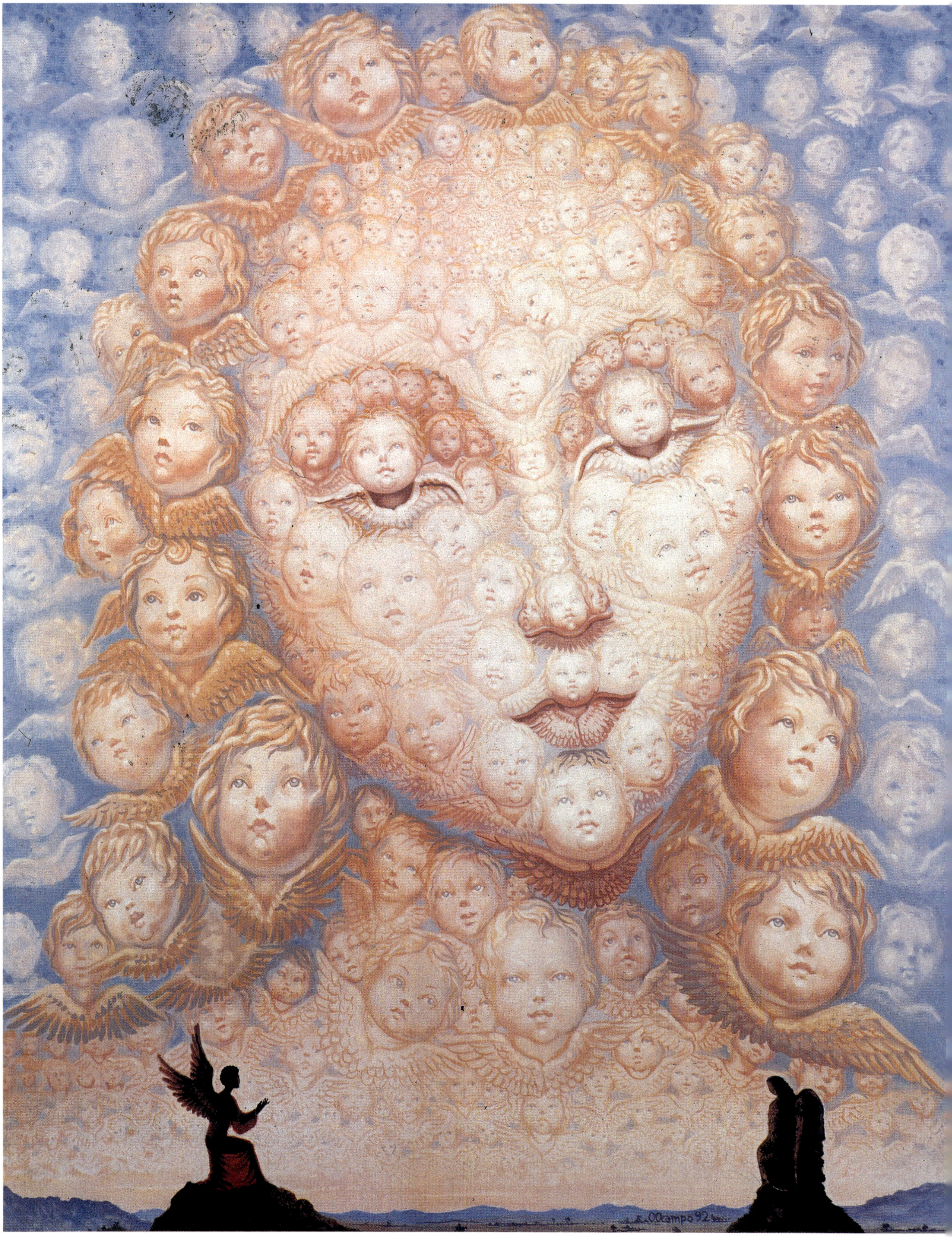
O.Ocampo 92

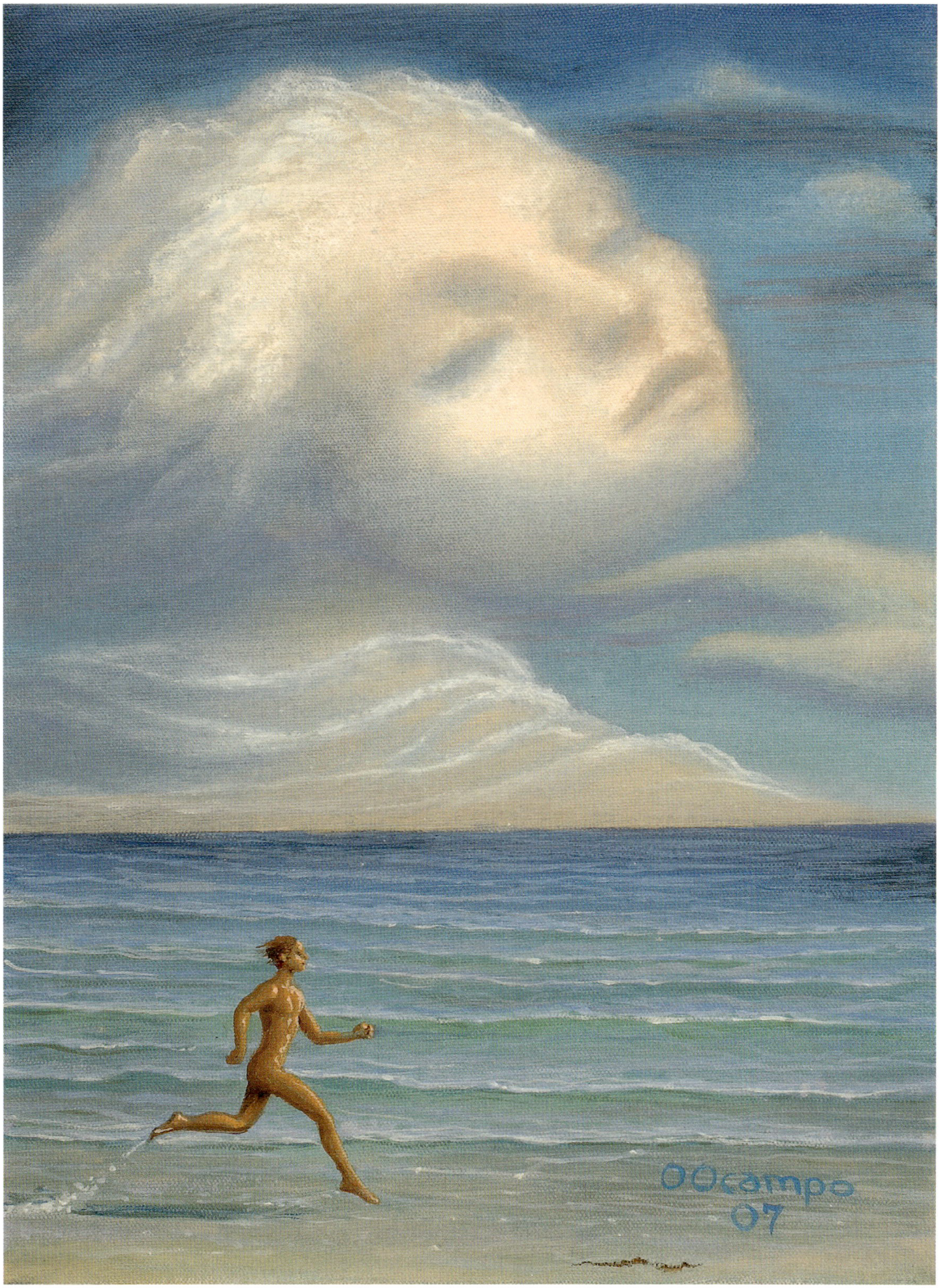

CORRIENDO CON EL AIRE 2007 (40 × 60)

Oil on canvas – Óleo sobre tela – Öl auf Leinwand – Huile sur toile

SUEÑO DEL ÁNGEL NEGRO 1992 (80 × 100)

Oil on canvas – Óleo sobre tela – Öl auf Leinwand – Huile sur toile

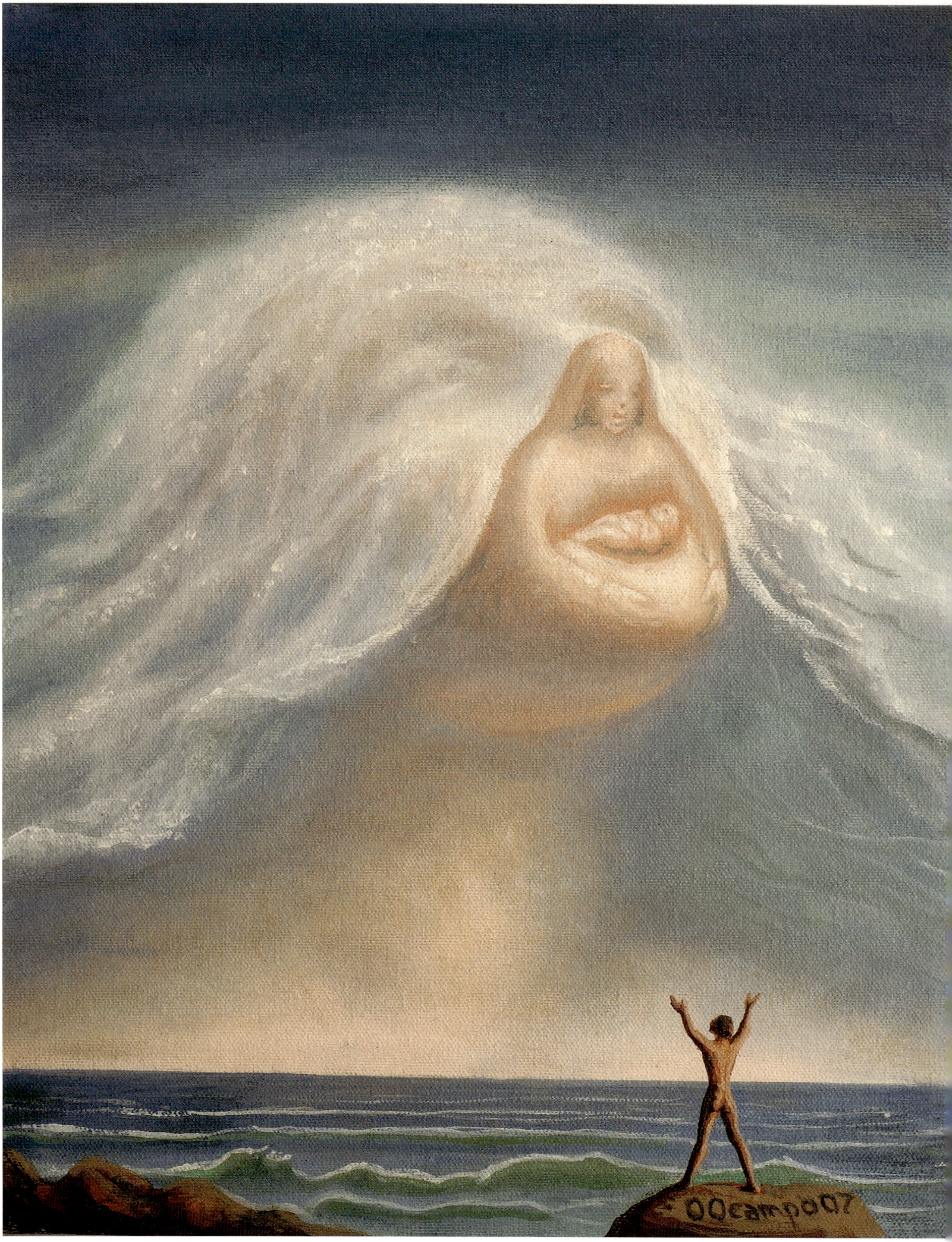
OOcampo07

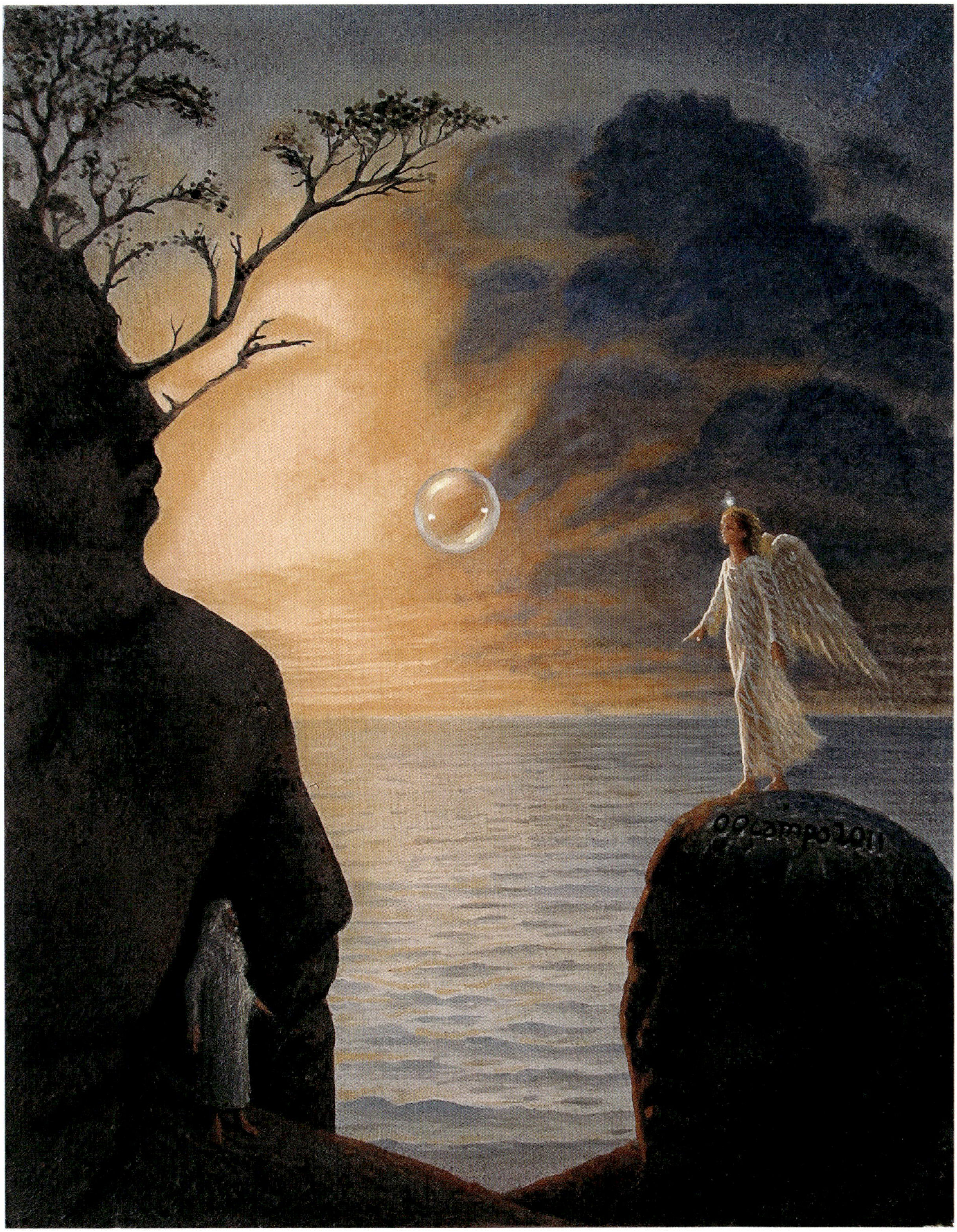

VISITA DEL ÁNGEL 2011 (71 × 92)

Oil on canvas – Óleo sobre tela – Öl auf Leinwand – Huile sur toile

REGALO DEL CIELO 2007 (35 × 28)

Oil on canvas – Óleo sobre tela – Öl auf Leinwand – Huile sur toile

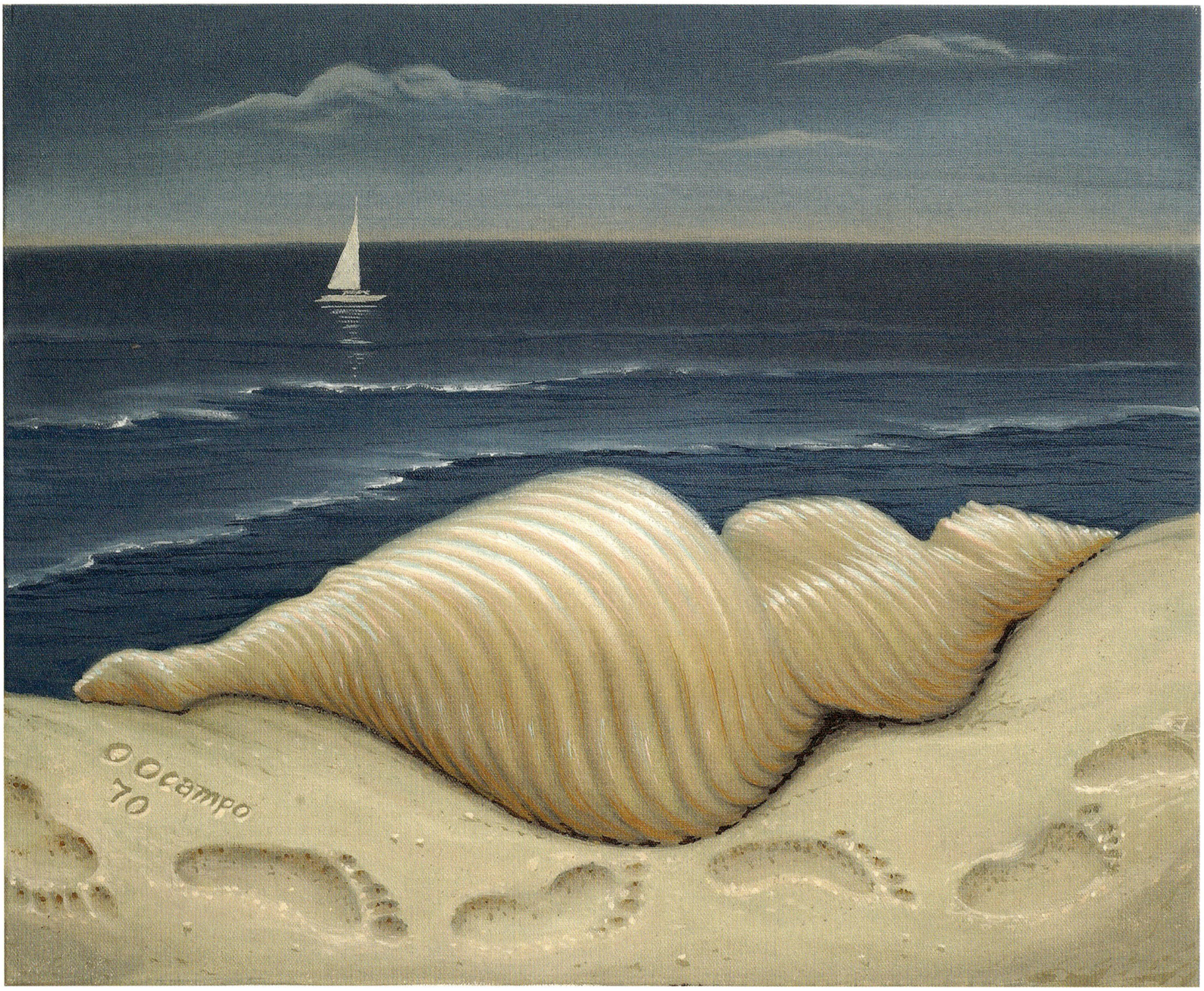

LA ESPERA DEL C ARACOL 2007 (50 × 40)

Oil on canvas – Óleo sobre tela – Öl auf Leinwand – Huile sur toile

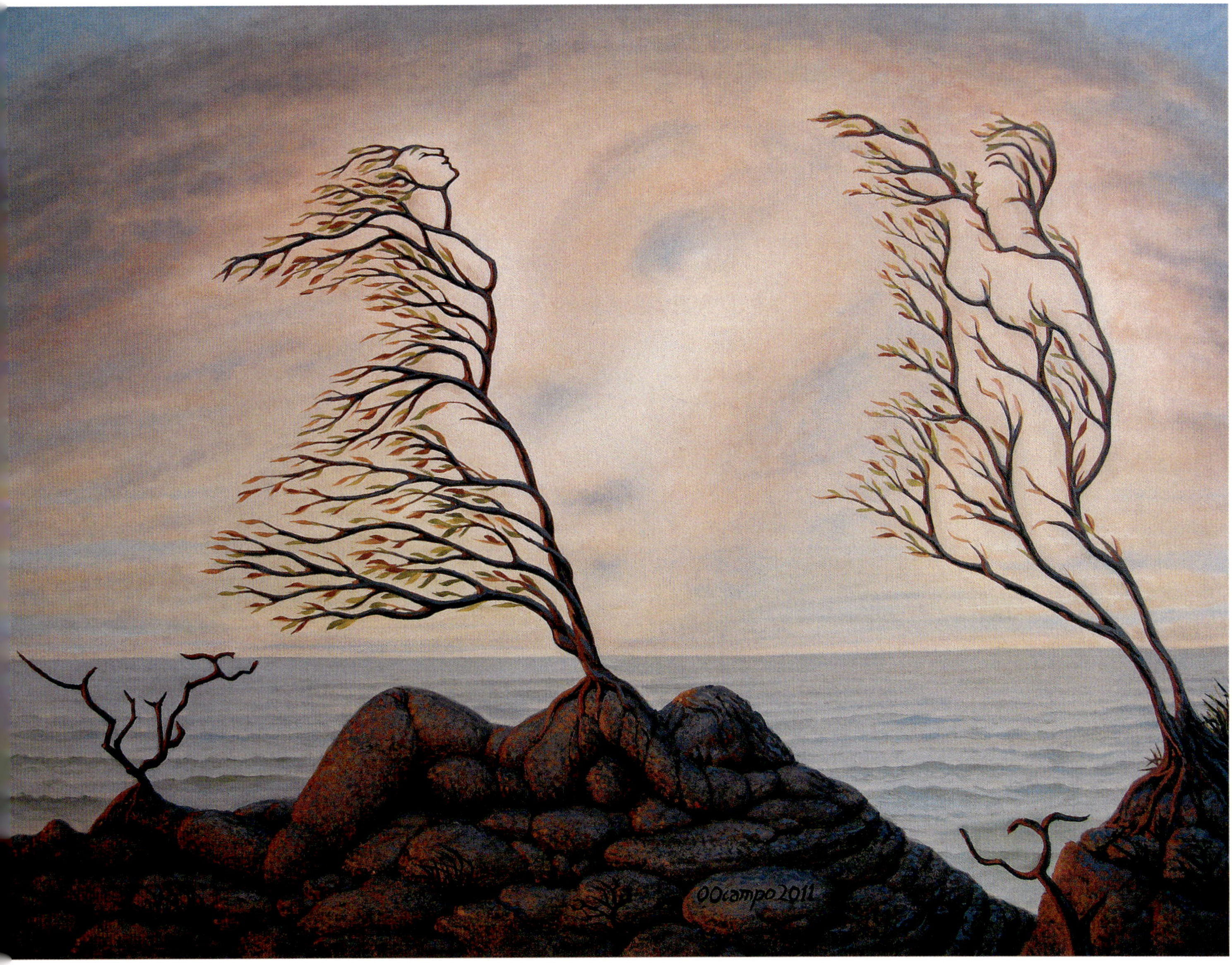

SOPLO 2009 (45 × 35)

Acrylic on canvas – Acrílico sobre tela – Acryl auf Leinwand – Acrylique sur toile

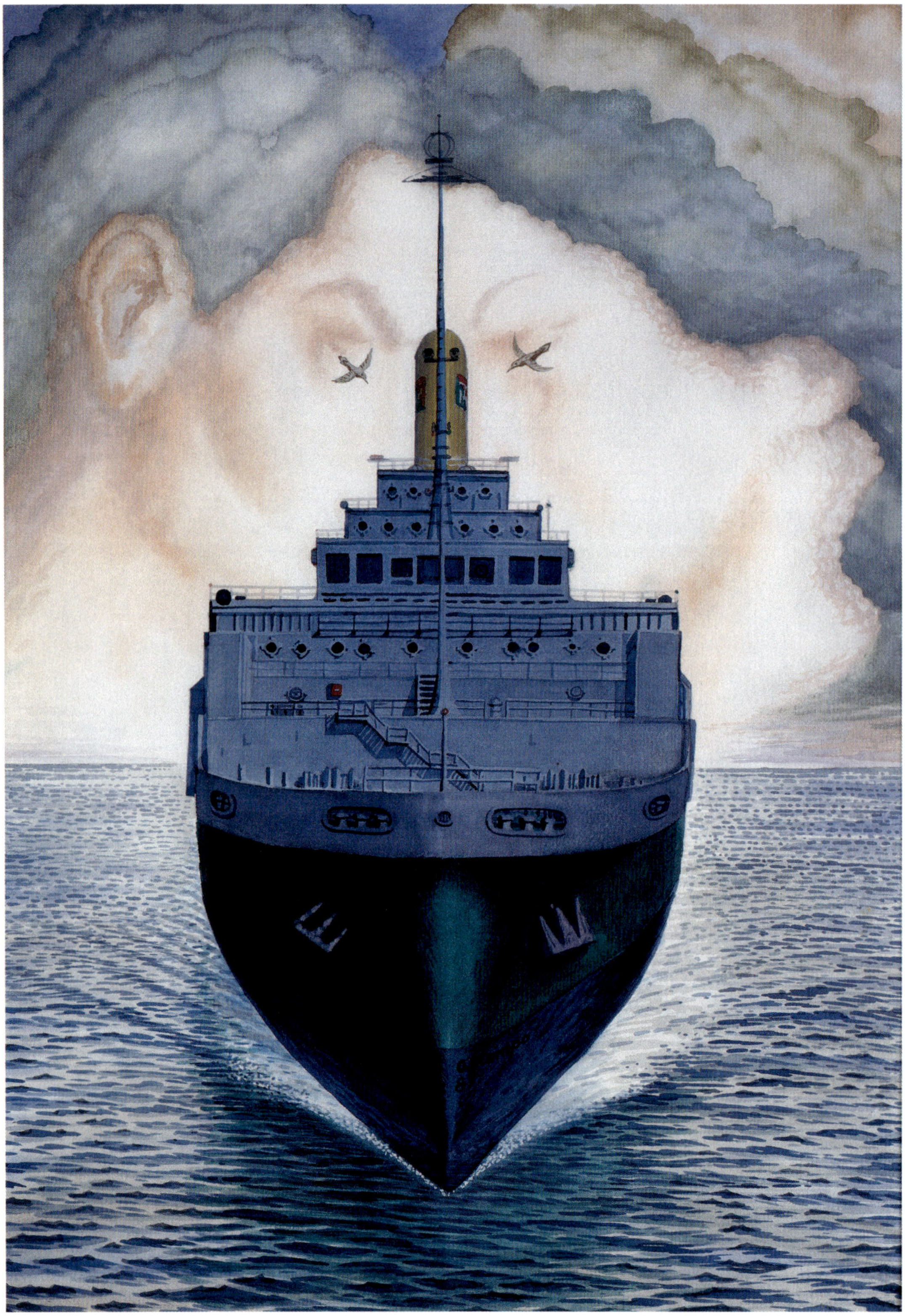

EL BUQUE 1987 (52 × 67)

Watercolor on paper – Acuarela sobre papel – Aquarell auf Papier – Aquarelle sur papier

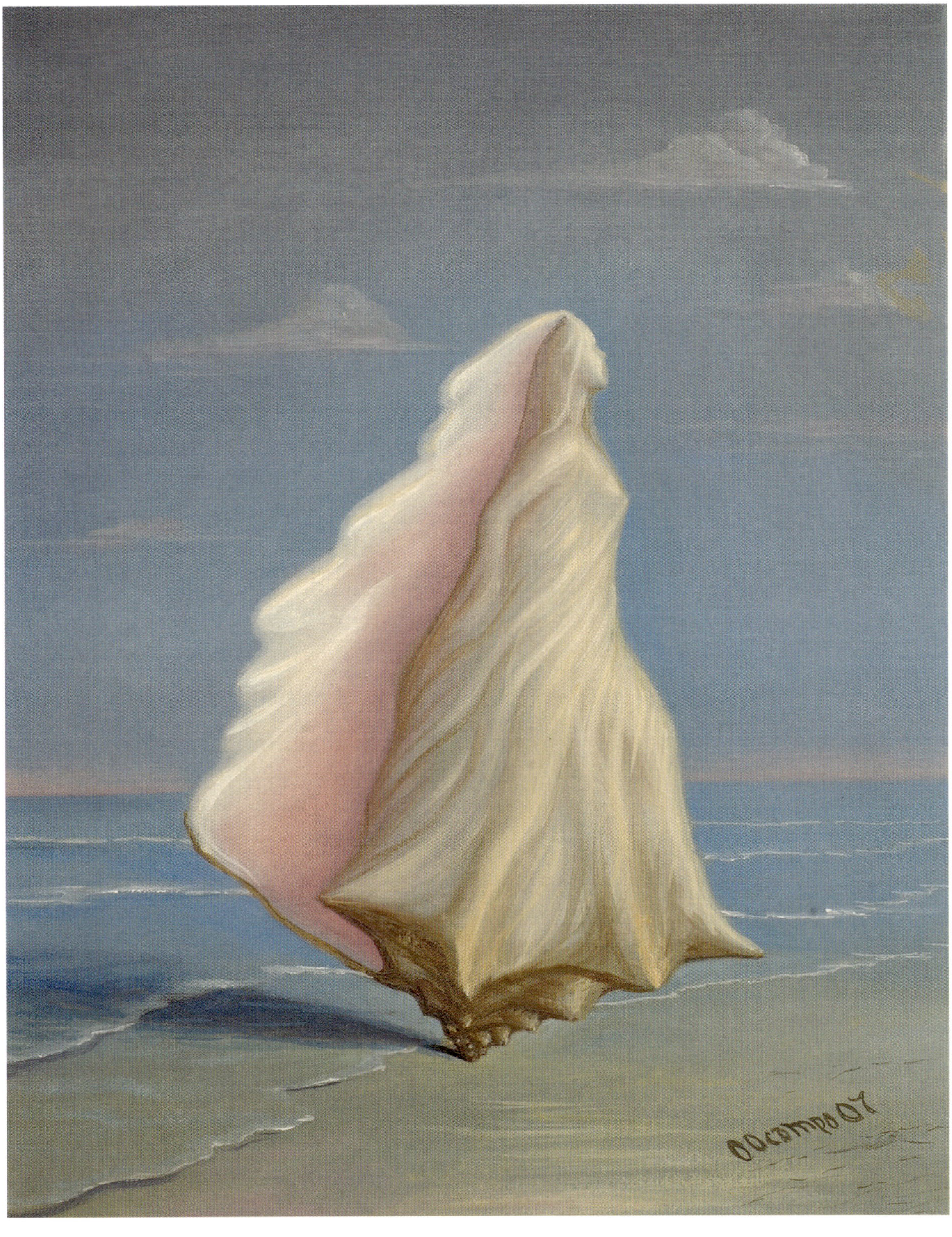

CARRERA DEL CARACOL 2007 (40 × 60)

Oil on canvas – Óleo sobre tela – Öl auf Leinwand – Huile sur toile

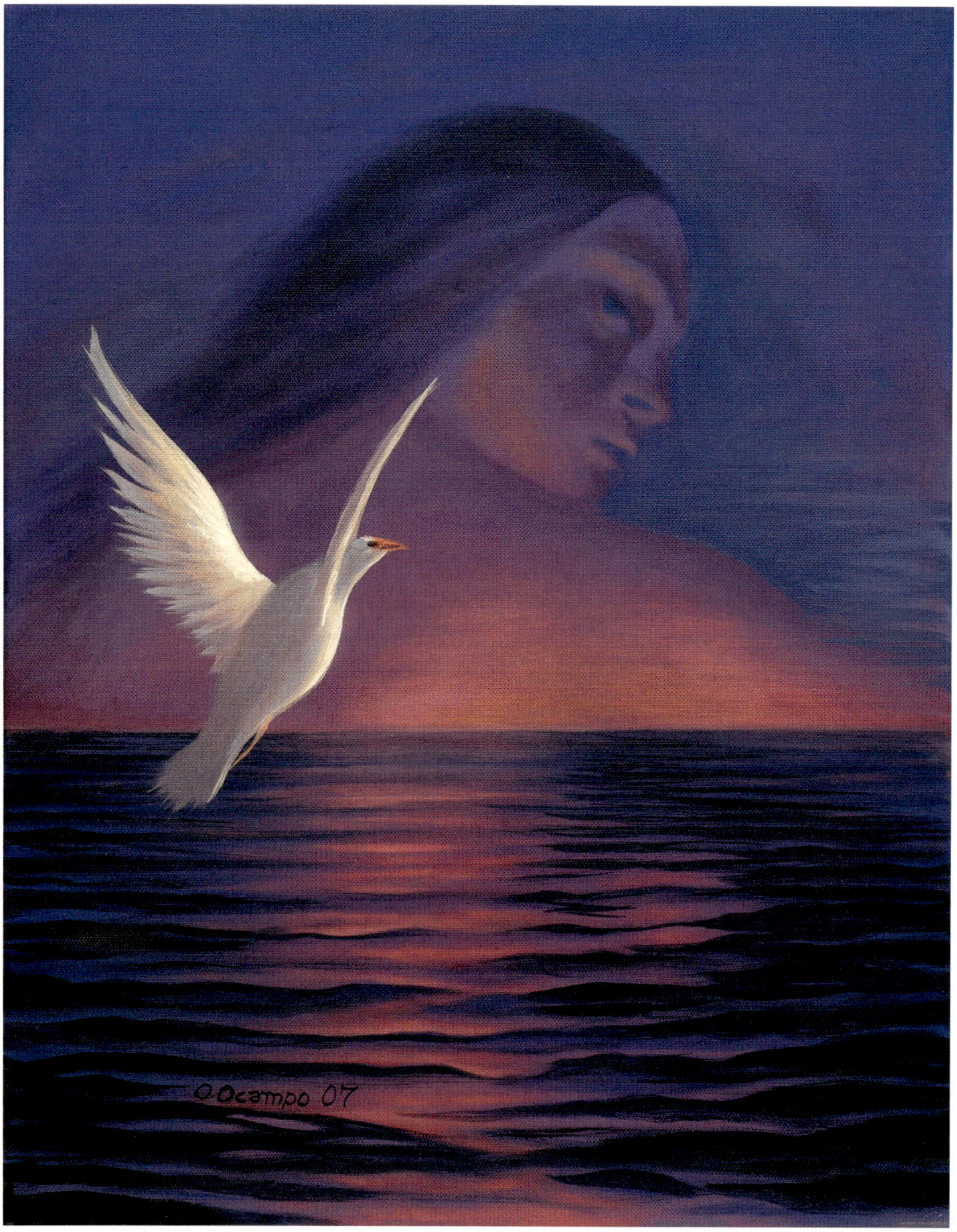

ÁNGEL DE LA TARDE 2007 (43 × 53)

Oil on canvas – Óleo sobre tela – Öl auf Leinwand – Huile sur toile

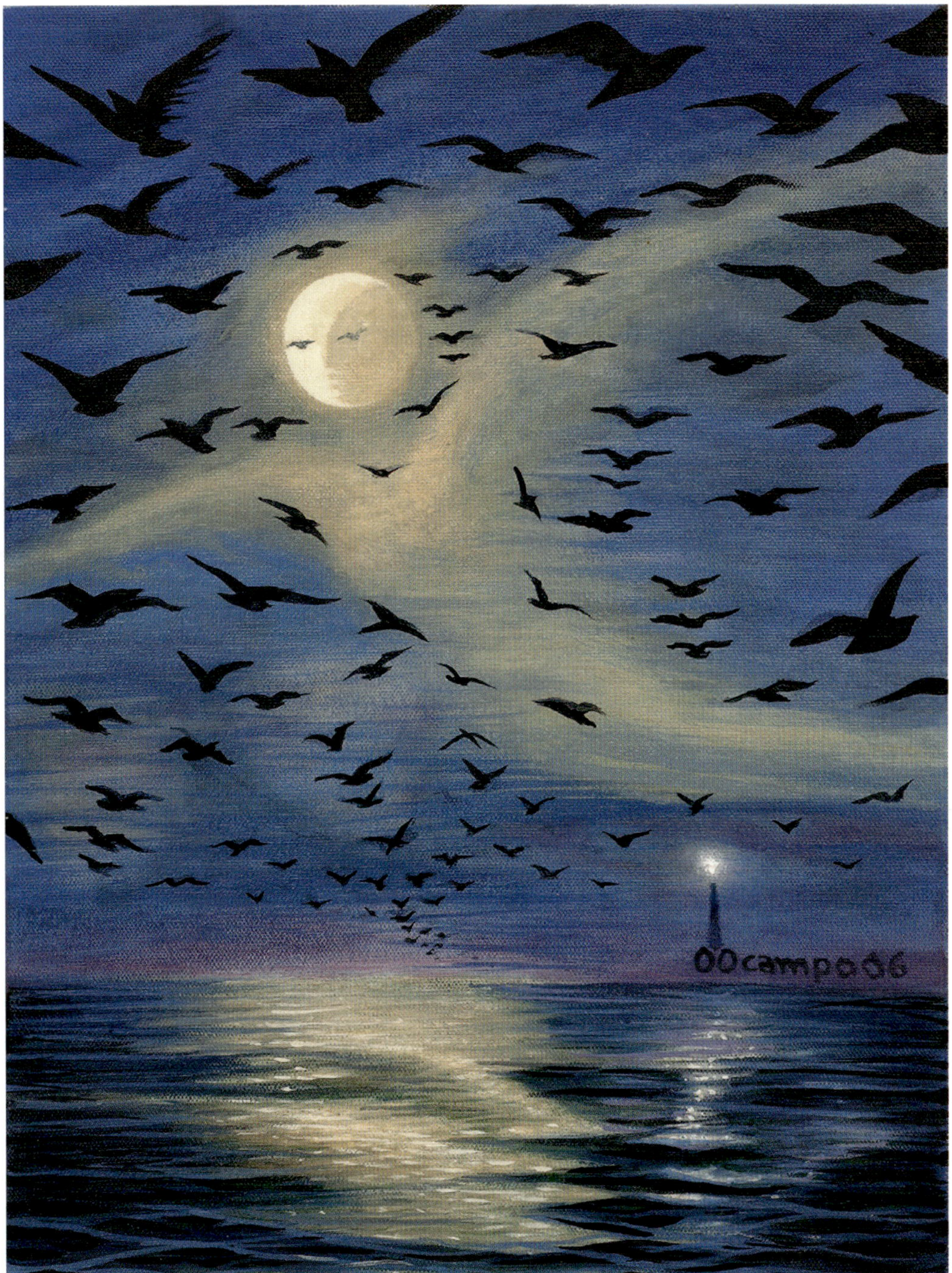

ÁNGEL DEL FARO 2006 (33 × 43)

Oil on canvas – Óleo sobre tela – Öl auf Leinwand – Huile sur toile

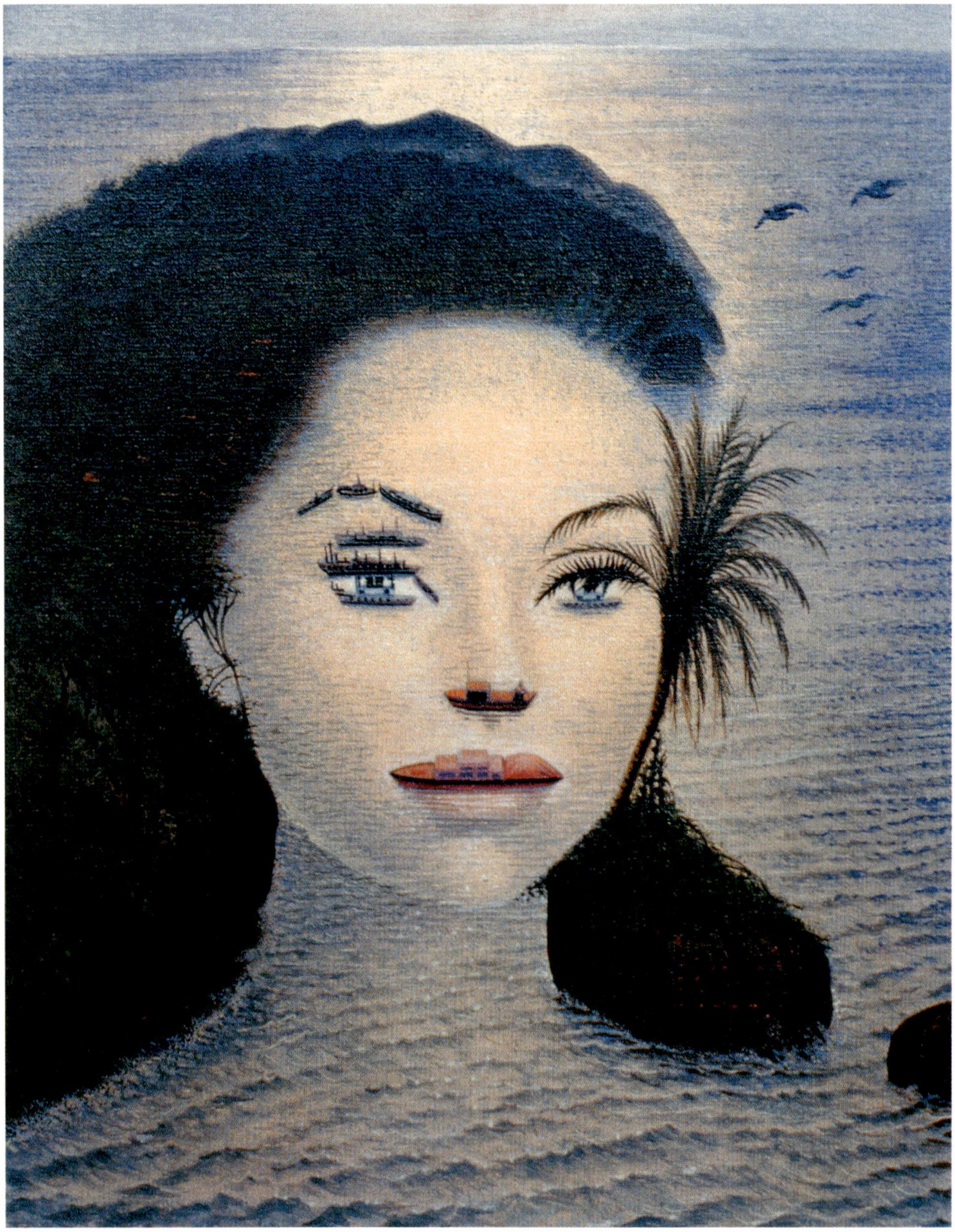

COSTEÑA 1987 (30 × 50)

Oil on canvas – Óleo sobre tela – Öl auf Leinwand – Huile sur toile

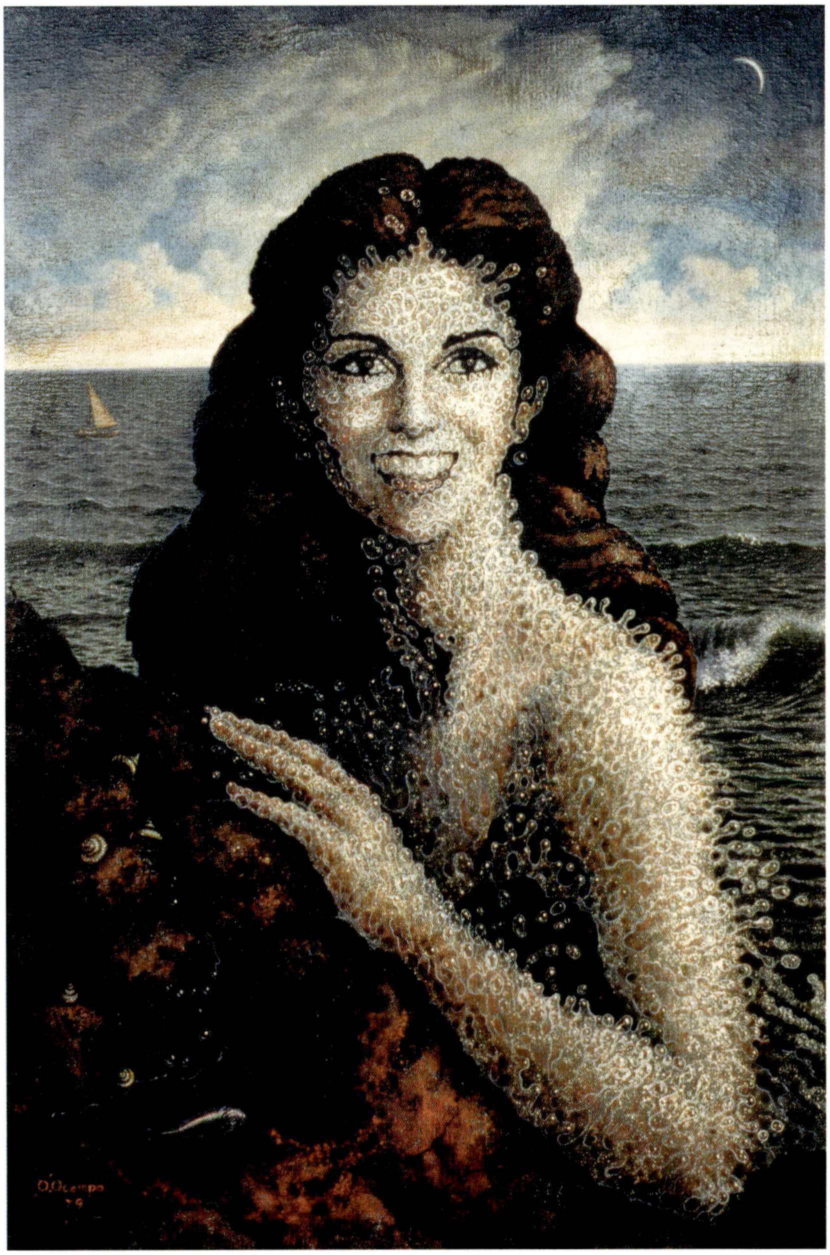

REGINA BURILLO 1978 (90 × 120)

Oil on canvas – Óleo sobre tela – Öl auf Leinwand – Huile sur toile

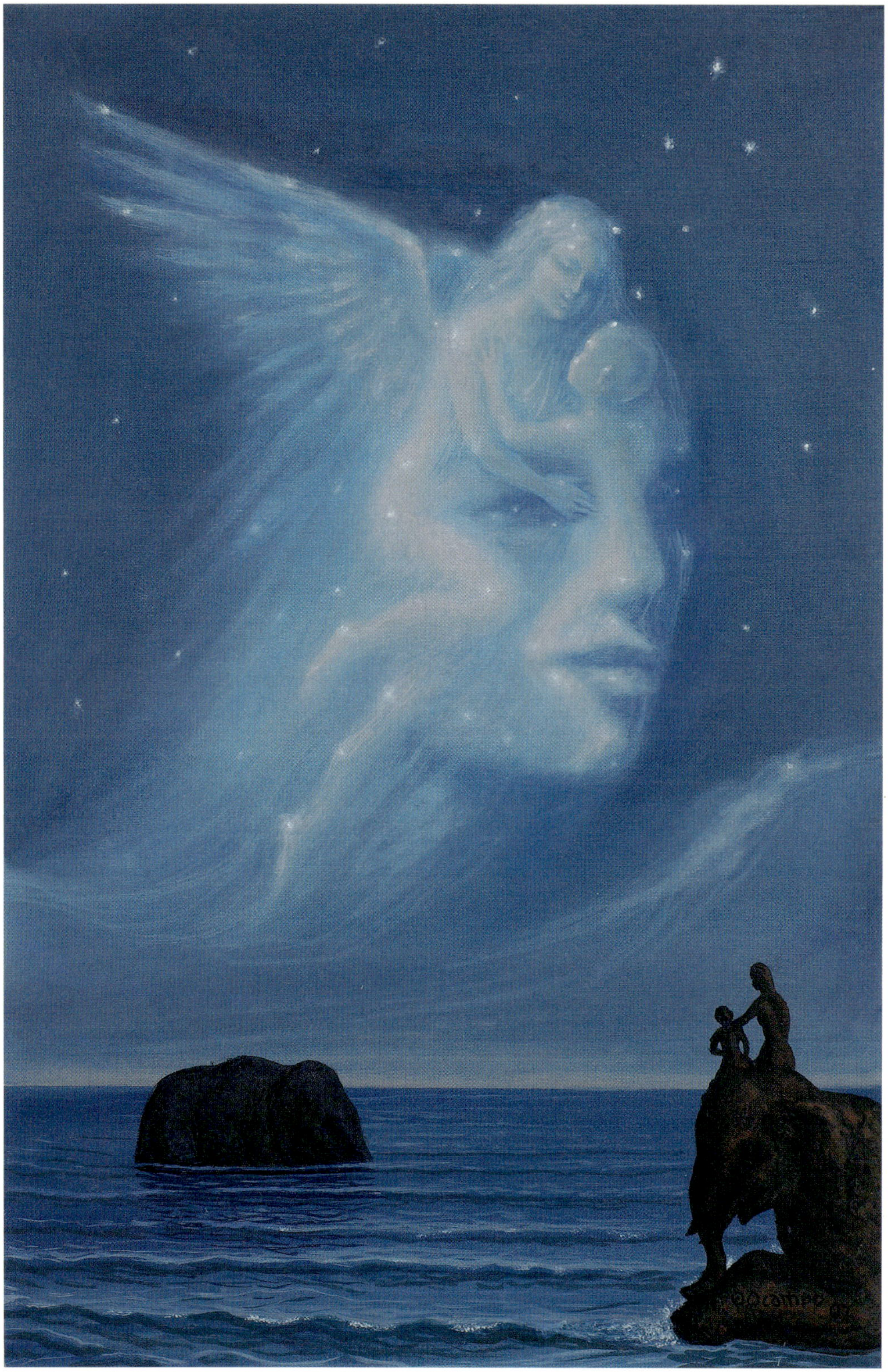

LA MATRIARCA 2007 (40 × 60)

Oil on canvas – Óleo sobre tela – Öl auf Leinwand – Huile sur toile

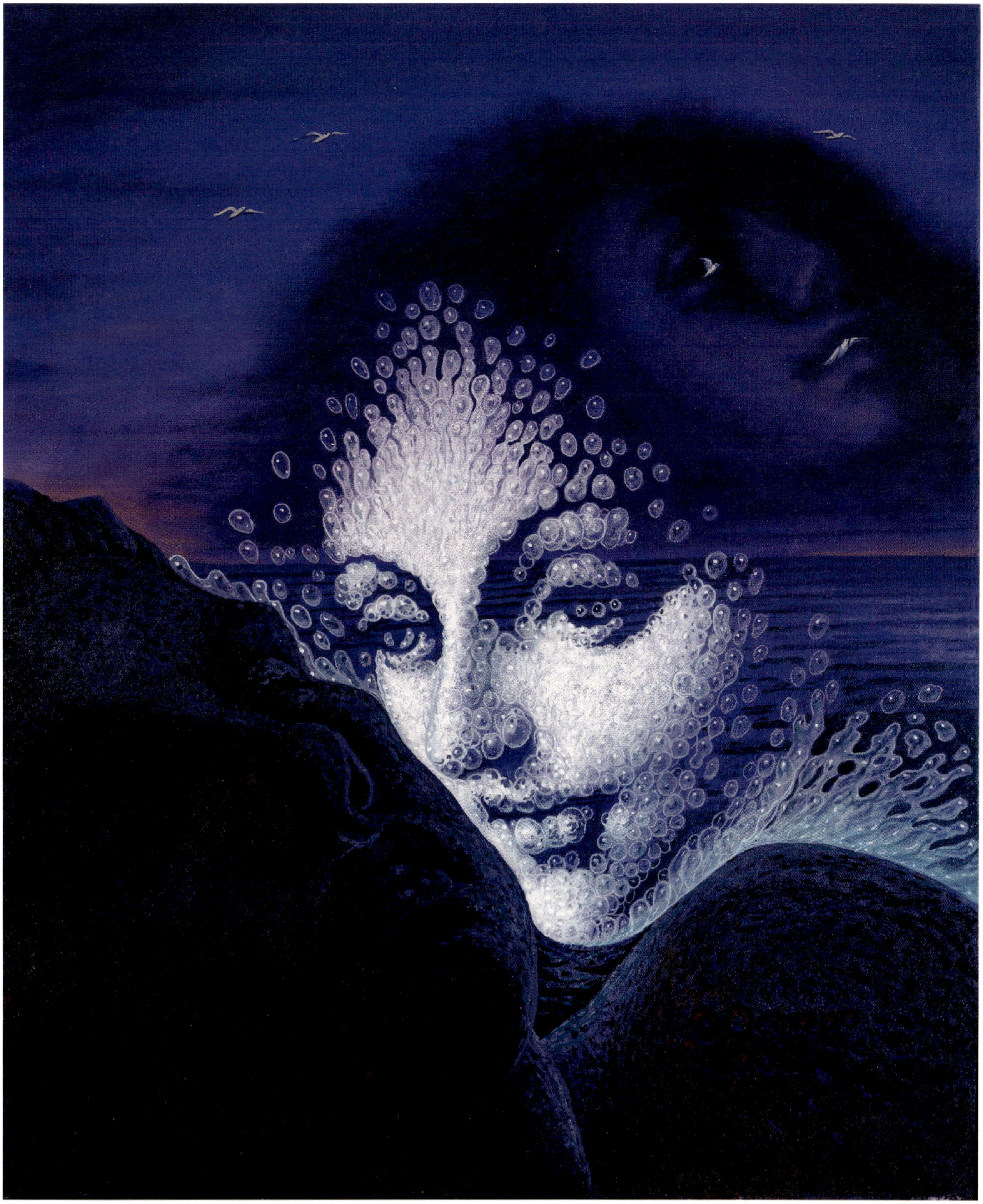

EL BESO DE LA OLA 2002 (50 × 60)

Oil on canvas – Óleo sobre tela – Öl auf Leinwand – Huile sur toile

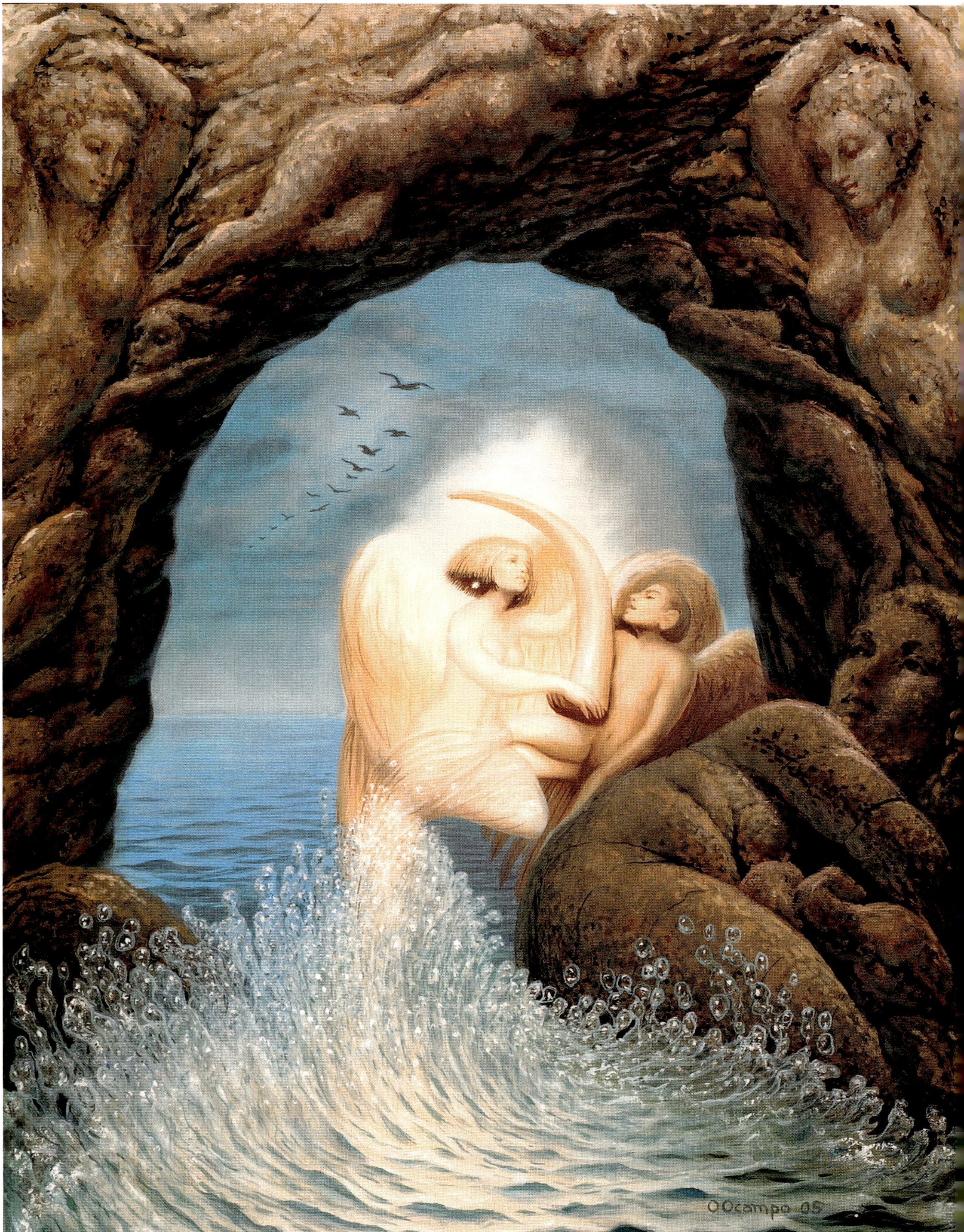
O.Ocampo 05

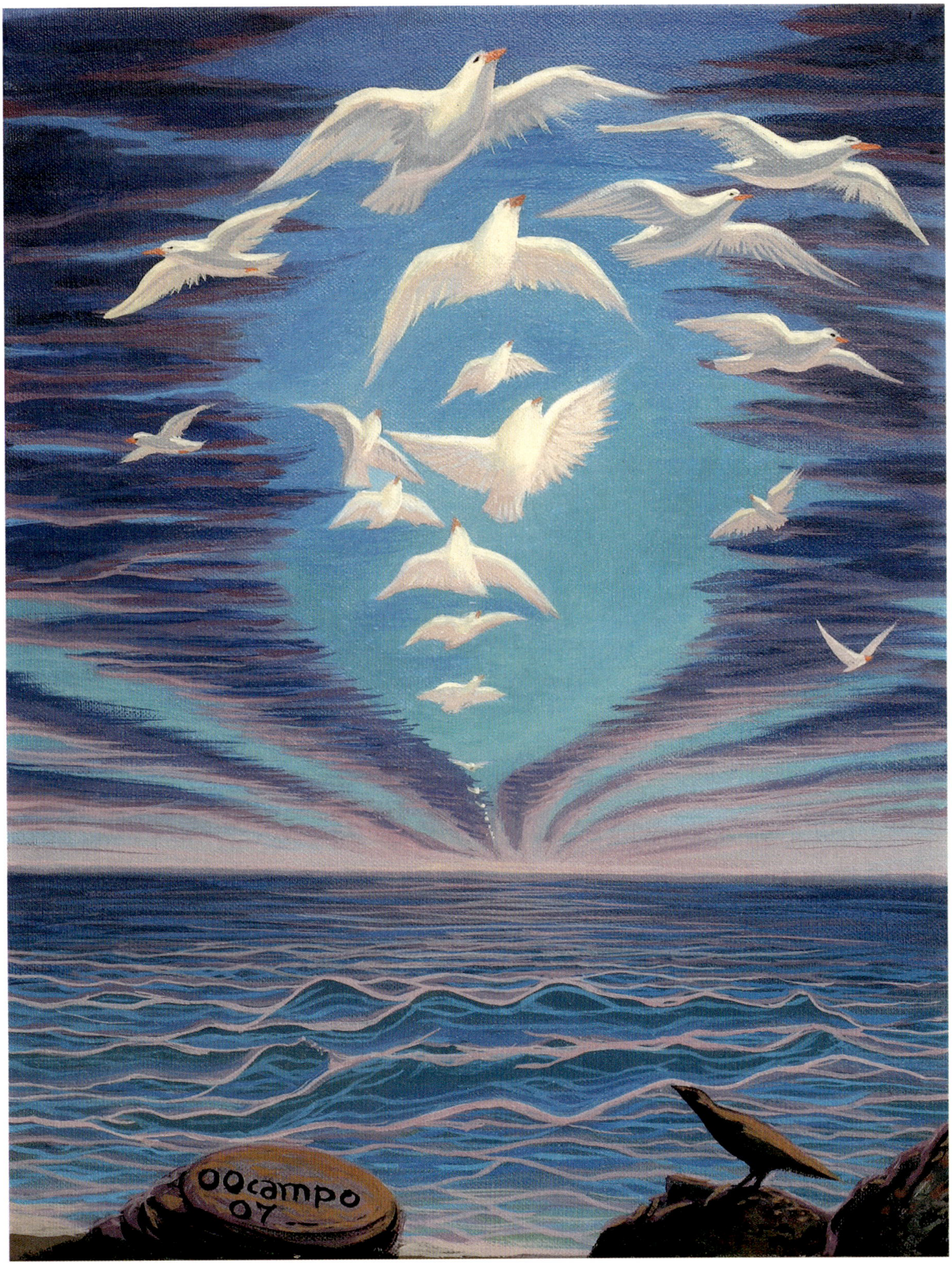

AVES DEL AMOR 2007 (36 × 46)

Oil on canvas – Óleo sobre tela – Öl auf Leinwand – Huile sur toile

MADONA DEL MAR 2005 (90 × 100)

Vinyl on canvas – Vinil sobre tela – Vinyl auf Leinwand – Vinyle sur toile

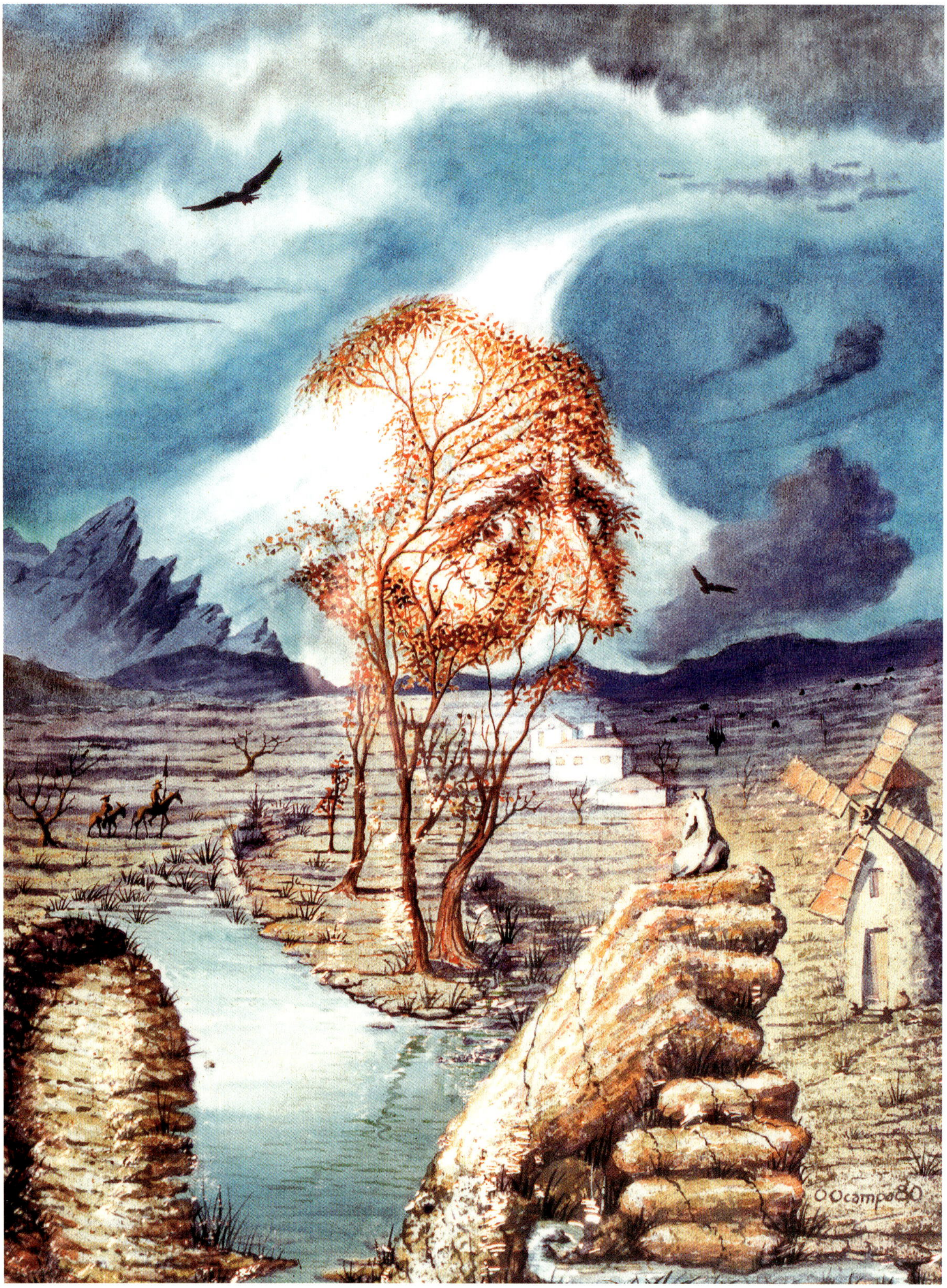

QUIJOTE 1980 (33,5 × 48)

Watercolor on paper – Acuarela sobre papel – Aquarell auf Papier – Aquarelle sur papier

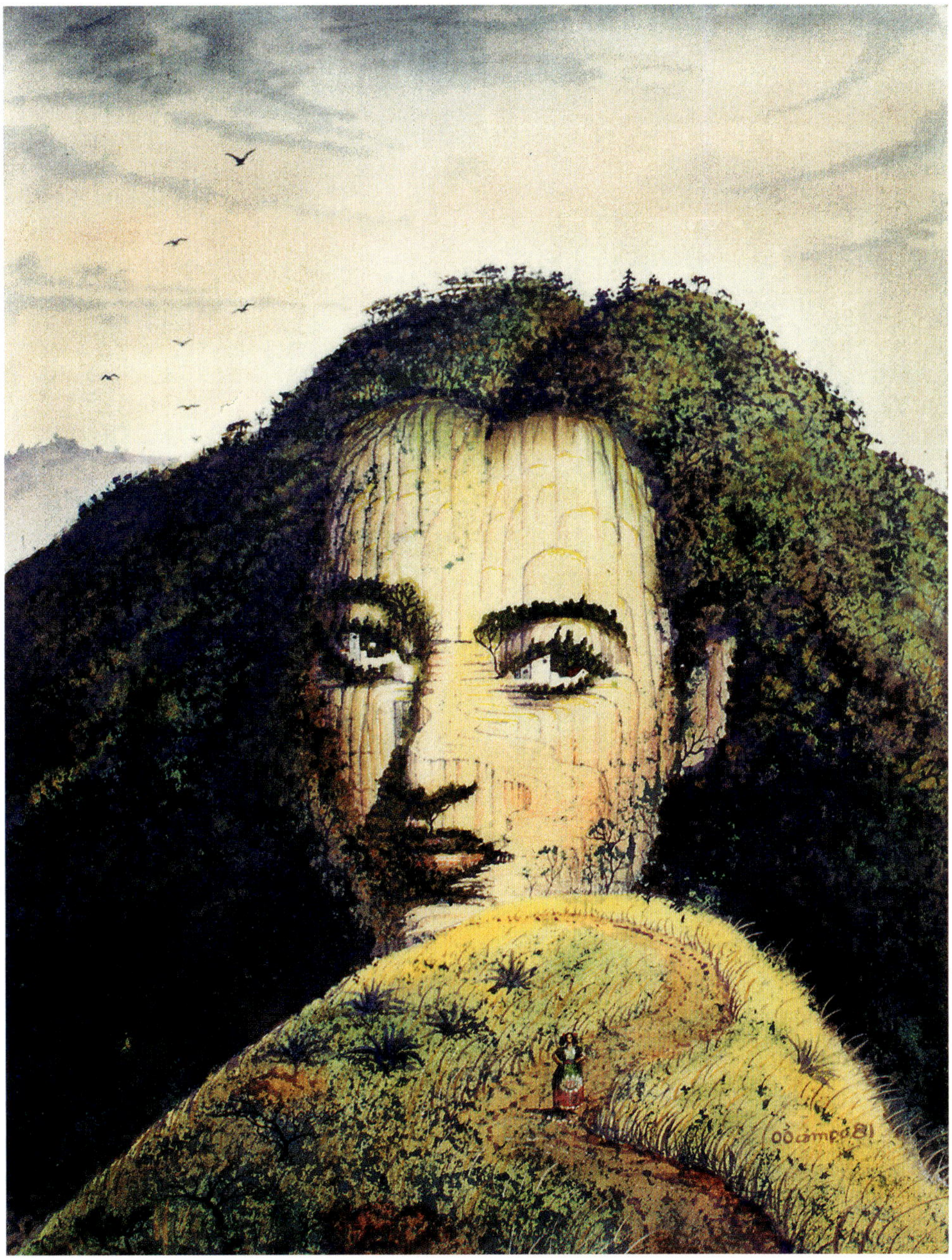

LUCHA REYES 1981 (38 × 51)

Watercolor on paper – Acuarela sobre papel – Aquarell auf Papier – Aquarelle sur papier

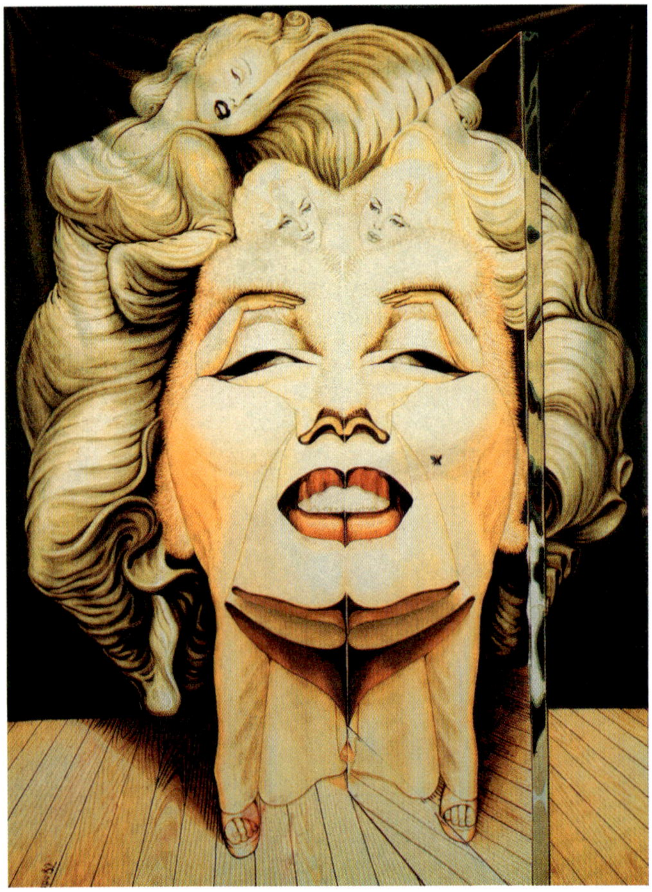

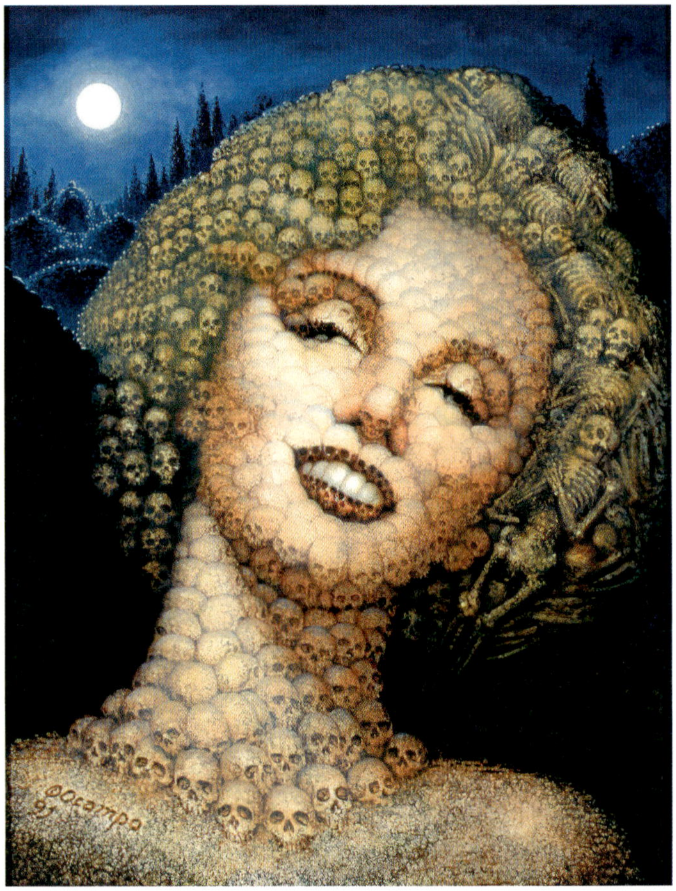

EL ESPEJO DE MARILYN 1982 (90 × 120)

Watercolor on cardboard – Acuarela sobre cartón – Aquarell auf Karton – Aquarelle sur carton

MATERIA Y ESPIRITU 1991 (50 × 65)

Oil on canvas – Óleo sobre tela – Öl auf Leinwand – Huile sur toile

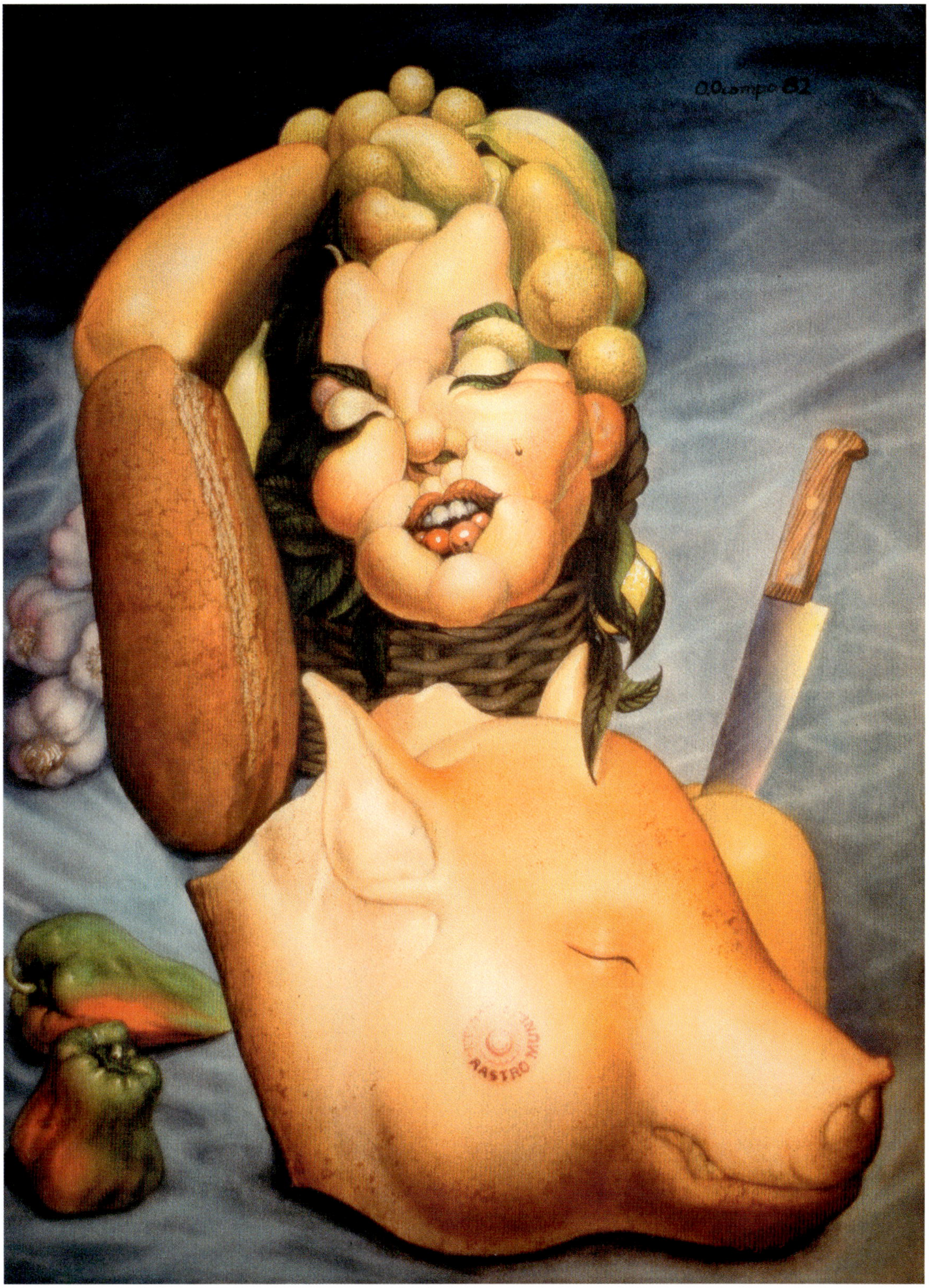

MARILYN FOOD 1982 (37 × 46)

Watercolor on paper – Acuarela sobre papel – Aquarell auf Papier – Aquarelle sur papier

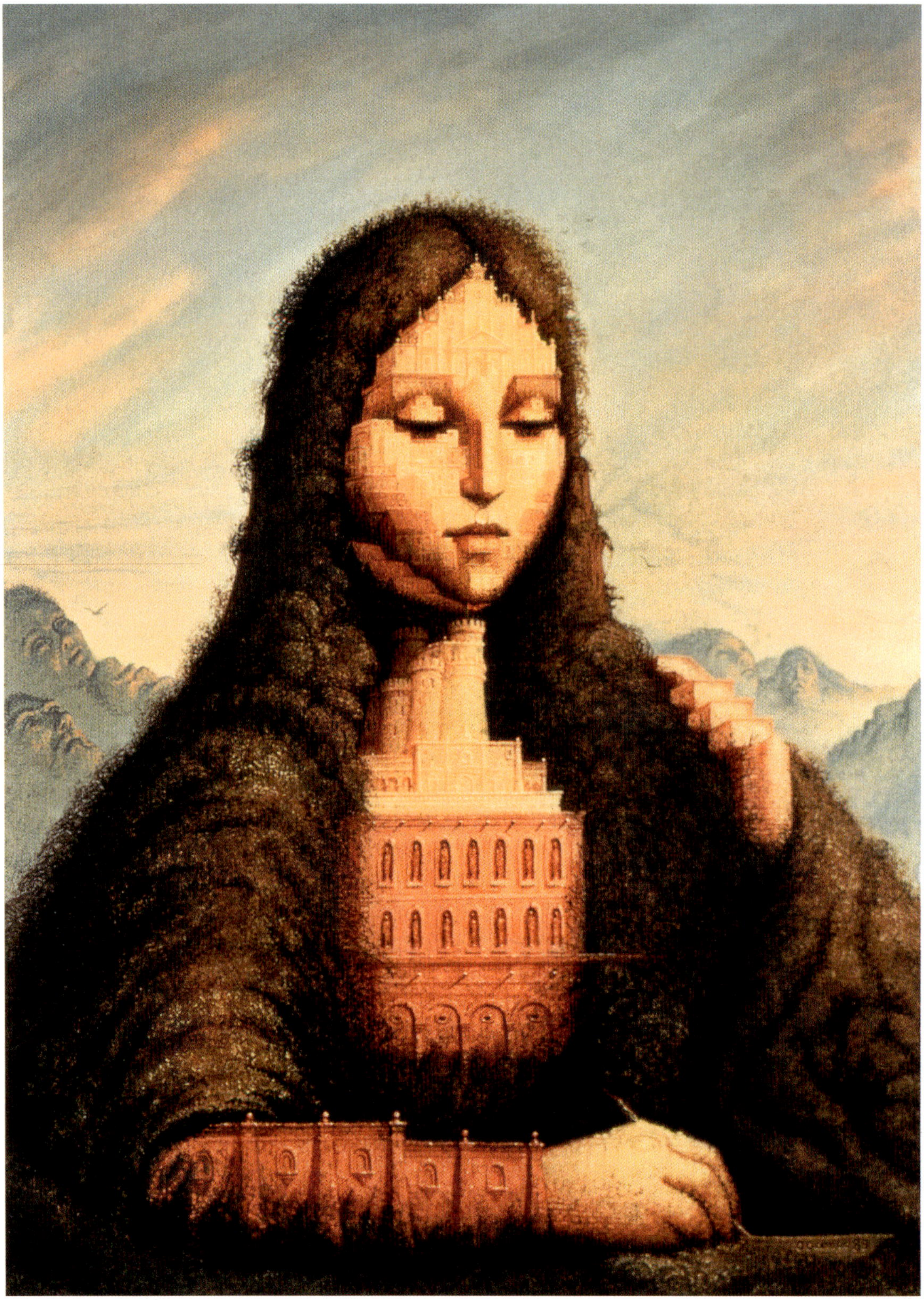

EL MENSAJE DE DULCINEA 1989 (23 × 30,5)

Oil on canvas – Óleo sobre tela – Öl auf Leinwand – Huile sur toile

LA SILLA DE LA GIOCONDA 1988 (80 × 100

Oil on canvas – Óleo sobre tela – Öl auf Leinwand – Huile sur toi

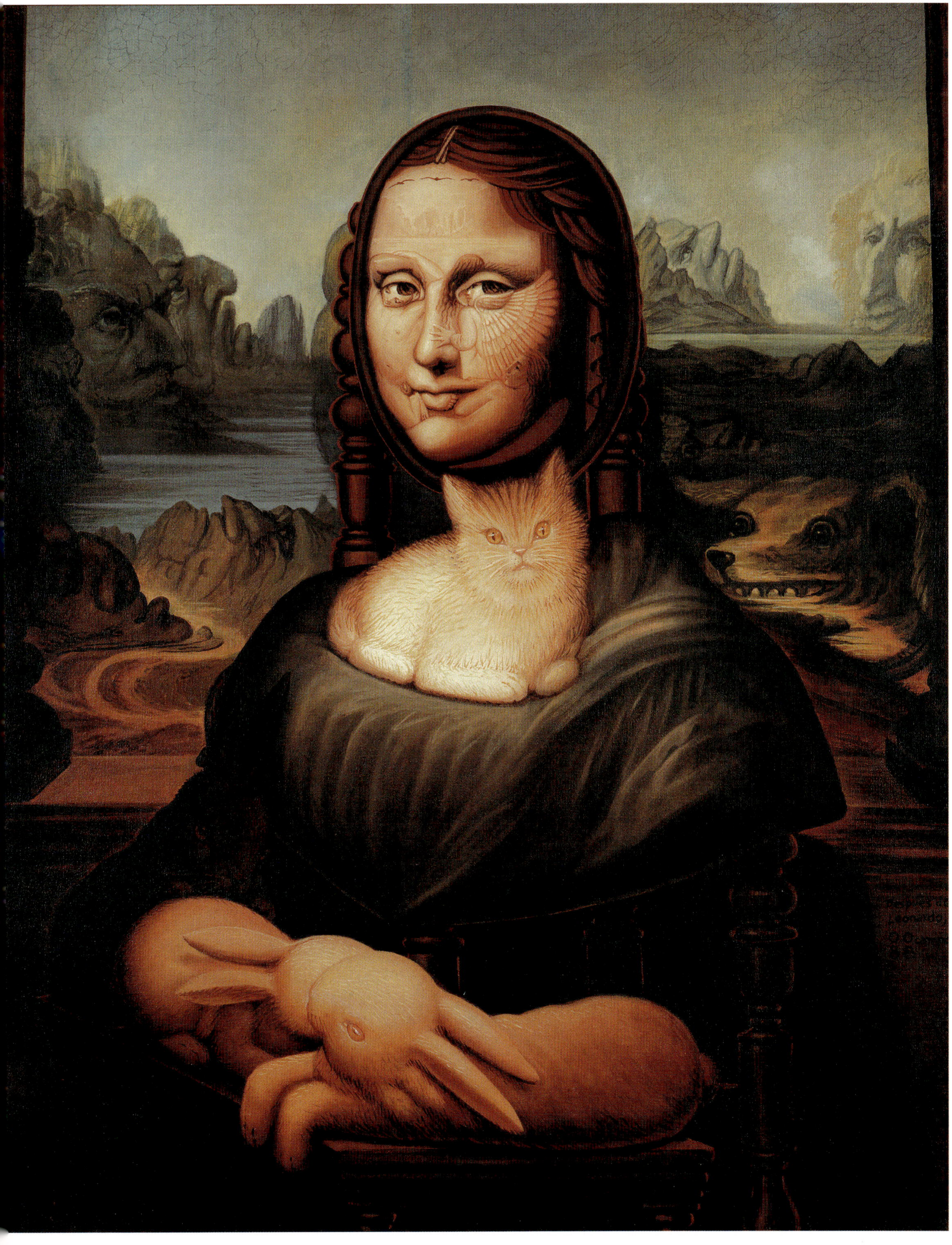

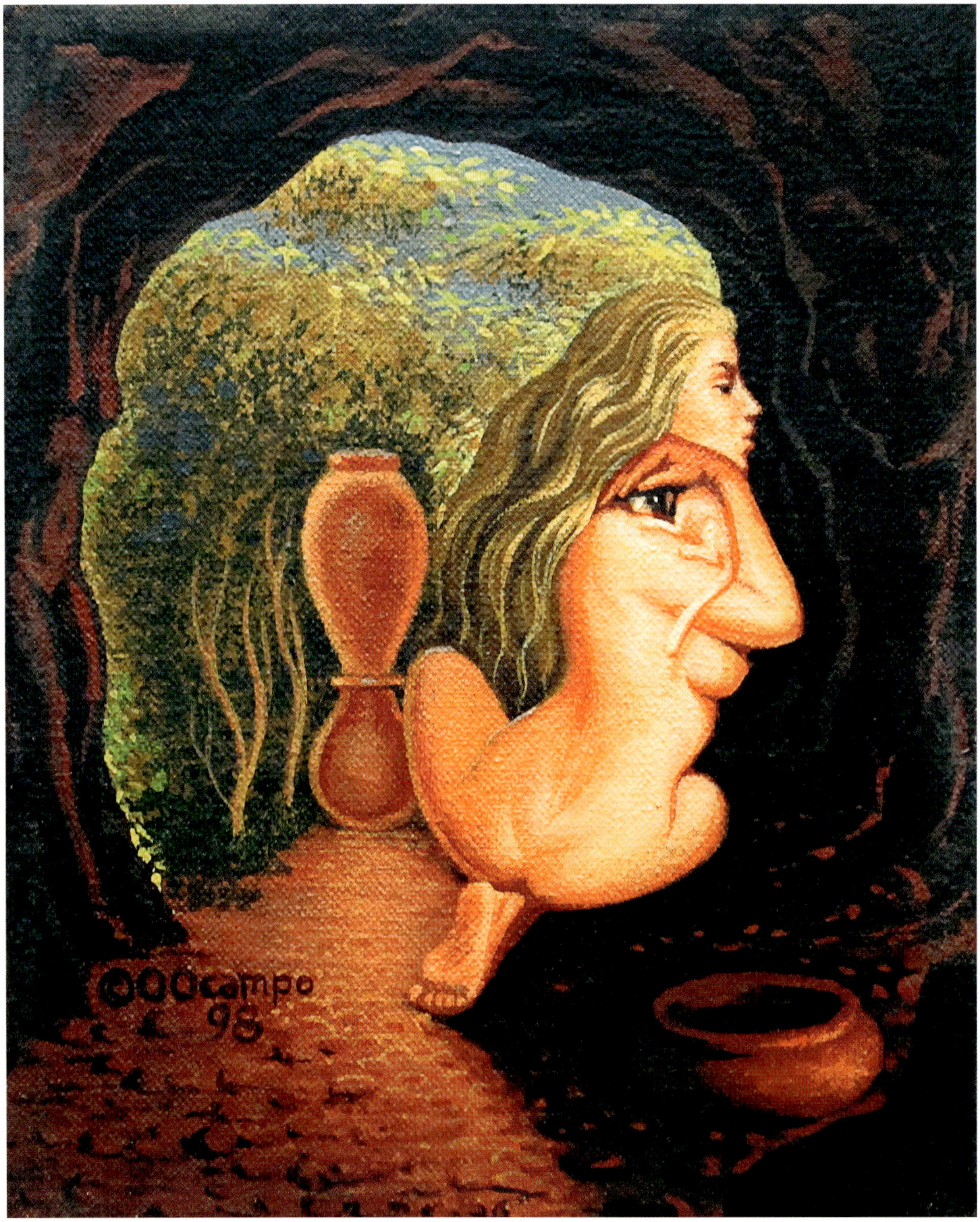

TE ESPERO EN LA CUEVA 1998 (19 × 24)

Oil on canvas – Óleo sobre tela – Öl auf Leinwand – Huile sur toile

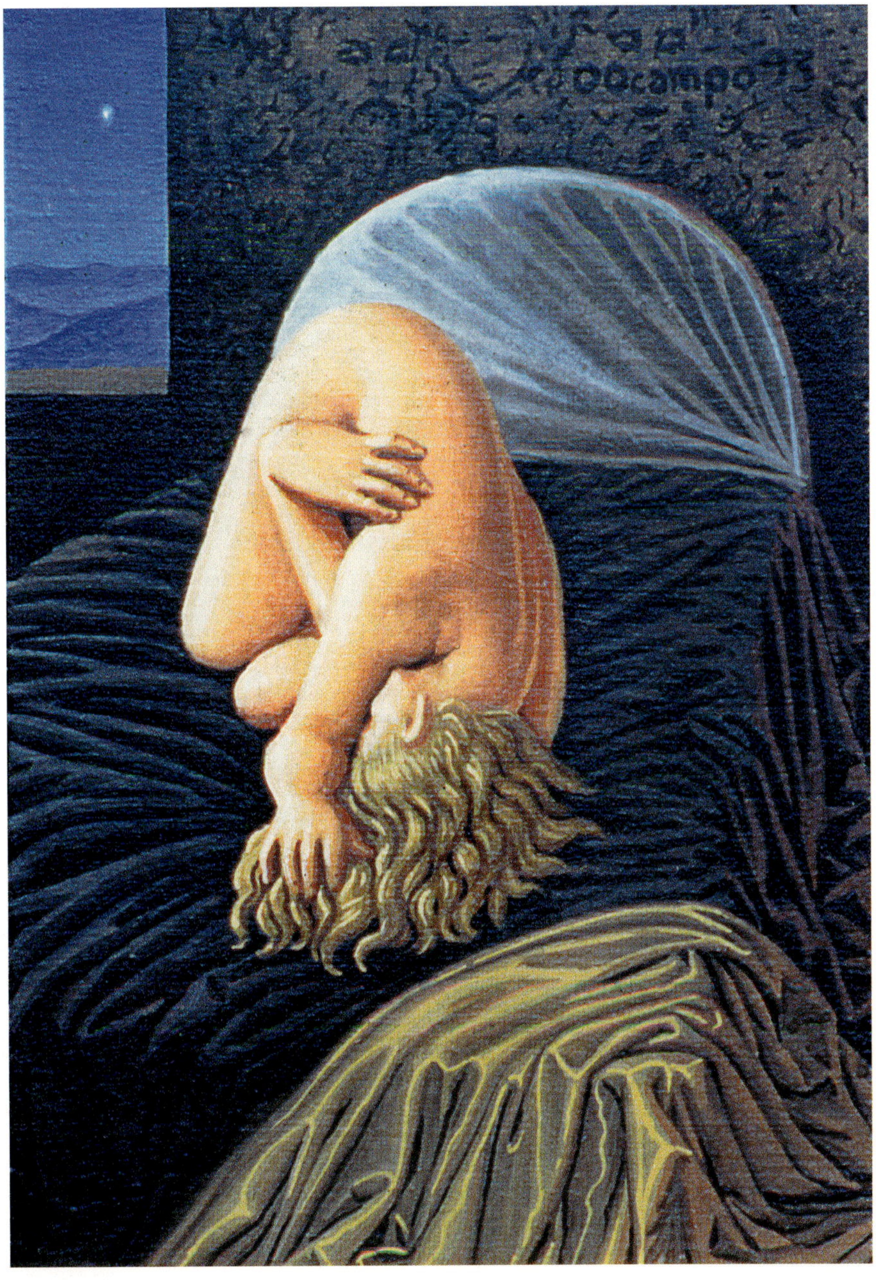

TE SUEÑO 1998 (31 × 35)

Oil on canvas – Óleo sobre tela – Öl auf Leinwand – Huile sur toile

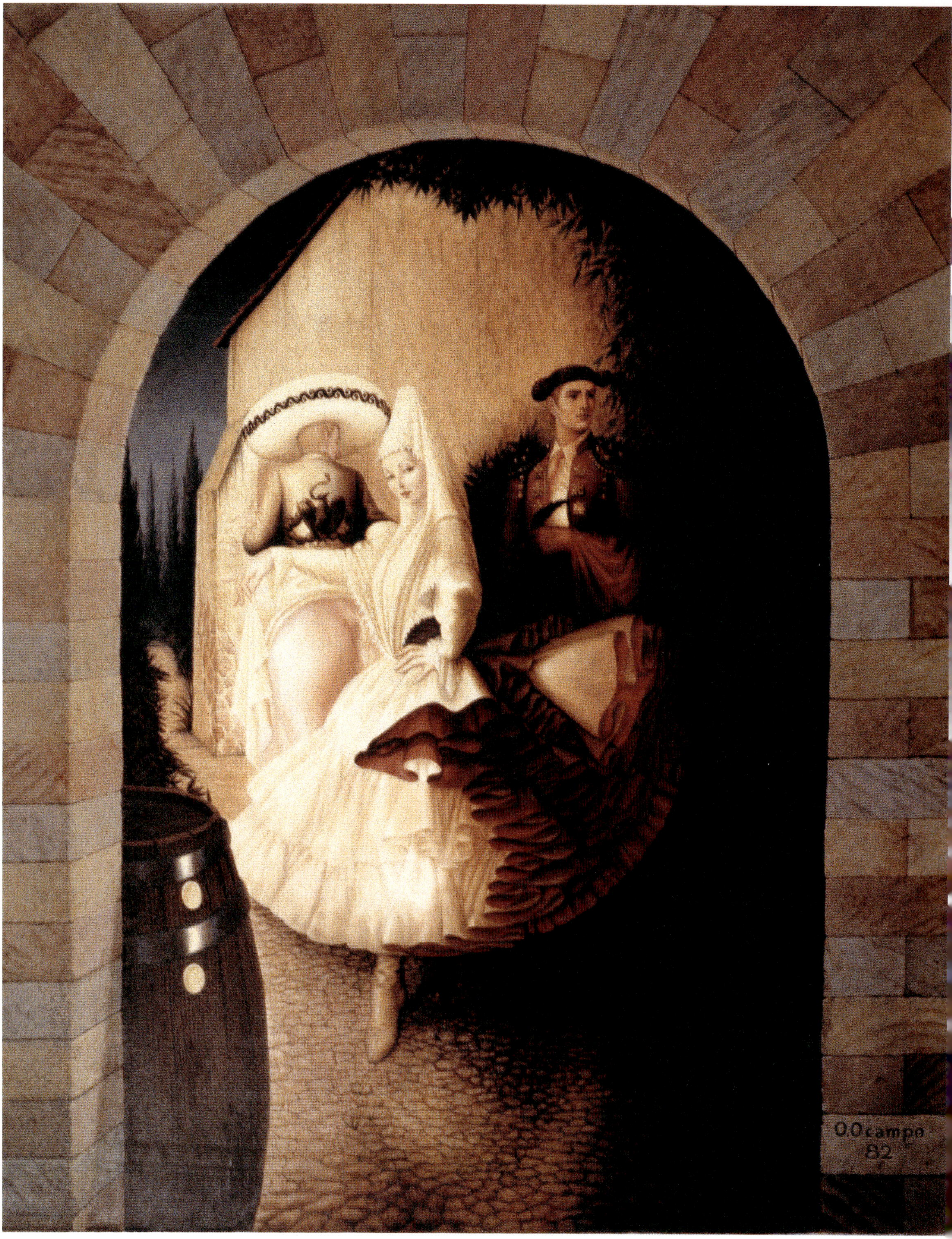
O.Ocampo
82

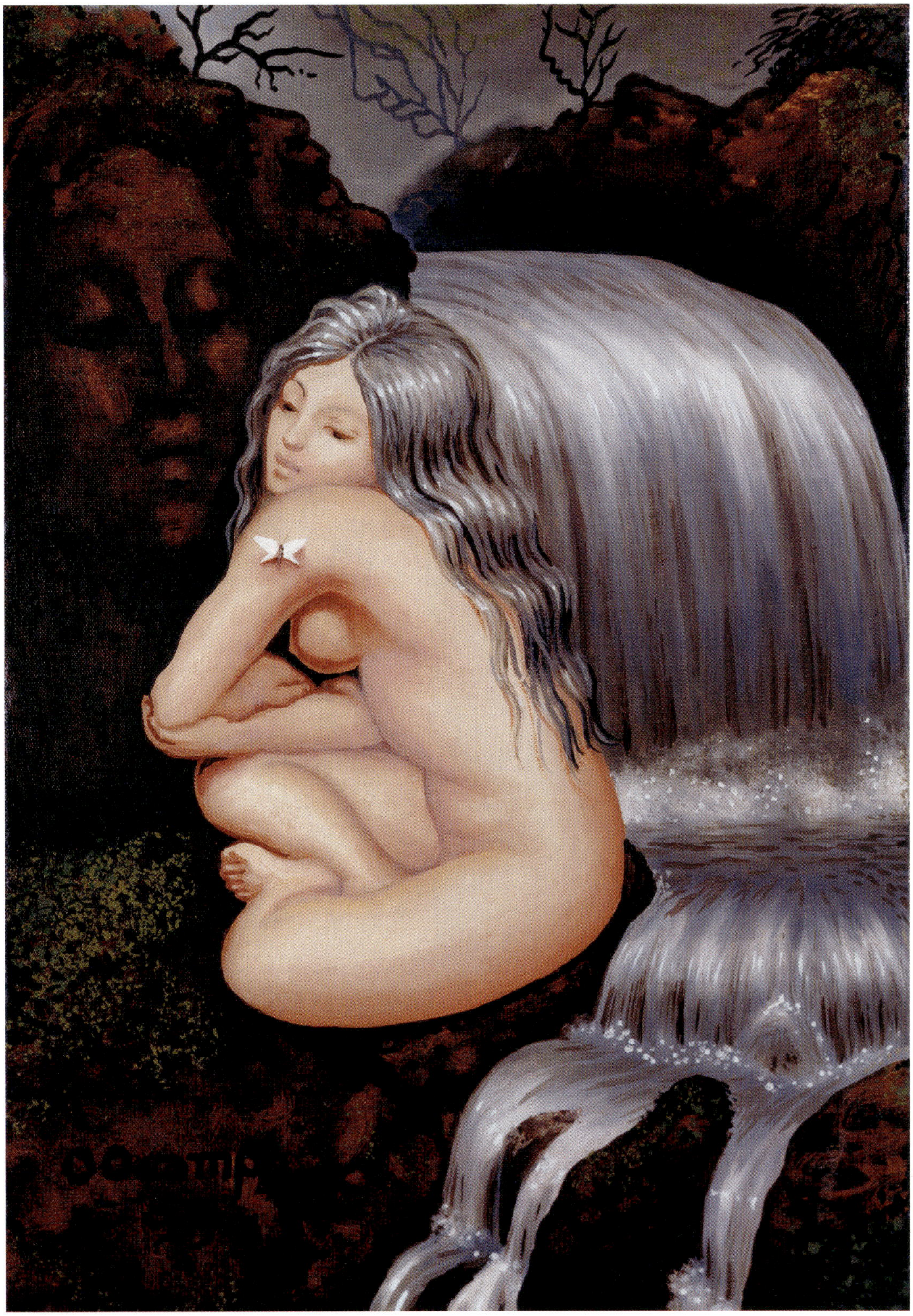

HILOS DE PLATA 1993 (24 × 35)

Oil on canvas – Óleo sobre tela – Öl auf Leinwand – Huile sur toile

LUPE VELEZ 1982 (80 × 100)

Oil on canvas – Óleo sobre tela – Öl auf Leinwand – Huile sur toile

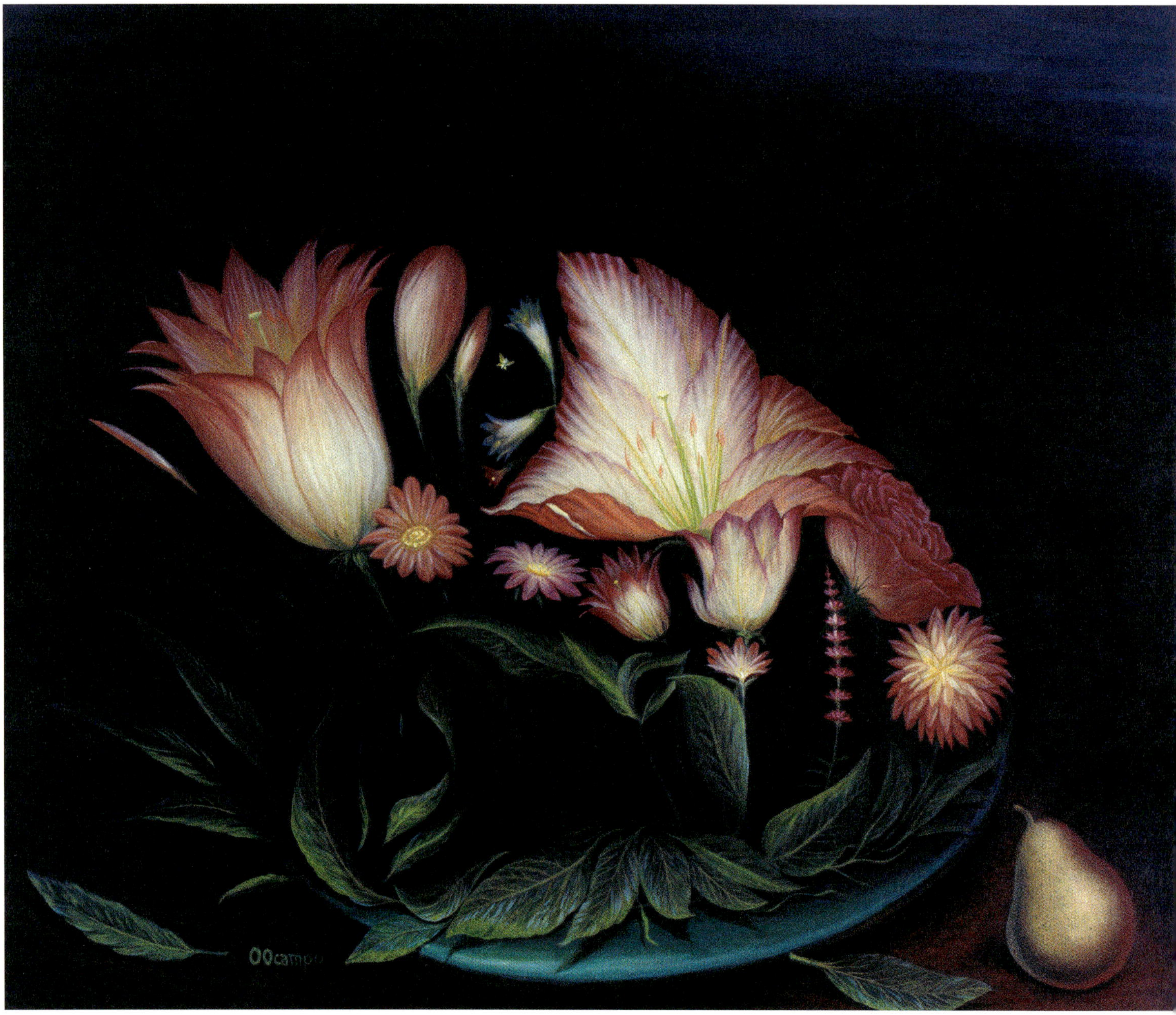

EL LADO OBSCURO 2003 (110 × 90)

Oil on canvas – Óleo sobre tela – Öl auf Leinwand – Huile sur toile

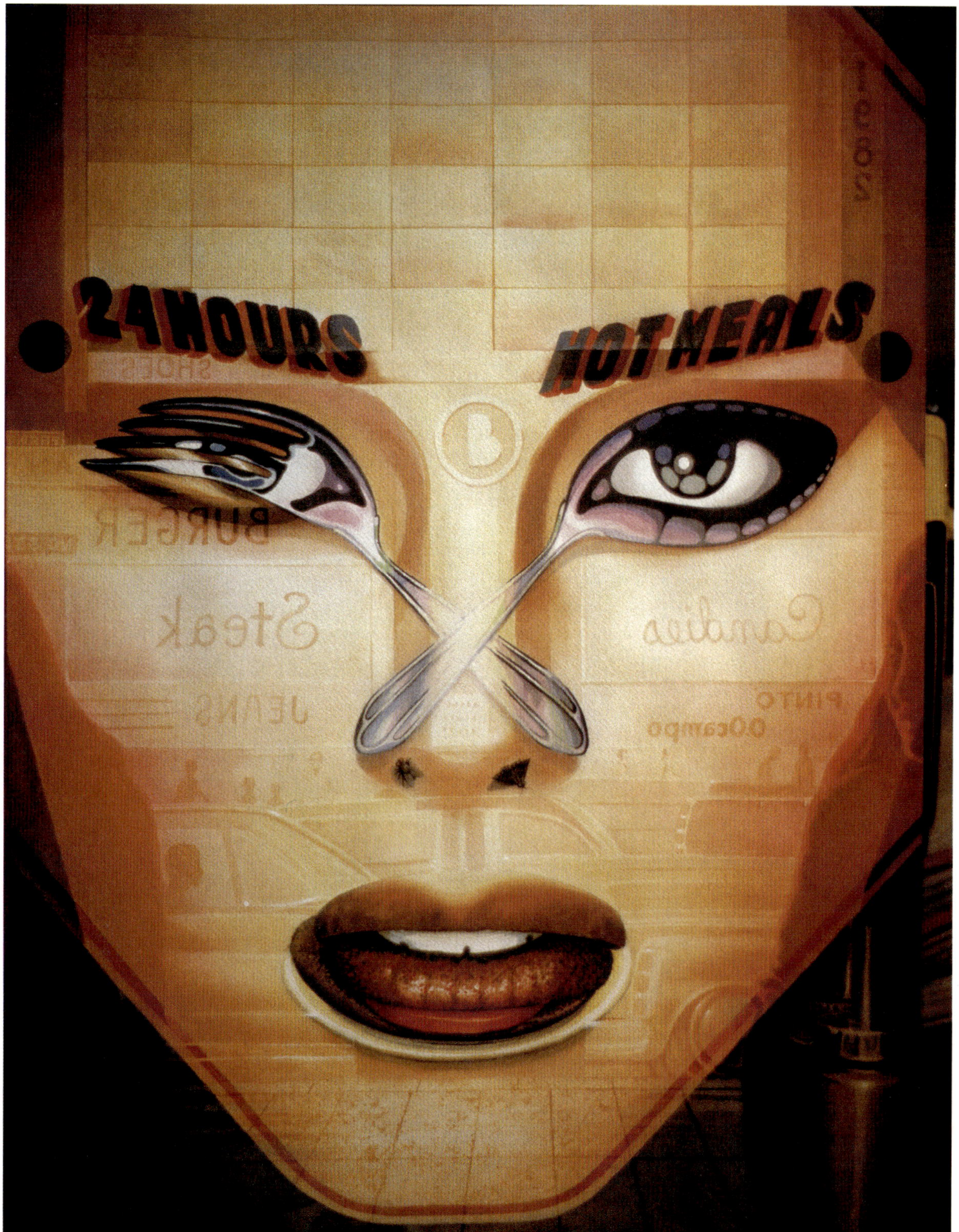

BROOKE SHIELDS 1982 (30 × 40)

Watercolor on paper – Acuarela sobre papel – Aquarell auf Papier – Aquarelle sur papier

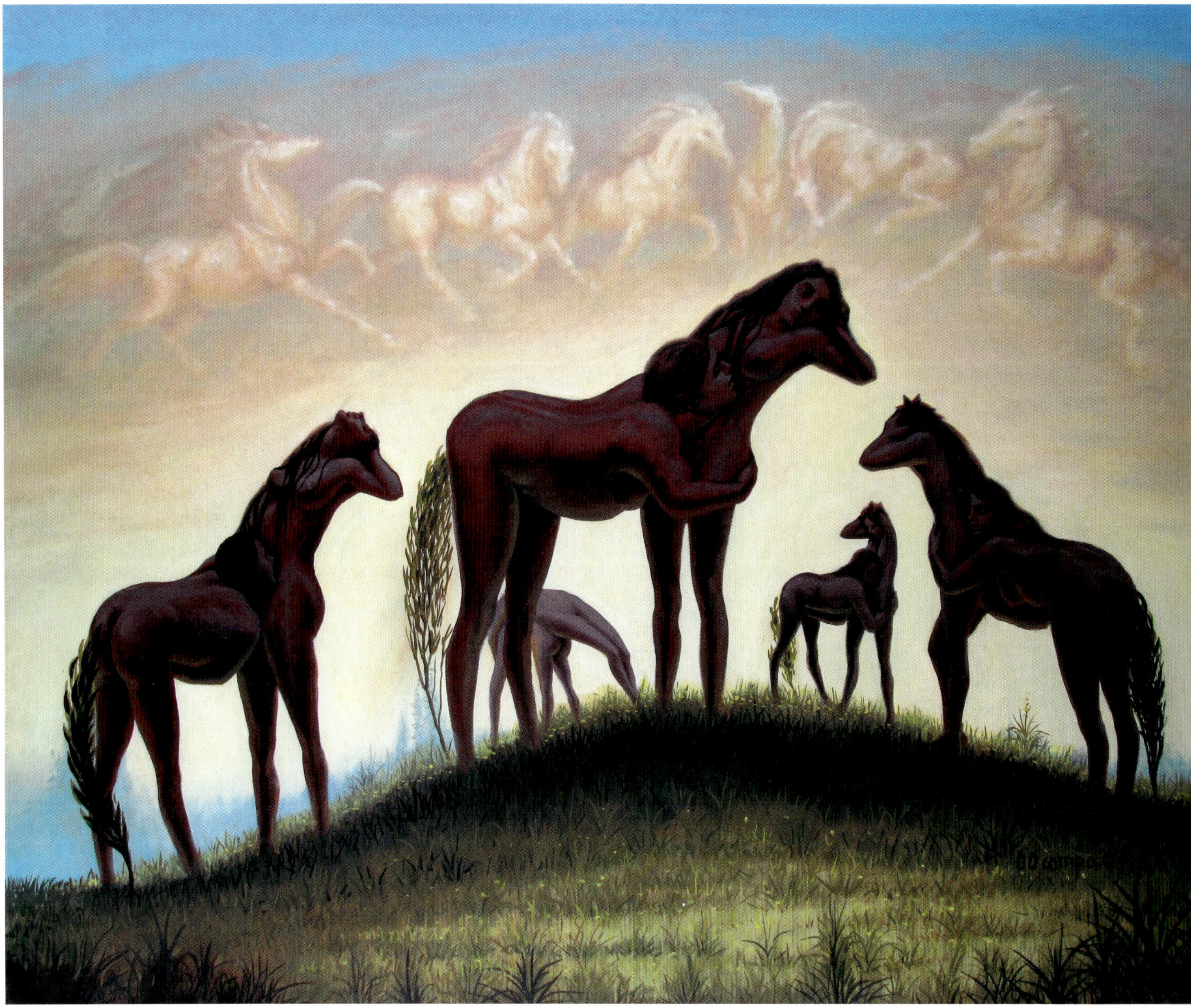

CABALLOS DEL AMOR 2004 (110 × 90)

Oil on canvas – Óleo sobre tela – Öl auf Leinwand – Huile sur toile

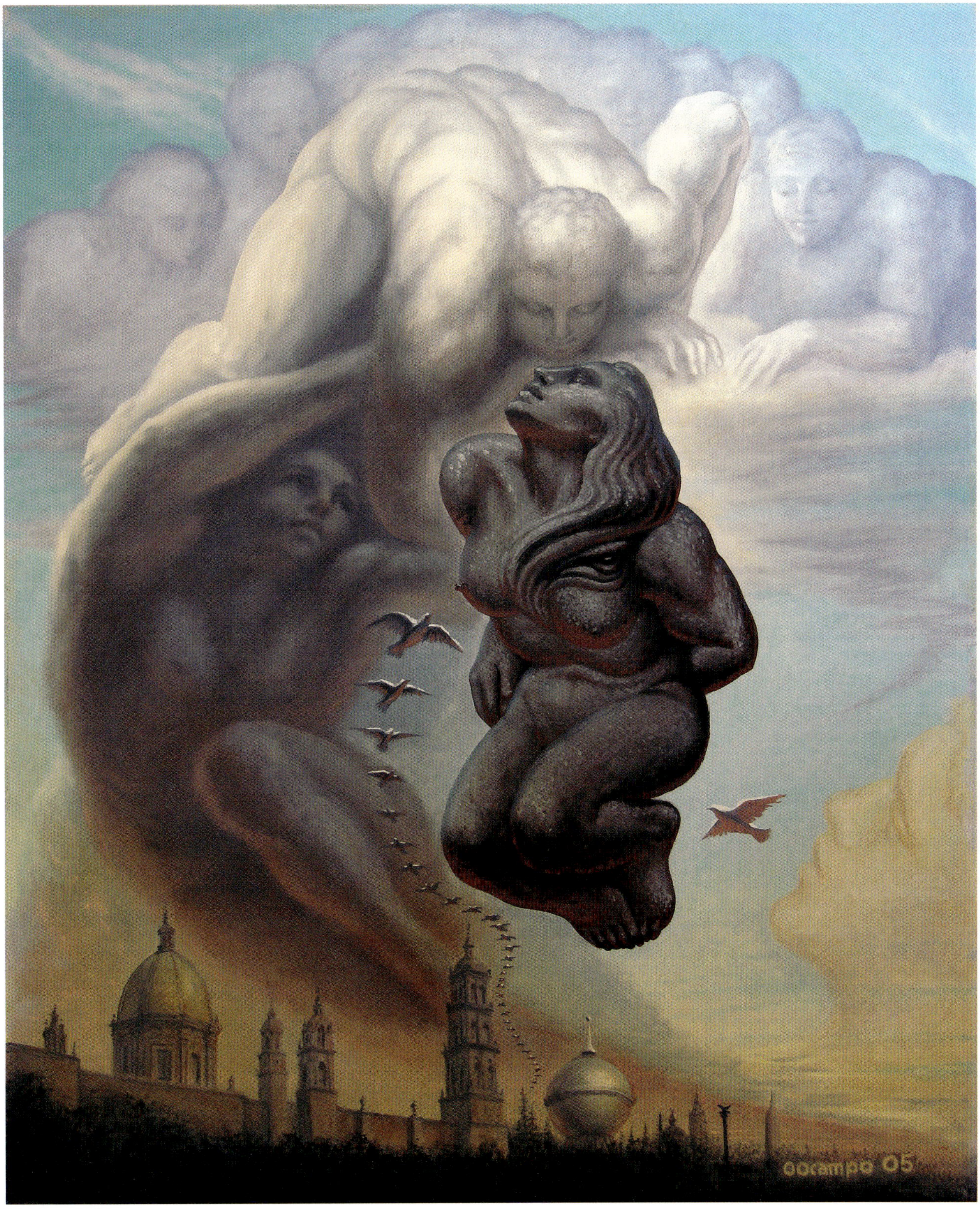

ARRIBA CELAYA 2005 (80 × 100)

Oil on canvas – Óleo sobre tela – Öl auf Leinwand – Huile sur toile

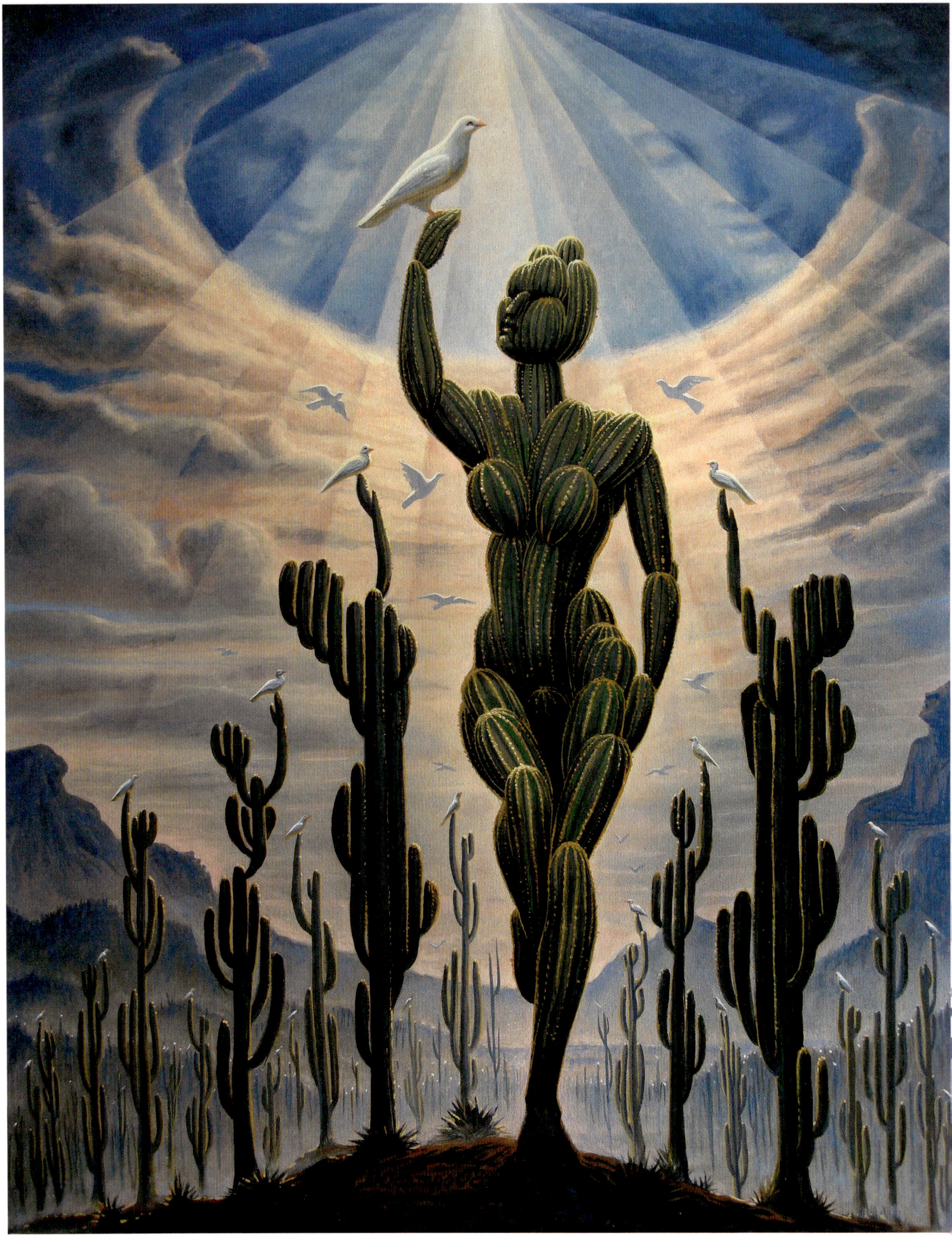

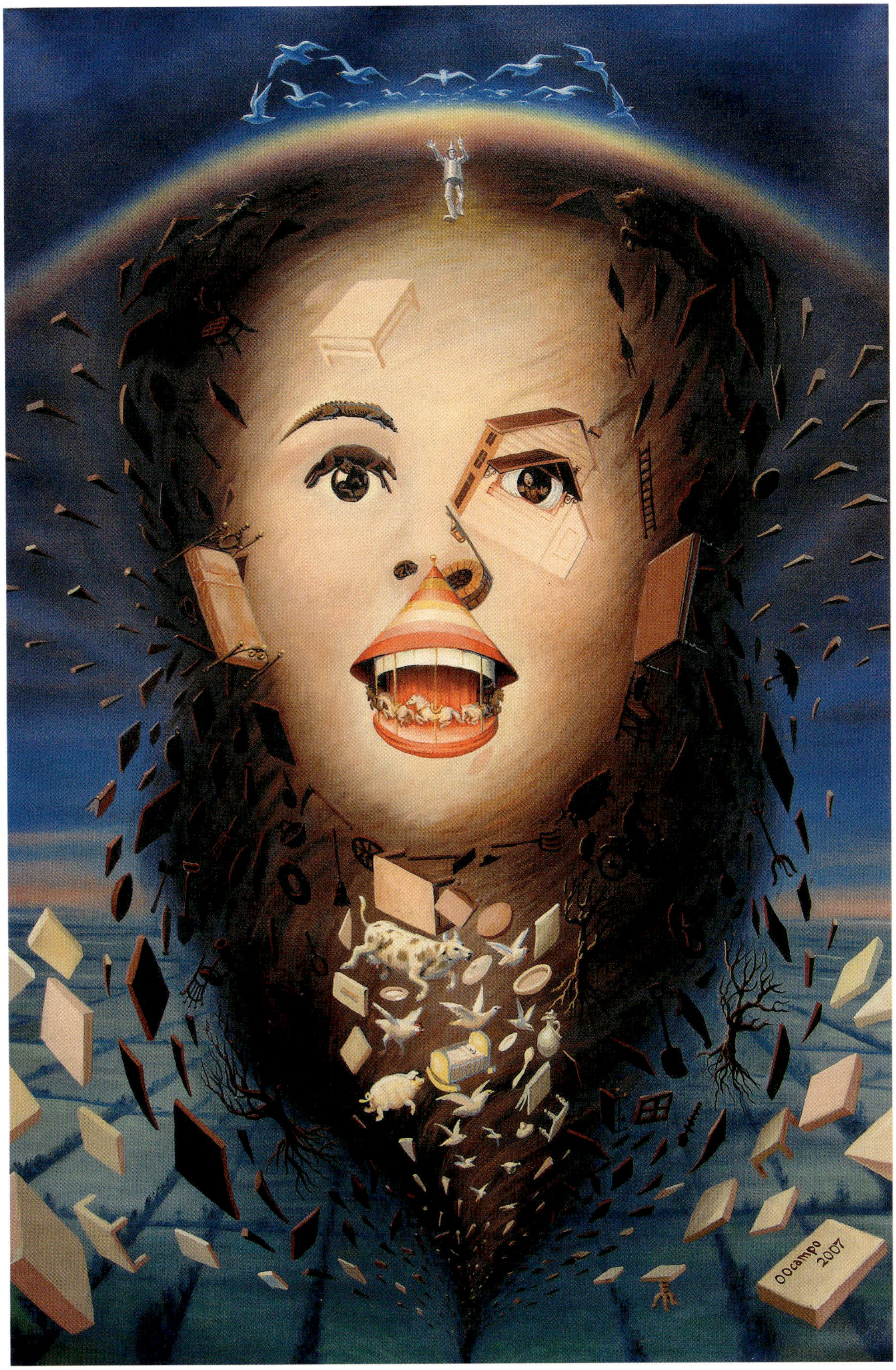

TORNADO 2007 (80 × 120)

Oil on canvas – Óleo sobre tela – Öl auf Leinwand – Huile sur toile

CACTUS POR LA PAZ 2008 (80 × 100)

Oil on canvas – Óleo sobre tela – Öl auf Leinwand – Huile sur toile

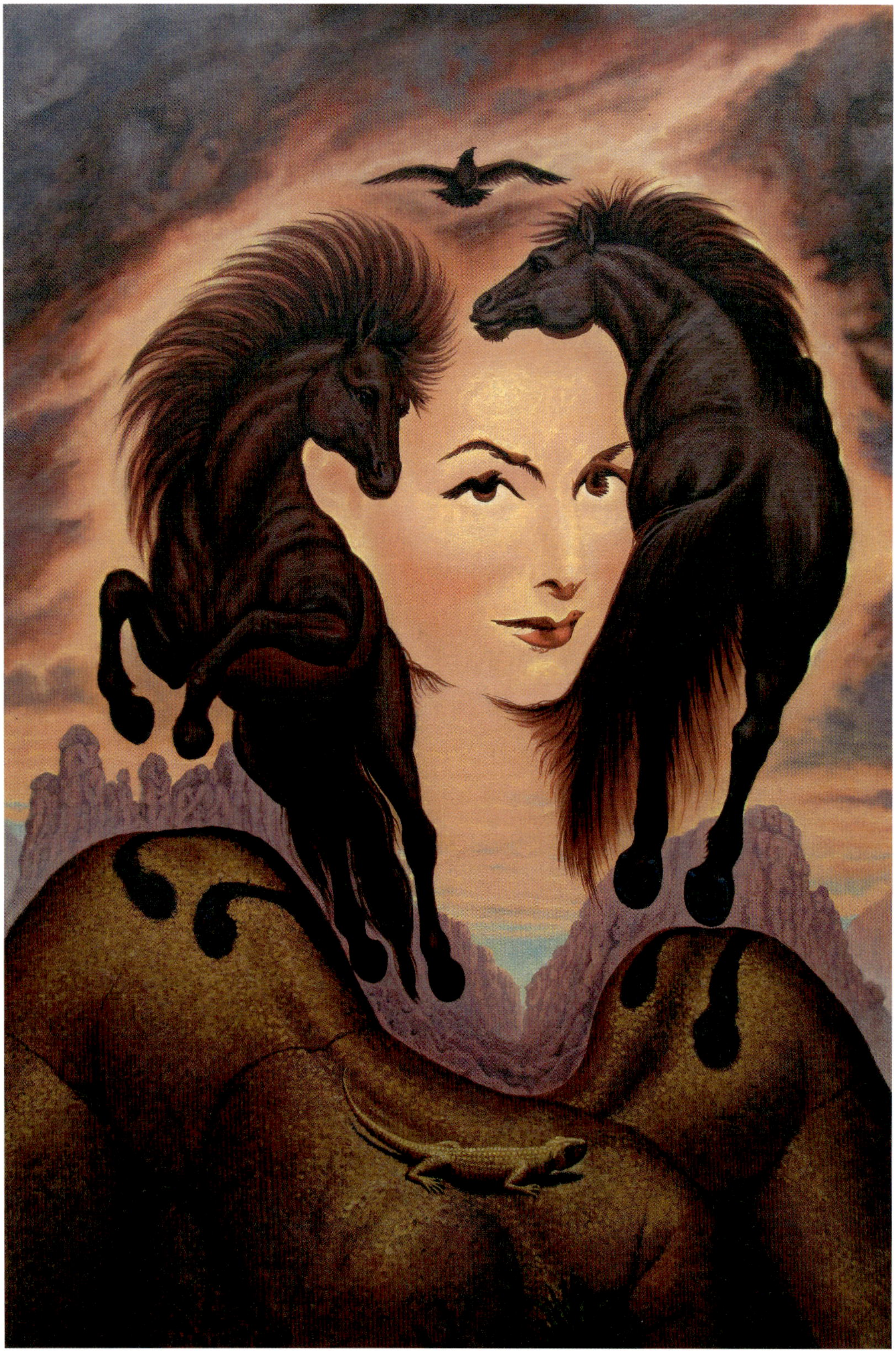

LA NORTEÑA 1998 (80 × 120)

Oil on canvas – Óleo sobre tela – Öl auf Leinwand – Huile sur toile

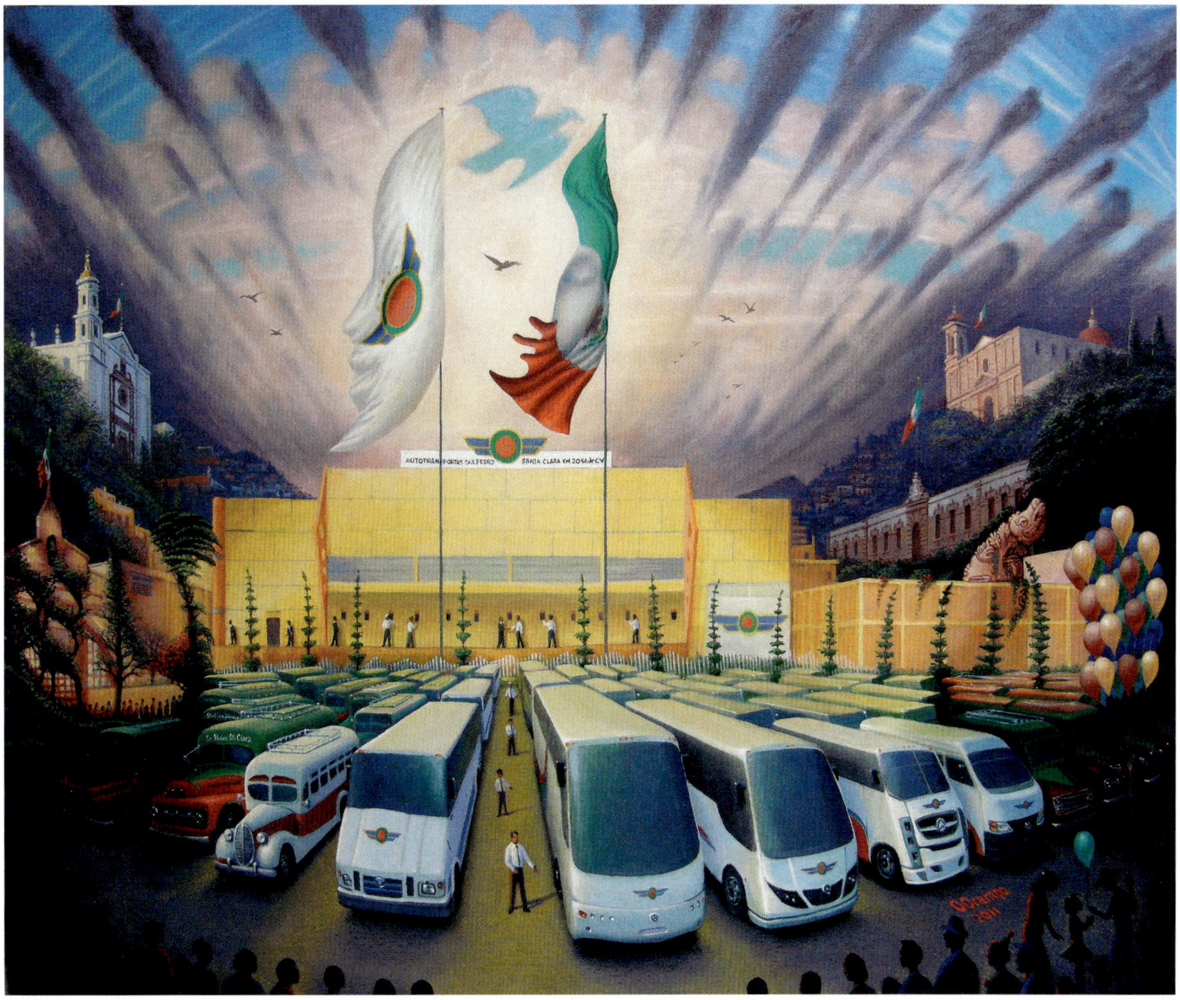

ALEGORÍA TRANSPORTES SAN PEDRO-SANTA CLARA 2011 (120 × 90)

Oil on canvas – Óleo sobre tela – Öl auf Leinwand – Huile sur toile

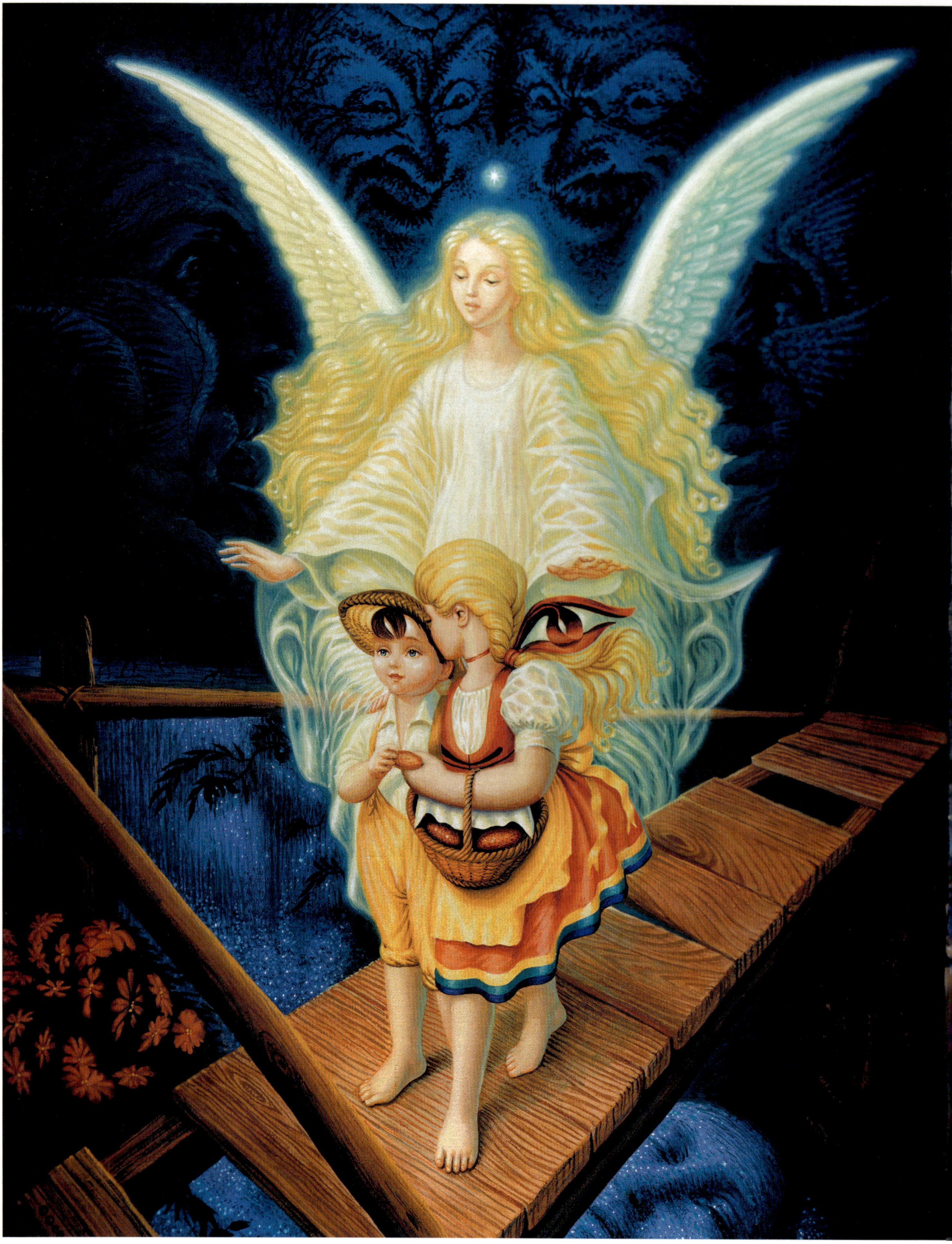

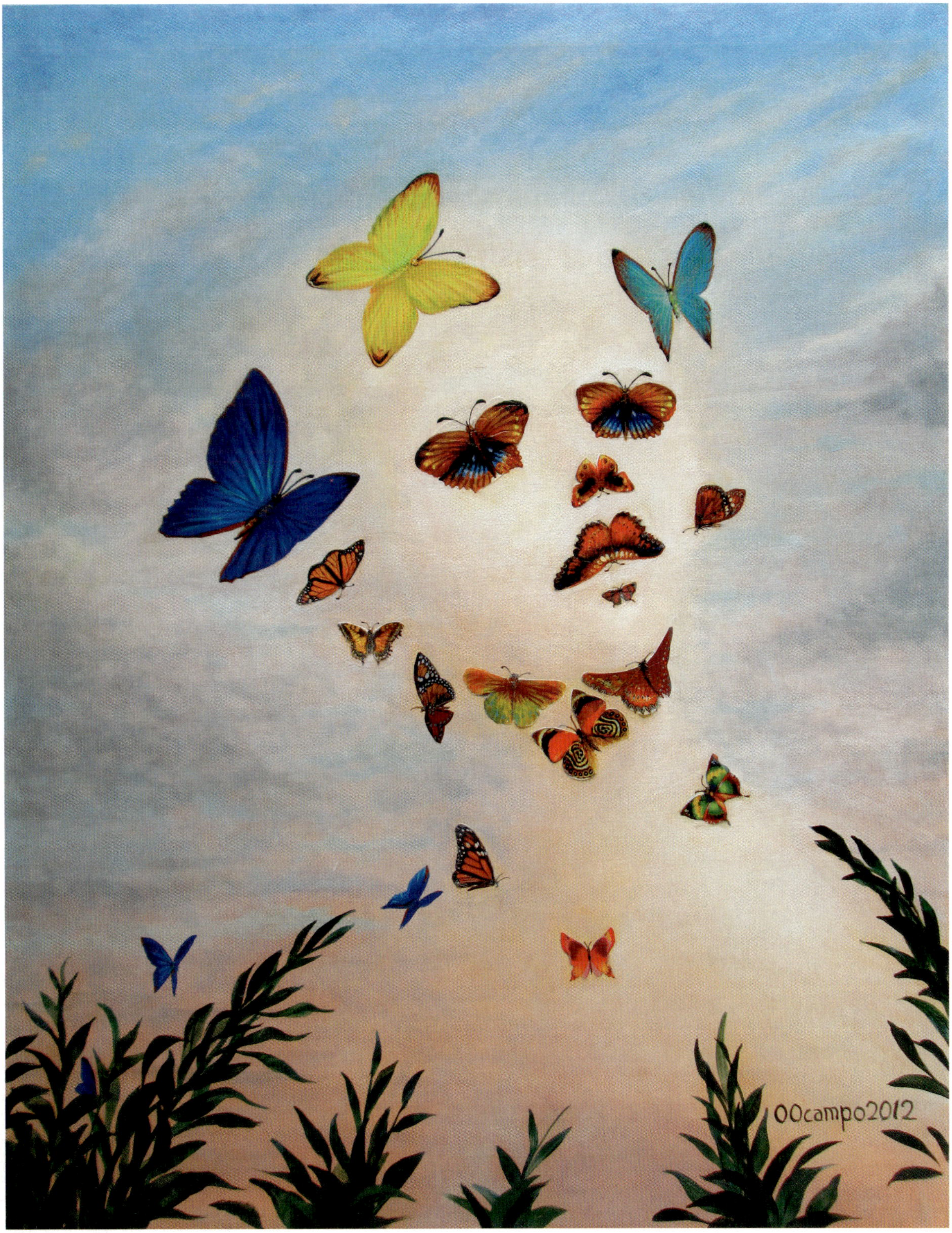

SIMPOSIUM DE MARIPOSAS 2012 (36,5 × 80,5)

Oil on canvas – Óleo sobre tela – Öl auf Leinwand – Huile sur toile

EL BIEN Y EL MAL 1995 (100 × 180)

Oil on canvas – Óleo sobre tela – Öl auf Leinwand – Huile sur toile

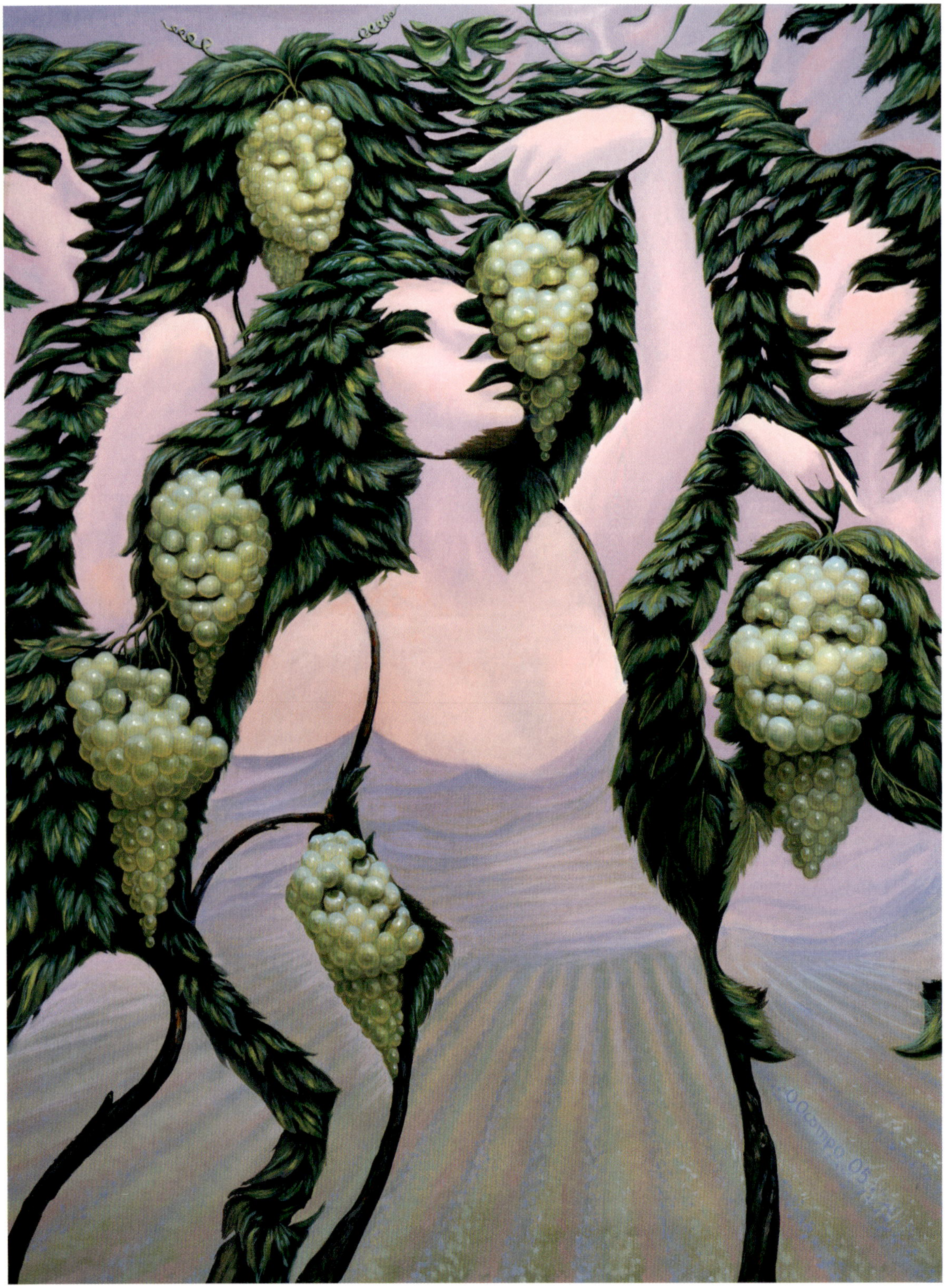

LAS BACANTES 2005 (90 × 120)

Oil on canvas – Óleo sobre tela – Öl auf Leinwand – Huile sur toile

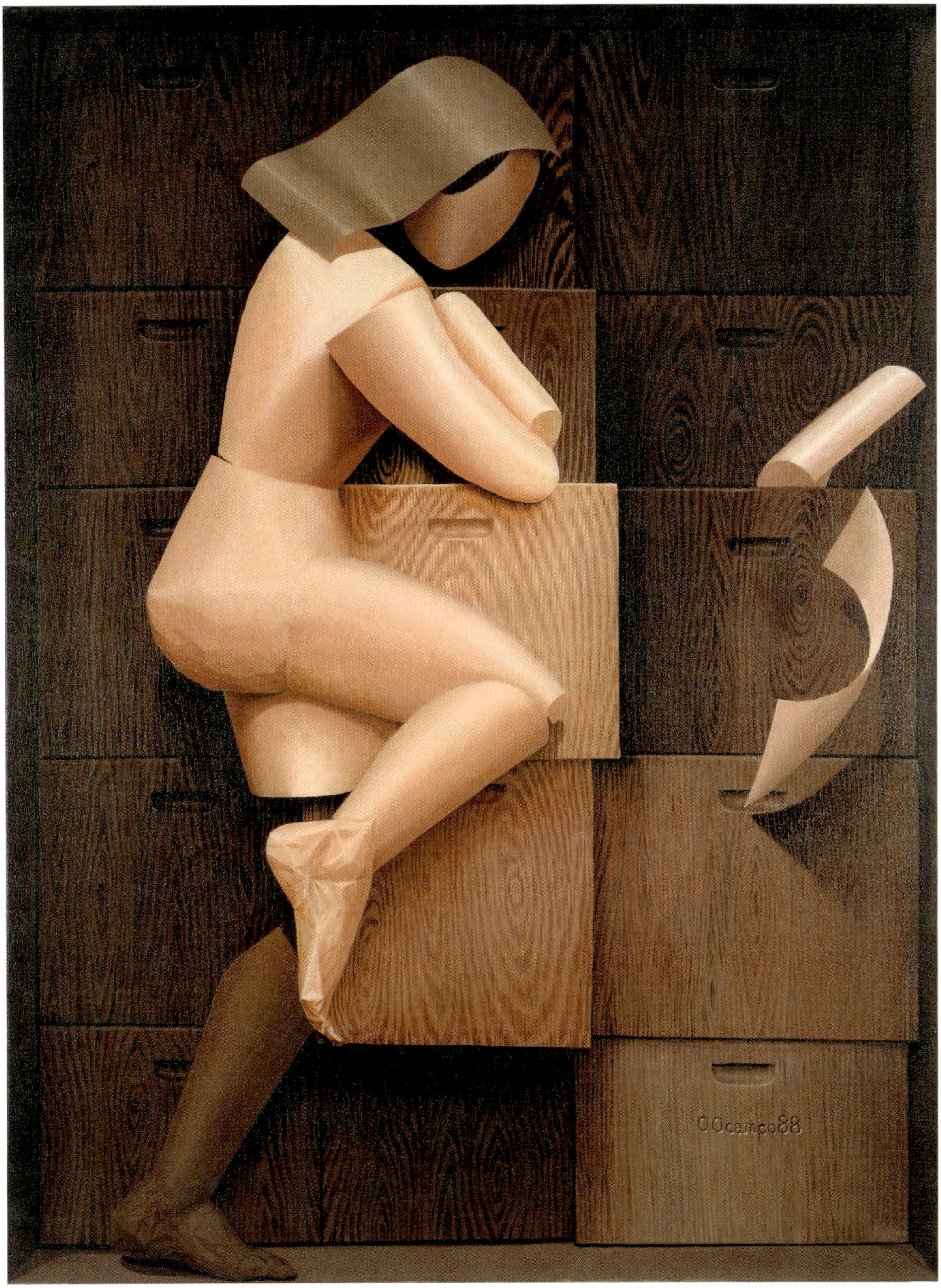

EL JEFE, LA SECRETARIA Y EL ARCHIVO 1988 (80 × 100)

Oil on canvas – Óleo sobre tela – Öl auf Leinwand – Huile sur toile

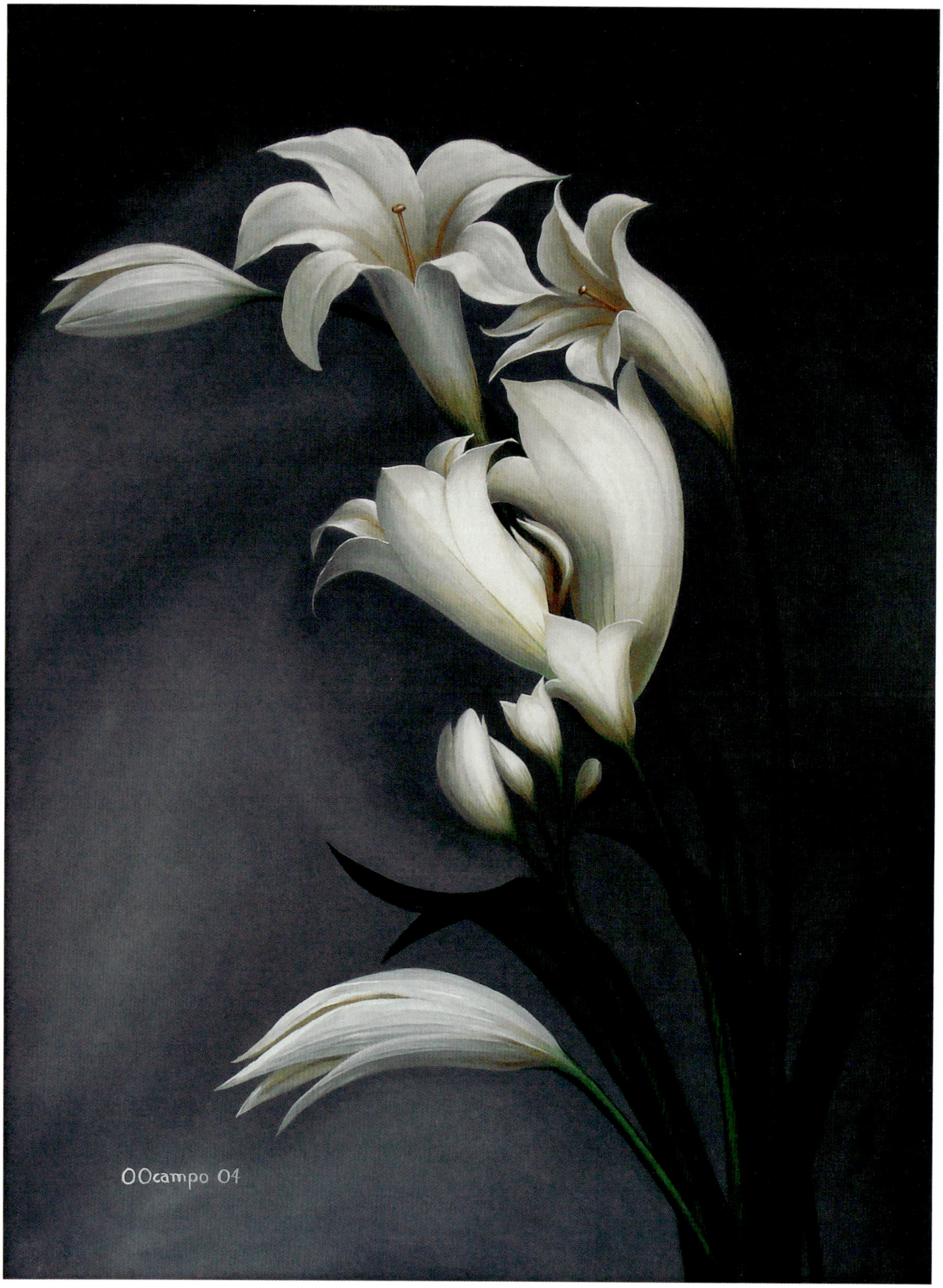

ÁNGEL DE LA AZUCENA 2004 (90 × 120)

Oil on canvas – Óleo sobre tela – Öl auf Leinwand – Huile sur toile

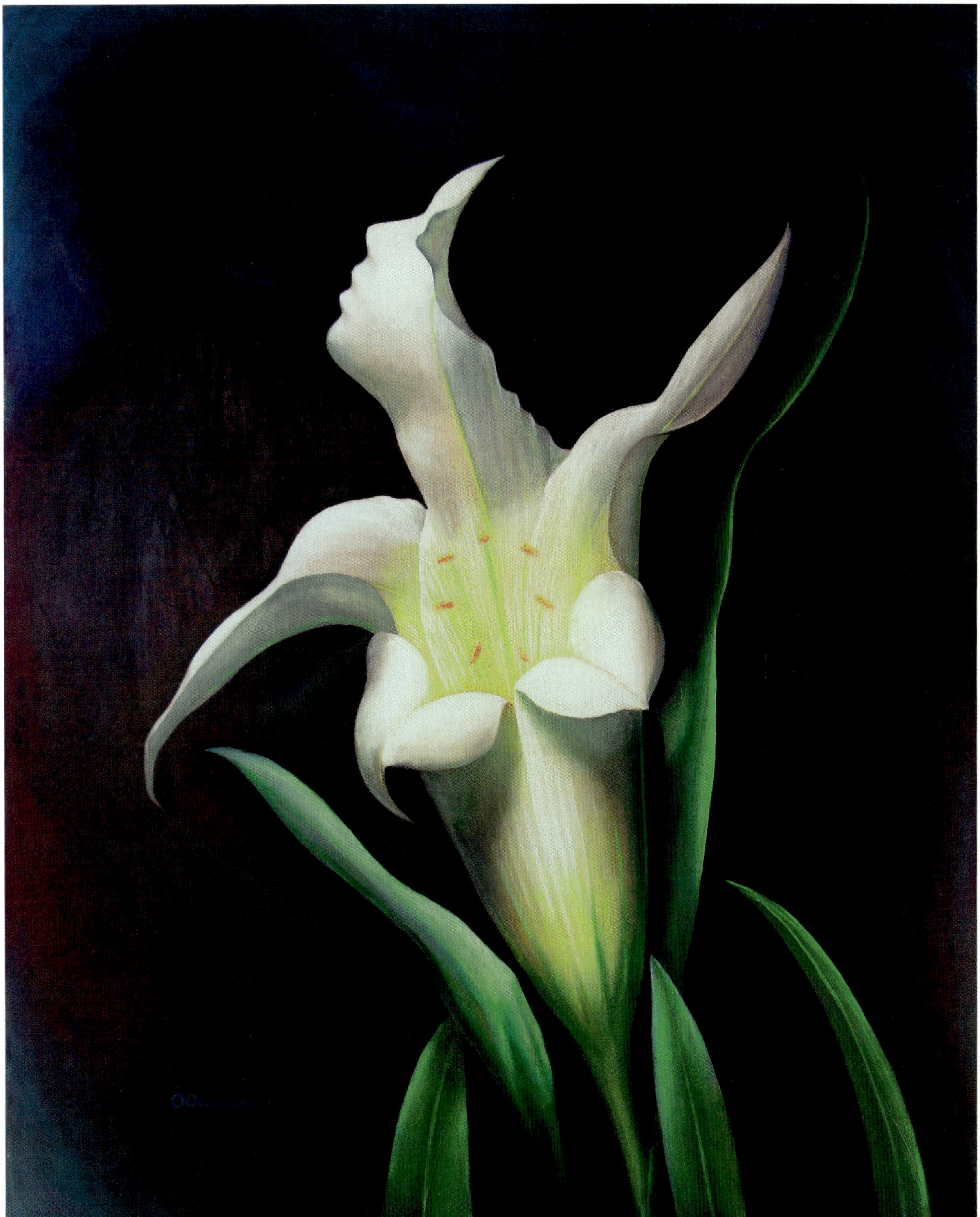

LOS AMANTES DE CASABLANCA 2004 (90 × 120)

Oil on canvas – Óleo sobre tela – Öl auf Leinwand – Huile sur toile

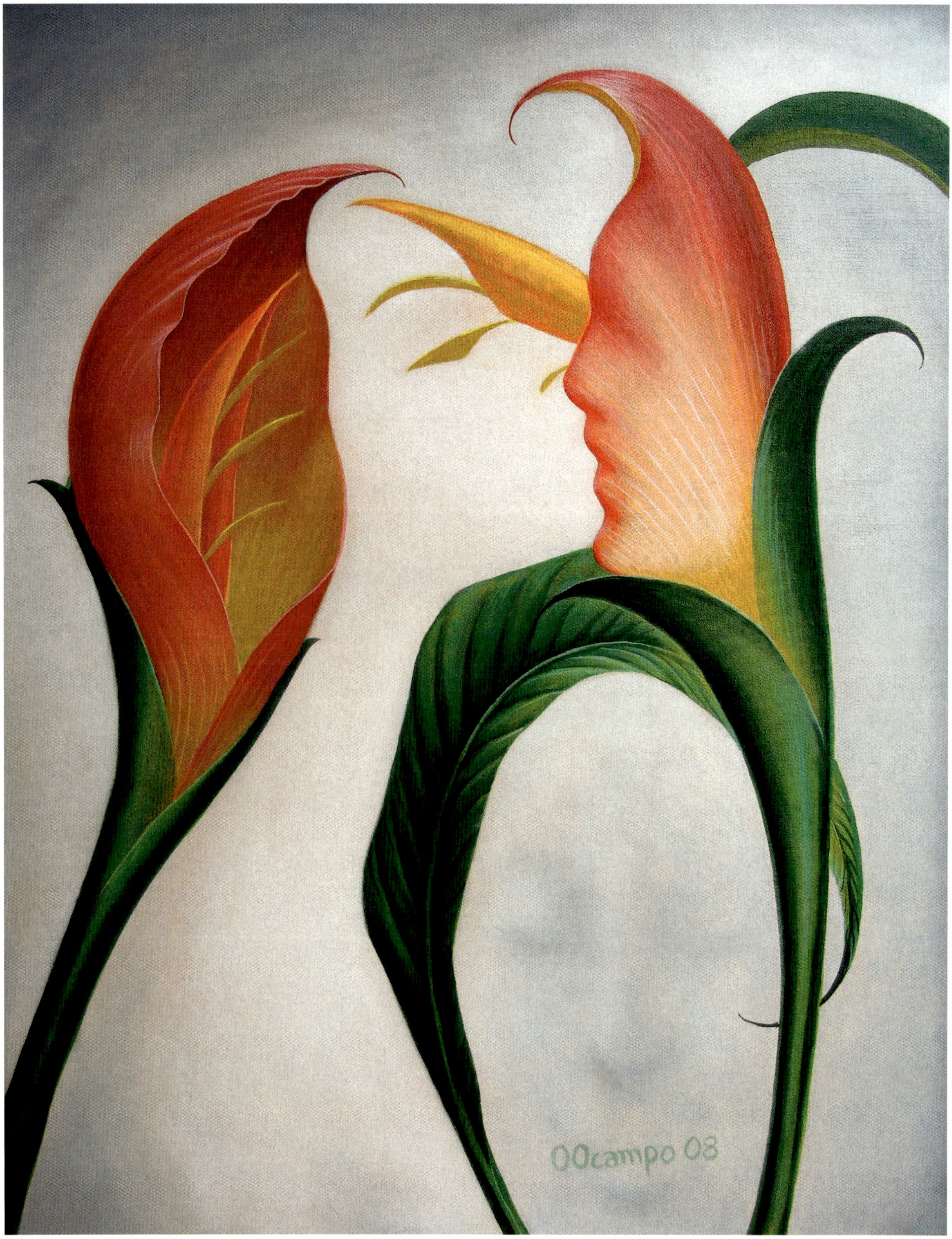

FLORES EXÓTICAS 2008 (70 × 90)

Oil on canvas – Óleo sobre tela – Öl auf Leinwand – Huile sur toile

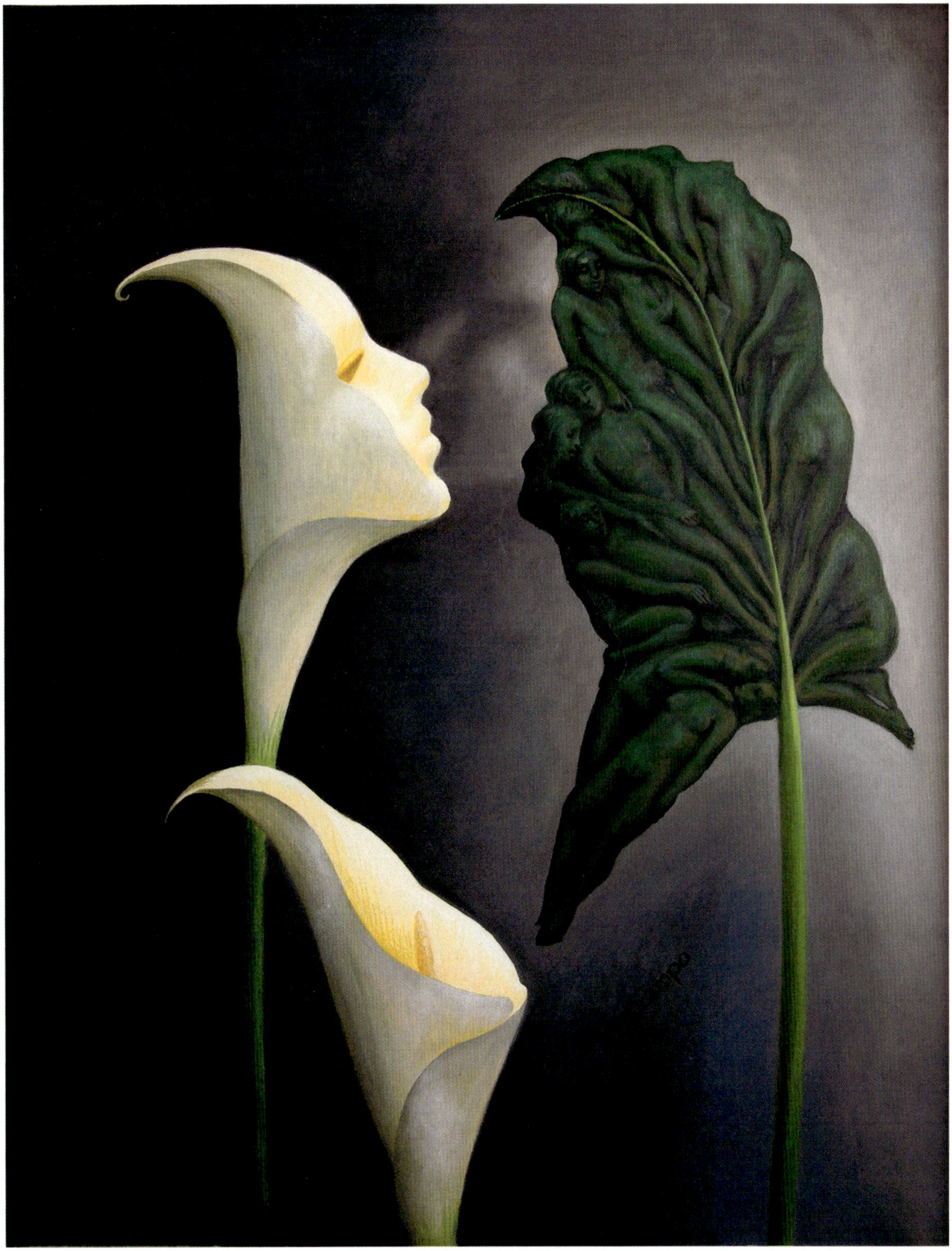

ALCATRACES AMAN LA HOJA 2009 (71 × 91)

Oil on canvas – Óleo sobre tela – Öl auf Leinwand – Huile sur toile

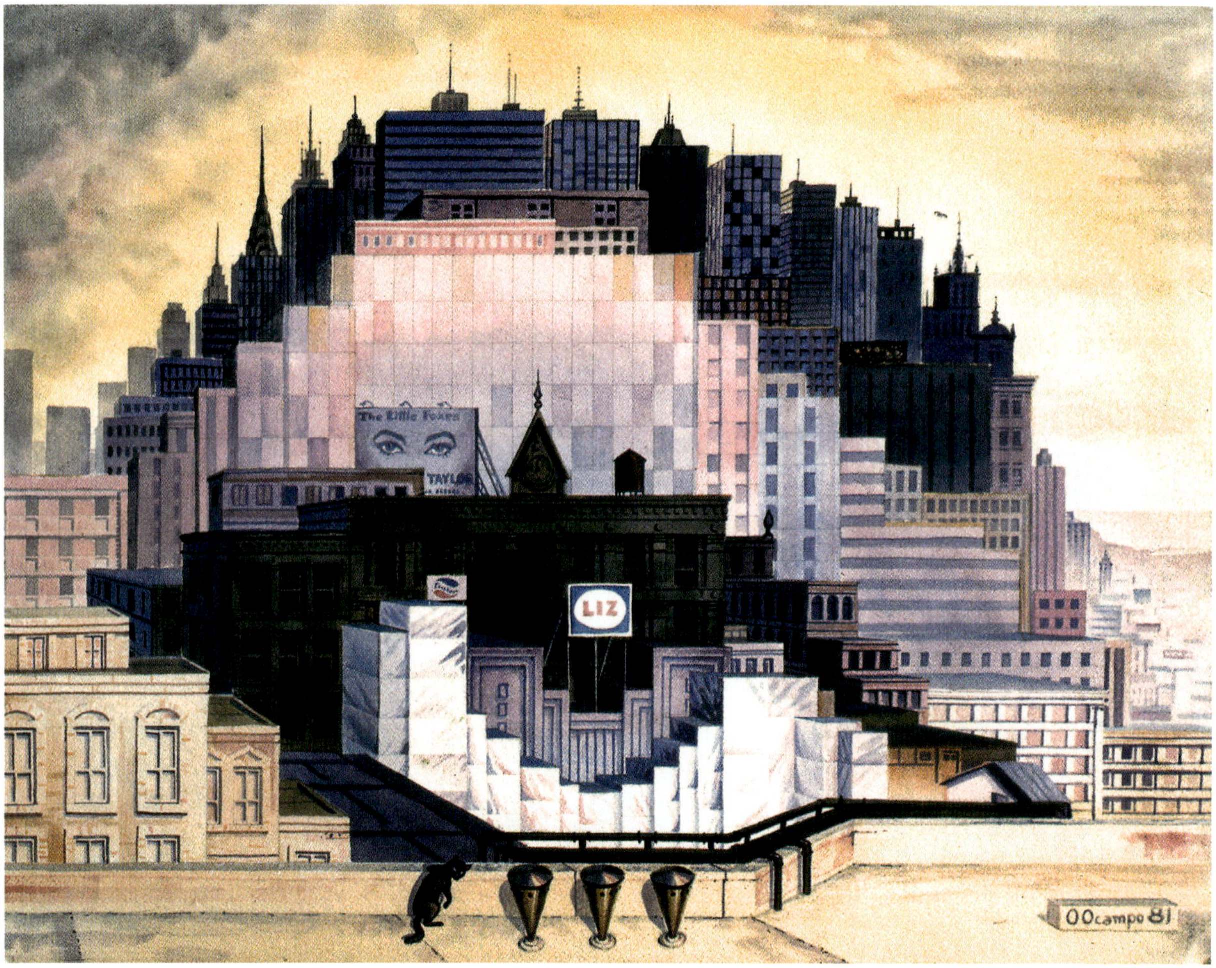

OJO DERECHO DE LIZ 1981 (45 × 35)

Watercolor on paper – Acuarela sobre papel – Aquarell auf Papier – Aquarelle sur papier

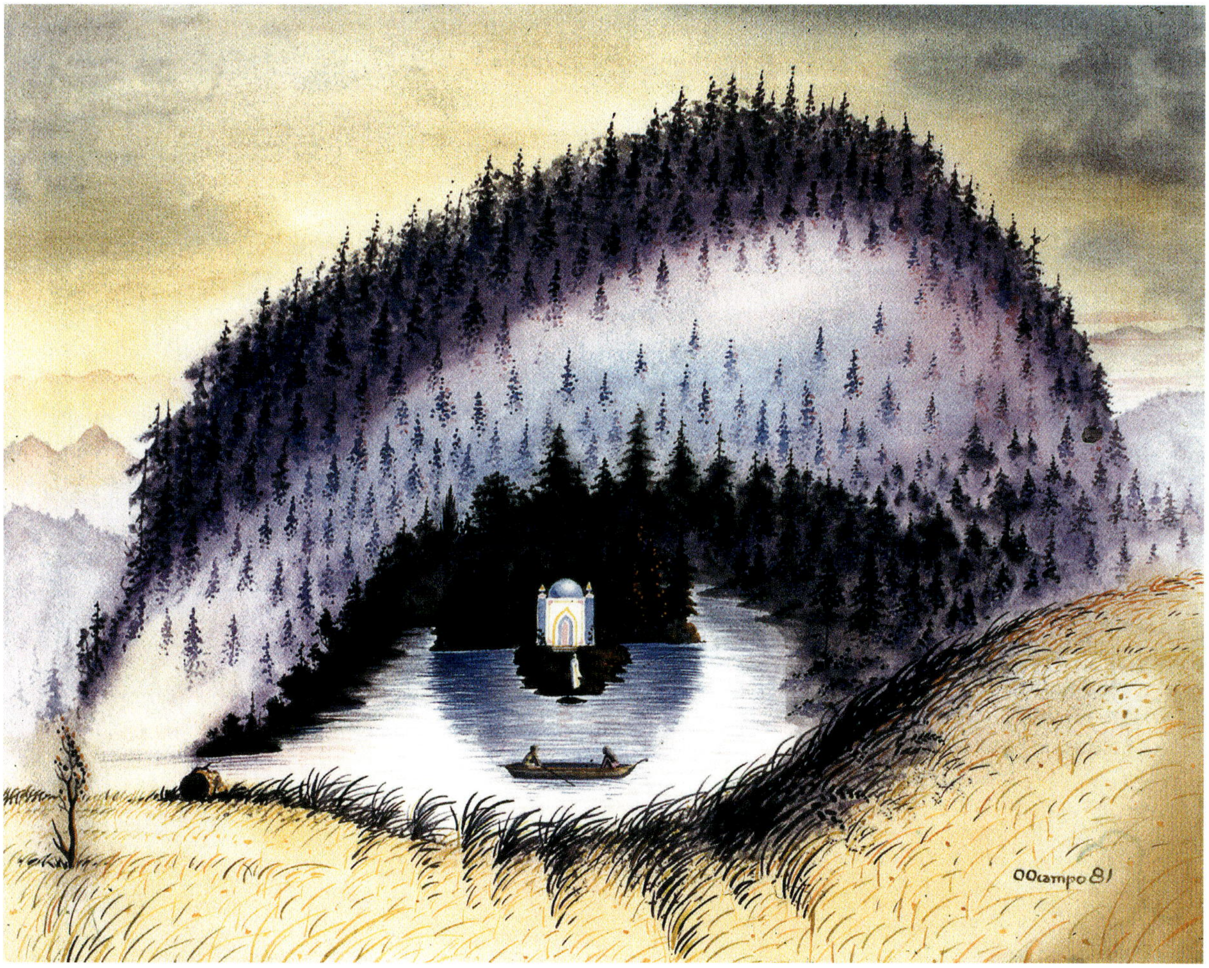

OJO IZQUIERDO DE LIZ 1981 (45 × 35)

Watercolor on paper – Acuarela sobre papel – Aquarell auf Papier – Aquarelle sur papier

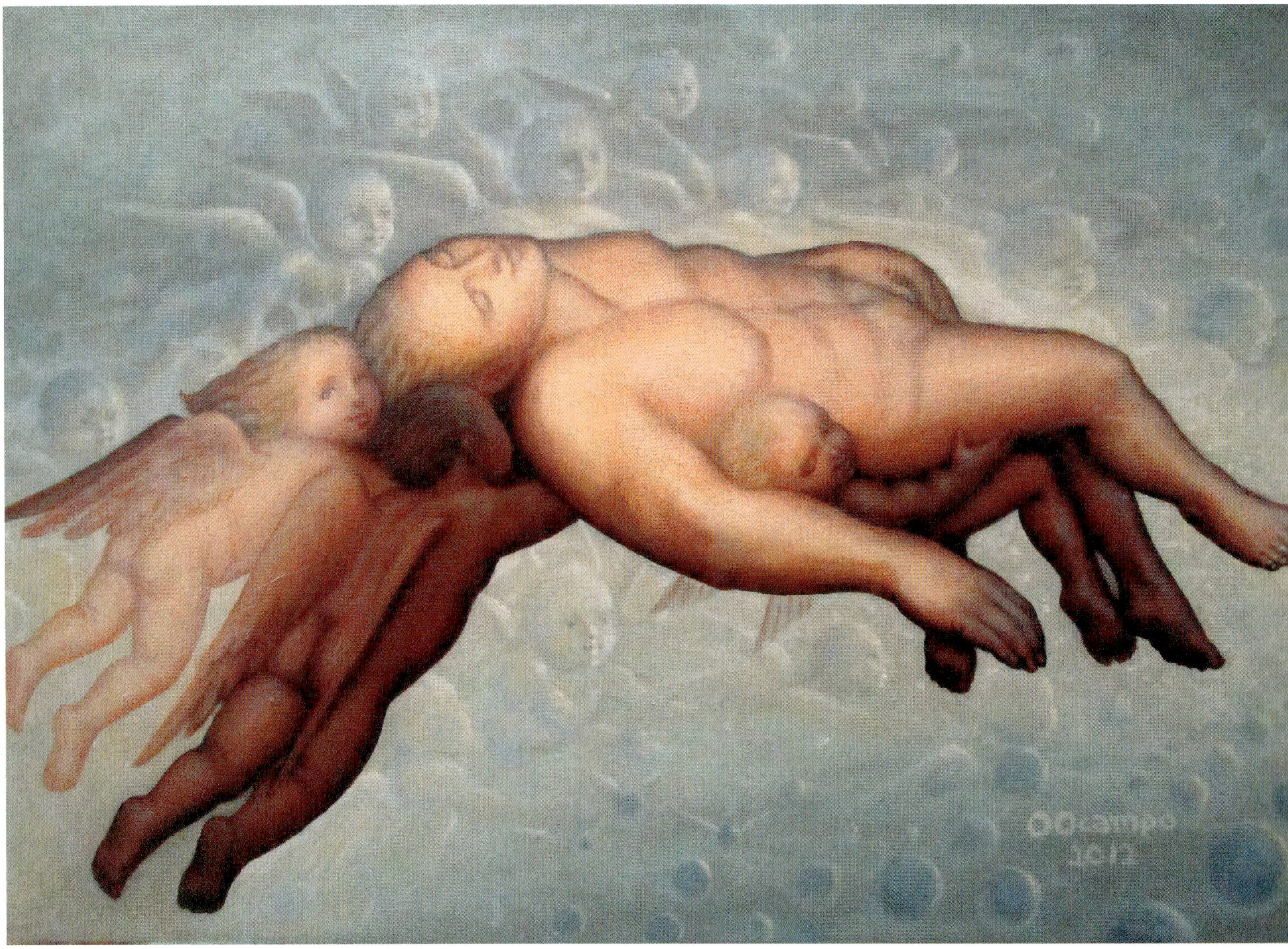

LA MANO DEL HOMBRE 2012 (65 × 45)

Oil on canvas – Óleo sobre tela – Öl auf Leinwand – Huile sur toile

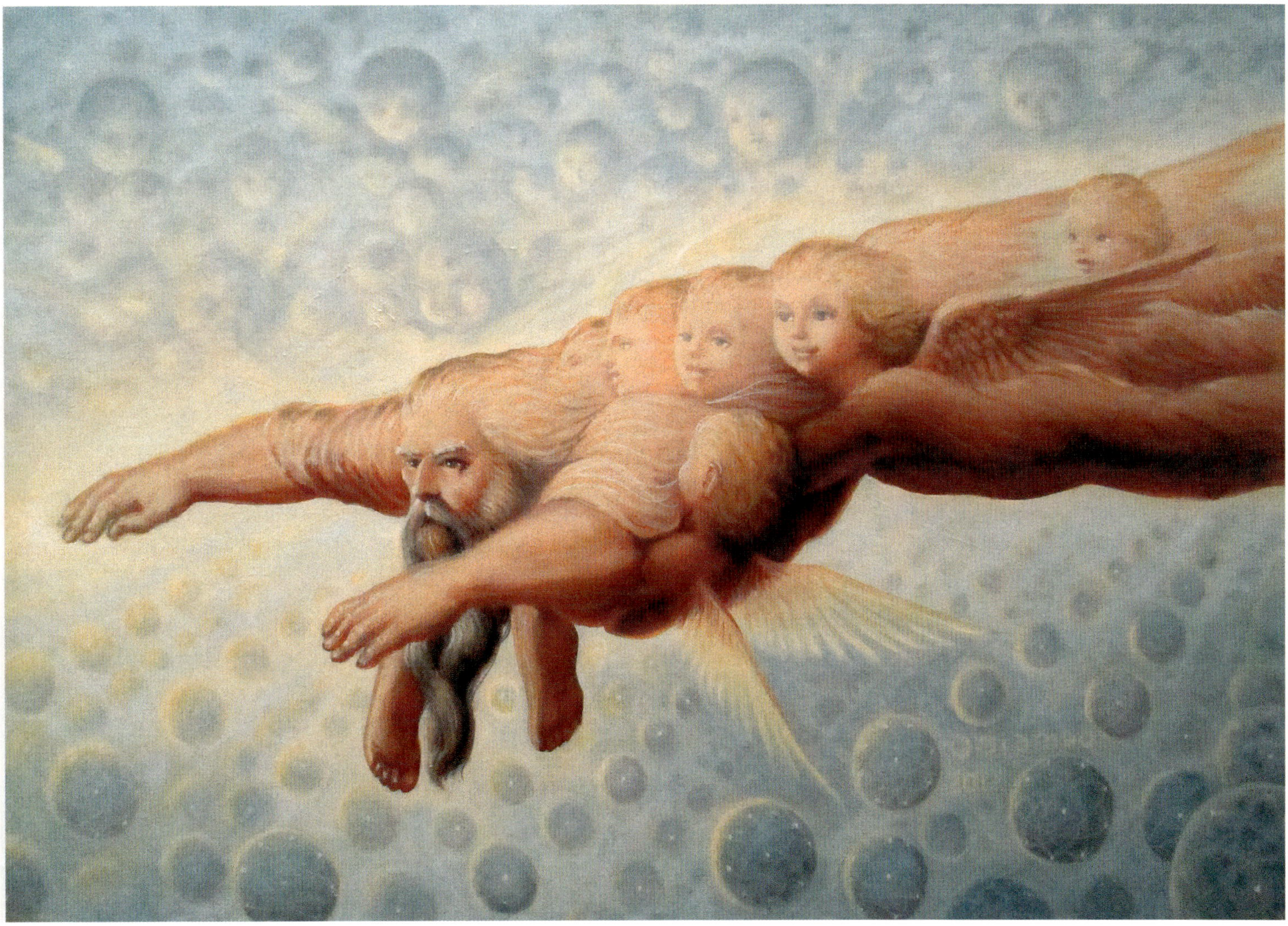

LA MANO DE DIOS 2012 (65 × 45)

Oil on canvas – Óleo sobre tela – Öl auf Leinwand – Huile sur toile

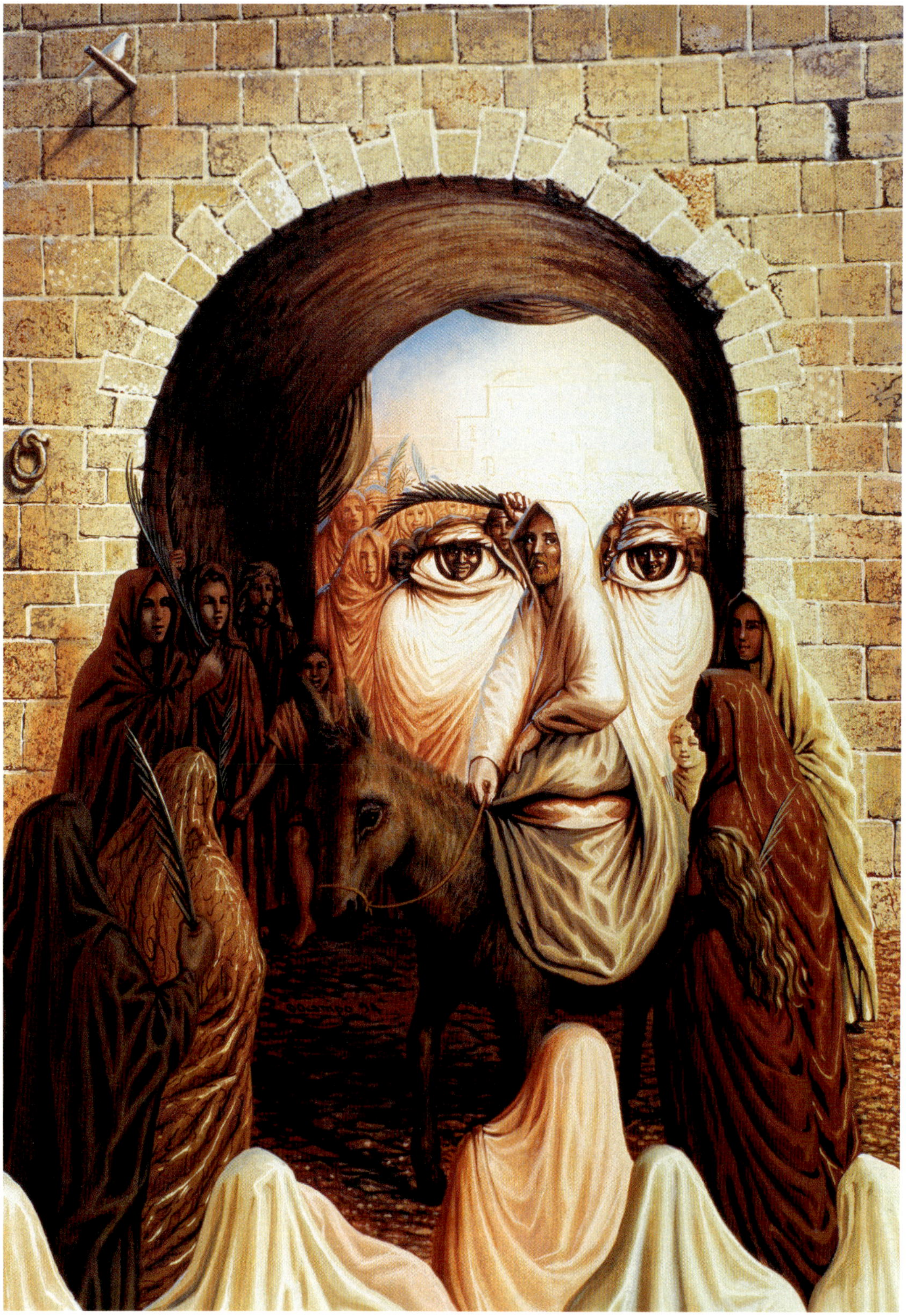

DOMINGO DE RAMOS 1994 (80 × 120)

Oil on canvas – Óleo sobre tela – Öl auf Leinwand – Huile sur toile

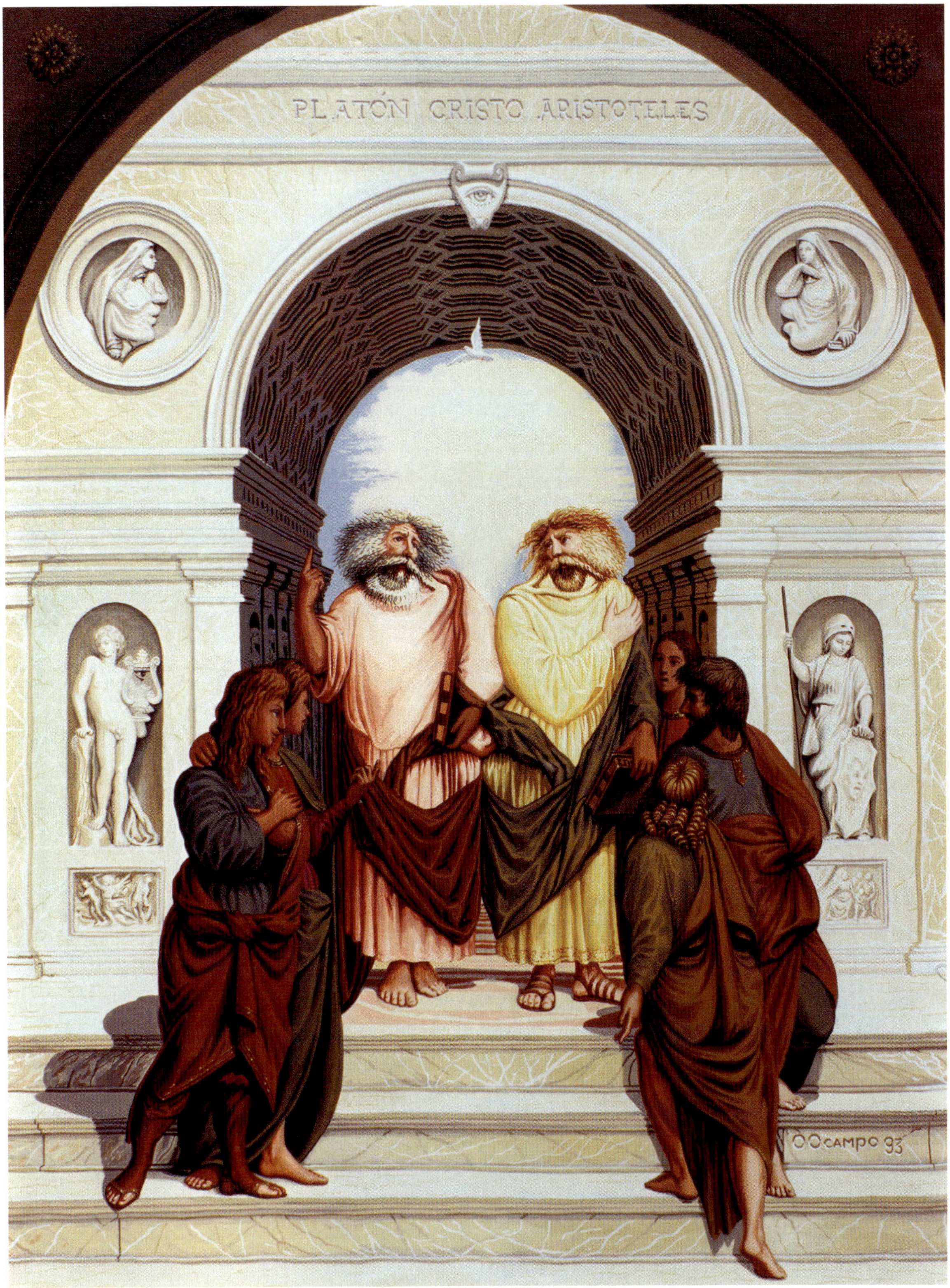

TRES FILÓSOFOS 1993 (80 × 100)

Oil on canvas – Óleo sobre tela – Öl auf Leinwand – Huile sur toile

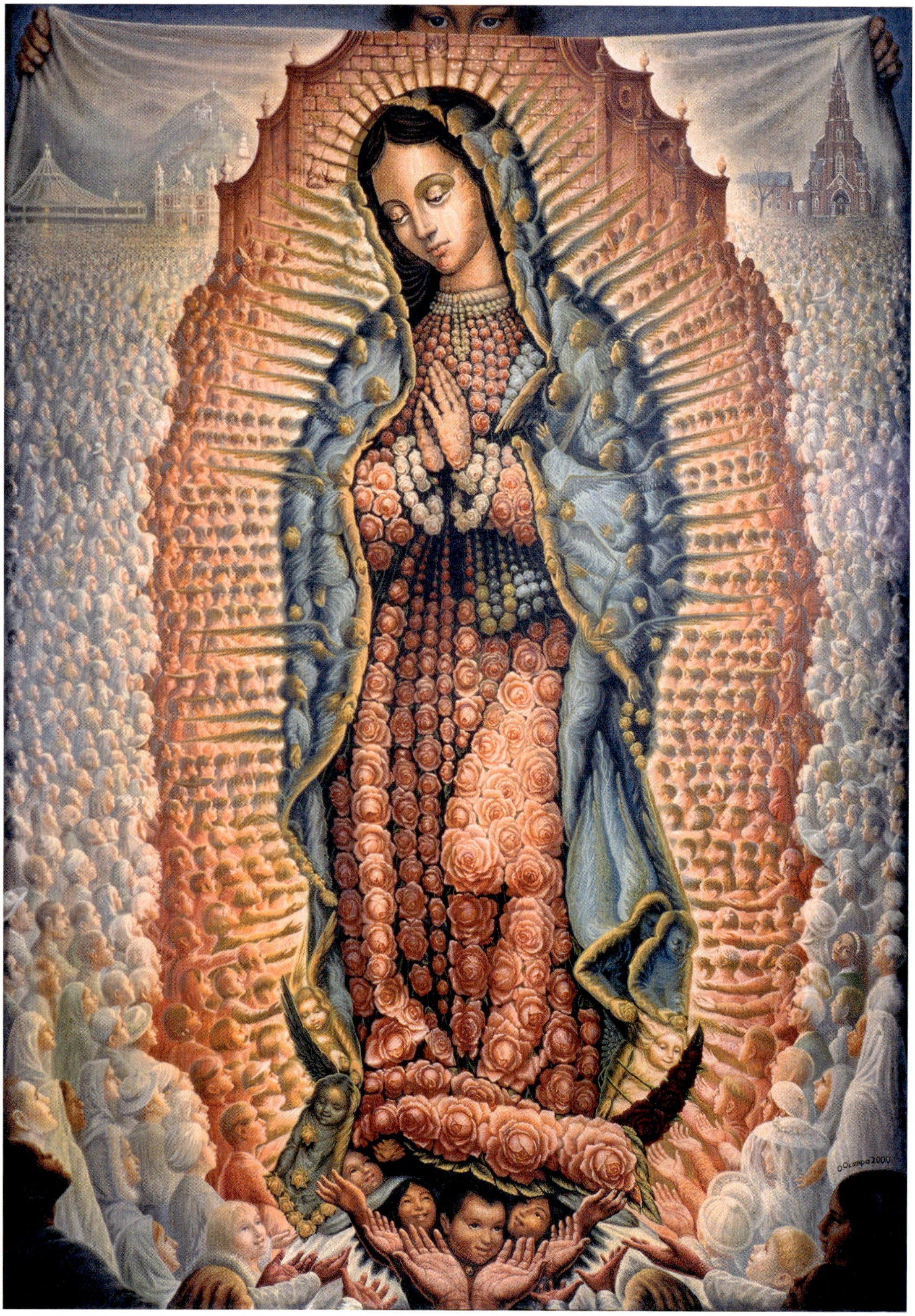

LOS DONES DE LA VIRGEN 200 (150 × 200)

Oil on canvas – Óleo sobre tela – Öl auf Leinwand – Huile sur toile

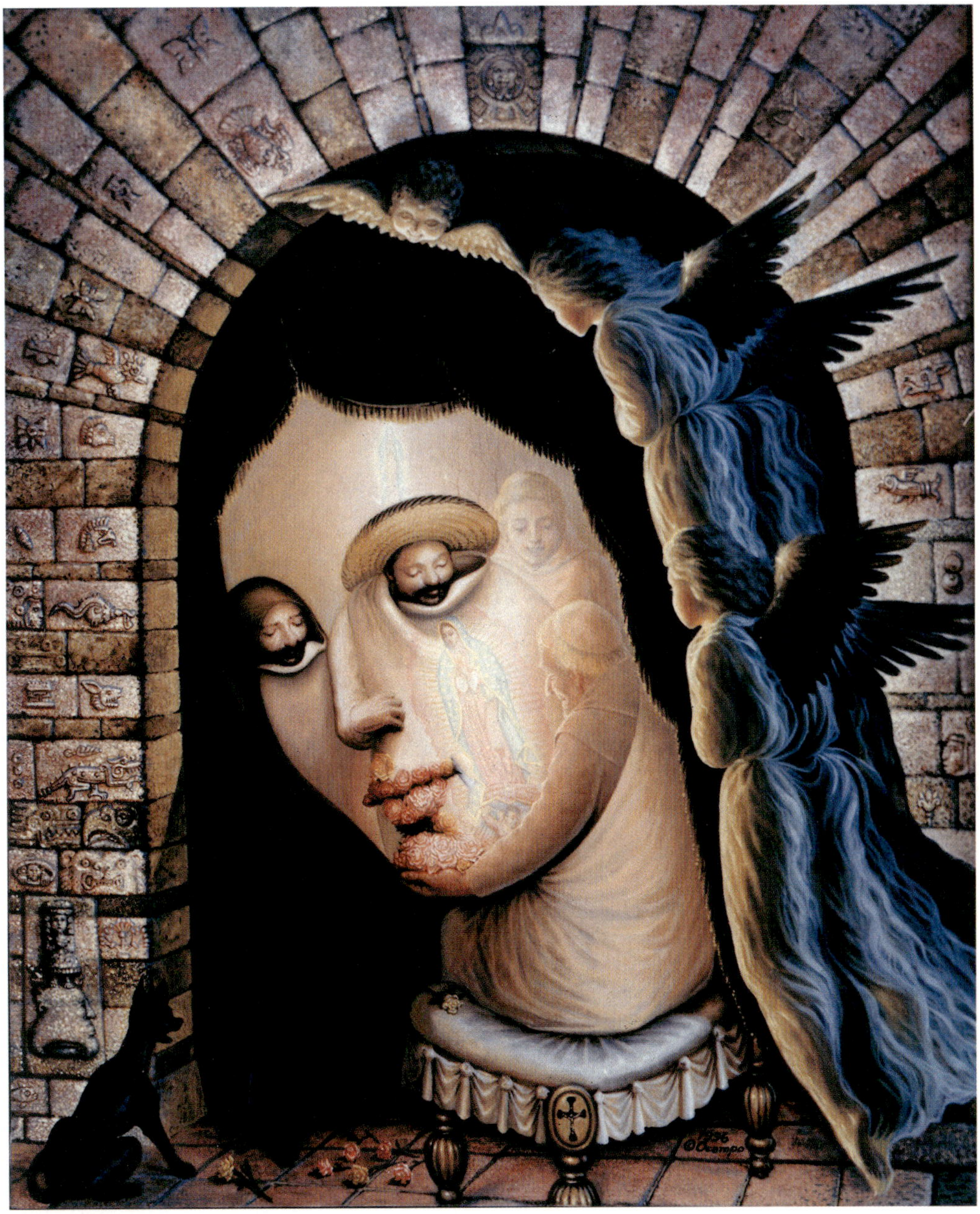

EL MILAGRO DE LAS ROSAS 1996 (100 × 120)

Oil on canvas – Óleo sobre tela – Öl auf Leinwand – Huile sur toile

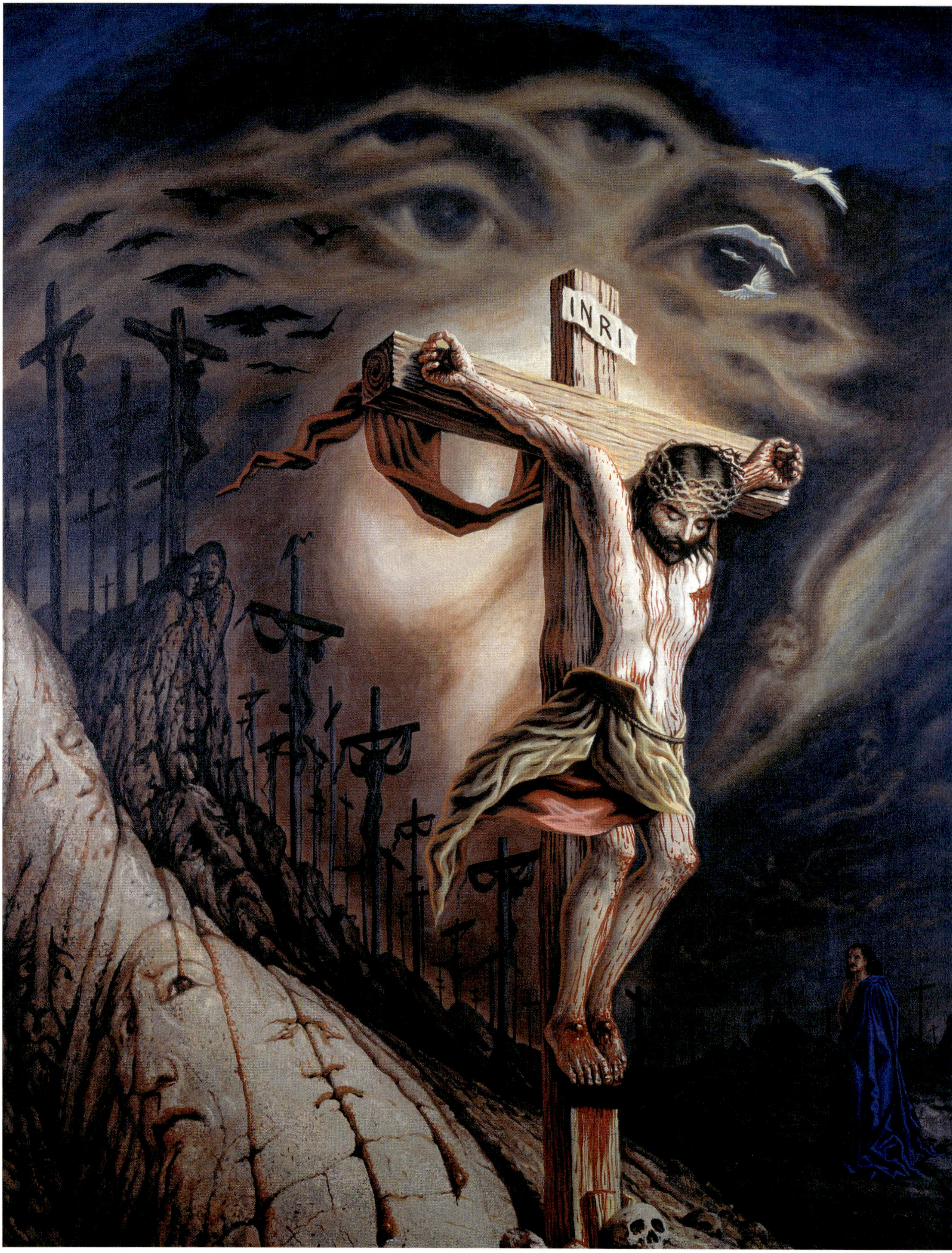
INRI

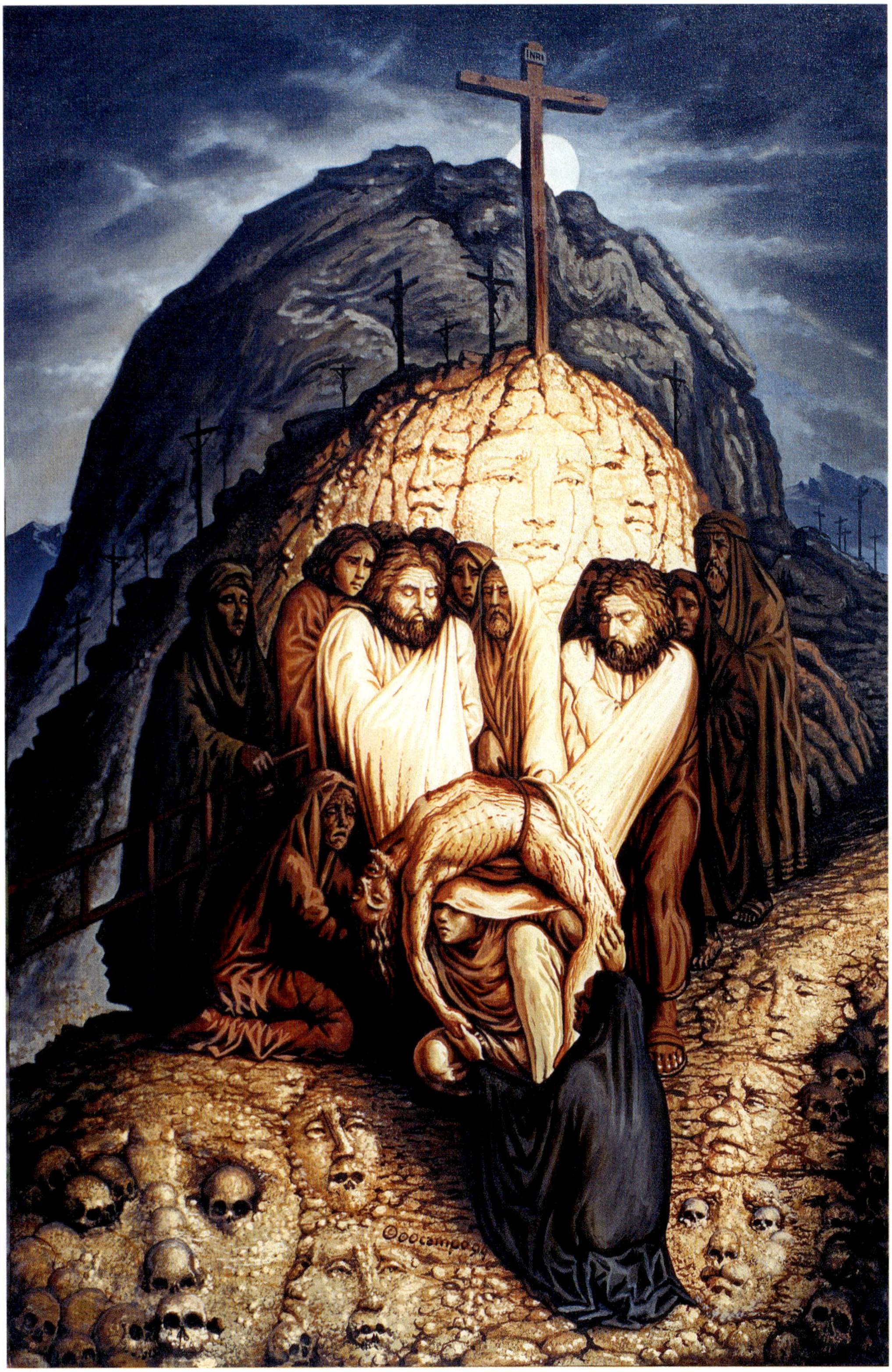

DESCENDIMIENTO 1995 (80 × 120)

Watercolor on paper – Acuarela sobre papel – Aquarell auf Papier – Aquarelle sur papier

EL CALVARIO 1995 (100 × 120)

Oil on canvas – Óleo sobre tela – Öl auf Leinwand – Huile sur toile

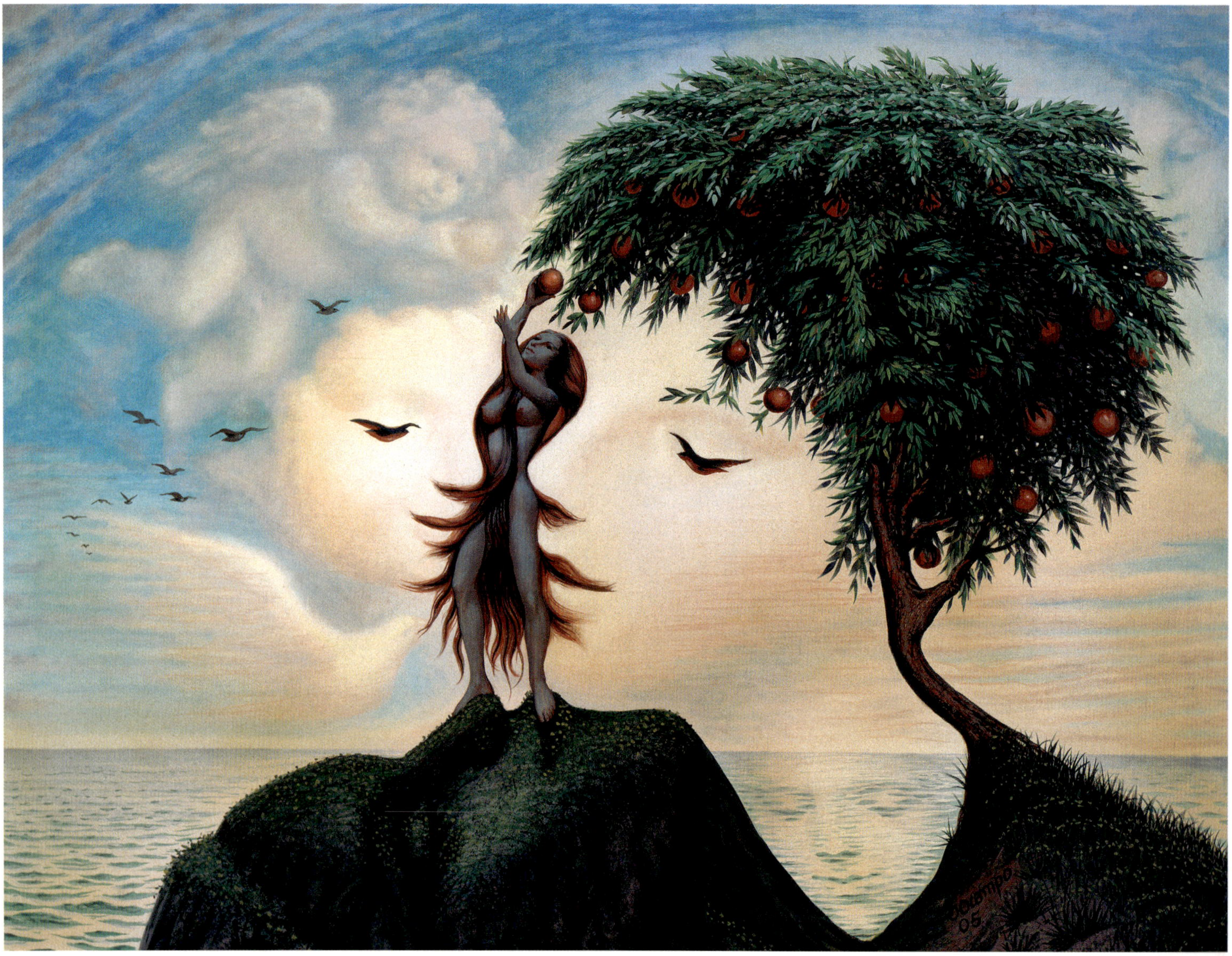

MANZANAS DEL AMOR 2005 (120 × 90)

Oil on canvas – Óleo sobre tela – Öl auf Leinwand – Huile sur toile

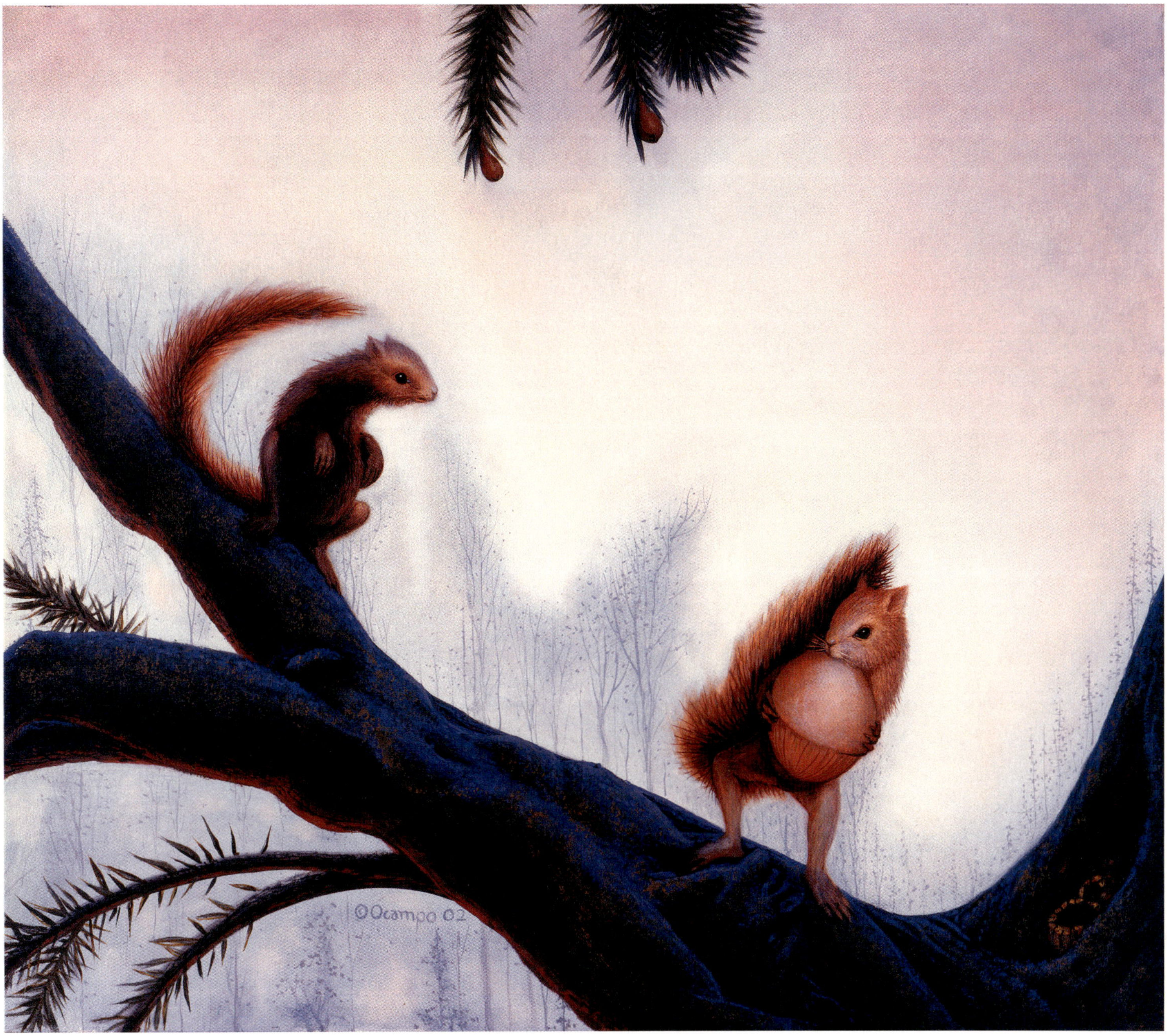

ARDILLAS EN EL ÁRBOL 2002 (110 × 90)

Oil on canvas – Óleo sobre tela – Öl auf Leinwand – Huile sur toile

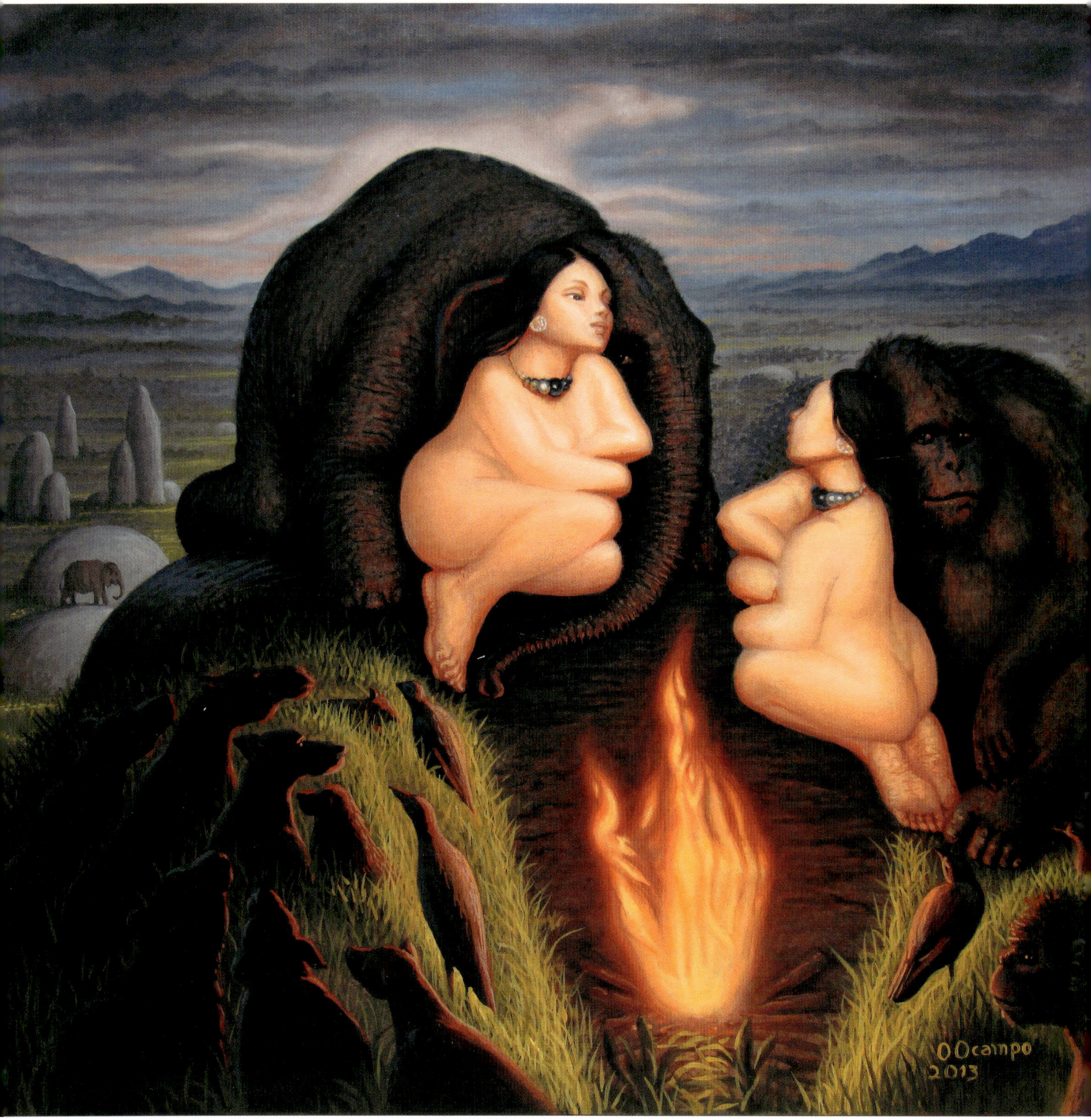

ANIMALERAS 2013 (84 × 67,5)

Oil on canvas – Óleo sobre tela – Öl auf Leinwand – Huile sur toile

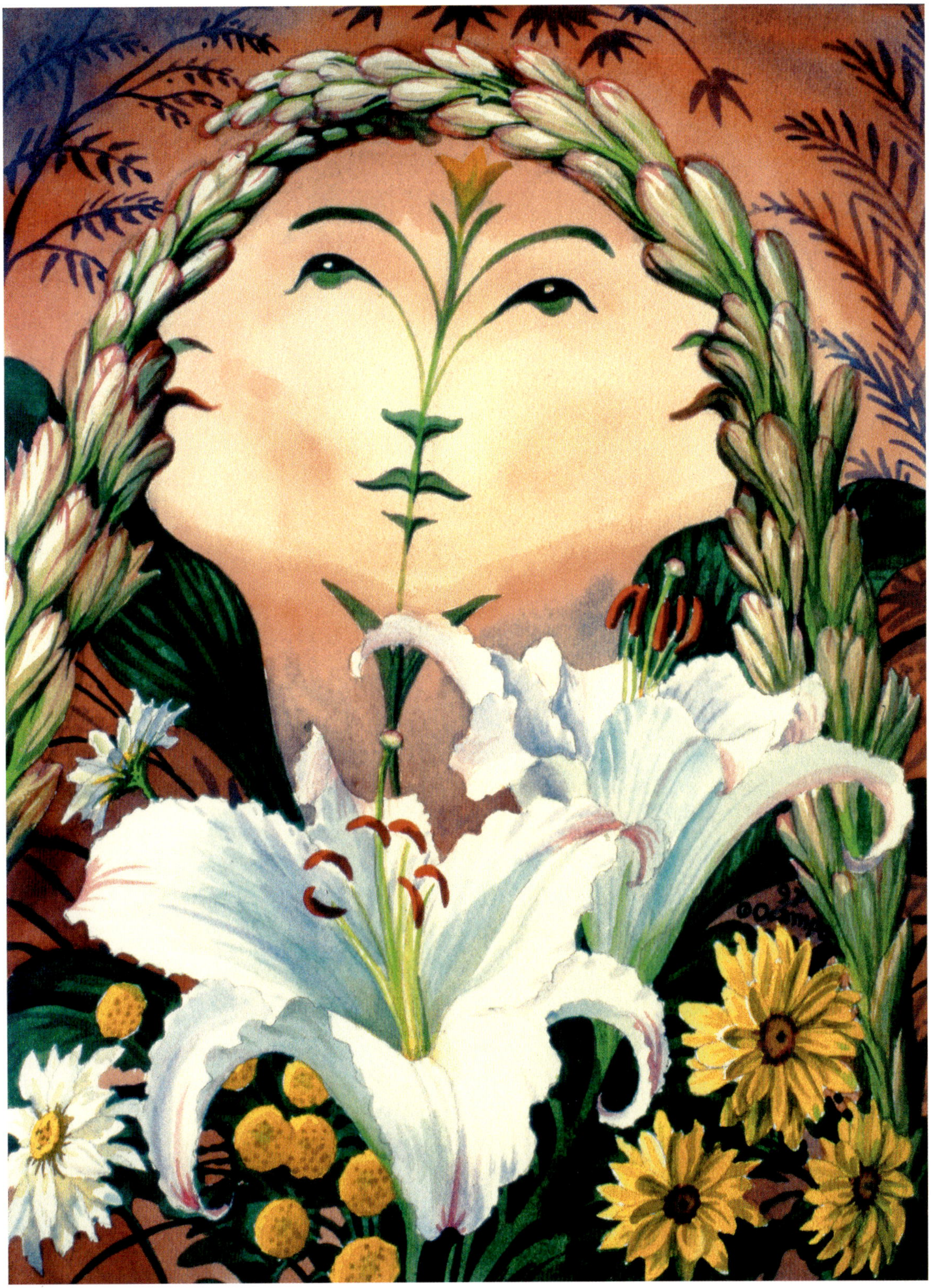

TRES CARAS DE FLOR 1997 (31 × 41)

Watercolor on paper – Acuarela sobre papel – Aquarell auf Papier – Aquarelle sur papier

Octavio Ocampo was born on February 28, 1943 in Celaya, Guanajuato. He is known for his unique style metamorphic. He has participated in over 80 solo exhibitions in Mexico and abroad as well as countless collective worldwide. Has more than 500 works of art and sculptural.

Octavio Ocampo nació el 28 de febrero de 1943 en la ciudad de Celaya, Guanajuato. Se le conoce por su peculiar estilo metamórfico. Ha participado en más de 80 exposiciones individuales en México y el extranjero, así como innumerables colectivas en todo el mundo. Cuenta con más de 500 obras plásticas y escultóricas.

Octavio Ocampo, geboren am 28. Februar 1943 in Celaya im mexikanischen Bundesstaat Guanajuato (GTO), hat sich mit seinem unvergleichlichen „metamorphischen„ Stil einen Namen gemacht. Er hat weltweit an über 80 Einzelausstellungen und zahllosen Sammelausstellungen teilgenommen und mehr als 500 Kunstwerke erschaffen.

Octavio Ocampo est né le 28 février 1943 à Celaya dans l'Etat de Guanajuato au Mexique. Il est célèbre pour son style unique qui fait de lui un maître des illusions optiques. Plus de 80 expositions lui ont déjà été consacrées au Mexique et à l'étranger – il a en outre participé à un très grand nombre d'expositions mixtes dans le monde entier. Son œuvre compte plus de 500 travaux artistiques et sculptures.

ACADEMIC
FORMACIÓN ACADÉMICA
KUNSTSTUDIUM
ÉTUDES D'ART

1952

Enrolled in the School of Plastic Arts of INBA, Celaya, Guanajuato, take classes with the sculptor and painter born in Querétaro, Don Salvador Zuniga.

Ingresa a la Escuela de Artes Plásticas del INBA, Celaya, GTO., toma clases con el escultor y pintor oriundo de Querétaro Don Salvador Zúñiga.

Ocampo besucht die INBA-Kunstakademie von Celaya und wird von dem Maler und Bildhauer Don Salvador Zúñiga unterrichtet.

Inscrit à l'Institut National des Beaux-Arts (INBA) de Celaya, Ocampo suit la classe du peintre et sculpteur Don Salvador Zúñiga.

1961—1965

At the suggestion of Maria Luisa ***la china*** Mendoza and Ruth Rivera, daughter of Diego Rivera, he moved to Mexico City to join the National School of Painting and Sculpture ***La Esmeralda*** INBA, Mexico City.

Por sugerencia de María Luisa ***La China*** Mendoza y de Ruth Rivera, hija de Diego Rivera, se traslada a la Ciudad de México para ingresar a la Escuela Nacional de Pintura y Escultura ***La Esmeralda*** INBA, México, D.F.

Auf Drängen von María Luisa ***La China*** Mendoza und Ruth Rivera, der Tochterdes Malers Diego Rivera, zieht er nach Mexiko-Stadt, um dort die Nationale Akademie für Malerei und Bildhauerei ***La Esmeralda*** zu besuchen.

Face à l'insistance de María Luisa ***La China*** Mendoza et de Ruth Rivera, la fille du peintre Diego Rivera, il part pour Mexico afin d'y poursuivre ses études à l'Académie Nationale de Peinture et Sculpture ***La Esmeralda.***

1971

He studied at the Art Institute of San Francisco, California, USA.

Estudia en el Art Institute de San Francisco, California, E.U.A.

Studium am San Francisco Art Institute in Kalifornien, USA

Études au San Francisco Art Institute en Californie, USA

SETS AND ACTION
ESCENOGRAFÍAS Y ACTUACIÓN
KULISSENBAU UND SCHAUSPIELEREI
DÉCORATEUR DE THÉÂTRE ET COMÉDIEN

Octavio Ocampo has a long experience as a set designer, costume designer and actor above his pictorial stage.

Octavio Ocampo cuenta con una larga experiencia como escenógrafo, vestuarista y actor que antecede a su etapa pictórica.

Octavio Ocampo sammelte Erfahrungen als Bühnenbildner, Kostümbildner und Schauspieler, bevor er sich ganz der Malerei zuwandte. Er war an folgenden Produktionen beteiligt:

Octavio Ocampo multiplie ses expériences en tant que décorateur de théâtre, costumier et comédien avant de se consacrer entièrement à la peinture. Il a participé aux productions suivantes :

1959—60

Play ***Las Salvajes Criaturas*** by Salvador Jaramillo in Celaya, Gto.

Obra teatral ***Las Salvajes Criaturas*** de Salvador Jaramillo en Celaya, Gto.

Las Salvajes Criaturas, Theaterstück von Salvador Jaramillo, Celaya

Las Salvajes Criaturas, pièce de théâtre de Salvador Jaramillo, Celaya

1960

Play ***Prohibido suicidarse en primavera*** by Alejandro Casona in Celaya, Gto.

Obra teatral ***Prohibido suicidarse en primavera*** de Alejandro Casona en Celaya, Gto.

Prohibido suicidarse en primavera, Theaterstück von Alejandro Casona, Celaya

Prohibido suicidarse en primavera, pièce de théâtre d'Alejandro Casona, Celaya

1964

Play ***El gran teatro del mundo*** by Don Pedro Calderón de la Barca in Tepoztlán, Mor.

Obra teatral ***El gran teatro del mundo*** de Don Pedro Calderón de la Barca en Tepoztlán, Mor.

El gran teatro del mundo, Theaterstück von Don Pedro Calderón de la Barca, Tepoztlán (MOR)

El gran teatro del mundo, pièce de théâtre de Don Pedro Calderón de la Barca, Tepoztlán (MOR)

1964

Play ***La pastorela de Metepec*** by Miguel Sabido in Tepotzotlán, Edomex.

Obra teatral ***La pastorela de Metepec*** de Miguel Sabido en Tepotzotlán, Edomex.

La pastorela de Metepec, Theaterstück von Miguel Sabido, Tepotzotlán (MEX)

La pastorela de Metepec, pièce de théâtre de Miguel Sabido, Tepotzotlán (MEX)

1964

Play ***Amor Médico*** by Del Valle Indán in Teatro de la Universidad in México, D.F.

Obra teatral ***Amor Médico*** de Del Valle Indán en el Teatro de la Universidad en México, D.F.

Amor Médico, Theaterstück von Del Valle Indán, Uni-Theater Mexiko-Stadt

Amor Médico, pièce de théâtre de Del Valle Indán, Théâtre universitaire, Mexico

1965

Play ***Escuela de Cortesanos*** by Wilberto Canton in Palacio de la Inquisición, México, D.F.

Obra teatral ***Escuela de Cortesanos*** de Wilberto Canton en el Palacio de la Inquisición, México, D.F.

Escuela de Cortesanos, Theaterstück von Wilberto Canton, Palacio de la Inquisición, Mexiko-Stadt

Escuela de Cortesanos, pièce de théâtre de Wilberto Canton, Palacio de la Inquisición, Mexico

1965

Play ***Ah, Wilderness!*** by Eugene O´Neill in México, D.F.

Obra teatral ***Ah, Wilderness!*** de Eugene O´Neill en México, D.F.

Ah, Wilderness!, Theaterstück von Eugene O'Neill, Mexiko-Stadt

Ah, Wilderness!, pièce de théâtre d'Eugene O'Neill, Mexico

1965—1970

Accepts job as head of the Department of ***Film Studies Set*** in America, where he made over 120 films.

Acepta en trabajo de Jefe del Departamento de Escenografía en los ***Estudios Cinematográficos América***, en donde realiza más de 120 películas.

Ocampo übernimmt die Leitung der Szenenbild-Abteilung der ***Estudios América*** und wirkt an über 120 Filmen mit.

Ocampo prend la direction du ressort décoration-scénographie de l'***Estudios América*** et apporte sa contribution dans plus de 120 films.

1966

Play ***Por Lucrecia*** by Jean Jiraudoux in Centro Cultural Coyoacán, México, D.F.

Obra teatral ***Por Lucrecia*** de Jean Jiraudoux en el Centro Cultural Coyoacán, México, D.F.

Por Lucrecia, Theaterstück von Jean Jiraudoux, Centro Cultural Coyoacán, Mexiko-Stadt

Por Lucrecia (Pour Lucrèce), pièce de théâtre de Jean Giraudoux, Centro Cultural Coyoacán, Mexico

1966

Play ***La Gatomaquia*** by Félix Lope de Vega in Teatro Jiménez Rueda, México, D.F.

Obra teatral ***La Gatomaquia*** de Félix Lope de Vega en el Teatro Jiménez Rueda, México, D.F.

La Gatomaquia, Theaterstück von Félix Lope de Vega, Teatro Jiménez Rueda, Mexiko-Stadt

La Gatomaquia, pièce de théâtre de Félix Lope de Vega, Teatro Jiménez Rueda, Mexico

1966

Participation as a set designer for the theater recital culmination of the festivities to celebrate the first centenary of the ***Teatro Degollado*** alongside actors Naciso Busquets, Mary Douglas and Ignacio Lopez Tarso.

Participación como escenógrafo durante el recital de teatro de culminación de los festejos para celebrar el Primer Centenario del ***Teatro Degollado*** junto a los actores Naciso Busquets, María Douglas e Ignacio López Tarso.

Anlässlich der Feierlichkeiten zum 100. Geburtstag des ***Teatro Degollado*** gestalten die Schauspieler Naciso Busquets, María Douglas und Ignacio López Tarso ein Recital, zu dem Ocampo das Bühnenbild liefert.

À l'occasion des 100 ans du ***Teatro Degollado,*** les comédiens Naciso Busquets, María Douglas et Ignacio López Tarso organisent un récital pour lequel Ocampo réalise le décor de scène.

1966

Film ***Los Caifanes*** by Juan Ibañez, where it participates as an actor and stage designer

Película ***Los Caifanes*** de Juan Ibañez en donde participa como actor y escenógrafo

Los Caifanes, Film von Juan Ibañez, in dem Ocampo auch eine Rolle übernimmt

Los Caifanes, film de Juan Ibañez, dans lequel Ocampo agit aussi en tant qu'acteur

1967

Play ***Te juro Juana que tengo ganas …*** by Emilio Carballido in México, D.F.

Obra teatral ***Te juro Juana que tengo ganas …*** de Emilio Carballido en México, D.F.

Te juro Juana que tengo ganas …, Theaterstück von Emilio Carballido, Mexiko-Stadt

Te juro Juana que tengo ganas …, pièce de théâtre d'Emilio Carballido, Mexico

1967

Play ***La Ronda de la Hechizada*** by Hugo Argüelles in México, D.F.

Obra teatral ***La Ronda de la Hechizada*** de Hugo Argüelles en México, D.F.

La Ronda de la Hechizada, Theaterstück von Hugo Argüelles, Mexiko-Stadt

La Ronda de la Hechizada, pièce de théâtre d'Hugo Argüelles, Mexico

1968

Film ***El Golfo*** by Juan Ibáñez

Película ***El Golfo*** de Juan Ibáñez

El Golfo, Film von Juan Ibañez

El Golfo, film de Juan Ibañez

1969

Soap opera ***El retrato de Dorian Gray*** by Oscar Wilde where does the picture that gave the effect of aging of Dorian Gray.

Telenovela ***El retrato de Dorian Gray*** de Oscar Wilde en donde realiza el retrato que dieron el efecto de envejecimiento de Dorian Gray.

Für die Telenovela nach der Vorlage von Oscar Wildes ***Bildnis des Dorian Gray*** malt Octavio Ocampo das Gemälde, das Grays Alterungsprozess zeigt.

Pour le feuilleton télévisé (telenovela) inspiré du roman d'Oscar Wilde ***Le portrait de Dorian Gray,*** Octavio Ocampo peint la toile qui montre le processus de vieillissement de Gray.

1969

Film ***El Topo*** by Alejandro Jodorovsky

Película ***El Topo*** de Alejandro Jodorovsky

El Topo, Film von Alejandro Jodorowsky

El Topo, film d'Alejandro Jodorowsky

1969

Film ***El Quelite*** by Jorge Fons

Película ***El Quelite*** de Jorge Fons

El Quelite, Film von Jorge Fons

El Quelite, film de Jorge Fons

1969

Film ***Santa*** de Emilio Gómez Muriel

Película ***Santa*** de Emilio Gómez Muriel

Santa, Film von Emilio Gómez Muriel

Santa, film d'Emilio Gómez Muriel

1969

Film ***El medio pelo*** de Carlos Velo

Película ***El medio pelo*** de Carlos Velo

El medio pelo, Film von Carlos Velo

El medio pelo, film de Carlos Velo

1970—1975

Independently performed sets, costumes and exhibits for movies, and several plays.

De manera independiente realiza escenografías, vestuario y participaciones para películas, además de diferentes obras de teatro.

Ocampo entwirft freiberuflich Kulissen und Kostüme für Film und Theater und wirkt immer wieder auch als Schauspieler mit.

Ocampo se met à son compte ; il crée des décors de scène et des costumes pour le cinéma et le théâtre, tout en intervenant aussi régulièrement comme acteur/comédien.

1970

Film ***Rosas Blancas para mi Hermana Negra*** by Abel Salazar

Película ***Rosas Blancas para mi Hermana Negra*** de Abel Salazar

Rosas Blancas para mi Hermana Negra, Film von Abel Salazar

Rosas Blancas para mi Hermana Negra, film d'Abel Salazar

1970

Film ***Paraíso*** by Luis Alcoriza

Película ***Paraíso*** de Luis Alcoriza

Paraíso, Film von Luis Alcoriza

Paraíso, film de Luis Alcoriza

1971

Film ***Tú, Yo y Nosotros*** by Guillermo Murray

Película ***Tú, Yo y Nosotros*** de Guillermo Murray

Tú, Yo y Nosotros, Film von Guillermo Murray

Tú, Yo y Nosotros, film de Guillermo Murray

1971

Film ***El Elegido*** by Servando González

Película ***El Elegido*** de Servando González

El Elegido, Film von Servando González

El Elegido, film de Servando González

1971

Film ***El Extraño Laberinto*** by Fernando Sánchez Mayans

Película ***El Extraño Laberinto*** de Fernando Sánchez Mayans

El Extraño Laberinto, Film von Fernando Sánchez Mayans

El Extraño Laberinto, film de Fernando Sánchez Mayans

1971

Film ***Apolinar*** by Julio Castillo

Película ***Apolinar*** de Julio Castillo

Apolinar, Film von Julio Castillo

Apolinar, film de Julio Castillo

1972

Film ***Vals sin fin*** by Rubén Broido en donde participa como actor

Película ***Vals sin fin*** de Rubén Broido en donde participa como actor

Vals sin fin, Film von Rubén Broido, bei dem Ocampo auch mitspielt

Vals sin fin, film de Rubén Broido, dans lequel Ocampo joue également

1972

Film ***El Elegido*** by Servando González

Película ***El Elegido*** de Servando González

El Elegido, Film von Servando González

El Elegido, film de Servando González

1972

Play ***El evangelio según San Mateo*** by Julio Castillo

Obra teatral ***El evangelio según San Mateo*** de Julio Castillo

El evangelio según San Mateo, Theaterstück von Julio Castillo

El evangelio según San Mateo, pièce de théâtre de Julio Castillo

1972

Film ***Apolinar*** by Julio Castillo

Película ***Apolinar*** de Julio Castillo

Apolinar, Film von Julio Castillo

Apolinar, film de Julio Castillo

1972

Film ***Victoria*** by José Luis Ibáñez

Película ***Victoria*** de José Luis Ibáñez

Victoria, Film von José Luis Ibáñez

Victoria, film de José Luis Ibáñez

1973

Play ***Los Insectos*** by Josef Capek in Teatro Universidad in México, D.F.

Obra teatral ***Los Insectos*** de Josef Capek en el Teatro Universidad en México, D.F.

Los insectos, Theaterstück von Josef Capek, Uni-Theater Mexiko-Stadt

Los insectos, pièce de théâtre de Josef Capek, Théâtre universitaire, Mexico

1973

Photo Novel ***Anillo de Amor*** in revista ***Chicas*** in México, D.F.

Foto Novela ***Anillo de Amor*** en la revista ***Chicas*** en México, D.F.

Anillo de Amor, Fotoroman in der mexikanischen Zeitschrift ***Chicas***

Anillo de Amor, roman-photo dans le magazine mexicain ***Chicas***

1973

Film ***El Padrino Lamberthier*** by Héctor Gómez

El Padrino Lamberthier de Héctor Gómez

El Padrino Lamberthier, Film von Héctor Gómez

El Padrino Lamberthier, film d'Héctor Gómez

1974

Soap opera ***El Manantial del milagro*** by Julio Castillo, where shares credit with Julissa and Lucia Tovar.

Telenovela ***El Manantial del milagro*** de Julio Castillo, en donde comparte créditos junto a Julissa y Lucía Tovar.

El Manantial del milagro, Telenovela (Regie: Julio Castillo)

El Manantial del milagro, feuilleton télévisé/telenovela (mise en scène : Julio Castillo)

1974

Play "***Orfeo 2000***" by Julio Castillo

Obra teatral "***Orfeo 2000***" de Julio Castillo

Orfeo 2000, Theaterstück von Julio Castillo

Orfeo 2000, pièce de théâtre de Julio Castillo

1975

Play ***El Pájaro Azul*** by Mauricio Meterlinck directed by Julio Castillo in México, D.F.

Obra teatral ***El Pájaro Azul*** de Mauricio Meterlinck dirigido por Julio Castillo en México, D.F.

El Pájaro Azul, Theaterstück von Mauricio Meterlinck (Regie: Julio Castillo), Mexiko-Stadt

El Pájaro Azul, pièce de théâtre de Mauricio Meterlinck (mise en scène : Julio Castillo), Mexico

1975

Play ***Jesucristo Superestrella*** by Andrew Lloyd Webber in Teatro Ferrocarrilero, México, D.F.

Obra teatral ***Jesucristo Superestrella*** de Andrew Lloyd Webber en el Teatro Ferrocarrilero, México, D.F.

Jesus Christ Superstar von Andrew Lloyd Webber, Teatro Ferrocarrilero, Mexiko-Stadt

Jesus Christ Superstar d'Andrew Lloyd Webber, Teatro Ferrocarrilero, Mexico

1976

Play ***Heroica*** by Osvaldo Dragún in México, D.F.

Obra teatral ***Heroica*** de Osvaldo Dragún en México, D.F.

Heroica, Theaterstück von Osvaldo Dragún, Mexiko-Stadt

Heroica, pièce de théâtre d'Osvaldo Dragún, Mexico

1977

Film ***El reventón*** by Archivaldo Burns

Película ***El reventón*** de Archivaldo Burns

El reventón, Film von Archivaldo Burns

El reventón, film d'Archivaldo Burns

MURAL PAINTING
MURALES
WANDGEMÄLDE
PEINTURE MURALE

1958

Las artes de México in Escuela Preparatoria y Profesional in Celaya, Gto.

Las artes de México en la Escuela Preparatoria y Profesional de Celaya, Gto.

Las artes de México in der Oberschule (Escuela Preparatoria y Profesional) von Celaya

Las artes de México à l'école préparatoire et professionnelle (Escuela Preparatoria y Profesional) de Celaya

1960

Stair access to the mayor of Celaya, Guanajuato, alluding to the theme of Mexican Independence and Revolution

Escalinata del acceso a la Presidencia Municipal de Celaya, Gto., sobre la Independencia y Revolución

Treppenaufgang des Rathauses von Celaya; thematische Auseinandersetzung mit dem mexikanischen Unabhängigkeitskrieg

Escalier de la Mairie de Celaya ; réflexion thématique sur la guerre d'indépendance du Mexique

1962

Santuario de Guadalupe in Celaya, Gto.

Santuario de Guadalupe en Celaya, Gto.

Wallfahrtskirche der Madonna von Guadalupe, Celaya

Église de pèlerinage de Notre-Dame de Guadalupe, Celaya

1978

Morelos Intelectual in Salón Morelos in the National Palace, México, D.F.

Morelos Intelectual en el Salón Morelos de Palacio Nacional, México, D.F.

Morelos Intelectual, Salón Morelos, Nationalpalast, Mexiko-Stadt

Morelos Intelectual, Salón Morelos, Palais National (Palacio Nacional), Mexico

1980

New murals in the Stair access to the mayor of Celaya, Guanajuato: ***Hidalgo, Conjurados de Querétaro y Batallas por la Independencia***; ***Morelos y abrazos de Acatempan***; ***Madero, retrato de grupo de revolucionarios y Batallas de Celaya***; ***Carranza, ferrocarril con revolucionarios y Álvaro Obregón*** y el plafón ***Alegorías del pueblo, de la Independencia y la Revolución***

Nuevos murales en el acceso a la Presidencia Municipal de Celaya, Gto.: ***Hidalgo, Conjurados de Querétaro y Batallas por la Independencia***; ***Morelos y abrazos de Acatempan***; ***Madero, retrato de grupo de revolucionarios y Batallas de Celaya***; ***Carranza, ferrocarril con revolucionarios y Álvaro Obregón*** y el plafón ***Alegorías del pueblo, de la Independencia y la Revolución***

Neue Wandbilder im Treppenaufgang des Rathauses von Celaya: ***Hidalgo, Conjurados de Querétaro y Batallas por la Independencia***, ***Morelos y abrazos de Acatempan***, ***Madero, retrato de grupo de revolucionarios y Batallas de Celaya***, ***Carranza, ferrocarril con revolucionarios y Álvaro Obregón*** und das Deckengemälde ***Alegorías del pueblo, de la Independencia y la Revolución***

Nouvelles peintures murales dans l'escalier de la Mairie de Celaya : ***Hidalgo, Conjurados de Querétaro y Batallas por la Independencia, Morelos y abrazos de Acatempan, Madero, retrato de grupo de revolucionarios y Batallas de Celaya, Carranza, ferrocarril con revolucionarios y Álvaro Obregón*** et la peinture du plafond ***Alegorías del pueblo, de la Independencia y la Revolución***

1982

Felinos in Grossenhacher Oil Company, Harlingen, Texas

Felinos en Grossenhacher Oil Company en Harlingen, Texas

Felinos, Grossenbacher Oil Company, Harlingen, Texas

Felinos, Grossenbacher Oil Company, Harlingen, Texas

1985

La Evolución del Hombre in Instituto Tecnológico de Celaya, Gto.

La Evolución del Hombre en el Instituto Tecnológico de Celaya, Gto.

La Evolución del Hombre, Instituto Tecnológico de Celaya (ITC), Celaya

La Evolución del Hombre, Instituto Tecnológico de Celaya (ITC), Celaya

1988

Unión de Trabajadores Mexicanos in Confederación Nacional de Organizaciones Populares (CNOP), México, D.F.

Unión de Trabajadores Mexicanos en la Confederación Nacional de Organizaciones Populares (CNOP), México, D.F.

Unión de Trabajadores Mexicanos, Sitz der Confederación Nacional de Organizaciones Populares (CNOP), Mexiko-Stadt

Unión de Trabajadores Mexicanos, siège de la Confederación Nacional de Organizaciones Populares (CNOP), Mexico

2002

José Alfredo Jiménez in Casa Museo José Alfredo Jiménez, Dolores Hidalgo, Gto.

José Alfredo Jiménez en la Casa Museo José Alfredo Jiménez, Dolores Hidalgo, Gto.

José Alfredo Jiménez, Casa Museo José Alfredo Jiménez, Dolores Hidalgo (GTO)

José Alfredo Jiménez, Casa Museo José Alfredo Jiménez, Dolores Hidalgo (GTO)

SOLO EXHIBITIONS
EXHIBICIONES INDIVIDUALES
EINZELAUSSTELLUNGEN
EXPOSITIONS EN EXCLUSIVITÉ

1971

Alianza Francesa de México, México, D.F.

Alianza Francesa de México, México, D.F.

Alianza Francesa de México, Mexiko-Stadt

Alianza Francesa de México, Mexico

1982

Palacio Legislativo de Guanajuato, Gto.

Palacio Legislativo de Guanajuato, Gto.

Palacio Legislativo, Guanajuato (GTO)

Palacio Legislativo, Guanajuato (GTO)

1983

Sings Gallery, New York, E.U.A.

Sings Gallery, New York, E.U.A.

Sings Gallery, New York

Sings Gallery, New York

1984

Pon Art Gallery, Los Angeles, California, E.U.A.

Pon Art Gallery, Los Angeles, California, E.U.A.

Pon Art Gallery, Los Angeles, Kalifornien, USA

Pon Art Gallery, Los Angeles, Californie, USA

1984

Instituto Tecnológico de Celaya, Celaya, Gto.

Instituto Tecnológico de Celaya, Celaya, Gto.

Instituto Tecnológico de Celaya (ITC), Celaya

Instituto Tecnológico de Celaya (ITC), Celaya

1985

House of Culture ***Enrique Ramírez***, México, D.F.

Casa de Cultura ***Enrique Ramírez***, México, D.F.

Casa de Cultura ***Enrique Ramírez***, Mexiko-Stadt

Casa de Cultura ***Enrique Ramírez***, Mexico

1985

Congreso Nacional de Arquitectos, Celaya, Gto.

Congreso Nacional de Arquitectos, Celaya, Gto.

Nationaler Architektenkongress, Celaya

Congrès National d'Architecture, Celaya

1986
Palacio Legislativo, México, D.F.
Palacio Legislativo, México, D.F.
Palacio Legislativo, Mexiko-Stadt
Palacio Legislativo, Mexico

1987
Gallery ***Las Brisas***, Acapulco, Gro.
Galería ***Las Brisas***, Acapulco, Gro.
Galerie ***Las Brisas***, Acapulco (GRO)
Galerie ***Las Brisas***, Acapulco (GRO)

1987
Buque Motor ***Lerma***, Yokohama, Japón
Buque Motor ***Lerma***, Yokohama, Japón
Frachtschiff ***Lerma***, Yokohama, Japan
Cargo ***Lerma***, Yokohama, Japon

1989
Allende Institute, San Miguel de Allende, Gto.
Instituto Allende, San Miguel de Allende, Gto.
Allende-Institut, San Miguel de Allende (GTO)
Allende-Institut, San Miguel de Allende (GTO)

1989
Burton Gallery, Los Angeles, California, E.U.A.
Burton Gallery, Los Angeles, California, E.U.A.
Burton Gallery, Los Angeles, Kalifornien, USA
Burton Gallery, Los Angeles, Californie, USA

1989
Jimmy Carter Museum, Atlanta, Georgia, E.U.A.
Museo Jimmy Carter, Atlanta, Georgia, E.U.A.
Jimmy Carter Museum, Atlanta, Georgia, USA
Jimmy Carter Museum, Atlanta, Géorgie, USA

1989
Museo Iconográfico del Quijote, Guanajuato, Gto
Museo Iconográfico del Quijote, Guanajuato, Gto.
Museo Iconográfico del Quijote, Guanajuato (GTO)
Museo Iconográfico del Quijote, Guanajuato (GTO)

1989
Gallery ***Galileo***, México, D.F.
Galería ***Galileo***, México, D.F.
Galerie ***Galileo*** , Mexiko-Stadt
Galerie ***Galileo***, Mexico

1989
Gallery ***La Alameda***, Celaya, Gto.
Galería ***La Alameda***, Celaya, Gto.
Galerie ***La Alameda***, Celaya
Galerie ***La Alameda***, Celaya

1990
Casa del Diezmo, Celaya, Gto.
Casa del Diezmo, Celaya, Gto.
Casa del Diezmo, Celaya
Casa del Diezmo, Celaya

1990
Escuela Preparatoria de Celaya, Celaya, Gto.
Escuela Preparatoria de Celaya, Celaya, Gto.
Oberschule (Escuela Preparatoria) von Celaya
École préparatoire (Escuela Preparatoria) de Celaya

1991
Art Museum, Brownsville, Texas, E.U.A.
Museo de Arte, Brownsville, Texas, E.U.A.
Kunstmuseum Brownsville, Texas, USA
Musée d'art de Brownsville, Texas, USA

1991
Guanajuato University, Gto.
Universidad de Guanajuato, Gto.
Universität Guanajuato (GTO)
Université Guanajuato (GTO)

1991
Ashland University, Oregon, E.U.A.
Universidad de Ashland, Oregon, E.U.A.
Ashland University, Oregon, USA
Ashland University, Oregon, USA

1991
Tlalpan House of Culture, México, D.F.
Casa de la Cultura de Tlalpan, México, D.F.
Casa de la Cultura Tlalpan, Mexiko-Stadt
Casa de la Cultura Tlalpan, Mexico

1991
Gallery of Jesus, Los Angeles, California, E.U.A.
Galería de Jesús, Los Angeles, California, E.U.A.
Gallery of Jesus, Los Angeles, Kalifornien, USA
Gallery of Jesus, Los Angeles, Californie, USA

1992
Gallery ***Las Brisas***, Acapulco, Gro.
Galería ***Las Brisas***, Acapulco, Gro.
Galerie ***Las Brisas***, Acapulco (GRO)
Galerie ***Las Brisas***, Acapulco (GRO)

1993
Casa de la Cultura, León, Gto.
Casa de la Cultura, León, Gto.
Casa de la Cultura, León (GTO)
Casa de la Cultura, León (GTO)

1993
Palacio Legislativo de Guanajuato, Gto,
Palacio Legislativo de Guanajuato, Gto.
Palacio Legislativo, Guanajuato (GTO)
Palacio Legislativo, Guanajuato (GTO)

1993
Gallery ***Arte para todos***, Tepoztlán, Mor.
Galería ***Arte para todos***, Tepoztlán, Mor.
Galerie ***Arte para todos***, Tepoztlán (MOR)
Galerie ***Arte para todos***, Tepoztlán (MOR)

1993
Casa de San José, San Juan, Puerto Rico
Casa de San José, San Juan, Puerto Rico
Casa de San José, San Juan, Puerto Rico
Casa de San José, San Juan, Puerto Rico

1994
Salón de Cabildos, Central Departament, México, D.F.
Salón de Cabildos, Departamento Central, México, D.F.
Salón de Cabildos, Departamento Central, Mexiko-Stadt
Salón de Cabildos, Departamento Central, Mexico

1995
Gallery ***Arte para Todos***, Cuernavaca, Mor.
Galería ***Arte para Todos***, Cuernavaca, Mor.
Galerie ***Arte para Todos***, Cuernavaca (MOR)
Galerie ***Arte para Todos***, Cuernavaca (MOR)

1995
Casa de la Cultura, Celaya, Gto.
Casa de la Cultura, Celaya, Gto.
Casa de la Cultura, Celaya
Casa de la Cultura, Celaya

1995
Archivo Histórico del Estado, Pachuca, Hgo.
Archivo Histórico del Estado, Pachuca, Hgo.
Historisches Staatsarchiv, Pachuca (HGO)
Archives historiques de la ville, Pachuca (HGO)

1995
Universitary Museum, Puebla, Pue.
Museo Universitario, Puebla, Pue.
Universitätsmuseum, Puebla (PUE)
Musée universitaire, Puebla (PUE)

1996
Cozumel Island Museum, Q.Roo, Mex.
Museo de la Isla de Cozumel, Q.Roo.
Museum Isla Cozumel (ROO)
Museum Isla Cozumel (ROO)

1996
Galería del ITESM, Campus Ciudad de México, D.F.
Galería del ITESM, Campus Ciudad de México, D.F.
ITESM-Galerie, Campus Ciudad de México, Mexiko-Stadt
ITESM-Galerie, Campus Ciudad de México, Mexico

1996
Museo Histórico, Córdoba, Ver.
Museo Histórico, Córdoba, Ver.
Historisches Museum, Córdoba (VER)
Musée historique, Córdoba (VER)

1996
Palacio Legislativo, Aguascalientes, Ags.
Palacio Legislativo, Aguascalientes, Ags.
Palacio Legislativo, Aguascalientes (AGS)
Palacio Legislativo, Aguascalientes (AGS)

1996
Palacio de Gobierno, Hermosillo, Son.
Palacio de Gobierno, Hermosillo, Son.
Palacio de Gobierno, Hermosillo (SON)
Palacio de Gobierno, Hermosillo (SON)

1996
Museo ***Casa del Diezmo***, Celaya, Gto.
Museo ***Casa del Diezmo***, Celaya, Gto.
Museum ***Casa del Diezmo***, Celaya
Musée ***Casa del Diezmo***, Celaya

1996
Antonio Narro University, Saltillo, Coah.
Universidad Antonio Narro, Saltillo, Coah.
Universität Antonio Narro, Saltillo (COAH)
Université Antonio Narro, Saltillo (COAH)

1997
Contemporary Movement Gallery, Kukulkán Plaza, Cancún, Q. Roo.
Galería Movimiento Contemporáneo, Kukulkán Plaza, Cancún, Q. Roo.
Galería Movimiento Contemporáneo, Kukulkán Plaza, Cancún (ROO)
Galería Movimiento Contemporáneo, Kukulkán Plaza, Cancún (ROO)

1997
Universitary Museum, Puebla, Pue.
Museo Universitario, Puebla, Pue.
Universitätsmuseum, Puebla (PUE)
Musée de l'Université, Puebla (PUE)

1997
Preparatoria Oficial de Celaya, Gto.
Preparatoria Oficial de Celaya, Gto.
Preparatoria Oficial, Celaya
Preparatoria Oficial, Celaya

1998
Central Tower of Pemex, México, D.F.
Torre Central de Pemex, México, D.F.
Torre Pemex, Mexiko-Stadt
Torre Pemex, Mexico

1998
Contemporary Movement Gallery, Kukulkán Plaza, Cancún, Q. Roo.
Galería Movimiento Contemporáneo, Kukulkán Plaza, Cancún, Q. Roo.
Galería Movimiento Contemporáneo, Kukulkán Plaza, Cancún (ROO)
Galería Movimiento Contemporáneo, Kukulkán Plaza, Cancún (ROO)

1998
Museum of Contemporary Art, Phoenix, Arizona, E.U.A.
Museo de Arte Contemporáneo, Phoenix, Arizona, E.U.A.
Museum of Contemporary Art, Phoenix, Arizona, USA
Museum of Contemporary Art, Phoenix, Arizona, USA

1998
Centro de Convenciones ITC, Celaya, Gto.
Centro de Convenciones ITC, Celaya, Gto.
Centro de Convenciones des ITC, Celaya
Centro de Convenciones de l'ITC, Celaya

1998

Casa de la Cultura, Celaya, Gto.

Casa de la Cultura, Celaya, Gto.

Casa de la Cultura, Celaya

Casa de la Cultura, Celaya

1998

Palacio Legislativo de Guanajuato, Gto.

Palacio Legislativo de Guanajuato, Gto.

Palacio Legislativo, Guanajuato (GTO)

Palacio Legislativo, Guanajuato (GTO)

1999

Casa de la Cultura de Irapuato, Gto.

Casa de la Cultura de Irapuato, Gto.

Casa de la Cultura, Irapuato (GTO)

Casa de la Cultura, Irapuato (GTO)

1999

Casa de la Cultura de Lagos de Moreno, Jalisco.

Casa de la Cultura de Lagos de Moreno, Jalisco.

Casa de la Cultura, Lagos de Moreno (JAL)

Casa de la Cultura, Lagos de Moreno (JAL)

1999

Misión del Sol Hotel, Cuernavaca, Mor.

Hotel Misión del Sol, Cuernavaca, Mor.

Hotel Misión del Sol, Cuernavaca (MOR)

Hôtel Misión del Sol, Cuernavaca (MOR)

1999

Casa M.I.M.A Museum, Guatemala, Guatemala

Museo ***Casa M.I.M.A.***, Guatemala, Guatemala

Museum ***Casa M.I.M.A.***, Guatemala, Guatemala

Musée ***Casa M.I.M.A.***, Guatemala, Guatemala

2000

Casa de la Cultura de Tabasco in México, México, D.F.

Casa de la Cultura de Tabasco en México, México, D.F.

Casa de Cultura del Estado de Tabasco, Mexico-Stadt

Casa de Cultura del Estado de Tabasco, Mexico

2000

Congreso Internacional de la Cultura Empresarial, Celaya, Gto.

Congreso Internacional de la Cultura Empresarial, Celaya, Gto.

Congreso Internacional de la Cultura Empresarial, Celaya

Congreso Internacional de la Cultura Empresarial, Celaya

2000

Casa de la Cultura de Zitácuaro, Michoacán

Casa de la Cultura de Zitácuaro, Michoacán

Casa de la Cultura, Zitácuaro (MIC)

Casa de la Cultura, Zitácuaro (MIC)

2000

Jardín Borda Museum, Cuernavaca, Mor.

Museo ***Jardín Borda***, Cuernavaca, Mor.

Museum ***Jardín Borda***, Cuernavaca (MOR)

Musée ***Jardín Borda***, Cuernavaca (MOR)

2001

Rotary International, Celaya, Gto.

Rotary International, Celaya, Gto.

Rotary International, Celaya

Rotary International, Celaya

2001

Gallery ***Atenea***, San Miguel de Allende, Gto.

Galería ***Atenea***, San Miguel de Allende, Gto.

Galerie ***Atenea***, San Miguel de Allende (GTO)

Galerie ***Atenea***, San Miguel de Allende (GTO)

2001

Metepec House of Culture, Edomex.

Casa de la Cultura de Metepec, Edomex.

Casa de la Cultura, Metepec (MEX)

Casa de la Cultura, Metepec (MEX)

2001

Casino Español de México, D.F.

Casino Español de México, D.F.

Casino Español de México, Mexiko-Stadt

Casino Español de México, Mexico

2001

Cozumel Island Museum, Q. Roo.

Museo de la Isla de Cozumel, Q. Roo.

Museum Isla Cozumel (ROO)

Musée Isla Cozumel (ROO)

2002

Art Expo New York, E.U.A.

Art Expo New York, E.U.A.

Art Expo New York, USA.

Art Expo New York, USA

2002

Misión del Sol Hotel, Cuernavaca, Mor.

Hotel Misión del Sol, Cuernavaca, Mor.

Hotel Misión del Sol, Cuernavaca (MOR)

Hôtel Misión del Sol, Cuernavaca (MOR)

2003

Casa de la Cultura de Irapuato, Gto.

Casa de la Cultura de Irapuato, Gto.

Casa de la Cultura, Irapuato (GTO)

Casa de la Cultura, Irapuato (GTO)

2003

Visions Fine Art, Sedona, Arizona, E.U.A.

Visions Fine Art, Sedona, Arizona, E.U.A.

Visions Fine Art, Sedona, Arizona, USA

Visions Fine Art, Sedona, Arizona, USA

2003

Misión del Sol Hotel, Cuernavaca, Mor.

Hotel Misión del Sol, Cuernavaca, Mor.

Hotel Misión del Sol, Cuernavaca (MOR)

Hôtel Misión del Sol, Cuernavaca (MOR)

2003

SEMARNAT, México, D.F.

SEMARNAT, México, D.F.

SEMARNAT, Mexiko-Stadt

SEMARNAT, Mexico

2003

Casa de la Cultura, Celaya, Gto.

Casa de la Cultura, Celaya, Gto.

Casa de la Cultura, Celaya

Casa de la Cultura, Celaya

2004

Universidad Autónoma del Estado de Hidalgo, Pachuca, Hgo.

Universidad Autónoma del Estado de Hidalgo, Pachuca, Hgo.

Universidad Autónoma del Estado de Hidalgo, Pachuca (HGO)

Universidad Autónoma del Estado de Hidalgo, Pachuca (HGO)

2004

Casa de las Bóvedas, Universidad Autónoma de Puebla, Pue

Casa de las Bóvedas, Universidad Autónoma de Puebla, Pue

Casa de las Bóvedas, Universidad Autónoma de Puebla (PUE)

Casa de las Bóvedas, Universidad Autónoma de Puebla (PUE)

2005

Colegio Cristóbal Colón de Cuernavaca S.C., Cuernavaca, Mor.

Colegio Cristóbal Colón de Cuernavaca S.C., Cuernavaca, Mor.

Colegio Cristóbal Colón de Cuernavaca S.C., Cuernavaca (MOR)

Colegio Cristóbal Colón de Cuernavaca S.C., Cuernavaca (MOR)

2005

IV Centenario del Quijote, Universidad de Celaya, Gto.

IV Centenario del Quijote, Universidad de Celaya, Gto.

400 Jahre Don Quijote, Universität von Celaya

400 ans Don Quichotte, Université de Celaya

2007

Jardín Borda Cultural Center, Cuernavaca, Mor.

Centro Cultural *Jardín Borda*, Cuernavaca, Mor.

Kulturzentrum *Jardín Borda*, Cuernavaca (MOR)

Centre culturel *Jardín Borda*, Cuernavaca (MOR)

2008

XVI Congreso Regional Casa Inn, Celaya, Gto.

XVI Congreso Regional Casa Inn, Celaya, Gto.

XVI. Regionalkongress Casa Inn, Celaya

XVIe Congrès régional Casa Inn, Celaya

2008

Casino Español de México, México, D.F.

Casino Español de México, México, D.F.

Casino Español de México, Mexiko-Stadt

Casino Español de México, Mexico

2008

Casa Museo José Alfredo Jiménez, Dolores Hidalgo, Gto.

Casa Museo José Alfredo Jiménez, Dolores Hidalgo, Gto.

Casa Museo José Alfredo Jiménez, Dolores Hidalgo (GTO)

Casa Museo José Alfredo Jiménez, Dolores Hidalgo (GTO)

2008

Universidad Lasallista Benavente, Celaya, Gto.

Universidad Lasallista Benavente, Celaya, Gto.

Universidad Lasallista Benavente, Celaya

Universidad Lasallista Benavente, Celaya

2009

San Pedro Art Museum, Puebla, Pue.

San Pedro Museo de Arte, Puebla, Pue.

San Pedro Museo de Arte, Pueplo (PUE)

San Pedro Museo de Arte, Pueplo (PUE)

2010

Centenarios Metamórficos in Casino Español de México, México, D.F.

Centenarios Metamórficos en el Casino Español de México, México, D.F.

Centenarios Metamórficos, Casino Español de México, Mexiko-Stadt

Centenarios Metamórficos, Casino Español de México, Mexico

2010

38° edition of Festival Internacional Cervantino, Guanajuato, Gto.

38° edición del Festival Internacional Cervantino, Guanajuato, Gto.

38. Internationales Cervantes-Festival, Guanajuato (GTO)

38e Festival international Cervantes, Guanajuato (GTO)

2010

Centenarios Metamórficos, Mesón de los Poetas, Guanajuato, Gto.

Centenarios Metamórficos, Mesón de los Poetas, Guanajuato, Gto.

Centenarios Metamórficos, Mesón de los Poetas, Guanajuato (GTO)

Centenarios Metamórficos, Mesón de los Poetas, Guanajuato (GTO)

2011

Sistema de Transporte Colectivo Metro, Estación *Pino Suárez*, México, D.F.

Sistema de Transporte Colectivo Metro, Estación *Pino Suárez*, México, D.F.

U-Bahn-Station *Pino Suárez*, Mexiko-Stadt

Station de métro *Pino Suárez*, Mexico

2011

Metamorfosis retro y presentación del libro ***Yo Metamórfico***, Casino Español de México, México, D.F.

Metamorfosis retro y presentación del libro ***Yo Metamórfico***", Casino Español de México, México, D.F.

Metamorfosis retro & Buchvorstellung ***Yo Metamórfico***", Casino Español de México, Mexiko-Stadt

Metamorfosis retro & Présentation de l'ouvrage ***Yo Metamórfico***, Casino Español de México, Mexico

2011

Autotransportes San Pedro- Santa Clara, Ecatepec, Edo. Mex.

Autotransportes San Pedro- Santa Clara, Ecatepec, Edo. Mex.

Autotransportes San Pedro Santa Clara, Ecatepec (MEX)

Autotransportes San Pedro Santa Clara, Ecatepec (MEX)

2011

Presentación del libro iconográfico ***Yo Metamórfico***, Museo del Quijote, Guanajuato, Gto.

Presentación del libro iconográfico ***Yo Metamórfico***, Museo del Quijote, Guanajuato, Gto.

Buchvorstellung ***Yo Metamórfico***, Don-Quijote-Museum, Guanajuato (GTO)

Présentation de l'ouvrage ***Yo Metamórfico***, Musée Don Quichotte, Guanajuato (GTO)

2012

Cozumel Island Museum, Q. Roo.

Museo de la Isla, Cozumel, Q. Roo.

Museum Isla Cozumel (ROO)

Museum Isla Cozumel (ROO)

PAINTINGS IN MEXICAN COLLECTIONS
COLECCIONES NACIONALES
GEMÄLDE IN MEXIKANISCHEN SAMMLUNGEN
TOILES DANS DES COLLECTIONS MEXICAINES

Miguel Alemán Foundation, Mexico City

Fundación Miguel Alemán, México, D.F.

Fundación Miguel Alemán, Mexiko-Stadt

Fundación Miguel Alemán, Mexico

AWARDS AND HONORS
PREMIOS Y DISTINCIONES
PREISE UND AUSZEICHNUNGEN
PRIX ET RÉCOMPENSES

2000

Presea Tlacaélel, Consejero Supremo del Rey (***Supreme Counselor of the King***)

Presea Tlacaélel. ***Consejero Supremo del Rey***

Presea Tlacaélel, ***Consejero Supremo del Rey***

Presea Tlacaélel, ***Consejero Supremo del Rey***

2003

Casino Español Award, 140th anniversary

Premio Casino Español, 140 Aniversario

Premio Casino Español, 140-jähriges Jubiläum

Premio Casino Español, célébration des 140 ans

2004

Arts Award ***Diego Rivera***, Congress of the State of Guanajuato

Premio estatal de artes ***Diego Rivera***, Congreso del Estado de Guanajuato

Staatlicher Kunstpreis ***Diego Rivera***, Kongress des Bundesstaates Guanajuatow

Prix d'Art national ***Diego Rivera***, Congrès de l'Etat de Guanajuato